Cinema as Pulpit

Cinema as Pulpit

Sherwood Pictures and the Church Film Movement

J. RYAN PARKER
Foreword by Terry Lindvall

McFarland & Company, Inc., Publishers
Jefferson, North Carolina, and London

LIBRARY OF CONGRESS CATALOGUING-IN-PUBLICATION DATA

Parker, J. Ryan, 1980–
Cinema as pulpit : Sherwood Pictures and the church
film movement / J. Ryan Parker : foreword by Terry Lindvall.
                    p.   cm.
Includes bibliographical references and index.
Includes webliography.

ISBN 978-0-7864-6990-1
softcover : acid free paper ∞

1. Sherwood Pictures. 2. Christian films—
United States—History and criticism. 3. Motion
pictures—Religious aspects—Christianity.
4. Religion in motion picutes. I. Title.
PN1999.S47P38 2012   791.43'682—dc23   2012018920

British Library cataloguing data are available

© 2012 J. Ryan Parker. All rights reserved

*No part of this book may be reproduced or transmitted in any form
or by any means, electronic or mechanical, including photocopying
or recording, or by any information storage and retrieval system,
without permission in writing from the publisher.*

Front cover images © 2012 Shutterstock

Manufactured in the United States of America

*McFarland & Company, Inc., Publishers
Box 611, Jefferson, North Carolina 28640
www.mcfarlandpub.com*

To Amy,
with love for patience embodied.
Without you, it all wouldn't have been nearly as much fun.

Table of Contents

Acknowledgements   viii
Foreword by Terry Lindvall   1
Preface   3
Introduction   5

1. A Very Brief History of Film and American Christianity   17
2. A Passionate Phenomenon   37
3. Low Budget? How About No Budget? Sherwood Baptist Church, Ministers of Movies, and *Flywheel*   57
4. *Facing the Giants*, Facing an Industry   73
5. *Fireproof* ... a Foolproof Plan   87
6. A *Courageous* Future   106
7. How Did We Get Here?   128
8. A New Church Film Movement   137
9. Critiquing the Films ... and Their Critics   166

Conclusion   177
Appendix: Internet Resources   185
Chapter Notes   187
Bibliography   198
Index   205

Acknowledgments

I must begin at the beginning by thanking my parents, George and Patsy, for always allowing me to follow my academic pursuits and supporting me even when I was unsure of what I was doing. It is not too much to say that I would not be where I am today without the support and encouragement of a handful of faith communities, beginning with Northside Baptist Church in Clinton, Mississippi, who found me at a spiritual and theological crossroads in my life and set me on my way. Bloomsbury Central Baptist Church in London, England, Providence Baptist Church in Mt. Pleasant, South Carolina, and Lakeshore Avenue Baptist Church in Oakland, California, have kept me on that path, nourishing me and giving me space to live out my love of film in a community of faith.

At the same time, professors at Mississippi College and the Divinity School at Wake Forest University inspired and challenged me along the way. Without Dr. David Miller's courage to ask tough theological questions and encouragement of his students to do so, I doubt that I would have transitioned to theological education in the first place. I am thankful to Dr. Katherine Amos, who first showed me that there was an academic future in the field of film and religion; her Faith and Film class changed the way I thought about and watched film. Dr. Bill Leonard was not only a formative professor but has since become a close friend and mentor. His advice and encouragement not only saw me through graduate school but also continue to guide me through life beyond it.

I would not have attended the Graduate Theological Union for doctoral study were it not for the presence of Professor Michael Morris, whose love of cinema and understanding of its theological and religious possibilities drew me to that place. His placement of film history within the broader realm of art history has enriched my viewing experiences in countless ways. I am thankful for his knowledge, guidance, and friendship, all of which made him the best advisor I could have hoped for. I am thankful to Professor Terry Lindvall for both his invaluable research and his willingness to participate on my dissertation committee at the completion of my doctorate. Professor Lindvall's groundbreaking research into the relationship between American Protestantism and film absolutely changed the direction of my doctoral studies early on in my time at the GTU. Without it, this book would not have been written, and I sincerely hope that this work is a small contribution to it. He has had a greater influence on me than a host of footnotes can possibly indicate. Without a doubt, any bloopers or mistakes in this book are the fault of this first-time "director."

Last, but certainly not least, I must thank my wife, Amy. Words cannot begin to describe my gratitude for her support of and belief in my work, which have sustained me as I worked on this book and kept me on the scholarly path when it would have been far easier to quit and find a "real job."

Foreword by Terry Lindvall

The archaeological excavation of seemingly insignificant bones often leads to impressive and surprising discoveries. One does not immediately recognize or appreciate what one has uncovered in the arduous task of digging and brushing and sorting such odd findings.

So J. Ryan Parker has performed an admirable historical task in taking the marginal categories of Evangelical films and bringing them to center stage. The remarkable success of Sherwood Pictures within the Church Film Movement strikes one as small stones in the pouch of David, being readied to face the giants of Hollywood's hegemony.

Leaving no stone unturned, Parker helps us to understand how contemporary churches have employed the previously suspect art of moviemaking for their mission. Films can provide uplift, evangelism, religious instruction, and inspiration to congregations, discovering that they could "adapt whatever means possible to win souls for Christ."

In the 1920s, Fleet Street journalist G.K. Chesterton visited America and observed that one of the problems of Americans was that they did not produce their own spiritual food in the same sense as their own material food. "They do not, like some peasantries, create other kinds of culture besides the kind called agriculture. Their culture comes from the great cities; and that is where all the evil comes from." He compared places like Oklahoma with Oberammergau and opined that "what goes to Oklahoma is not the peasant play but the cinema. And the objection to the cinema is not so much that it goes to Oklahoma as that it does not come from Oklahoma."

What Parker has done so well is to show that cultural products are being produced in the hinterlands, in the religious pockets of the American landscape. In 1929, the Rev. Thomas Opie from North Carolina connected Shakespeare's ability to see "sermons in stones" with the churches' call to see "sermons in pictures." Parker has clearly shown that churches from Albany, Georgia to Yorba Linda, California, have answered a call to engage giants with their sermons in pictures. He has indeed made an invaluable contribution in studying and illuming these cinematic artifacts and helping us to understand their place in both film history and church history.

Terry Lindvall, Ph.D., is the C. S. Lewis Professor of Communication and Christian Thought at Virginia Wesleyan University. Among his books are *The Silents of God: Selected Issues and Documents in Silent American Film and Religion, 1908–1925*; *Sanctuary Cinema: Origins of the Christian Film Industry*; and *Celluloid Sermons: The Emergence of the Christian Film Industry, 1930–1986*.

Preface

The aim of this book is to broaden the discussion of religion and film by examining contemporary independent Christian (church-based) filmmaking. Current conversations around religion and film largely follow two paths, theological and historical. The first, and most widespread, is the analysis of film from a religious or theological perspective. That is, critics and scholars consider the ways films embody certain theological concepts such as sin, forgiveness, evil, and so on, or depict particular religious communities or practices. The second avenue is smaller but gaining popularity among not only religious studies but in film history circles as well. These scholars and historians analyze the influence of religion on the development of American cinema and vice versa. A popular vein of study on one side would be the role of the Catholic Church in the creation of the Production Code, for example. On the other hand, a few historians are now considering the ways in which Protestant ministers embraced (or rejected) the cinema as a means to uplift, instruct, and entertain members of their faith community.

This book follows the second trajectory, even though elements of the first undergird my analysis of the films that I discuss. From the perspective of film history, I consider both the ways in which religion and film relate to one another but also the ways in which changes in filmmaking technology and industry practices have opened doors for greater participation in the film industry on the part of Evangelical Christians, a group that often views itself as marginalized *vis a vis* contemporary American popular culture. As such, this book provides a view into both American evangelical Protestantism and independent religious filmmaking (with implications for secular filmmakers as well).

My goals in this book are to briefly trace the broad histories of both the relationships between religion and film and the religious film, show how contemporary church-based filmmakers constitute a new movement that fits into this broader history, and suggest ways in which this movement might experience greater creative (and theological) diversity in the future. In the process, I focus on a decidedly small number of films, especially considering the vast number of straight-to-DVD releases that fill (on-line) store shelves. I limit my consideration to theatrically released films because doing so provides a more manageable set of films with which to work and reveals that theatrical exhibition is now a reality for even the most low-budget filmmakers. Finally, the inclusion of all contemporary Christian films would have turned this book into an encyclopedia.

Even as I am confident that this book provides a much-needed voice in the conversation, there are important questions for consideration that are beyond its scope. I hint at two of them in my analysis of these filmmakers' work and audiences' reactions to it. First is the consideration of filmmaking as spiritual and religious practice. What religious or spiritual meaning do these filmmakers and countless volunteers create both individually and within community as they undertake production of decidedly evangelical films? The second is closely linked to the first and that is the notion of film-watching as spiritual practice. In what ways do audiences make religious, theological, or spiritual meaning by watching these films alone or in community with one another? How can or do these films shape viewers' beliefs and actions? In both cases, answers to these questions will benefit from interviews with filmmakers and both individual and groups of viewers. Perhaps these questions will be the groundwork for a second book.

Finally, as with most books on film and religion or theology, this one is unfinished. On a weekly basis, it seems, I read about a new film in production or another church taking up cameras. This is a strong and growing movement. With the democratization of cinema and increasing avenues of exhibition, it will only grow stronger. I am especially thankful to Michael Morris and Terry Lindvall, whose research and teaching have helped lay the historical foundation for this work. Their encouragement of and belief in my more contemporary research has helped bring this book to life.

Introduction

> *The church would perform its greatest service if it would teach Hollywood by example rather than precept. Let the Federal Council or some other religious group produce a pious epic that grosses a million dollars. Everyone knows what imitators the magnates are: There will be an immediate stampede to dramatize purity and sanctity.* — Alva Johnson, 1931[1]

From its humble beginnings, film has endured a tumultuous relationship with American religion. At times this relationship has been contentious and at others cooperative, but it has never been boring. Numerous film historians have claimed that the history of American cinema is the history of America itself.[2] To narrow this equation further, I argue that, whether as Hollywood blockbuster or church-based experiment, the history of religious films is, in a very real way, the history of American cinema itself. Religious films marked almost every technological advancement in filmmaking or rapidly attempted to exploit those advancements for either financial gain or to more effectively engage their audience. Some of the very first motion pictures envisioned *The Passion Play*, which had previously been relegated to the stage for centuries. Some of the early black-and-white film versions of the life of Jesus even included hand-tinted scenes, an early version of color production. The first feature-length film with synchronized dialogue sequences, *The Jazz Singer* (Warner Bros., 1927), tells the story of Jackie Rabinowitz (Al Jolson), an aspiring jazz singer who wrestles with his father's traditional Judaism and expectations that he succeed him as cantor. In the 1950s, when 20th Century–Fox created CinemaScope to counter the growing popularity of television and boost declining movie audiences, the studio first utilized it for *The Robe* (1953), a sword-and-sandal epic about the Roman centurion (Richard Burton) in charge of Jesus' crucifixion. Similar widescreen religious epics helped keep the film industry afloat as their narratives appealed to a sizable pious American Christian audience while their scantily clad characters and large-scale battles simultaneously satisfied a craving for sex and violence.

Yet with social and political upheaval on the horizon in the mid–1960s and the demise of the studio system, which had until then defined the style of Hollywood productions for nearly four decades, such films soon became culturally irrelevant and financially destructive for the studios.[3] As a result, mainstream, Hollywood productions of religious films rapidly declined. When Hollywood films did include religious elements, the filmmakers often approached them from a highly skeptical or cynical point of view, which mirrored the wider culture's changing view of religion. Few mainstream religious productions made a significant splash in the film industry and society at large until Martin Scorsese's *The Last Temptation of Christ* (Universal, 1988) and DreamWorks' *The Prince of Egypt* (1998), the former for its sexual controversy and the latter for its animated piety.

However, the history of film and American Christianity transcends mainstream, Hollywood religious productions. From the beginning, American Christians have been influential in the formation of film content beyond actual filmmaking. Chief among these efforts is the Catholic Church's role in the creation of the Production Code, a list of dos, don'ts, and "be carefuls" that governed representations of sex, violence, and religion, among many other topics, from 1930 to 1968. At the same time, the Catholic Church created the Legion of Decency, a watchdog organization that warned of objectionable content in films and provided their own ratings and recommendations. Bolstered by strong organization and leadership, Catholics presented a force that Hollywood filmmakers could not ignore. Far less organized, but no less important, Protestants also joined the effort to ensure "clean" pictures. Numerous Protestant ministers and laity saw the potential for films to morally uplift viewers while others saw the cinema as a healthy alternative to the saloon. In fact, the temperance movement and efforts to clean up motion pictures were closely aligned. However, if Protestant participation in censorship efforts seems lacking, it could be due to the fact that they were busier making films than censoring them.

As such, we find a third avenue through which to approach the history of film and American Christianity. It might come as a surprise to many readers, but the history of Protestant responses to the cinema, even among its most conservative denominations, is surprisingly diverse. Most people will be familiar with conservative Protestant notions of the cinema as the handmaiden of the devil, a poison for the minds of youth and the mentally or spiritually infirm. Contemporary Christian opponents of motion pictures still bemoan the prevalence of sex and violence in motion pictures and their influence on younger viewers. On the other hand, with the birth of cinema, many Protestant ministers and laity saw the emergence of a new universal language that could unite humankind and potentially bring about world peace. These same ministers saw a new tool for evangelism that would be more effective than a thousand eloquent sermons. Soon, they set about producing their own films and organizing production and distribution companies that would provide wholesome films to congregations across the country. The quote from Alva Johnson that opens this introduction epitomizes the hopes that ministers had for the cinema and the confidence in their ability to bring them to fruition. Unfortunately, harsh economic realities, poor organization, and the emergence of radio largely derailed these hopes and dreams. Though independent religious film production would continue throughout the twentieth century, it would largely remain ghettoized until the beginning of the twenty-first century.

In February of 2004, an established Hollywood superstar and a little-known independent film studio came closest to realizing Johnson's prophetic vision from over seventy years before. Though it was not church-based, Mel Gibson and Icon Pictures' *The Passion of the Christ* was a religious epic that grossed well over $599 million worldwide to become the highest-grossing R-rated independent religious film ever produced.[4] Not since the days of Cecil B. DeMille's *The King of Kings* (DeMille Pictures, 1917) or *The Ten Commandments* (Paramount, 1956) had a religious film so strongly captured the public's attention. Within weeks of *The Passion*'s release, the Hollywood magnates did show what imitators they truly are as studios began to green-light religious productions and create boutique faith-based production and distribution arms for their corporations. The same studios that refused to back Gibson's film because of its controversial religious nature soon found themselves "chasing *Passion* dollars," scrambling to connect with the previously ignored evangelical Christian audience that had made Gibson's film such a phenomenon.[5] Hollywood studios and established Christian production companies struck while the iron was hot and began to invest millions of dollars in faith-based feature-length films. Unfortunately, none of these films came close to replicating *The Passion*'s success as many of them struggled to break even at the box office and only made a profit through DVD sales.

While *The Passion* was dominating box offices around the world and Hollywood frantically discussed how best to tap into a newfound market, two amateur filmmakers at a Baptist church in a small town in Georgia were hard at work on a film that would revolutionize the world of religious filmmaking. In 1999 and 2001, respectively, brothers Alex and Stephen Kendrick joined Sherwood Baptist Church in Albany, Georgia, as associate ministers. Both were eager to embrace the role of media, particularly filmmaking, in the life of the church. Having read a survey that stated that films had more influence in popular culture than the church, they set out to make films that provided an uplifting, transformative, evangelical Christian message. In 2003, they established Sherwood Pictures and produced an incredibly low-budget ($20,000) feature-length film entitled *Flywheel*, which they only ever intended to screen at their local movie theater. However, through word of mouth, it spread to theaters beyond their hometown, was broadcast on conservative Christian cable networks, and even enjoyed a profitable DVD release. All of this exceeded the Kendricks' wildest imaginings and encouraged them to dream bigger and begin production on their second feature-length film. This time, things would be different.

Bolstered by the significant financial performance of *Flywheel*, the Kendrick brothers released *Facing the Giants* in Fall 2006. Through a partnership with Provident Films and Carmel Entertainment, Sherwood Pictures connected with mainstream Hollywood companies Sony Pictures and Samuel Goldwyn Films, which assured them a broader theatrical release. Releasing in 441 theaters (still a small number considering that *The Passion* played in over 3,000), *Facing the Giants* went on to earn $10,178,331 in box office receipts.[6] While these returns seem minuscule compared to most Hollywood standards, *Facing the Giants* also had a production budget ($100,000) that was a fraction of many independent films. Eventually adding $20,103,602 in DVD sales to those box office receipts, *Facing the Giants* enjoyed financial success on a *Passion* level.

By drawing from a wealth of volunteers from their church to keep production costs low, only hiring professionals for key production roles like cinematography and lighting, and relying on word-of-mouth advertising, the Kendrick brothers discovered a method for producing religious films that would be both spiritually and financially successful. In terms of the former, the lack of outside investors allowed the Kendricks to stay faithful to their conservative evangelical Christian message by avoiding any restrictions on it that such investments might require. In terms of the latter, even a more modest box office performance would have allowed them to recoup their investment, ensuring funds for future productions. Though the production budget of their third feature-length film, *Fireproof* (2008), increased to $500,000, their box office returns and DVD sales nearly tripled to over $60 million.

Although Hollywood has responded to the Kendricks' productions (each subsequent film enjoys a broader theatrical release), they have not been the only ones to do so. In light of Sherwood Pictures' success, other churches have entered into the business, and ministry, of filmmaking. New Song Community Church in Oceanside, California, Yorba Linda Friends Church in Yorba Linda, California, New Harvest Bible Chapel in Chicago, Illinois, and Calvary Church of the Nazarene in Memphis, Tennessee, have all released feature-length films in theaters or will do so in the near future. Like Sherwood Pictures' productions, these films cost a fraction of their Hollywood counterparts and, whether or not they recoup their investments from the box office, are all sure to perform well through DVD sales and rentals. Taken together, these congregations form a contemporary church film movement that harkens back to Protestant uses of and expectations for cinema in the early 1900s.

This book tells the story of the emergence of Sherwood Pictures as not only the leading player in the contemporary church film movement, but a prominent figure in the broader world of independent film production. It also analyzes a small number of the other participants in this movement to reveal their influence Sherwood has had on the evangelical filmmaking community. A complete account of every participant in this new church film movement is nearly impossible, as new church-based film production companies and consulting groups seem to emerge on a monthly basis. By looking back to the history of Protestant uses of and expectations for cinema, this book also situates this contemporary movement in a broader history of Protestant engagement with film. The Kendrick brothers' desires, and those of their evangelical filmmaker peers, have not changed much from those of their predecessors in the early 1900s. What has changed, however, are the means of production, distribution, and exhibition that inhibited those earlier Christian filmmakers from enjoying the success that the Kendrick brothers have found. Moreover, changes in communication with the emergence of the Internet and accompanying social media and networks like YouTube, Facebook, and Twitter have empowered independent filmmakers (religious or not) in ways unimaginable only a decade ago. As such, this book is also a study of the changes in technology and communication that have affected the broader independent filmmaking industry in which Sherwood Pictures plays a small part. Finally, because the Kendrick brothers foreground their deep religious commitments at every phase of filmmaking from production to exhibition, this book provides further insight into contemporary American evangelical Christianity and its relationship with the broader popular culture in which it is situated.

Coming Attractions ... or a Chapter Outline

While this book primarily focuses on contemporary film history, it must be situated in a broader history to determine the ways in which these events are simultaneously unique and reiterations of movements that have taken place before them. After this introduction, Chapter 1 offers a three-fold overview of this broader history. First, I will highlight the varieties of mainstream Hollywood religious productions that characterize Hollywood's (and the broader culture's) changing relationship with religion throughout the 1900s. Broadly speaking, these phases can be summarized as pious (1900–1930), spectacular (1940–1960), and cynical (1970s onward). Here, we will see that the more recent reactions of Hollywood studios to *The Passion of the Christ* do indeed have historical precedent as studios have always attempted to follow one financial success, be it religious or not, with another. Second, I will outline the role that Christians, both Catholic and Protestant, played in the shaping of film content through censorship efforts in the mid–1900s. Though Catholic efforts benefited from stronger organization and leadership, Protestant efforts, though less familiar, were no less influential and important in helping "clean up" the motion picture industry and creating "morally uplifting" films.

Finally, I will summarize the Protestant uses of and expectations for cinema that have only recently been uncovered through the work of film and religion historian Terry Lindvall, who reveals that a wealth of optimism characterized much of the initial Protestant reaction to the cinema and religious filmmaking. I will highlight some of the more concerted efforts on the part of both individual ministers and denominations, through the likes of the Christian Herald Motion Picture Bureau, Sacred Films, the International Church Film Corporation, and the Church Film Company, to not only produce feature-length films but to establish networks of distributors and exhibitors to provide congregations with films and the means to exhibit them. Unfortunately, financial constraints, poor organization, technological limitations, and the advent of the radio squashed this optimism. Faith-based filmmaking (that is, films produced by congregations or religious organizations) would operate well below the broader cultural radar until the release of *Facing the Giants* in 2006. Though Billy Graham's World Wide Pictures, Donald Thompson's Mark IV Pictures, and Peter and Paul Lalonde's Cloud Ten Pictures all invested millions of dollars in production, their films did not enjoy broad theatrical releases and often released directly to DVD, where they also struggled financially.

Chapter 2 examines the watershed moment in religious film history that took place with the release of Gibson's *The Passion of the Christ* and Hollywood's reaction to it. The film has been academically dissected from nearly every possible angle except, perhaps, the most interesting one, Hollywood's response. This chapter will provide a quick account of the financial performance of Gibson's film, along with religion and film scholars' reactions to it, before looking at the creation of boutique faith-based production and distribution companies in major Hollywood studios like 20th Century–Fox, the Weinstein Company, and Sony Pictures and the films that emerged from them. Here, the public statements of the participants in the development of these departments (studio executives, producers, marketing agents, etc.) provide rich insight to what might simultaneously be seen as financial opportunism and a genuine desire to market to an underserved audience. I will also provide a financial analysis and critique of a handful of films released after *The Passion*, particularly those released in 2006 that are most certainly reactions to *The Passion* given the two-year timeframe that allowed adequate time for production and marketing. Despite their producers' best intentions, none of these films captured evangelical attention as effectively as *The Passion* did. As a conclusion to this chapter, I will offer theories as to why they failed to do so.

Chapter 3 provides an introduction to Sherwood Baptist Church through a brief overview of its history and its core beliefs, particularly the notion that they can "change the world from Albany, Georgia." Their theological and cultural worldviews mirror much of the conservative Christian evangelical community of which they are a part. These worldviews find unwavering expression in their films, which is part of their appeal to a conservative evangelical Christian audience. This chapter concludes with an analysis of the production, distribution, exhibition, and reception of their first feature-length film, *Flywheel*. I will not devote an entire chapter to this film because, unlike the productions that followed, its lack of a proper theatrical release severely limited the availability of film critics' and viewers' reactions to it that factor prominently in my engagement with their subsequent releases. However, with the production of *Flywheel*, the Kendrick brothers, and the rest of the Sherwood Pictures team, uncover a system to which they will return with each subsequent project.

Chapters 4, 5, and 6 closely follow the structure of the last half of Chapter 3 as they continue the four-fold analysis of Sherwood Pictures' films, *Facing the Giants*, *Fireproof*, and *Courageous*. I will analyze the production of these films through extant interviews with the cast and crew in the press and in behind-the-scenes featurettes and director's commentaries available on the DVD versions of each film. In terms of production, I will pay close attention to the role of volunteers in the creation of these films and not only how their involvement helps cut costs but also how they see their work as a ministry. The films' low budgets also have theological implications. Because Sherwood Pictures does not rely on outside funding, no theological or narrative constraints are placed on their films. In short, they can say what they believe and believe what they say.

At first glance, to analyze the marketing of these films might seem rather pointless because they devote little in the way of financial resources to it. However, to only think of marketing in dollars and cents is to miss a critical way in which evangelical Christians market their films. Here, I will pay close attention to the ways in which the Kendrick brothers preview and promote their films, particularly the ways in which they create an "us vs. them" mentality between their productions and mainstream Hollywood films. The narrative they create surrounding their films contributes to the broader "Culture War" in which many evangelical Christians believe themselves engaged. Furthermore, the geography of these films' exhibition sites (urban vs. rural) and the sites themselves (traditional theaters vs. church exhibition) provide valuable insight into both the current and future states of independent film exhibition. Rather than attempting to win over a few large markets like New York or Los Angeles, some filmmakers, like the Kendrick brothers, opt for smaller markets that might be more open to their message. Of course, this strategy is full of assumptions that ignore the presence of potential audience members in those larger markets. In places where theaters cannot or will not exhibit their product, these filmmakers make their movies available, for a small licensing fee, to groups like churches and schools who can then screen them for their broader community.

Finally, an analysis of the reception of Sherwood Pictures' films must take into consideration both secular and religious film critics' reviews of them as well as audience feedback through posts on websites like Beliefnet, Hollywood Jesus, the Internet Movie Database, and even Amazon. These reviews and comment posts provide a snapshot of the diversity of both religious and non-religious reactions to these films. Furthermore, the diversity of responses from within the evangelical Christian community itself reveals the difficulty of talking about this group as some monolithic entity, which is one of the reasons that mainstream Hollywood executives have failed to effectively connect with them. Overall, this four-fold analysis tells the story of Sherwood Pictures' rise from an amateur production studio to a full-fledged independent powerhouse complete with ancillary products and a branded image. As they find their filmmaking feet in *Flywheel*, they make a name for themselves with *Facing the Giants*, and use that name in a brilliant marketing and product strategy to great effect with their promotion of *Fireproof*. With *Courageous*, thanks to YouTube, blogs, Twitter feeds, and an old-fashioned publicity campaign, Sherwood Pictures' has harnessed the power of a networked culture that will aid in the creation, marketing, and distribution of what could be their most financially successful production yet.

Chapter 7 provides a bit of a diversion in the story as I re-examine film history to show the changes in production that allowed Sherwood Baptist Church to produce feature length films in the first place, much less see millions of dollars in return on a few hundred thousand dollars investment. This chapter will also briefly analyze the world of evangelical Christian pop culture from which these films come and into which they move. In terms of my re-examination of film history, I will explore how changes in both the makeup of the Hollywood industry and filmmaking technology have allowed marginalized voices to be heard (and seen) on a broader scale. While independent or avant-garde cinema has always existed alongside mainstream productions, it was not until the 1960s and 1970s, with their accompanying cultural revolutions and technological advancements, that such films impacted mainstream society. Ironically, we can find early parallels to Sherwood Pictures in the work and leadership of controversial filmmakers like Roger Corman and Russ Meyer, whose sexual, violent, and sexually violent films challenged the staid status quo. Another, more recent production that paved the way for Sherwood Pictures was *The Blair Witch Project* (Haxan Films, 1999), whose low budget and word-of-mouth advertising were greatly enhanced by the growing influence of the Internet. Of course, the digitalization of filmmaking has played an important role in decreasing production costs and increasing avenues for distribution and exhibition as well.

This chapter will conclude with an analysis of contemporary evangelical pop culture and the challenges that evangelicals must face in attempting to impact the broader culture in which they live and work. The research of Heather Hendershot and Daniel Radosh will show the ambiguity of much of contemporary evangelical media that betrays their commitment to moral absolutes and biblical inerrancy, for example. Drawing from the work of Mara Einstein and Lynn Schofield Clark, I will consider the ways in which Sherwood Pictures has become, or is becoming, a faith brand, an easily recognizable product among a sea of options from which consumers have to choose.

Chapter 8 is, in a way, a continuation of my analysis of the reception of Sherwood Pictures' films as it looks at the various churches that have begun film production in response to the success of *Facing the Giants* and *Fireproof*. Ministers in churches from Tennessee to Illinois to California have taken up the camera in an effort to spread the gospel message. I will provide a similar, but more brief, four-fold analysis of films that have been released thus far and consider the production and marketing of films that will be released soon. Comparisons between both the content of and reaction to these films and Sherwood Pictures' productions will be inevitable, especially since some of these faith communities even consulted the Kendrick brothers to help plan their production schedule. Though these films emerge from a variety of denominations, they all espouse similar conservative theological and cultural worldviews.

Chapter 9 returns to a closer examination of both the positive and negative reactions to the films from the church film movement and uses Frank Burch Brown's writings on kitsch and ecumenical aesthetics to moderate this conversation. I hope that this conversation will temper both the criticism that ignores the context from which these films emerge and to which they are targeted and the uncritical praise that ignores their aesthetic shortcomings and theologically problematic narratives. Ironically, some of the staunchest opponents of this church film movement and its productions come from a religious context. Not surprisingly, so do the majority of its supporters. Here, I argue that these films' harshest critics fail to fully consider the context of these films and, at times, are unfair in their stinging criticism of them. On the other hand, viewers who continually praise these films without fully acknowledging their aesthetic weaknesses or, for example, the ways in which the religious components often feel tacked on, actually do the movement a disservice by not demanding improvements in future productions that might aid in the crossover appeal of these films.

In the conclusion to this book, I look at the ways in which Sherwood Pictures represents the future of independent filmmaking while suggesting other possible futures for the church film movement that include a broader array of theological and cultural voices. Burch Brown's vision for the future of an artistic Christianity, as well as criticisms of evangelical Christian media from evangelicals themselves, all imply the need for greater diversity in the church film movement. Beyond shared theological and cultural worldviews, most if not all of the participants in the church film movement are wealthier congregations that have the financial and technological resources available to undertake such massive projects. I am well aware that, particularly in this economy, smaller and perhaps more theologically or socially progressive congregations do not enjoy either the financial wellbeing or the technological know-how necessary to undertake film production. However, my brief discussion of the work of Act One, an organization working to improve Christian filmmaking, and the production of *Blue Like Jazz*, a film saved by its fans, points to a brighter future for the church film movement. Even churches with limited financial resources can make their cinematic dreams a reality thanks to the current practices of crowd-sourcing and crowd-funding.

Behind the Scenes: A Word on Sources

This book is both descriptive and evaluative, based primarily on research and not field study. As I mentioned in the chapter outline above, my examination of the contemporary church film movement is four-fold, considering production, distribution, exhibition, and reception. In each case, I will draw from familiar sources like the mainstream press (*The New York Times*, *USA Today*, etc.), religious publications (*Christianity Today*, *The Baptist Press*, etc.), and scholarly texts on media, film, and religion and their relationship with one another. However this only provides a limited understanding of the church film movement. In his essay "Hollywood Chronicles: Toward an Intersection of Church History and Film History," film and religion historian Terry Lindvall calls for a deeper understanding of and more comprehensive research into the relationship between church history and film history.[7] One of the ways that we can attain this, Lindvall argues, is by looking to often-ignored or unlikely source material. In the past, such sources included industry trade publications like *Variety* or *Motion Picture World* and even, for Lindvall, religious publications like church newsletters and bulletins. Today, more often than not, these ignored or unusual resources are digital in nature, located online in the form of websites, blogs, discussion forums, comment posts, and customer feedback posts. Consulting these sources, most notably the production blogs that accompany some of these films and viewer feedback on sites like the Internet Movie Database and Amazon, will augment the information gleaned from the more traditional sources listed above. Combining traditional and "unusual" resources helps paint a clearer picture of who is watching these films and how they are responding to them.

In *Into the Dark: Seeing the Sacred in the Top Films of the 21st Century*, film and theology scholar Craig Detweiler consults the users of the Internet Movie Database (www.imdb.com) to create his list of the top films of the 21st century. His discussion of the importance of this "unconventional research tool" is helpful for my analysis of the response to the films emerging from the church film movement. Though Detweiler focuses specifically on IMDb, his comments could apply to the other unconventional, online sources that I have consulted. Detweiler describes IMDb as a "receptor-oriented database, culling from the collective wisdom of the global film-watching community," one that is "driven by love and devotion and fueled by passionate opinions."[8] He also argues that IMDb is important because people freely and frequently offer up their unguarded responses and no one is paid for their reviews. He adds:

> The IMDb offers both a long view of cinematic history and an immediate snapshot of a film's relative popularity and power.... For film scholars, what used to be guesswork rooted in hunches or slow, scientific surveys has been replaced by ongoing data gathering [as thousands] of ratings and reviews are posted on the site irrespective of merit. Yet the IMDb also offers an important corrective — reviews of the reviews. Each capsule review can also be voted on.[9]

Because most of the films discussed in this book had relatively limited theatrical releases, few mainstream critics had the opportunity to see and review them. In some cases, an audience member's response to a particular film might be more insightful than a professional film critic's, especially when, as is often the case, that audience member evidences a clear(er) understanding of the faith tradition from which that film emerges.

The anonymity of reviewers on Amazon and IMDb might be problematic. Authors of positive reviews could be participants in the production of the film or either related to or close friends with someone who is. If that is the case, then positive reviews, at best, become efforts to increase the popularity of a loved one's work and, at worst, nothing more than veiled self-promotions. On the other hand, negative reviews could come from individuals who are simply out to attack every religious film they encounter, despite its aesthetic quality. However, we could also view this on-line anonymity as an opportunity for viewers to be more honest in their reactions to a particular film: Secular viewers are free to praise it while members of the evangelical Christian community are free to be highly critical of it. In the end, the viewers' comments that I quote throughout this book serve as an accurate representation of both the support of and attacks on Sherwood Pictures' productions and other movies from the church film movement.

Other often-overlooked resources include the special features on the DVD versions of these films. In an effort to boost DVD sales, filmmakers offer a vast amount of bonus features that include behind-the-scenes footage, making-of featurettes, and commentary tracks by the directors, cast, and crew. In the case of the films from Sherwood Pictures, these special features furnish a wealth of production information unavailable elsewhere. The director's commentary tracks on these DVDs also provide further insight into the theological underpinnings of these films, both on the screen and behind the scenes. The statements that Alex and Stephen Kendrick make, for example, reveal their hopes for their films and how they want to present them as alternatives to a corrupt Hollywood industry.

A Film Studies Mash-Up: Why This Book Matters

First and foremost, this book is significant because it links film history and church history in ways that few texts have done thus far, answering the call of Lindvall and other film and religion scholars to seek out new avenues of study in the field. Much of the hybrid history of religion and film, or theology and film, has dealt with the role of Catholicism in shaping the Production Code, the ways in which the Bible or Christians and Christianity have been portrayed on screen, or the ways in which films embody or challenge particular theologies. While Protestants and film have often received less scholarly attention, this has begun to shift with Lindvall's research and work in both *Sanctuary Cinema: Origins of the Christian Film Industry* and *The Silents of God: Selected Issues and Documents in Silent American Film and Religion, 1908–1925*, both of which provide the historical framework for my more contemporary research. In his conclusion to *Sanctuary Cinema*, Lindvall briefly refers to a revival of Protestant filmmaking after it appeared to lie dormant for nearly five decades. For me, this conclusion was an invitation to continue this research, and it is my hope that this book is a contribution to that discussion.

Few scholars of religion and film have considered issues of production, distribution, marketing, exhibition, and reception to see the ways in which both producers and consumers of films make religious and/or theological meaning. At the same time, few critics of religious films are knowledgeable of the theological and religious contexts from which these films emerge. Lindvall argues that a more sophisticated understanding of the relationship between film and American Christianity is necessary for a clearer picture of both the film industry and religion in contemporary American culture. He writes, "[U]nfortunately, readers of film history are rarely provided with theologically informed narratives or critiques. Likewise, we might confess that church historians are oblivious (and many happily so) to the relevance of popular culture to their tasks of mapping out theological trends and events." He continues, "[A] writing of church history in the twentieth century requires competency in the study of popular culture, and particularly, film."[10] This book combines both an awareness of the context(s) from which the films of the church film movement emerge as well as the modes of production, distribution, marketing, and exhibition that either contribute to or distract from the mission of these church-based production studios.

Furthermore, the fact that this book focuses on independent religious cinema goes a long way to curbing a shortcoming that Lindvall finds in the field of religion and film studies. He writes, "Bias against independent religious films, for example, distorts any kind of careful and fair analysis of materials thought to be sentimental, trivial, or exploitative. Such blatantly dispensational films as the Mark IV production of *A Thief in the Night* might be worthy of cavalier dismissal, but the text should be considered in light of its purpose and effects as much as its aesthetic and technical constraints."[11] As such, he continues, "The need for a fresh interdisciplinary writing involves not only demographic differences, but also a category we might call theographics, wherein we seek to understand how different theological traditions ... might approach the interpretation of films."[12] Here, Lindvall is very close to Burch Brown's notion of "ecumenical aesthetics," to which I will refer in Chapter 9. Though the films discussed here will not be immune from strident critical analysis, this book also conveys an awareness of the ways in which many audience members make genuine religious and theological meaning of them and enjoy genuine emotional and spiritual experiences through them. Again, the use of unusual sources like discussion forums, product reviews, and comment posts allow individual viewers to speak for themselves rather than forcing the author to speculate on possible responses. As such, this book also fulfills Lindvall's assertion that contemporary religion and film histories must examine the people who watch religious films to determine "the functions that media play in fulfilling people's needs and what influence the media have in attracting target audiences by way of satisfying certain needs."[13]

This book is also a significant contribution to the study of evangelical popular culture. The majority of scholarly texts on evangelical culture, Hendershot's *Shaking the World for Jesus* for example, take a broader view of the culture, simultaneously analyzing a variety of industries including music, publishing, merchandise, and film. Unlike most of those texts, this book is an attempt to delve further into one of those industries, filmmaking, through an in-depth analysis of a small number of films from one studio and what they, in turn, might tell us about that industry and evangelical Christianity's engagement with pop culture as a whole. Though this book focuses on the specific contexts from which these films emerge, it is also aware of the broader context of contemporary American evangelicalism to which they appeal. An awareness of this broader context helps us to better understand the antagonistic relationship that participants of the church film movement appear to have with Hollywood, even as they acquiesce to it.

Implications for religious studies aside, this book also makes contributions to the broader field of film studies. First, it simultaneously considers the impact that Gibson's *The Passion of the Christ* had on the broader filmmaking industry and the limitations of that impact. Though the film can be seen as a watershed moment in religious film history, perhaps it did not change the broader filmmaking industry in ways that commentators initially thought it would. Second, as a result, this book reveals the power that independent film, even independent religious film, now has over the broader filmmaking industry. As such, an analysis of the production, distribution, marketing, and exhibition of Sherwood Pictures' films simultaneously provides insight into the state of the independent filmmaking industry today. The work of Sherwood Pictures represents a shift of power that is currently taking place in the broader context of film production from larger studios to independent producers. This is a direct result of the digitalization of film production and exhibition, cheaper production and editing equipment and software, and enhanced means of communication via the Internet and social networking that improve and cheapen advertising and publicity. This book draws from research in contemporary film studies in ways that few (if any) other religion and film texts do. Again, as I will show, religious cinema has often found itself at the forefront of, or at least in the center of, changes in filmmaking.

Chapter 1

A Very Brief History of Film and American Christianity

The relationship between Hollywood and American Christianity is a complex one. For clarification, however, we could divide it into three separate areas of study: representations of Christianity (its sacred texts and practitioners) in mainstream Hollywood films, the role of Christians in the industry, and the work of specifically Christian film productions that, formidable or not, set themselves up as sacred opponents to their secular counterparts. Each of these areas could be further divided into narrower topics, each of which would most certainly inspire multiple books. For the purposes of this book, a summary of these three broad areas, with a reference to existing literature on them, will have to suffice. Here, I simply want to set the historical context in which the contemporary church film movement is situated. We will see that the contemporary efforts of both mainstream studios to tap into a religious audience and religious efforts to embrace filmmaking for evangelism, education, inspiration, and even entertainment, each of which benefit from new technologies, are actually just the latest chapter in the relationship between American film and Christianity that dates back to the late 1800s and early 1900s.

Hollywood Gets Religion

Of the three areas of study that I have delineated here, most readers will be familiar with the first, Hollywood's representation of Christianity's sacred texts and practitioners. Before Hollywood even existed, the earliest filmmakers turned to stories from the Judeo-Christian tradition for cinematic inspiration. These stories were beneficial for early filmmakers on three levels: they were free and not bound by copyright, appealed to a sizable religious population in America at the time, and helped legitimize the new medium, which many cultural critics decried as a lower-class form of entertainment. In *Sanctuary Cinema*, Lindvall refers to a minister who defends a film version of *The Passion Play* by linking the film to classical illustrations by Dore. Lindvall writes, "Connecting the religious moving picture to pious historical religious illustrations extended legitimacy and credibility to the novel medium."[1] On the other hand, filmmakers quickly began to recognize that a good word from a religious production could do wonders for their film's popularity. Lindvall adds, "Along with the use of religious rhetoric, secular producers garnered support for their products from various ecclesiastical movers and shakers."[2] A good word by evangelist Billy Sunday, for example, could literally boost box office business for a particular film.

Throughout film history, secular representations of Christianity's sacred texts and its practitioners have followed a path, some might say downward, from the pious to the cynical, or from the sacred to the scandalous. While each decade might see films of both types, this general trajectory holds true. Commenting on the reservations of the earliest filmmakers to depict Jesus on screen, film and religion professor Michael Morris summed up the history of secular filmmakers' approach to religion and argued that by the end of the 1920s, the question among potential filmmakers of Jesus films had become not "Should we?" but "How reverently does this film treat the Jesus story?" By the 1970s, the question had seemingly become not "How reverently does this film treat the Jesus story?" but "How far can we take it?"[3] Between the early 1930s and mid–1960s, Hollywood largely ensured reverence for religion through the implementation of the Production Code, a system of self-censorship highly influenced by the Catholic Church. The Code strictly forbade the ridicule of religion and the representation of ministers as comic or villainous characters. Of course, filmmakers always found ways to bend or subvert these rules, but for the most part they obliged. Yet with the demise of the Code in 1968, all bets were off. Filmmakers began to take more cynical, critical approaches to religion, many of which mirrored the cultural revolutions of the day that were critical of authority in any form, especially religious. It is almost impossible to imagine the production and exhibition of *Life of Brian* (HandMade Films, 1979) or *The Last Temptation of Christ* before 1968. Furthermore, one wonders if *The Passion of the*

The unrelenting violence with which Mel Gibson depicted Jesus' torture and crucifixion would have kept *The Passion of the Christ* (Icon Pictures, 2004) off the silver screen during the Production Code era. Jim Caviezel as Jesus is unrelentingly tortured by two Roman guards.

The humor with which the Monty Python comedy troupe approached crucifixion would have offended most religious sensibilities in the 1930s and 1940s. Eric Idle (left) as Lead Singer Crucifee and Graham Chapman (right) as Brian Page lead their fellow crucified in the uplifting song, "Always Look on the Bright Side of Life."

Christ would have seen the light of day (or a darkened theater) before the demise of the Production Code and its prohibitions against showing brutal killings in detail.

Although Adele Reinhartz focuses solely on Jesus films in *Jesus of Hollywood*, her analysis of them has important implications for my discussion of films that depict Biblical or Christian epics or feature ministers as main characters. She writes, "[The] historical Jesus, the canonical Jesus and the biopic Jesus [Jesus depicted in film] are equally preoccupied with the interests, concerns, and anxieties of their own time and place."[4] As I have already hinted, filmmakers used religious films to navigate the broader experiences of which they and the broader culture were a part. Whether it be Victorian piety in early Jesus films, the Cold War through the Exodus story, or the counter-culture movement of the late '60s and early '70s in Jesus musicals, as Professor Morris argues, filmmakers of all ethnic, racial, gender, and political groups have adopted religious subject matter to advance their own creative visions and political or cultural agendas.[5] In the next few pages, I want to highlight a few of the films that illustrate secular filmmakers' ever-changing approach to religion, some of which are directly responsible for the efforts of Christians to create their own films. I recognize that in each case, I am leaving out far too many films that could further reveal the diversity of secular approaches to religious films.

Jesus Films

With the advent of film as a modern art form at the end of the 19th and beginning of the 20th centuries, there was an initial mistrust of the propriety of showing Jesus on the silver screen due to fears of idolatry and the low reputation of the cinema at that time. Surprisingly, filmmakers' reservations with depicting Jesus would last well into the 1950s, and, for reasons unknown, there is a hesitation with employing full-bodied depictions of Jesus from the 1930s to the 1950s. For instance, in the films *The Last Days of Pompeii* (RKO Pictures, 1935) and *Quo Vadis?* (MGM, 1951), the portrayals of Jesus go no further than the glimpse of a hand or a foot; never a profile or full-faced image. Nevertheless, fearless filmmakers persevered and some of the oldest remaining films available for viewing today portray the life of Jesus. In the late 1800s and early 1900s, filmmakers from the Lumiere, Gaum, Pathe, and Kalem studios all attempted to capture the life of Jesus on film. Today it is difficult to understand what all the fuss was about, given the piety and sincerity with which these filmmakers approached the subject matter.

La Passion (Lear, 1897), a five-minute French film which no longer exists, was the first to chronicle the life of Jesus and probably the first motion picture to be based on any portion of the Bible. Many early Jesus films experimented with new filmmaking technology and techniques as the gospel accounts of Jesus' miracles presented filmmakers with the opportunity to test the new medium. French filmmaker Georges Méliès' Jesus film, *Le Christ marchant sur les flots [Christ Walking on Water]* (Melies, 1899), used trick photography to show Jesus walking on water. The French *The Birth of Jesus* (1909), was one of the earliest films to employ color as the filmmakers hand-tinted some of the scenes. Kalem's *From the Manger to the Cross* (1912) was, perhaps, the most important American religious production of its time. Directed by Sidney Olcott, it cost a whopping $100,000 and was shot entirely on location in Egypt and Palestine. Like many early Jesus films, its intertitles quoted scenes of scripture and the images that surrounded them acted out those scenes. The lack of descriptions and the limited amount of intertitles suggest a familiarity with the subject matter on the part of the audience. Olcott's film would be the standard for all Jesus films until the arrival of one of the most popular productions in the history of film, religious or not, fifteen years later.

Historians estimate that over a billion people have seen Cecil B. DeMille's Jesus film *The King of Kings* (DeMille Pictures, 1927). This is the most extravagant depiction of Jesus on the screen during the silent era and reflects sensitivity to the kind of common piety characteristic of American popular culture in the first half of the twentieth century. However, it also reflects a subversion of that piety in its representation of Mary Magdalene as a seductive courtesan who fears she is losing her man, Judas, to Jesus, implicitly establishing a scandalous love triangle. Audiences may have flocked to see Jesus, but DeMille hooked them with a scantily clad Mary. DeMille also re-captured any waning attention with an epic scene (an earthquake at Jesus' crucifixion) that shows the director at his disastrous best. Despite these embellishments, DeMille made every effort to ensure a faithful production as three ministers, including a Jesuit priest and a minister from the Federal Council of Churches, were present to give advice throughout shooting. On top of that, members of the cast and crew celebrated Mass every morning before shooting began, and the first day of shooting opened with prayer by Protestant, Catholic, Jewish, Buddhist, and Muslim representatives.[6] Generations of viewers were deeply impacted by the film and it remains an effective viewing experience to this day. Shortly after the film's release, an American minister told H.B. Warner, the actor who played Jesus, "'I saw you in *The King of Kings* when I was a child and now, every time I speak of Jesus, it is your face I see.'"[7]

DeMille's beloved silent film would reign as the premier Jesus film for nearly three decades. Perhaps filmmakers' continued reservation about portraying Jesus on film or the fact that DeMille was still such a strong presence in the industry made it so. However, in 1954, Irving Pichel and John T. Coyle directed *Day of Triumph* (Century Films), which starred Robert Wilson as Jesus. The head of Century Films, Rev. James K. Friedrich, produced this film for distribution to churches, but the color production proved so attractive that Century Films issued it to theaters in 1954 to considerable popularity. Friedrich set out to tell the story of Jesus with a fictional plot that revolved around a secret group in Jerusalem, of which Judas was a member, that wanted to use Jesus to start a revolt against the ruling Romans. Protestant, Catholic, and Jewish clergy praised its action, pageantry, suspense, and human emotion, and the film remains a perfect example of 1950s Christian taste.

In 1961, Nicholas Ray directed *King of Kings* for MGM and cast Jeffrey Hunter as Jesus and Rip Torn as Judas. The film is in no way similar to DeMille's earlier version, save for the title and the subject, and should not be considered a remake. Nearly every critic reviled it and the public proved apathetic to its release. The blame for the film's failure surely rests with director Ray and screenwriter Philip Yordan, whose script was hokey and frequently at odds with scripture. Like *Day of Triumph*, it followed the narrative of Jesus serving as a potential tool for political radicals to overthrow Roman rule and, as a result, emphasized spectacular battle scenes while downplaying Biblical events. As a sign of the times, the film alludes to important events in recent history that occurred between the release of DeMille and Ray's films, specifically the Holocaust of the Jews and the conflict between Jews and Arabs after the establishment of Israel. The portrayal of Jesus here is that of a Messiah of Peace (the words "peace" and "love" are frequently associated with him throughout the film), which is not coincidental given the 1960s Cold War mentality and threat of nuclear war.

Few films characterize the typical Technicolor style as effectively as *The Greatest Story Ever Told* (United Artists, 1965), directed by George Stevens and starring Max von Sydow as Jesus and Charlton Heston as John the Baptist. It originally aired in Cinerama and attempted to be the end-all-be-all of Jesus films. Stevens flooded his production with big-name superstars, whose appearances distracted from the overall story. Just over a decade later, Franco Zeffirelli directed a made-for-television Jesus film, *Jesus of Nazareth* (1977), which starred Robert Powell as Jesus and Anne Bancroft as Mary Magdalene. Unlike Stevens, Zeffirelli was able to fill his production with household names without distracting from the story. Though it told the life of Jesus in great detail, numerous Protestant viewers and organizations criticized it for its inaccuracy. Critics disagreed and argued that it was a reverent and inspirational retelling of the Jesus story.

With the arrival of the 1970s, moviegoers were treated to two counter-cultural Jesus musicals, *Godspell* (Columbia Pictures) and *Jesus Christ Superstar* (Universal Pictures), both released in 1973. The former, based on the book of Matthew, was derived from the Broadway play of the same name, while the latter, drawing heavily from the Gospel of John, was an effective media event that began with an album (in 1968), a touring concert, a stage show, and finally the film. Both targeted the growing youth culture of the early '70s, but the actors in *Godspell* frolic around an abandoned New York City, while the events in *Jesus Christ Superstar* take place in Israel. In 1979, the Monty Python comedy troupe used the gospel story to provide the narrative framework for the life of the titular character in *Life of Brian*. The film tells the story of Brian, a young man in first-century Roman-occupied Palestine, whom people begin to believe is the Messiah. The filmmakers do not necessarily attempt to make fun of the Jesus story, but rather of how Jesus' followers have appropriated, or misappropriated, that story.

By far one of the most controversial Jesus films to make it to the silver screen was

Martin Scorsese's *The Last Temptation of Christ*, starring Willem Dafoe as Jesus and Harvey Keitel as Judas. Based on Nikos Kazantzakis' novel of the same name, the film is an effort to portray Jesus' struggle between the flesh and the spirit. A concluding scene in which Jesus *dreams* of coming down from the cross and having a family with Mary Magdalene sent religious viewers, organizations, and critics into a frenzy, and local police often had to separate protesters from moviegoers. Most critics did not care for the film, although a few argued that Scorsese had made a masterpiece.

Two more recent productions evidence a filmmaker's attempt to advance a political or cultural agenda by co-opting the Jesus story. Haitian-American filmmaker Jean-Claude La Marre directed two films, *Color of the Cross* (Nu-Lite Entertainment, 2006) and *Color of the Cross 2: The Resurrection* (Nu-Lite Entertainment, 2008), in which he also starred as a black Jesus. La Marre uses the films to argue that Jesus was a black man whose death was a racially motivated hate crime. Neither film enjoyed significant theatrical exhibition and quickly went to DVD.

A significant body of literature is available for readers interested in the depiction of Jesus in film. Reinhartz's *Jesus of Hollywood* is perhaps the most insightful of all as she unpacks the representations of, not only Jesus, but also his mother, father(s), disciples, Mary Magdalene, Judas, Satan, the Pharisees, Caiaphas, and Pilate in 41 films. In *Jesus at the Movies: A Guide to the First Hundred Years* (Polebridge Press, 2004), W. Barnes Tatum looks at 14 Jesus films and considers their narrative trajectory (whether they attempt to present a comprehensive portrayal of Jesus or take an alternative approach), the way in which they portray Jesus, and the response of critics and viewers to them. Richard Walsh, in *Reading the Gospels in the Dark* (Trinity Press International, 2003), brings the canonical gospels into conversation with five Jesus films and American culture and discusses how each illuminates the other. Richard C. Stern's *Savior on the Silver Screen* (Paulist Press, 1999) analyzes nine Jesus films and unpacks the insights they offer into the time and cultures from which they emerged. More than the other texts listed here, this book is designed for discussion groups in congregations and

Few directors of films about Jesus have embraced the narrative for their own purposes as intensely as director-actor Jean Claude La Marre, who argued that Jesus' crucifixion was a racially motivated hate crime. Here is a publicity poster for the film *Color of the Cross* (Nu-Lite Entertainment, 2006).

even in college courses. Finally, though not specifically about film, Phillip Yancy's *The Jesus I Never Knew* reveals the power of film (in this case films about Jesus) to influence religious consciousness.

Old Testament and Christian Epics

Like their Jesus films counterparts, biblical epics (primarily representations of Old Testament narratives) and Christian epics (stories of newly converted Christians or Christian persecution under Roman rule), also reveal the changing approaches to religious subject matter on the part of secular filmmakers. One could argue that they do so in a more rapid fashion given the absence of Jesus from their narratives and accompanying preoccupations with how to portray him. While many early biblical epics were created to educate and uplift religious audiences in pious fashion, others set out to exploit their subject matter, particularly their sexual and violent elements, to dazzle, titillate, and entertain large audiences. Though the Production Code was still in effect during the production of many of these films, filmmakers could get away with scandalous portrayals of sex and violence under the auspices of re-telling, and remaining faithful to (wink-wink), a biblical narrative.

Chief among such filmmakers was DeMille, who revealed his abilities for mixing the scandalous and the sacred to great effect in *The King of Kings*. However, Old Testament narratives gave him more salacious source material with which to work. Most readers are familiar with his 1956 production *The Ten Commandments* (Paramount), perhaps the most popular religious film of all time. However, in 1923, he produced a black-and-white silent version in which the story of the Exodus and Moses' acquisition of the Ten Commandments serves as a precursor to a modern story of two brothers, one who is faithful to their mother's pious Christianity and one who is not and breaks, often laughably so, every commandment on the list. This use of a scriptural backdrop to a more modern story was a common practice among many filmmakers who worked with biblical subject matter at that time. In 1929, Michael Curtiz employed it in *Noah's Ark* (Warner Bros.), paralleling the biblical story with the wild jazz age. Both parallel narratives show not only the importance of the biblical narrative in modern times but also how filmmakers and viewers subverted it.

Cecil B. DeMille was the master of walking the tightrope between the sacred and the scandalous. In *The Sign of the Cross* (Paramount, 1932), Claudette Colbert plays an evil temptress, Empress Poppaea, whose wardrobe-staging malfunction slipped past censors at the time.

Two alternative approaches to biblical epics stand out in the 1930s. In 1933, James Sibeley Watson and Melville Webber produced and directed a short black-and-white film, *Lot in Sodom*. It centered on themes of homosexuality and familial structures and openly placed sexual politics, power, and desire within the context of avant-garde film. In 1936, Warner Brothers released the fascinating *Green Pastures*, directed by Marc Connelly. It was the first major Hollywood film to feature an all-black cast and recounts the major Old Testament events up to the coming of Christ as visualized by a young African American girl listening to her Sunday school teacher. The film was banned in cities across the United States and in England because it portrayed God on the screen. Because it was directed by a white man, many critics, then and now, viewed it as a highly racist film.[8]

Far more typical of biblical epics were DeMille's *Samson and Delilah* (Paramount, 1949), Henry King's *David and Bathsheba* (20th Century–Fox, 1951), and King Vidor's *Solomon and Sheba* (Edward Small Productions, 1959), all of which play out like soap operas. *Samson and Delilah* starred Hedy Lamarr as the breasty Delilah and Victor Mature as Samson, whose chest size competed with his female co-star's. Paramount was wary of producing another biblical epic until DeMille showed them the sexy costume designs for Lamarr's Delilah, which they knew would draw a crowd. *David and Bathsheba* featured Gregory Peck and Susan Hayward as the titular lovers but was ultimately a dry re-telling of the scandalous biblical story. *Solomon and Sheba* was a reverent production that featured political intrigue and romance as the queen of Sheba (Gina Lollobrigida) betrays the pharaoh of Egypt to fall in love with the king of Israel (Yul Brynner).

We must step away from Old Testament narratives to briefly consider one of the most exploitative "biblical" epics of all time. In 1955, MGM released *The Prodigal*, which was directed by Richard Thorpe and starred Lana Turner as Samarra, a pagan priestess who tempts the infamous prodigal son of parable fame. This is a highly fictional account of the biblical parable and ultimately serves as a vehicle for Turner to trot around in seductive costumes while she tempts the wayward son. Ironically, the film was based on a script by Joseph Breen, the son of Joseph I. Breen, the infamous head of the Production Code Administration in charge of censoring objectionable film content.

Few films top the grandeur and pageantry of DeMille's epic classic *The Ten Commandments* (1956). For better *and* for worse, it stands as the definitive biblical epic of all time. It starred Charlton Heston, Yul Brynner, Anne Baxter, and Yvonne De Carlo. Even now, more than fifty years since its theatrical release, cable and network television stations still replay it in its entirety. For generations of moviegoers, Heston became Moses ... or Moses became Heston. Biblical infidelity aside, DeMille's uncanny ability to link the intimate with the spectacular is on full display here. In one moment he is able to glimpse the fear and uncertainty of a Jewish family plagued by Egyptian rule and, only a few scenes later, capture the magnificence of the Exodus. Not until DreamWorks' production *The Prince of Egypt* (1998) would a film so effectively portray the story of Moses. In fact, its animated scenes of the Exodus and the parting of the Red Sea are some of the most spectacular ever created.

Perhaps the most epic attempt to film the biblical narrative came in 1960 when producer Dino DeLaurentiis decided to film the entire Old Testament, a feat comparable to the construction of the Tower of Babel, which he managed to capture on film as well. For all his hopes and dreams, DeLaurentiis only managed to release three hours of footage covering the first 22 chapters of Genesis. The result was *The Bible* (20th Century–Fox, 1966), directed by John Huston, who also stars as a humorous Noah and supplies the voice of God. The film is one of the few biblical epics to feature Abraham (George C. Scott) and Sarah (Ava Gardner). While it is a highly reverent film, it is, unfortunately, far too boring for its length.

Closely linked to the Biblical epics in style and theme are Christian epics set in apostolic times. Perhaps the cheesiest Christian film of all time is DeMille's *The Sign of the Cross* (Paramount, 1932), which is the scandalous exception to the pious rule of secular approaches to religious filmmaking. Of all of DeMille's films, it is perhaps the one most associated with his not-so-subtle, lurid flourishes that he snuck in under the protective umbrella of a "religious film." The film included an epic arena battle with scantily clad Amazon women impaling pygmies, a gorilla attacking a naked woman tied to a post, and elephants and crocodiles attacking Christians. Charles Laughton plays a delightfully nasty Nero while Claudette Colbert played Empress Poppaea. In one of the film's more memorable scenes, she bathes in a pool of asses' milk and entices a female courtesan to take off her clothes and join her. The filmmakers' efforts to measure the height of Colbert's nipples and to fill the pool with enough milk to cover them did not prevent frontal exposure that somehow slipped past the censors as well. This scene, and others of Roman wealth, contrasted sharply with what American audiences were experiencing during the Great Depression, as many could not afford the $1.50 admission fee. DeMille re-released the film in 1944 to coincide with wartime sensibilities and included a new prologue that shows Protestant and Catholic army chaplains flying in a B-17 bomber on a mission to drop leaflets over Rome. DeMille also trimmed footage offensive to the Catholic Legion of Decency, which had risen to power at that time.

Far more reverent, though no less epic, are the *Quo Vadis?* and *Ben-Hur* "trilogies," all of which are far more tasteful, even in their scenes of gladiatorial combat or Christian persecution. An early version of *Quo Vadis?* was filmed in Paris in 1902 and was followed by three remakes, all filmed in Italy. The most popular version would be MGM's 1951 production starring Robert Taylor, Deborah Kerr, and Peter Ustinov as Nero. At a cost of $8.5 million, it was the most expensive film to date and went on to be both a financial and critical success (it was nominated for eight Oscars). MGM also produced two of the three versions of *Ben-Hur*. The first was a 1907 Kalem feature directed by Sidney Olcott, who also directed *From the Manger to the Cross*. The 1925 MGM version starred Ramon Novarro and Francis X. Bushman and cost the studio $4 million. It would go on to gross over $9 million. The 1959 MGM remake was directed by William Wyler and starred Charlton Heston. This final remake was both a box office and critical success, taking home nine Academy Awards, including Best Picture. In each version, the famous chariot battle scene is the most memorable and one of the most iconic images of film history.

The Robe (20th Century–Fox, 1953) told the story of the Roman centurion, Marcellus Gallio (Richard Burton), in charge of Jesus' crucifixion who eventually wins Jesus' robe in a dice game at the foot of the cross. Soon, the robe begins to exert a mystical influence over the centurion. The film is most famous for being the first production in CinemaScope, 20th Century–Fox's extra-large, widescreen response to the growing popularity of television. The film inspired a sequel, *Demetrius and the Gladiators* (1954), in which Marcellus' slave Demetrius (Victor Mature) moves to the forefront to keep the robe out of Caligula's possession.

Like Watson and Webber did with *Lot in Sodom*, Derek Jarmann used a religious narrative to foreground themes of homosexuality, sexual power, and desire in his 1976 production *Sebastiane* (Cinegate Ltd.). While it was made as a gay film, it reached a wider audience and played in art house cinemas throughout the United States. The film posited that Sebastian was in fact the lover of the Emperor Diocletian and a captain in his Imperial guard. When Sebastian converts to Christianity and no longer submits to the emperor's desires, Diocletian sends him away to be tortured, and finally executed, in his archers' target practice.

Biblical narratives still appeal to filmmakers in the twenty-first century. In 2009, Harold Ramis directed *Year One* (Columbia Pictures), which stars Jack Black and Michael Cera as bumbling prehistoric losers who stumble throughout famous Old Testament scenes. Expelled from their tribe, the two meet Cain and Abel on a fateful day, stop Abraham from killing Isaac, become slaves, and reach the city of Sodom where their tribe is now enslaved. Critics reviled the film, asserting that it failed to live up the tradition of more thoughtful, satirical epics like *Life of Brian*.

Several texts provide valuable insight into the production of biblical and Christian epics. Most notable among these is Jon Solomon's *The Ancient World in the Cinema* (Yale University Press, 2001), in which the author discusses a wealth of films that feature not only Old and New Testament narratives but Greek and Roman mythology, along with a number of films set in Babylon, Egypt, Persia, and the Ancient Orient. Two biographies of Cecil B. DeMille, *Cecil B. DeMille: A Life in Art* (Thomas Dunne Books, 2007) by Simon Louvish and *Empire of Dreams: The Epic Life of Cecil B. DeMille* (Simon & Schuster, 2010) by Scott Eyman, provide valuable information about the life and work of the most famous director of biblical epics in film history. J. Stephen Lang's *The Bible on the Big Screen: A Guide from Silent Films to Today's Movies* (Baker Books, 2007) provides information on the logistics of biblical films (credits, release dates, running times, etc.), the motives behind making the movies, critics' reactions to them, and other behind-the-scenes information. In *Big Screen Rome* (Wiley-Blackwell, 2005), Monica Silveira Cyrino discusses nine films set in ancient Rome and considers the ways in which they both wrestled with the social concerns of the times in which they were created and the implications they might have for contemporary audiences.

Ministers on Film

In his book *Christians in the Movies: A Century of Saints and Sinners* (Rowman & Littlefield Publishers, 2009) Peter E. Dans notes a historical transition in the way secular films portray Christians, which also parallels the way filmmakers approached religion in general. Organizing his survey chronologically by decade, Dans notes an "arc of the portrayal of Christians as 'saints' or favorably in the early decades [that became] progressively less [favorable] as the millennium approached."[9] While Dans shows that each decade offered films with both positive and negative portrayals of Christians, he ultimately argues that the trend holds.

One of the first popular films to feature a minister in the lead role was *The Miracle Man* (Paramount, 1919), starring Lon Chaney. In the pious fashion of the times, the film tells the story of a gang of crooks who evade the police by moving their operations to a small town. There, the gang's leader encounters a faith healer and uses him to scam the gullible public of funds for a supposed chapel. However, when a real healing takes place, a change comes over the gang. The Sadie Thompson "trilogy" included the films *Sadie Thompson* (Gloria Swanson Pictures, 1928), *Rain* (Feature Productions, 1932), and *Miss Sadie Thompson* (Columbia Pictures, 1953). All of the versions of this Somerset Maugham story feature a corruptible, inept minister who attempts to save the soul of Sadie Thompson (most likely a prostitute), who has fled San Francisco and landed in the South Pacific. The minister ends up falling for her (but kills himself after spending the night with her) before she is to be sent back to face her punishment stateside.

In 1929, King Vidor directed MGM's *Hallelujah!*, a film that was advertised as an authentic look at African Americans and their religious sensibilities. Most critics claimed that it, like *The Green Pastures*, simply reinforced white prejudices about African Americans and continued to stereotype them.[10] One of its many problems was the way in which it linked religious fervor with sexuality, highly sexualizing the former in the process. Frank Capra's *The Miracle Woman* (Columbia Pictures, 1931) is a satirical glance at the more questionable activities of America's religious fringe with Barbara Stanwyck playing an Aimee Semple MacPherson–type character. The film also includes an awkward love story that employs a creepy puppet.

Catholic priests fared well in a variety of Hollywood films. In *Angels with Dirty Faces* (Warner Bros., 1938), Pat O'Brien plays Father Jerry Connolly opposite James Cagney's Rocky Sullivan, who gets wrapped up in a life of crime. Connolly, and the censors, eventually forced Sullivan to show remorse for his sinful life of crime as he approaches the electric chair. This was a drastic shift for a character who portrays a tough-as-nails personality throughout the majority of the film. Also in 1938, Spencer Tracy starred in *Boys Town* (MGM) as the real-life Father Flannagan, a priest who founded Boys Town, an orphanage that sought to redeem troubled boys. It inspired a sequel, *Men of Boys Town* (MGM, 1941). In 1944, Bing Crosby starred in *Going My Way* (Paramount) as Father O'Malley, a performance that earned him an Academy Award for Best Actor. In the film, Father O'Malley serves as the youthful assistant to the older, gruff Father Fitzgibbon (Barry Fitzgerald), who attempts to relieve the mortgage-ridden parish of its debt. Crosby's Father O'Malley was a kinder, cooler priest, and one who could carry a tune as well. For Catholics who were often ghettoized in American popular culture, this film was wildly popular. In 1946, Crosby reprised his role as Father O'Malley in *The Bells of St. Mary's* (Rainbow Productions) and tries to soften up an authoritarian Mother Superior (Ingrid Bergman). This film was even more successful than its predecessor.

One of the most artistic, haunting American films ever made happens to feature a maniacal minister as its main character. Charles Laughton's *The Night of the Hunter* (Paul Gregory Productions, 1955) starred Robert Mitchum as a psychotic country preacher who tries to track down the widow of a man recently hanged for murder. He is convinced that she, or her children, can show him where the proceeds of her husband's robbery are hidden. He eventually kills the widow and later hunts the fleeing children through the moonlit countryside. This was the only film that Laughton ever directed and must surely stand as one of the greatest cinematic one-hit-wonders of all time.

In 1964 and 1965, Richard Burton played a defrocked Episcopal priest and a headmaster at an Episcopal school, respectively, in *The Night of the Iguana* (MGM) and *The Sandpiper* (Filmways Pictures). In the former, he was turned out of his church because "the kneeling position turned into the reclining position" and becomes a guide to a party of Baptist spinsters on a tour of Mexico. Just before production of *The Sandpiper* began, Burton married Elizabeth Taylor, and in the film, the newlyweds play two characters who fall in love with one another. Burton's character was married to Claire (Eva Marie Saint), whom he forsakes in order to satisfy his lust for the hip, bohemian Laura (Taylor).

Perhaps the most famous of all huckster minister films is *Elmer Gantry* (United Artists, 1960), an adaptation of Sinclair Lewis' attack on commercialized, show-biz revivalism. It stars Burt Lancaster in the lead role as a traveling salesman who discovers the lucrative aspect of hell-fire and damnation preaching. Lancaster received an Oscar for Best Actor while Shirley Jones won for Supporting Actress and Richard Brooks won for Best Screenplay.

In *The Night of the Hunter* (Paul Gregory Productions, 1955), Robert Mitchum plays the murderous Rev. Harry Powell, here in his now iconic pose highlighting his LOVE and HATE tattoos.

More recently, *The Apostle* (Butcher's Run Films, 1997), which Robert Duvall both directed and starred in, is a highlight of the genre because of the complexity of its lead character, a troubled Pentecostal preacher on the lam for attacking his ex-wife's boyfriend. He settles in a small Louisiana town where he starts a new church until the law finally catches up with him. This is one of Duvall's greatest performances, and the sincerity with which he approaches the topic is evident in both the film and his commentary on it. In 2007, P.T. Anderson directed *There Will Be Blood* (Paramount Vantage), a story of oil and religion in post-wild west America. Daniel Day-Lewis plays Daniel Plainview, a tough-as-nails oil man who strikes it rich in California. His main opposition comes in the form of Eli Sunday (Paul Dano), an up-and-coming minister at the Church of the Third Revelation, who questions Plainview's business practices and the destination of his soul. When Sunday runs into financial troubles, he turns to Plainview for help with tragic consequences.

While there are fewer texts that focus on the portrayal of ministers in film, especially compared to Jesus and biblical narratives, there are a few worth mentioning. Dans' *Christians in the Movies* takes a broader approach to the genre, considering films that include both Catholic and Protestant ministers. Although they are focused on the portrayal of Catholics, Colleen McDannell's edited collection of essays *Catholics in the Movies* (Oxford University Press, 2007) and Anthony Burke Smith's *The Look of Catholics: Portrayals in Popular Culture from the Great Depression to the Cold War* (University Press of Kansas, 2010) provide valuable insight into the changing ways in which filmmakers have portrayed ministers throughout film history.

Christians Behind the Scenes

While most viewers will be familiar with many of the films that I discussed above, few will be familiar with the role that Christians and Christian organizations played in shaping the industry of Hollywood as a whole through both censorship and production. For the remainder of this chapter, I want to highlight this involvement, particularly Protestant efforts to produce, distribute, and exhibit their own productions. I will conclude with a brief consideration of the reasons why these production efforts were so short-lived.

Censorship

To put it simply, both Catholics and Protestants played a role in regulating film content through censorship. The former, however, played a much more substantial part for a variety of reasons, not the least of which was their established institutional organization. Their ability to mobilize in support of or against a film made Catholics a key audience to help boost a film's potential success at the box office. Two specific Catholic efforts that demand attention are the Catholic Legion of Decency and the Hollywood industry's Production Code, which was highly influenced by Catholic leadership and Catholic theology. Though Catholics like Joseph Breen and Daniel Lord shaped the document, Hollywood executives turned to a Protestant, Will H. Hays, a Presbyterian elder and postmaster general, to implement it and run the Motion Picture Producers and Distributors of America (MPPDA) that screened films to rate them before their release.

The Catholic Legion of Decency stood apart from both the Hollywood filmmaking industry and its Production Code and was dedicated to identifying and combating objectionable content in motion pictures. Its members would view films and provide them with their own ratings. Where the MPPDA issued ratings of G or R, for example, the Legion of Decency would rate films as A (morally unobjectionable), B (morally objectionable in part), or C (condemned by the Legion of Decency). They broke the A rating into age groups as well, further rating films suitable for all audiences (A-I) or suitable for adults with reservations (A-IV). Catholics, or at least those who took the Legion seriously, would faithfully follow these recommendations. Even now, there are generations of Catholics who still remember reciting a pledge of allegiance to the Legion during Mass, which read, in part:

> I wish to join the Legion of Decency, which condemns vile and unwholesome moving pictures. I unite with all who protest against them as a grave menace to youth, to home life, to country and to religion. I condemn absolutely those salacious motion pictures, which, with other degrading agencies, are corrupting public morals and promoting a sex mania in our land.... Considering these evils, I hereby promise to remain away from all motion pictures except those which do not offend decency and Christian morality.[11]

Such religious involvement in Hollywood was, no doubt, two-fold. Not only did it work to shape film content, but it also led to the liberal backlash of the '60s and '70s that I will discuss later in Chapter 7. The Catholic involvement in Hollywood has been well documented in works like Frank Walsh's *Sin and Censorship: The Catholic Church and the Motion*

Picture Industry (Yale University Press, 1996), Gregory D. Black's *The Catholic Crusade Against the Movies, 1940–1975* (Cambridge University Press, 1998), and Thomas Doherty's *Hollywood's Censor: Joseph I. Breen and the Production Code Administration* (Columbia University Press, 2009).

Many Protestants were just as concerned with improving film content but were not as organized as their Catholic counterparts. Protestant ministers who supported the cinema hoped that it would change the world by more effectively spreading the Gospel in ways that transcended language and cultural barriers. For example, D.W. Griffith, a Methodist and one of American cinema's most famous and influential directors, believed that motion pictures presented a whole new "universal language" that would usher in the immanent Kingdom of God. At the same time, many Protestant ministers hoped that morally uplifting and educational films could improve the lives of faithful viewers and those who had wandered from the faith. Jane Addams, founder of Hull House, a settlement house that worked for social reform, believed that "moving pictures and nickel theaters could be 'made instructive' and thus productive of social virtue and moral growth if they were more closely supervised by the police and citizen groups." She even set up a model nickel theater in Hull House, which *Moving Picture World* referred to as "the uplift theatre." This experience convinced Addams that, in time, "'schools and churches will count films as among their most valuable equipment.'"[12]

The Early Church Film Movement

Even less familiar than Protestant participation in film censorship are the Protestant efforts at embracing the technology of this young medium and the emerging church film movement that emerged during the first few decades of the 1900s. Over the past decade, Lindvall has led the effort to uncover this vibrant and diverse Protestant response to the advent and rapid growth in popularity of the cinema. Lindvall reveals that, far from being the conservative, fundamentalist resisters to new technology (though there were some among them), many Protestants embraced, and even had grand dreams for, the possibilities of motion pictures. The Protestant embrace of the cinema was, in part, a natural progression from its use of slide projectors to illustrate sermons and lectures and to project hymn lyrics during worship. Missionaries used slides to teach the illiterate and non–English speakers around the world while also using them to illustrate lectures about the missionary efforts to congregants back home. Lindvall argues that by embracing "the display of these marvels through optical illusion, the church of the nineteenth century embraced a celebratory exhibition of visual art" and further readied itself for the birth of cinema.[13] Here, I want to simply highlight a few of the Protestant uses of the cinema from Lindvall's research that find parallels in the contemporary church film movement that I will discuss later.

Lindvall notes that those who embraced motion pictures among the Protestant community did so on a three-fold level, "to achieve their mission of attracting new audiences, of instructing and entertaining their congregations, and of exploiting nontheatrical films to serve the Kingdom of God and their parishes."[14] By 1913, the church reaction to motion pictures had become so positive and widespread that the Edison Company arranged to supply the Presbyterian Board of Publications with films and projectors, "with a subsequent heavy increase in projector sales to the churches of the Mid-west in the following year."[15] The efforts on the part of the Edison Company to reach out to congregations is especially interesting because it reveals that the church use of film did not simply take place in big cities along the East Coast but in small towns across the country as well.

The major event at that time that epitomizes Protestant expectations for motion pictures was the 1919 Methodist Episcopal Centenary in Columbus, Ohio. The leaders of this conference created an open-air movie screen measuring 136 feet high and 146 feet wide that could seat over four million viewers. Hollywood dignitaries like Adolph Zukor and D.W. Griffith were on hand to lend their blessings to the proceedings. Lindvall writes, "In conjunction with Griffith, [the Rev Dr. Christian] Reisner and a dozen Methodist laymen devised 'ways and means to raise a fund of $120,000,000 for the purchase of entertainment devices to be placed in the churches of this denomination.' ...The grand vision was to enable a mature Methodist Church to become 'one of the most important film producing and distributing concerns in the world.'"[16] Along with the Edison Company's plans to provide churches with films and projectors, the Methodists' desire to invest in technology for their churches reveals the first major role that churches played in relation to the cinema, that of exhibition site.

At the height of the church-film movement, the church became such a prominent site of exhibition that neighboring theater managers complained, arguing that churches were stealing their business. Churches screened films during morning and evening Sunday worship services in the sanctuary or in classrooms during Sunday school. Some churches even began screening films (and not just specifically religious productions either) every day of the week. Most often, these films included "actualities" (or what film historian Tom Gunning calls a "Cinema of Attractions"), usually documentary footage of people, places, and events.[17] In a church setting, actualities could also include images of the Middle East and the Holy Land accompanied by a lecture from the minister or a visiting speaker on the significance of the images that appeared (and moved) before the congregants' eyes. As films developed a narrative, these same ministers and lecturers could use melodramas to teach a moral lesson. No matter the type of film shown, church-exhibited motion pictures guaranteed both a safe viewing location and, most often, unobjectionable content. As a result, they became an effective alternative to saloons and even other movie houses that might have been both physically or morally harmful to their patrons.

Other organizations, while not equipping churches with the means to exhibit films, began recommending the use of motion pictures in the life of the church. As Lindvall refers to them, these Better Picture Movements recommended "good" pictures to religious organizations and warned of "bad" ones. One, actually entitled the Better Films Movement, vehemently opposed censorship in favor of honest character, even as it preferred ethical subjects of religious, dogmatic material. They were also aware that the church use of motion pictures could have a positive reverse effect, lifting up the industry at all levels from production to exhibition.[18] Churches and denominations also took matters into their own hands to recommend good films. Perhaps the most effective was the Methodist church's "White List," a parallel to Catholic efforts with the Legion of Decency. A publication of the Methodist Committee on Conservation and Advance, the list included "1,001 films available for church and school use" that went out to more than two thousand Methodist pastors.[19] Other nonsectarian groups got in the recommendation business as well, specifically the National Board of Review's National Committee for Better Films and the Committee on Visual Education of the International Council of Religious Education. Both released publications recommending films for educational and church use.[20] Again, religious individuals and organizations' responses to these lists, which included secular films, were mixed. Some valued wholesome Hollywood features while others continued to advocate for a separate film industry driven by church-based productions.

Finally, during this time, some ministers, dissatisfied with simply recommending or exhibiting certain motion pictures, began to produce their own films.[21] The first major Christian production effort occurred in 1913 with the International Bible Students Association's eight-hour (broken into three separate features) *Photo-Drama of Creation*. The production was presented for free at major cities across the country and was a mixture of colored slides, tinted movies, phonographic lectures, and musical accompaniment.[22] However, expenses soon began to mount and the producers and exhibitors would be forced to encourage audiences to make financial contributions. In 1919, the Episcopal Rev. Dr. James K. Shields produced and directed *The Stream of Life*. The film tells the story of a farm boy who becomes a financial CEO, drifts into "secular" life, loses his daughter, sees his wife ameliorate her grief through faith, and comes to faith himself. Interestingly enough, the film does not simply end with his conversion, but shows him devoting his post-conversion life to the service of others. If any religious viewers were offended by the film's non-biblical content, its supporters simply reminded them of "Jesus' methods of using pictures and parables for dramatic effect."[23] Shields also organized ministry teams to accompany screenings for follow-up ministry. Perhaps more important than Shields' film is his vision for the future of the church and the cinema. Lindvall writes:

> [Shields] explained that in addition to preaching evangelists and singing evangelists, the church would one day commission "motion picture evangelists, men and women who will, with the same divine consecration, pour the heart of the Gospel into simple stories and great dramas for the screen that will draw and grip the hearts of thousands and millions that the preaching and singing evangelists can never reach because of their physical limitations."[24]

Soon, organizations began to emerge that devoted themselves to the production of nontheatrical films for church use. These included groups like Sacred Films Incorporated, the International Church Film Corporation, the Historical Film Corporation, the Bible Film Company, and New Era Films.

The two major organizations, that produced and distributed non-theatrical religious films were the Christian Herald Motion Picture Bureau and the Religious Motion Picture Foundation. Despite fits and starts from other organizations, Lindvall argues that the "most comprehensive movement toward a church-film association occurred in the boardrooms and pages of the *Christian Herald* magazine."[25] The members of the Christian Herald Motion Picture Bureau (CHMPB) had the grand vision of making churches "completely independent of any output by the theatrical motion picture interests." To do so, they would supply churches with a plethora of productions, films "written only by 'consecrated Christian men, acted by Christian men and women,' and produced under the most talented and inspired direction with all the technical excellence of Hollywood."[26] Unfortunately, Lindvall points out that "most of the pictures that the *Christian Herald* released seemed more concerned with Prohibition and good citizenship than with Christian doctrine."[27] The CHMPB soon succumbed to a variety of both internal and external forces.

Founded in 1925, the Religious Motion Picture Foundation built a network of Presbyterian, Congregational, Episcopal, Lutheran, Methodist and Reform Churches.[28] The RMPF was led by William Elmer Harmon and would soon become known as the Harmon Foundation. It was, according to Lindvall, "the last major attempt of big business to enter the non-theatrical field during the silent film era."[29] The RMPF had a particularly successful output, with films strong in visual quality but weaker in drama. They produced four films on the life of Christ and also hired consultants to instruct ministers on the use of these films as sermon illustrations. Because of limited funds, the RMPF only hired professional actors for leading roles and employed amateurs and volunteers for supporting roles, all while shooting in a small studio loft.[30]

Why the Movement Stalled

As passionate as many of these ministers were and as successful, for a time, as many of the production efforts were, their dreams of a viable church film movement to counter Hollywood productions were short-lived. A number of factors contributed to its demise: lingering religious resistance, inadequate finances, the emergence of radio, and a limited production output. Despite a number of religious supporters of motion pictures, many ministers maintained a negative opinion of the new medium. Of course, Hollywood scandals in the 1920s, epitomized by the Roscoe "Fatty" Arbuckle case in San Francisco, fueled these ministers' fire.[31] That a significant number of ministers chose to remain highly critical of Hollywood motion pictures rather than attempting to help create "cleaner" alternatives certainly struck a blow to the early church film movement.

Disagreeing ministers aside, participants in the church film movement did themselves few favors by underestimating the financial commitment required to sustain viable film production, distribution, and exhibition efforts. The arrival of sound to motion pictures only increased the costs of exhibiting films as both theaters and churches would be required to wire their buildings for sound, an undertaking that proved cost-prohibitive to many congregations. Of course, the impending Depression only made it more difficult for churches to undertake an already costly business. Despite the appeal of motion pictures and their ability to spread their message, the advent of the radio presented ministers with a cheaper medium for evangelism, one that was even more suitable for preaching.[32]

Ultimately, a major fault lies in the productions that emerged from this early church film movement. The majority of ministers and organizations trafficked in biblical and missionary films and failed to craft narratives that appealed to a broader audience. Though Lindvall refers to the *Christian Herald*'s departure from film production, he might as well be referring to the church as a whole and the ways in which it forever altered its relationship to motion pictures. Lindvall writes, "[In] the film world of the brazen serpent [the *Christian Herald*] completely relinquished its creative production potential. It traded its birthright to supply the churches with fresh Christian film narratives for a bowl of critical opinions. In an effort to shape better pictures, it chose to critique movies rather than create them."[33]

After the Demise

As we just saw, Christian film production began to wane in the mid–1920s. It would lie dormant for almost three decades as filmmakers like DeMille, Vidor, and King took charge of the biblical and/or Christian epics discussed earlier in this chapter. However, Lindvall does note three significant production efforts on the part of Christian filmmakers, one of whom I have already discussed. The Rev. James K. Friedrich, Carlos Octavia Baptista, and Dr. Irwin Moon briefly re-energized Christian film production.[34] Friedrich revived black-and-white biblical pictures while also producing *Day of Triumph*, Baptista filmed an animated version of *Pilgrim's Progress*, and Moon created experimental films called "Sermons from Science." A few decades later, Billy Graham would sustain Christian filmmaking through his production company World Wide Pictures, which produced *Two a Penny* (1967) and *The Hiding Place* (1975) and continues to produce straight-to-DVD features today. These Protestant efforts parallel the development and work of the Catholic production company Paulist Pictures, which later produced *Romero* (1989) and *Entertaining Angels: The Dorothy Day Story* (1996).

I was tempted to include this film in the list of Jesus films above, but it fits better here because it was an independent Christian production designed more to reap a spiritual profit than a financial one. In 1979, John Heyman directed *Jesus*, starring Brian Deacon in the title role. Primarily basing their movie on the gospel of Luke, Heyman and his cast and crew attempted to persuade viewers of the truth of Jesus, and before production began, they circulated a preliminary script for several hundred religious leaders and biblical scholars to proofread for scriptural and historical accuracy. A seven-minute commentary at the end of the film represents a cinematic counterpart to the traditional altar call in many Protestant churches, inviting viewers to follow Jesus and enter into a relationship with him. Campus Crusade for Christ uses the film aggressively in its evangelism work and argues that it is the most widely viewed film in history. With the help of the Jesus Film Project, they claim that over six billion people have seen the film, which has been translated into 1,100 languages, and that over 200 million "decisions for Christ" resulted form those screenings.[35]

Around the same time, Donald Thompson, an evangelical Christian filmmaker, founded Mark IV Productions, which specialized in apocalyptic films. His films, *A Thief in the Night* (1972), *A Distant Thunder* (1978), and *Image of the Beast* (1981), dominated evangelical filmmaking in their time. Unlike many of their Christian film counterparts, as Hendershot points out, "their evangelical interpretations of Biblical prophecy are so complex that several films in Thompson's series actually grind to a halt as a character uses a giant wall chart to explain the most perplexing passages form Daniel, Ezekiel, and Revelation."[36] Yet these low-budget features (*A Thief in the Night* cost only $68,000) had a great influence on evangelical life and filmmaking. Hendershot speculates, "It is only a slight exaggeration to say that *A Thief in the Night* affected the evangelical film industry the way sound or color affected Hollywood."[37]

A couple of decades later, Christian filmmaking brothers Peter and Paul Lalonde founded Cloud Ten Pictures. Following in Thompson's footsteps, they also focused on rapture and apocalyptic films. Beginning in 1998, Cloud Ten Pictures undertook two separate apocalyptic film series, one of which was an adaptation of the wildly popular *Left Behind* novels. Both series were commercial and critical failures that suffered from poor filmmaking and, in one case, a literally unbelievable marketing strategy. Their first apocalyptic series include the films *Apocalypse: Caught in the Eye of the Storm* (1998), *Revelation* (1999), *Tribulation* (2000), and *Judgment* (2001). These films cost $1, $5, $9, and $11 million respectively. We can only assume that their limited DVD sales of around 300,000–400,000 copies each allowed them to continue producing these films.

In the midst of this series, Cloud Ten also produced *Left Behind* (2000), *Left Behind II: Tribulation Force* (2002), and *Left Behind III: World at War* (2005), all starring former child television actor turned Christian film star Kirk Cameron. The first *Left Behind* film cost $17.4 million and became, at that time, the most expensive Christian film ever made. Although Lalonde wanted to release it in over 2,500 theaters, abysmal marketing and a ridiculous release strategy (he released the DVD before the theatrical release in an effort to increase word-of-mouth publicity) ensured the failure of the film (it took in only $4.2 million at the box office). The sequels cost an estimated $3.8 and $4.6 million respectively. The third film in the series was released in over 3,200 churches on a single opening weekend, which parallels the number of venues into which many Hollywood blockbusters release. Cloud Ten Productions claims that they have sold over ten million DVD copies of these films worldwide.[38] If this is even remotely true, then they have most likely seen a return on their investments. Cloud Ten has recently reclaimed the film rights to the *Left Behind* series and is currently securing funding for a big-budget remake of the first film in the series.[39] No doubt the sudden rise in popularity of Christian films has inspired this remake.

Following in this apocalyptic trend, Matthew Crouch produced *The Omega Code* (1999) and *Megiddo: The Omega Code 2* (2001) through his company, Gener8xion Entertainment. The films cost $7 and $22 million respectively. Unlike the Lalondes' productions, *The Omega Code* had a brief theatrical release and earned $2 million in its first weekend. As of July 2001, it had grossed $12.6 million from all markets.[40] *Megiddo* finished its theatrical run with earnings of just over $6 million.[41] Crouch is the son of Jan and Paul Crouch, the founders of Trinity Broadcasting Network (TBN), which has proven to be a great treasure chest of funds from which he could draw. Hendershot writes:

> As a not-for-profit ministry, TBN cannot sell ads, but viewers donate an estimated $80 million to the network each year. TBN is a privately owned network with twelve full-power and more than three hundred low-power stations nationwide. TBN also has five thousand cable outlets accessible to over seventy million households. TBN received the initial exclusive rights to air *Omega Code* on television, as well as an undisclosed percentage of the box office returns.[42]

Not only does TBN provide financial resources for these and other productions, but its extensive networks ensure maximum exposure to the evangelical community to which these films are targeted.

All of these films best fit Lindvall's definition of Christian cinema concerning films of the first two decades of the 1900s. They do not aspire to, or at least do not appear to aspire to, high aesthetic values, had no or extremely limited theatrical release, seek to educate and uplift believers, and have had virtually no crossover appeal (despite their producers' assertions, the numbers do not lie). These films play on evangelical Christians' anticipation (and fear?) of the rapture and apocalyptic tribulation while also giving voice to some Christians' feelings of oppression and suffering on Earth here and now.

Their lack of crossover success could be attributed to two factors, their lack of respect for non–Christian characters and their theology and prophecy, which are confounding to outsiders and problematic to many insiders. Hendershot argues that this is because "the filmmakers fail to realize that prophecy is in many ways a self-enclosed system that means nothing to outsiders."[43] For insiders, the films are problematic for two reasons. Christians who might share similar theological worldviews often criticize them for their unclear salvation message. Hendershot writes, "While [the films imply] that the heroes are saved by showing them praying, [they do] not outline exactly how to repent and be saved."[44] On the other hand, to Christians who do not share a similar theological worldview, these films are deeply troubling. Biblical scholars like Barbara Rossing are bringing scathing critiques of the evangelical obsession with the Rapture, its lack of scriptural support, and its implications for world politics into the mainstream.[45]

I have drawn attention to these apocalyptic films because they stand in stark contrast to the films from the contemporary church film movement that I will discuss later in this book. The shortcomings of the Lalonde brothers' and Crouch's films will help further explain the success and, if limited, crossover appeal of Sherwood Pictures' productions. In this chapter, I have both intentionally and unknowingly overlooked a host of Christian productions. Furthermore, I am aware that Lindvall has just published another book on Christian film production from the point at which he leaves off in *Sanctuary Cinema* until the 1980s. He has uncovered film production efforts on the part of Baptists, Lutherans, Episcopalians, and Presbyterians and has delved further into the work of Billy Graham's Worldwide Pictures and Gateway Films.[46] There have been a host of other straight-to-DVD Christian films that appeared at the end of the 1990s and in the early 2000s. One of these is the made-for-television *The Bible Collection*, a series that includes films like *Abraham* (1993), *Jacob* (1994), *Joseph* (1995), *Moses* (1995), *Samson and Delilah* (1996), *David* (1997), *Solomon* (1997), *Esther* (1999), and *Jesus* (1999). All of these films were produced by the Beta Film Company but flew under the critical radar given their lack of a theatrical release. Many of these DVD releases are now available through distribution outlets that I will discuss in the next chapter. Even with these omissions aside, I have at least drawn attention to the rich history of the interactions between American cinema and Christianity. Yet as vibrant as this history was, nothing could prepare Hollywood insiders or religious outsiders for what was to come in 2004.

Chapter 2

A Passionate Phenomenon

The Passion of the Christ opened on Wednesday, February 25, 2004, earning $83.8 million in its opening weekend. Final domestic box office figures amounted to almost $370.8 million, while foreign receipts brought in just over $241 million, for a total of almost $611.9 million.[1] These receipts made *The Passion* the highest-grossing R-rated film of all time.[2] When the film premiered on DVD in August 2004, 4.1 million copies flew off the shelves on the first day. These figures are even more impressive when we consider the fact that this independent film had a "paltry" $30 million production budget, a great portion of which Gibson financed himself. Both the film and audiences' reactions to it demanded analysis.

Even before its release, critics and scholars began to pick apart Gibson's film, focusing on its violent images of the torture and crucifixion of Jesus and its potential to incite anti–Semitism. After its release, they approached *The Passion* from almost every conceivable angle, resulting in several books and a host of articles about the film and audiences' reactions to it. In his article "Lights! Camera! Action!," Jose Marquez argues that we can better understand the film in light of the action movie genre in which Gibson had so much prior success.[3] Taking a completely different tack, William G. Little examines *The Passion* in light of our makeover-obsessed culture.[4] Given the controversy over its perceived anti–Semitism and Gibson's conservative Catholic leanings, other critics have placed the film in broader ecclesial and theological contexts.[5] Still other scholars examine the art historical influences on Gibson's production.[6] Yet perhaps the most difficult, and intriguing, studies seek to determine just how the film became so popular and financially successful. In their introduction to *Mel Gibson's Bible*, Timothy K. Beal and Tod Linafelt ask quite simply, "How do we understand the overwhelmingly positive response of so many viewers to this unusual mix of Hollywood, biblical narrative, and conservative Christian theology?"[7]

The analyses of audience reaction to *The Passion* reveal, in part, three main reasons for the film's success: controversy, marketing, and genuine spiritual connection. First, as countless news reports and many essays have shown, controversy surrounded Gibson's film from the start. This controversy involved accusations of anti–Semitism, fidelity to scripture, and the violence with which Gibson intended to depict Jesus' torture and crucifixion. Despite all of this criticism, Gibson insisted that he was being faithful to scripture and that his critics ultimately did not have a problem with him, but rather with scripture. Whether or not Gibson's film was faithful to scripture became a point of contention within the Christian community, while charges of anti–Semitism raised tension between Christian and Jewish groups.

Beyond the well-documented accusations of anti–Semitism, the controversy intensified around Gibson's use of violence. Sharon Waxman, an entertainment journalist who extensively covered *The Passion*'s release, notes a strange source of publicity that was no doubt responsible for thousands of ticket sales. She writes, "The film has been promoted on horror-fan websites, and young men seem to be drawn by reports that the movie is gory."[8] Another horror website described it as "'the bloodiest, goriest, flesh-rippingest film your church-going grandma will ever want to see. Jesus' ripped flesh becomes a horror makeup artist's dream.'"[9] Peter Guber, chairman of Mandalay Entertainment added, "'*The Passion* was brilliantly marketed through *controlled* political and religious controversy, and there are people going to see it for the R-rated violence, but the key question for the rest of us is whether its sweet spot is its religious fervor.'"[10] Guber's comment picks up on the other two reasons for *The Passion*'s success, marketing and religious fervor.

Prior to the film's release, Gibson engaged his film in an unprecedented marketing strategy. Though producers of religious films have offered advance screenings to religious organizations throughout film history, none have exhibited the level of control over both audience makeup and response.[11] In his article on market segmentation, mass marketing, and the promotion of *The Passion*, Peter A. Maresco writes that the producers sent out "personal invitations to many high profile church and religious leaders" and that "churches whose leaders had been specifically invited to view a preview of the film on their own encouraged their congregations to purchase large blocks of tickets."[12] While this is not necessarily new (Moresco gives examples of the ways in which producers marketed *The King of Kings* and *The Greatest Story Ever Told*), what is unique about Gibson's marketing strategy is how specific these preview audiences were. Mark Silk, in his essay "Almost a Culture War: The Making of *The Passion* Controversy," provides a clearer understanding of the implications of these invitations. He writes:

> [Flocks] of evangelical ministers were invited to screenings around the country; all they had to do was sign a pledge in which they agreed to keep confidential their "exposure, knowledge and opinions of the film"—while at the same time they were "free to speak out in support of the movie and your opinions resulting from today's exposure to this project and its producer." This clever marketing campaign resulted in waves of enthusiasm from the like-minded pundits and pastors, while almost all those who might be critical were left waiting for the movie to appear.[13]

Moreover, when Gibson and his supporters did encounter negative criticism about anti–Semitism or violence, they went on the offensive. J. Shawn Landres and Michael Berenbaum write, "[Gibson's] defenders turned their allegations on its head: the film was not anti–Semitic, but the attacks on it were anti–Christian. The more Jewish spokespersons protested, the stronger the 'defense' of Christianity against its 'attackers.'"[14]

Maresco also notes the promotional materials available to churches that included door hangers, invitation cards, church bulletin inserts, Bible excerpts and study guides. He catalogues a host of product tie-ins, from cross necklaces made out of nails to the *Passion* logo on the hood of a NASCAR racecar.[15] Along with Maresco, William J. Cork sees the parallel rise of blogging and social interaction via the Internet as a key ingredient in the film's success due to this unprecedented free publicity.[16] Yet none of these promotional materials or Internet discussions would have mattered had the film not resonated spiritually and emotionally with millions of viewers.

Thus, we see a final reason for *The Passion*'s success. Though controversy and marketing no doubt drew in countless viewers, the subject matter had to appeal to a great portion of the audience. Of all the articles about the success of *The Passion*, only Terry Lindvall, William J. Brown, and John D. Keeler's provides a quantitative analysis of it.[17] They considered the controversy surrounding the film and its marketing strategy but also conducted on-line surveys to determine why people attended the film and how it affected them after they watched it. They write of their findings, "The first reason given by 46.2 percent of the respondents was 'for personal spiritual growth.' The second most common reason, given by 30.5 percent of respondents, was that they had an 'interest in the story.' The third most common reason was that respondents were 'curious about the controversy,' but this was a much smaller group (only 7.3 percent of the sample)."[18] Lindvall, Brown, and Keeler also show that a majority of the respondents felt that the news media had greatly exaggerated the controversy and thus concluded, in part, that the "tremendous box office success of this film can be explained in part by its strong emotional and spiritual effects."[19] Moreover, these strong emotional and spiritual effects, the authors argue, explain why many viewers saw the film multiple times, taking guests with them to each screening.

Hollywood Reacts

Scholars and critics were not the only ones to take note of *The Passion*'s success. As domestic box office returns soared into the hundreds of millions of dollars, the same Hollywood studios that refused to financially back Gibson's production struggled to both understand and cash in on the phenomenon. In their article "Moving from Films to Digital Movies," Terry Lindvall and Andrew Quicke write:

> The tremendously unexpected success of Mel Gibson's *The Passion of the Christ* opened the floodgates of evangelically themed moviemaking in the early 2000s.... It sparked frantic discussion in Hollywood boardrooms about the potential market of religious viewers that the industry had neglected. *The Passion of the Christ* made so much money that no studio in Hollywood could ignore the implications that there could be a Christian crossover market to which they should cater.[20]

In her coverage of Hollywood's reaction to *The Passion*, Waxman wrote, "Mainstream Hollywood, after decades of ignoring the pious — or occasionally defying them ... — is adjusting to what it perceives to be a rising religiosity in American culture. [... Producers], directors, studio executives and marketing specialists have been looking either to mollify or entice an audience that made its power felt with last year's *Passion of the Christ*."[21] Few members of mainstream Hollywood jumped into the faith-based market more earnestly than 20th Century–Fox.

In Fall 2006, 20th Century–Fox Home Entertainment announced the launch of a new distribution company, Fox Faith. This new company, with its motto "Films You Can Believe In," signified the seriousness with which a major Hollywood film company approached both Christian films and a Christian audience. Fox Faith is a branded distribution label created to house and distribute its growing portfolio of morally driven, family-friendly programming. To be a part of Fox Faith, a movie has to have overt Christian content or be derived from the work of a Christian author. The company hopes to acquire as many as twelve new films per year that focus on specifically Christian content, half of which will be in limited theatrical release, specifically in AMC Theaters and Carmike Cinemas.[22] Since its debut, Fox Faith has already shipped over 30 million faith-based DVDs and sold over 15 million copies of *The Passion of the Christ* on DVD.

These numbers reveal the purchasing power of the audience that led to the creation of Fox Faith in the first place. Steve Feldstein, senior vice-president of 20th Century–Fox

Home Entertainment, commented on the inspiration for Fox Faith Films: "'It's really simple. We saw an opportunity to fill a need in the marketplace. The Christian market, in terms of filmed entertainment, has been drastically underserved, and we intend to correct that.'" Feldstein makes a direct correlation to this new company and the success of *The Passion of the Christ*, arguing that the latter's financial success "[opened] all of Hollywood's eyes." Yet Feldstein's comments are full of tension and contradictions. He speaks in market terms about recognizing a "need in the marketplace," which sounds financially opportunistic; however, in the same interview, he asserts that Fox Faith had been in the works before the popularity of Gibson's film. Furthermore, Feldstein also emphasizes Fox Faith's devotion to quality over quantity as proof of their sincerity. He adds, "We intend for all of [our films] to be of the highest production value.... Every one of these movies will have a message of faith. Some will be more overt than others, but that is the common link amongst all of them.'" Another tension arises as he assures viewers, "We are in the business of entertainment. First and foremost, Fox Faith releases will be quality entertainment. We have no agenda and we are not in the business of proselytizing or preaching."[23] The difference between "having a message of faith" and "not being in the business of preaching" must be the fine line that a secular company has to walk in the process of wooing a religious audience.

Fox Faith was not alone in trying to cash in on the mythical audience that created *The Passion*'s popularity. Though he is one of the most powerful figures in Hollywood, Harvey Weinstein has not broken into the faith-based genre like he might have hoped. Only two months after the emergence of Fox Faith, the Weinstein Company announced they would create a faith-based label. Whereas Fox Faith targets the home video market, the Weinstein Company planned to partner with other production companies, especially Christian companies like Impact Entertainment, to distribute their films to theaters. Their first two reported projects are adaptations of the books of Joyce Meyer and Max Lucado, two wildly popular conservative Christian authors. Weinstein commented on their strategy, "'This is a rapidly emerging and important area in the entertainment industry, and this deal fits perfectly into our strategy of acquiring and producing films that target niche audiences.'"[24] Executives at the Weinstein Company recognize the importance of hiring marketing specialists that know how to target Christian audiences. They acknowledge that "these titles more than those in other genre labels, [require] creative marketing ideas, such as courting pastors not just ahead of release but before a project goes into production."[25] Unfortunately, production information on the Meyer and Lucado projects remains unavailable.

Though they came to the faith game a bit later, Sony launched Affirm Films in 2008. The company sees itself as "the home of quality entertainment that inspires, uplifts, challenges and captivates. Through compelling films, thought-provoking documentaries, treasured children's classics and timeless stories, we deliver on the promise of wholesome and trusted entertainment."[26] Affirm Films is responsible for the DVD releases of classics like *Barabbas* (Columbia Pictures, 1961) and *Florence Nightingale* (Cypress Point Productions, 1985), family-friendly films like *Hachi: A Dog's Tale* (Inferno Production, 2009) and *The Waterhorse: Legend of the Deep* (Spectrum Films, 2007), and the films of Sherwood Pictures and New Song Community Church that I will discuss in depth in subsequent chapters. Affirm Films' website provides links to purchase these films as well as free downloadable PDF study guides for each film, which include scriptural references, scenes for suggested group viewing, and topics and questions for discussion.

Fox Faith, Weinstein's efforts to serve a niche market, and Sony's creation of Affirm Films represent post–*Passion* Hollywood creations that attempt to cater to the audiences that made Gibson's film both a financial and spiritual success. However, other mainstream production companies were in the business of producing morally uplifting, family-friendly fare before *The Passion*'s release. Companies like Walden Media and Bristol Bay, though less overtly Christian, are no less concerned with targeting an audience that desires morally uplifting productions. Walden Media chooses many of its projects based on classic and award-winning books and themes for children and young adults, and develops them into films to be enjoyed by the whole family. Walden Media's focus on film's educational ability to "inspire curiosity, creativity, and demonstrate the rewards of learning," though secular in tone, falls in line with early twentieth-century views of the cinema as a source of moral and educational uplift for young viewers.[27] Their films include *The Chronicles of Narnia* series (2005, 2008, and 2010), *Charlotte's Web* (2006), *The Bridge to Terabithia* (2007), and *Because of Winn-Dixie* (2005).

Bristol Bay Productions is similar to Walden Media as it too finances and produces feature-length films of all genres that "tell uplifting stories appropriate for audiences of all ages." They also draw from sources similar to Walden Media's, "popular books that have engaged millions, from the lives of influential people, and from timeless heroes and events that have inspired us all."[28] Bristol Bay specifically limits their productions to G, PG, or PG-13 ratings only. Their films include *Ray* (2004), *Sahara* (2005), and *Amazing Grace* (2006).

Another similarity exists between Bristol Bay and Walden Media: they both fall under the umbrella of the Anschutz Film Group, headed by Phillip Anschutz, a conservative, evangelical Christian billionaire who uses part of his resources to finance morally uplifting films. His cinematic investments represent what Kathy Bruner calls "filmanthropy..., he trend for wealthy individuals or groups to create documentary media in support of particular causes," even though Anschutz's are narrative rather than documentary in nature.[29] The Anschutz Film Group is one of the leading production companies in business today with films in active development with Walt Disney Pictures, Paramount Pictures, 20th Century–Fox, MGM, and Universal Pictures.[30] Though some critics see Walden Media as a shrewd combination of Anschutz's "business acumen with his religious principles," he remains committed to making movies that "have a positive effect on people's lives and on our culture" and that are "uplifting productions for all the family."[31]

Finally, there is one more leading player in the production and distribution of faith-based, family-friendly films, Provident Films, which is part of the Nashville-based Provident Music Group. Provident Films is committed to renewing viewers' faith in films and believes that "movies can make a difference. They can be something the entire family enjoys together. They can be stories you recommend to your friends and neighbors. They can literally leave you cheering." Their website offers an interesting description of their commitment to renewing audiences' faith in films:

> [These] days, it's awfully hard to find movies like those that helped make Hollywood, well, Hollywood. You know, movies where real life is conveyed in a meaningful story. Movies about ordinary people who want to make a difference. Movies where inspiration, celebration, humor, and tears intermingle. Movies that renew your passion ... and your purpose. Stories of hope, love, and faith that touch the hearts and lives of everyday people in extraordinary ways. In other words, the kind of movies that Provident Films is committed to bringing you through our theatrical and direct-to-DVD releases.[32]

Provident Films has been involved in the production and distribution of numerous family-friendly films including *The Second Chance* (2006), *The Lost and Found Family* (2009), and

Bringing Up Bobby (2009). They have been an integral partner in the theatrical distribution of Sherwood Pictures' films as well.

Along with new production and distribution companies and their accompanying films and "filmanthropists," the surge of Hollywood's interest in religious media brought even more power players to the forefront. Lindvall and Quicke recognize that companies not only began to seek out specifically Christian or religious material, but also began to look for the crossover potential of mainstream movies to evangelical audiences. They write, "The leading promoter is Grace Hill Media, owned by Jonathan Bock. *Premier* suggested Bock might be 'the most powerful Christian in Hollywood, but you'd never know it.'"[33] Bock's company maintains a commitment to "highlighting entertainment for the faith community which shares in their beliefs, that explores their values, and that enhances and elevates their view of the world."[34] Grace Hill helps conduct pre-screenings of films, like the *Chronicles of Narnia* series, that might appeal to Christian viewers. At these screenings, they conduct surveys to gather information that they either share with the producers themselves for potential edits or with marketers to help them promote the films. Along with these promotional organizations, the renewed interest in religious productions has fueled the work of conservative film critics like Ted Baehr, who no doubt feel a sense of vindication with the emergence of more Christian-family–friendly productions.[35]

I now want to turn to some of the religious films that emerged after *The Passion of the Christ*. I will offer information on their financial performances at both the box office and in DVD sales and rentals as well as a brief overview of critical and audience reaction to them. I will conclude this chapter with a discussion of why, perhaps, they failed to capture the attention of evangelical audiences in ways that *The Passion* did and why mainstream Hollywood production efforts may no longer be the way in which faith-based films come to life.

The Chronicles of Narnia: The Lion, the Witch and the Wardrobe *(2005)*

The Chronicles of Narnia: The Lion, the Witch and the Wardrobe (Walt Disney Pictures and Walden Media), directed by Andrew Adamson, might be the most financially and critically successful religious film in a post–*Passion* world (even though its production began well before the release of Gibson's film). It had a domestic box office return of just over $290 million dollars (with an additional $457 million in foreign receipts) along with over $352.3 million in DVD sales so far, all against a production and advertising budget of around $240 million.[36] Of course, its sizable production budget makes it difficult to attain the financial percentage of success that Gibson's film acquired. Yet, coupling these returns with product tie-ins like video games and toys results in a financially viable franchise. In fact, Walden Media and Walt Disney were so pleased with its success that they approved production of both *Prince Caspian*, which premiered on May 16, 2008, and *The Voyage of the Dawn Treader*, which premiered on December 10, 2010.

The *Chronicles of Narnia* series opens as the Pevinsie children, Peter, Susan, Edmund, and Lucy, are sent to the countryside for safety during the London Blitz in World War II. While playing in Professor Kirke's mansion, they find a wardrobe that transports them to the magical world of Narnia. Unbeknownst to the Pevinsies, they fulfill an ancient prophecy by helping Aslan, the lion-ruler of Narnia, defeat the wicked White Witch and become kings and queens of Narnia forever, or at least until they stumble back through the wardrobe some years later. The story contains all the ingredients for a good fantasy complete with talking mythical creatures, gorgeous scenery, and a triumphant final battle.

It was not necessarily a post–*Passion* religious production, but Walt Disney and Walden Media targeted Christian audiences during the marketing and pre-production of *The Chronicles of Narnia: The Lion, the Witch and the Wardrobe* (Walt Disney Pictures, 2005).

One cannot ignore the possibility that the producers of *The Chronicles of Narnia* banked on the success of the *Lord of the Rings* (2001, 2002, 2003, New Line Cinema) trilogy by C.S. Lewis' colleague, J.R.R. Tolkien. *The Lion, the Witch and the Wardrobe* received rave reviews from mainstream and religious critics, with the former even embracing the story's Christian allegory. *The San Francisco Chronicle* film critic Mick LaSalle wrote, "That the film is a Christian allegory is beyond dispute. This element is in no way disguised, nor should it be, as it's a major source of the story's power.... Thus, despite its enormous secular appeal, *The Chronicles of Narnia* could also be called the most effective and moving religious picture since Nick Ray's *King of Kings*."[37] Along with other critics, Roger Ebert made the inevitable comparison with the *Lord of the Rings* series: "These events, fantastical as they sound, take place on a more human, or at least more earthly, scale than those in *Lord of the Rings*.... That the battle owes something to Lewis' thoughts about the first two world wars is likely, although nothing in Narnia is as horrible as the trench warfare of the first or the Nazis of the second."[38] Here, Ebert hints at the relatively tame representation of violence in the film, a point that even conservative Christian reviewers picked up on and to which I will return later.

The Chronicles of Narnia: Prince Caspian *(2008)*

Walt Disney Pictures and Walden Media released the second installment of the *Narnia* series on May 16, 2008. It too had a production budget of around $200 million, and while it took in only $141.6 million at domestic box offices, its foreign receipts brought in an additional $278 million. DVD sales, to date, have surpassed $76.2 million.[39] Once again, the Pevinsie children return to Narnia; there, 1,300 years have passed since they left as kings

This promotional material for *The Chronicles of Narnia: Prince Caspian* (Walt Disney Pictures and Walden Media, 2008) features several key elements that appeal to fans of the series, from its fantasy setting (right) to the Christ-like lion Aslan (middle) to the armored Prince Caspian (Ben Barnes) and Pevensie children (left, from top to bottom: William Moseley, Anna Popplewell, Skandar Keynes, and Georgie Henley). Though prepared for battle, the Pevensie children's weapons will never see a drop of blood.

and queens. The Telmarines, humans who long ago banished the magical creatures of Narnia to the wilderness, now rule the land. The Pevinsies eventually lead the exiled Narnians in an uprising, resulting in numerous battles that make the sequel considerably darker than its predecessor. In the process, it also downplays the Aslan-as-Christ theme.

The reviews were considerably more mixed the second time around for Adamson and crew. Given the film's darker storyline, most negative criticisms decried the absence of the magic and spirit that made the first film so memorable. In his review for *Christianity Today*, Peter T. Chattaway commented on what appeared to be Adamson's desire to stage big epic fantasy battles and that, "in steering the film closer to his own vision, Adamson steers it away from Lewis's, and so it loses some of the book's core spiritual themes."[40] However, if the plot is darker, it does not always come across in the action. Kenneth Turan of *The Los Angeles Times* wrote, "[*Prince Caspian*] fits squarely in the tradition of the kind of teenage movies the Disney organization used to make before teens discovered horror and gore."[41] Again, the issue of violence takes center stage. Though the religious and spiritual aspects of the series are toned down here, religious critics still found a message to tout. In his review for ChristianAnswers.net, David Criswell wrote, "The lesson is that we are never to 'do it alone.' Only with God by our side can we hope to achieve victory."[42]

The Nativity Story (2006)

New Line Cinema released *The Nativity Story* on December 1, 2006, at a cost of $26 million in production and marketing. This film wasn't warmly received and had a brief theatrical run that yielded just over $37 million at domestic box offices, $5.7 million from foreign receipts, but almost $26 million in DVD sales.[43] Most critics panned its bored retelling of Jesus' birth and recognized that it was obviously geared towards religious audiences looking for a holiday movie. However, A.O. Scott of *The New York Times* gave it a positive review, writing, "*The Nativity Story* sticks to the familiar details of the narrative and dramatizes them with sincerity and good taste.... Rather than trying to reinterpret or modernize a well-known, cherished story, the filmmakers have rendered it with a quiet, unassuming professionalism."[44]

The Nativity Story, directed by Catherine Hardwicke, reveals the very real scandal of Mary's pregnancy and the difficult position in which it placed Joseph. Oscar Isaac's performance as Joseph is one of the true highlights of a film that plays very much like a love story to Jesus' earthly father, who is shown as kind, devoted, loving, and faithful. However, certain elements of the film betray simple storytelling, especially for religious audiences. The film's soundtrack begins with "O Come, O Come, Emanuel" and concludes with "Silent Night." Thus, the film becomes a chance for Christian audiences to engage this story in an even more familiar way. Though the words to these hymns were not necessarily sung in the film, a Christian audience cannot help but hear the words in their heads and connect them to the images on the screen. Moreover, one of the wise men asks another, "How's your faith now?" but given that he addresses the camera in a medium shot, he might as well be asking the audience. The spotlight of the star shining on the stable where Jesus is born might blind audiences to the film's liberating conclusion. "Silent Night" plays as Mary, Joseph, and Jesus make their way to Egypt, and Mary narrates the "Magnificat." In the end, the film serves as a reminder of Jesus' stance *for* the poor, but unfortunately, some may be too blinded by the spotlight and deafened by the carols to see it.

The baby Jesus is ready for his close-up as Joseph (Oscar Isaac) and Mary (Keisha Castle-Hughes) look on in *The Nativity Story* (New Line Cinema, 2006).

One Night with the King (2006)

One Night with the King (Gener8Xion Entertainment) is by far the poorest critically received film of the group and also the least financially successful, bringing in almost $13.4 million from domestic box offices (it did not have a foreign release) and $20.4 million in DVD sales, both against a $20 million production and advertising budget.[45] The film tells the story of Esther, a Jew, and her experiences in the Persian King Xerxes' court. When the king's prime minister, Haman the Agagite, convinces him to wipe out all the Jews, Esther comes to the rescue. The film boasts high production values with gorgeous sets and even cameos by legendary actors Peter O'Toole and Omar Sharif. In his review for *Christianity Today*, Russ Breimeier writes, "Esther's wedding day offers the same elegant pageantry that established Cecil B. DeMille during the golden age of Hollywood."[46] Unfortunately, the lead roles of Esther (Tiffany Dupont) and King Xerxes (Luke Goss) are poorly cast and even more poorly performed. Though Gener8xion Entertainment conducted a three-week preview screening tour for pastors, youth leaders, and other faith workers in Philadelphia, New York, Nashville, Dallas, and fifteen other cities, the film only opened in 850 theaters, as opposed to the more than 3,000 in which *The Passion* opened.

Matthew Crouch, Gener8xion's CEO, claims that his company is committed to "producing motion pictures that not only entertain and inspire, but that will stand up to critical scrutiny."[47] Unfortunately, this release does not. *One Night with the King*, directed by Michael O. Sajbel, takes an otherwise epic, sexually scandalous story, sanitizes it, and turns it into a love story for its religious audiences. Despite the high production values, the film moves at a terribly slow pace thanks to a script that has virtually no direction or consistency.

Like the Biblical epics of Hollywood's Golden Era, *One Night with the King* (Gener8xion Entertainment, 2006) benefits from impressive production values. Unfortunately, that is the film's only positive attribute.

The tag line for *End of the Spear* (Every Tribe Entertainment, 2006), "Dare to Make Contact," not only describes the missionaries whose story it tells but encourages Christian viewers to do so as well.

The few positive reviews of the film noted Esther's bravery and humanity, rather than divine intervention, as a source of her triumph. This film reminds its religious audience, especially its young women, to stay faithful to God first and then to their men. In the end, the film, contrary to the biblical story, is as sexually pure as possible, hammering home the ultimate message of "no sex before marriage."

End of the Spear *(2006)*

End of the Spear (Every Tribe Entertainment) premiered at a small number of theaters on January 20, 2006. The film took in almost $12 million from the box office and over $21 million in DVD sales and rentals thus far, both against an almost $12 million production and marketing budget.[48] Like *The Passion of the Christ*, *End of the Spear*'s website offered information on performance licenses for private organizations to screen both *End of the Spear* and *Beyond the Gates of Splendor* (Bearing Fruit Entertainment, 2002), the documentary about the same story, an option that is no doubt responsible for the film's financial success on DVD.

End of the Spear, directed by Jim Hanon, tells the story of five missionaries to the Waodani tribe in the eastern rain forest of Ecuador. This violent tribe, defined by revenge killing, speared these missionaries to death when they first made contact. Rather than fleeing, the missionaries' families moved into the rain forest with the Waodani tribe. One missionary's son, Steve Saint (played by Chad Allen), narrates as he reflects on his father's work to reach the Waodani and his own personal journey to return to the rain forest, a journey that uncovers the true meaning of love and forgiveness. The film's tagline challenges audiences to "Dare to make contact." By glorifying the missionaries who gave their lives in service to the Gospel, the film implicitly challenges its audience to "make contact" with the "lost" as well, even in the face of potential conflict.

This film barely appeared on secular critics' radars, yet religious critics picked up on it and celebrated the sacrifices that the missionaries made for their faith. However, even reviewers for the conservative website, HollywoodJesus.com, noticed some shortcomings. In his review, Greg Wright commented, "This is not a perfect movie. [… The] screenplay presents us with so many characters that only a couple of them really become completely three-dimensional. We never really understand what makes these missionaries tick, for instance."[49] If a religious viewer expresses an inability to understand the missionaries, the film has little hope for crossover appeal.

Amazing Grace *(2006)*

Perhaps the best made film of the group and of any recent religious production is Bristol Bay's *Amazing Grace*, financed in large part by Philip Anschutz to the tune of $28 million. The film brought in almost $28 million in worldwide box office receipts and earned just over $25 million in DVD sales.[50] In 1999, Anschutz met producer Ken Wales; Anschutz wanted to make a film about William Wilberforce, the British parliamentarian who helped abolish slavery in the English empire, while Wales hoped to make a film about John Newton, a former slave ship captain who repented, became a minister, and eventually wrote the hymn "Amazing Grace." Newton would later become Wilberforce's pastor, close friend, and an advisor during his fight for abolition. Anschutz (and his money) won out as Walden Media released *Amazing Grace* in February 2007, on the 200th anniversary of the British parliament's vote to abolish the slave trade.

Ioan Griffud stars as the famous British abolitionist William Wilberforce in *Amazing Grace* (Bristol Bay Productions and Walden Media, 2006), perhaps the best post–*Passion* film discussed here.

Next to *The Lion, the Witch and the Wardrobe*, *Amazing Grace* is perhaps the most critically well received film discussed here. Directed by Michael Apted, it's a simple, straightforward account of a most important story and benefits from a terrific cast of British stars. The film follows something of a cycle in and out of Parliament, focusing on both Wilberforce's public and private life. In the end, *Amazing Grace* reveals that Christian faith and effective socio-political activism do indeed go hand in hand. I will return to audiences' responses to this film shortly.

In *Amazing Grace*, legendary actor Albert Finney stars as the ex-slave trader John Newton, who pens the titular hymn and mentors Wilberforce as he attempts to abolish the slave trade.

The Ultimate Gift *(2006)*

This low-budget yet surprisingly well-made film only took in $3.4 million

The popularity of Abigail Breslin, star of *Little Miss Sunshine* (Fox Searchlight, 2006), could not boost the box office performance of *The Ultimate Gift* (Dean River Productions, 2006).

at domestic box offices, just allowing the producers to break even.⁵¹ Although I have not been able to find accurate numbers, various reports suggest that it fared well in DVD rentals and sales, finishing in the Top 20 in both categories in its first two weeks on the market. Directed by Michael O. Sajbel (who also directed *One Night with the King*), the film tells the story of Jason Stevens (Drew Fuller), an improvident, trust-funded twenty-something who truly comes of age only after he partakes in a unique self-improvement program initiated by his wealthy, but estranged grandfather.

Shortly after its theatrical run, Rick Eldridge, one of the film's producers, said the film might have done much better in theaters had it not been released under the Fox Faith label. "I really felt this story had strong values that would hit home with the general market," Eldridge said when his film debuted on DVD. "Then we got pigeonholed into this little 'Christian' niche. [... I think] that caused some people to distance themselves from this movie. There was no need for that to happen."⁵² Of course, poor box office performance can be attributed to a number of factors including insufficient advertisement, limited release, or simply a bad script.

What success the film did have might also be attributed in large part to the casting of Abigail Breslin (hot off her hilarious performance in *Little Miss Sunshine*) as a feisty young leukemia patient who decides that Jason would be a swell match for her single mom. Joe Leydon of *Variety* noted that it "soft-pedals its religious elements — discussions of faith and God are fleeting, almost subliminal — without stinting on the celebration of wholesome family values."⁵³ Mark Olsen of *The Los Angeles Times* said that it felt "less like a sermon and more like a film with a good, if somewhat sappy, heart."⁵⁴ The film's poor performance at the box office is even more difficult to comprehend because, like few of the films discussed here, the filmmaking is first rate, even if the lead actor's performance is a bit stiff.

A Tough Act to Follow

We have just seen that a film's association with Fox Faith, for example, can be both a blessing and a curse: it helped sell 15 million copies of the *Passion of the Christ* DVD, but the producer of *The Ultimate Gift* felt like it alienated potential viewers. Yet many things can sink a film aside from its affiliation with a faith-based distributor. Moreover, this analysis begs the question of how we define "unsuccessful" in this context. Just because a film does not reap massive financial returns like *The Passion* does not mean that it was unsuccessful. Most of these films broke even at the box office, at least, and picked up significant revenue in DVD sales. For some, simply releasing to theaters in the first place was cause for celebration (*End of the Spear* and *One Night with the King*, for example). Yet none of these films resonated with Christian audiences or generated the same energy as *The Passion*, despite their producers' and marketers' best efforts. I now want to suggest a few possible reasons for this before turning to a successful model for the future of religious filmmaking in a post–*Passion* world.

Content and Controversy, or Lack Thereof

In his review of *The Nativity Story*, A.O. Scott asks a crucial question: "How do you make piety entertaining without seeming impious?"[55] Another question follows close behind: How do you make a religious film without being overly pious? In 1917, Rev. Harry E. Robbins had strong words for filmmakers who failed in this latter respect: "In trying to be sure they were harmless they became merely dull. Drama is one of the greatest teachers in the world, and to make it preachy or goody-goody only weakens it and kills its real value."[56] While content and style are important considerations for all filmmakers, they seem to be doubly so for religious filmmakers. Mel Gibson benefited from both content that included a built-in audience and a controversial style that attracted thousands more.

At first glance, it seems that some of these post–*Passion* films would have benefited from their built-in audiences as well. *The Chronicles of Narnia* has long been a favorite series among even conservative Christians. Both *One Night with the King* and *The Nativity Story* tell Biblical stories that one would think are attractive to Christian audiences. However, a closer consideration of these two films reveals otherwise. Though *One Night with the King* tells the story of Esther, it is a Jewish story rather than a Christian one, and God, as a character, does not even make an appearance in the story. No doubt New Line Cinema hoped that *The Nativity Story* would reap financial rewards like *The Passion*. Although the film visualizes the birth of Jesus, it does not happen until the closing minutes. Therefore, the story centers on Mary and Joseph, not nearly the central figures in conservative, evangelical Protestant life that Jesus is. Religion and film professor Michael Morris claims that both *One Night with the King* and *The Nativity Story* also suffer from poor titles. He observes, "Bad advertising! For instance, *One Night with the King* is too sexy a title for church-goers and not specific enough for flesh-peddlers."[57] Regarding *The Nativity Story*, Morris claims that the title gives away everything, as people know full well what they will see before entering the theater, echoing Scott's recognition of the story's familiarity. Of course, we can not deny that audiences were already familiar with the subject matter of Gibson's film.

Aside from the mild controversy surrounding *The Nativity Story* (its unwed lead actress, Keisha Castle-Hughes, became pregnant around the time of filming), none of these films drummed up any significant pre-release publicity. Of course, as family-friendly fare, the producers might have preferred it this way. Yet their style, the ways in which some of these filmmakers treat potentially scandalous material, reveals an unwillingness to take risks. If we can say anything about Gibson's production, it is that it was a risky one. The problem with *The Passion*'s successors is that they shy away from the more controversial components of their narratives. The violence in both *Narnia* films and *End of the Spear* always takes place just outside the frame. Reviewing *Prince Caspian* for the conservative website Christian Answers, David Criswell wrote, "In one scene, Peter even pulls his sword out of a victim, but the sword appears clean!"[58] Writing about *End of the Spear* for Hollywood Jesus, Greg Wright commented, "[The] cut-away editing of the story's countless murders, while undoubtedly necessary to avoid an R rating, is mistimed just enough that it calls attention to itself in a sometimes jarring way."[59] The massacre scene in *End of the Spear* shows little, if any, blood with all stabbings located just outside the frame. Paralleling its contemporaries, *Amazing Grace* implies everything but actually shows little to none of the brutality that the slaves suffered under British rule. Ironically, all these films seem to operate under the conservatism of the 1934 Production Code. Joseph Breen, head of the Production Code Administration, wrote in response to violence in cinema, "We suggest that you trim all these scenes of torture, hanging, men pierced with arrows, etc., as impressionistically as possible, avoiding any specific details or close-up shots that might be offensive."[60] Over seventy years later, some filmmakers are still happy to oblige.

In *One Night with the King* (Gener8xion Entertainment, 2006), the story of Esther (Tiffany Dupont) and King Xerxes (Luke Goss) is transformed from a sexually scandalous Biblical narrative into something along the lines of a pro-abstinence high school love story.

Along with violence, censors and critics have paid close attention to representations of sex(uality) in film. Thus, brief reconsideration of what should have been the most sexually scandalous film of the group is in order. The producers of *One Night with the King* totally de-sexualize a sexually scandalous story. Could we imagine the pre-release press for the film if it intended to depict the stripteases that entertained King Xerxes? What if the producers decided to film King Xerxes and Esther's first night together rather than cutting away? Since the filmmakers play it safe, the film, again, becomes something of a saccharine high school romance.

Evangelical Assumptions and Marketing

As many scholars have noted, Gibson employed a brilliant marketing strategy. Though they tried, most of the films discussed in this chapter failed to replicate it. Braving difficult circumstances, Walt Disney decided to market *The Lion, the Witch and the Wardrobe* directly to Christians, a risky move given evangelicals' mistrust of all things Disney. In "The Reader, the Evangelists, and the Wardrobe," reviewer Mark I. Pinsky writes:

> In the months leading up to the film's pre–Christmas release, media attention focused on Disney's delicate predicament. The studio reached out to the large evangelical market by hiring some of the same firms that worked with Mel Gibson on *The Passion of the Christ* to emphasize the film's Christian content. At the same time, Disney executives downplayed the effort to avoid scaring off the even larger pool of mainstream moviegoers.[61]

But Disney had the financial backing to overcome these obstacles, offering numerous pre-screenings. Pinsky continues, "[Millions] flocked to special, church-sponsored screenings the day before the general release — Rick Warren's Southern California mega-church booked 13 screens for its 20,000 members."[62]

On the other hand, the producers of *End of the Spear* and *One Night with the King* simply could not afford anything larger. Moreover, their films did not have wide enough appeal to sacrifice millions of dollars for pre-screenings. Yet one of these films, *Amazing Grace*, used its medium-sized budget to fund a smart marketing-release strategy. As I hinted at in my initial analysis with this film, it is hard not to draw contemporary socio-political parallels when watching it. Indeed, director Michael Apted commented, "If the film can in some way draw attention to the world we live in, that would be great."[63] In fact, the film was released and promoted in conjunction with a campaign called the Amazing Change in an effort to end the practice of human slavery that still exists today. The campaign also encouraged churches to participate in an Amazing Grace Sunday in which they would all sing "Amazing Grace" and pledge their support to the campaign. The film's marketers also distributed informational packets that included a history of slavery and abolition, a DVD with clips from the film, and discussion guides for group leaders.

Unfortunately, several religious groups drew other connections to the world in which we live, no doubt contrasting Apted's original concerns. After seeing the film, these audiences used its message of uncompromising faith and determination to fuel their socio-political stance against issues like abortion and stem cell research. Rather than fully participating in the effort to raise awareness of the still-present evils of slavery, they saw the film as an encouragement to continue their fight against other contemporary evils. Richard Land, Southern Baptist Ethics & Religious Liberty Commission president, argued, "'You'd have to be deaf, dumb, and blind not to see the parallels between, first of all the abortion issue and slavery, and, second, the general condition of the culture then and now.'"[64] Charles

Colson wrote, "Wilberforce's efforts remind us we must tirelessly persevere in battles against modern moral horrors: abortion, embryonic stem-cell research, AIDS."[65]

This situation shows how difficult it is for secular filmmakers to determine the conservative, evangelical Christian response to their films, a reality that might undo these newly formed companies and impede further production of religious films. The reality of the relationship between Christians and Hollywood is much more complex than Hollywood simply being out-of-touch with "traditional family values," as so many conservative critics often claim. Waxman writes, "Many in Hollywood make the mistake of assuming Christian moviegoers are vastly different from the average audience."[66] To complicate matters, she refers to a study conducted by MarketCast, a leading Hollywood marketing firm, that suggests that American Christians watch mainstream entertainment and that even the most conservative among them are attracted to violent productions. The survey found that religious and non-religious audiences do not differ in their tastes regarding popular films. Joseph Helfgat, president of MarketCast, revealed that "people with conservative religious doctrine are the most likely to see movies rated R for violence. If you compared it to liberals, it's a third more." He concluded that "catering to the religious audience was trickier than it might first appear and that Hollywood would do well to explore those complications."[67] Perhaps the decision to non-violently film the violent scenes in films like the *Narnia* series or *End of the Spear* backfired for their producers.

This complexity is a symptom of a much deeper identity crisis among a sizeable religious population that transcends its relationship to popular culture. Quentin J. Schultze and Robert H. Woods, Jr., note, "We are intentionally ambiguous about the meaning of *evangelical* because evangelicals themselves do not agree completely on what makes one an evangelical."[68] Though they remain ambiguous about the nature of evangelicals and evangelicalism, they highlight a characteristic of evangelical engagement with media. They write:

> [There] is no single tribe of evangelicals.... Constructive criticism from one tribe can look like knee-jerk disloyalty to another.... In fact, being a faithful evangelical media critic in North America is a balancing act. On one side is praise for outstanding evangelical media efforts — creative, authentic, virtuous and the like. On the other side is blame for poorly done, propagandistic, even unbiblical media efforts. Both can be accurate assessments.[69]

Lest we think this is some terribly post-modern development within the religious community, Lindvall references Mary Beattie Brady, a champion for religious films during the difficult decades of the 1920s and '30s who conducted extensive research on the use of films in congregations. In analyzing the troubled relationship between Hollywood and religious audiences, she first blamed it on a dearth of films that resulted from "producers treating religious communities as one vast, non-discriminating market upon which it could unload irrelevant product."[70] Of course, as we have also seen, the Christian ministers and organizations that entered into the business of filmmaking also failed to turn out productions with broad appeal.

Given this historic complexity, the following statements from contemporary studio executives sound even more shortsighted. Russell Schwartz, president of theatrical marketing at New Line Cinema, cavalierly claimed, "There's definitely more of an awareness, but it's just another group to be marketed to, albeit a very strong one, with incredible grass-roots tentacles." Marc Shmuger, vice chairman of Universal Pictures added, "It's a well-formed community, it's identifiable, it has very specific tastes and preferences and is therefore a group that can be located and can be directly marketed to."[71] On the other hand, Waxman mentions some higher-ups' insightful recognition of the complicated nature of this phenomenon. She writes, "Many Hollywood executives argue that the success of *The Passion* cannot be easily replicated by simply making more Bible stories. The movie is not just a portrayal of the Crucifixion, they say, but a political religious statement driven by the intensity of Mr. Gibson's conservative Catholicism."[72] This awareness has also bred pessimism in other observers. The president of production at Warner Brothers, Jeff Robinov, most likely echoed a larger portion of mainstream Hollywood when he admitted, "I wouldn't know how to duplicate this."[73] Furthermore, he expressed a lack of interest in even marketing to the audience that made *The Passion* a success.

Yet even if Hollywood does everything right, some religious audiences will be skeptical of its products. We have already seen the secular-sacred balancing act that Disney had to walk as they promoted the first *Narnia* film. Though Fox Faith might feel that its products are right up evangelicals' alley, other observers are more cautious. Suzanne Goldenberg notes, "Christian retailers and commentators were skeptical that the company that helped make Paris Hilton a household name and produced TV programs such as *Nip/Tuck* and *The Simpsons* was serious about making movies without swearing and sex scenes."[74] As a result, we could see Fox Faith's efforts to partner with Christian organizations like the Dove Foundation as attempts to allay this skepticism.

The complexity of the evangelical community and the skepticism of Hollywood among some evangelicals make Gibson's success all the more surprising. Berenbaum and Landres write, "*Gibson's wealth and standing* gave him the capacity to use the medium of film to challenge what he apparently perceives as the liberalism not only of Hollywood but also of the Roman Catholic Church."[75] This is especially ironic because Gibson has the very same liberal Hollywood, in which he shamelessly thrived for years, to thank for the wealth and standing that allowed him to make his film. How could Gibson, a paragon of Hollywood, break through this complexity and skepticism?

Conviction

In her discussion of the Contemporary Christian Music industry (CCM), Hendershot discusses the failure of some Christian music videos to appeal to a wider evangelical audience. She writes, "One reason that some Christian music videos do not successfully advance a Christian message is that they are not made by evangelicals."[76] Perhaps the same can be said of the failure of these post–*Passion* films to garner a more loyal evangelical fan base. In the end, Gibson's unyielding conviction in not only his beliefs, but also his project, helped fuel its success. This brings me to my final and perhaps most tenuous explanation for why the post–*Passion* films failed to connect with Christian audiences. Few of the filmmakers discussed here openly talked about their religious convictions around the release of their films as publicly as Gibson did and certainly not in ways that were as inflammatory. Throughout the entire director's commentary on *The Lion, the Witch and the Wardrobe*, Adamson never once makes reference to the spiritual aspects of the story. Of course, the producers of *One Night with the King* and *End of the Spear* are highly religious, yet they were not able to sufficiently insert themselves into the mainstream conversation given their limited budgets. While I recognize that this is a slippery argument, Lindvall, Brown, and Keeler's conclusion that a sizable portion of *The Passion*'s audience connected to the film on a spiritual level seems to justify a correlation between the beliefs of the filmmaker and its audience. Moreover, throughout history, filmmakers' religious convictions have not only influenced their productions, but audience responses to them as well. DeMille, Pier Paolo Pasolini, Martin Scorsese, and, most recently, Gibson all come to mind.

As we have seen, the films discussed in this section failed to capture audiences in ways that *The Passion* did. The waning of Hollywood *production* of faith-based films and the emphasis that these secular companies place on the *distribution* of faith-based films might indicate a shift in the faith-based film industry. That is, the reason that this religious fervor has not taken hold in Hollywood is because secular producers will always be telling the story from an outsider's perspective. What if, like Gibson, more insiders had access to the resources needed to produce films and theatrically distribute them? What if the future of faith-based film production is no longer centered in Hollywood the way it once was in the 1950s for example? What if there is no longer a filmmaking center at all? To get a glimpse of this future, we need to turn to a church in southern Georgia, where amid the scandal surrounding the production of *The Passion*, two untrained filmmakers quietly made a film that would change the landscape of faith-based filmmaking forever and re-ignite a movement that had lay dormant for nearly eighty years.

Chapter 3

Low Budget? How About No Budget? Sherwood Baptist Church, Ministers of Movies, and *Flywheel*

On the surface, Sherwood Baptist Church in Albany, Georgia, is no different from any other Southern Baptist Church in the South. Its architecture is similar to the prevalent style of the almost-megachurch-size congregations within the denomination. It has traded a couple of aisles and rows of pews for stadium seating and comfortable theater seats. Screens adorn the "stage," and theater-quality projectors display hymn and praise song lyrics, announcements, scripture verses, and short films. The church has a massive family life center with exercise rooms and even a giant recreational park. Yet like most large congregations, Sherwood Baptist had humble beginnings.

Sherwood Baptist Church has a rich history in its community. This history is one of consistent, rapid growth from its early days in 1955 when a small group of men and women began meeting at the U.S. Army Reserve building for Sunday school. Within a year, the group had grown to over 300 members and, after acquiring a plot of land in the Sherwood Acres subdivision, enrolled as Sherwood Baptist Church in both the Mallary Baptist Association and the Southern Baptist Convention.[1] Two years later, their first pastor, Albert Caldwell, oversaw construction of an educational building that could seat 750 people. Only five years after its birth, Sherwood had grown large enough to sponsor its own mission, Radium Springs Baptist Church, in East Albany. In 1968, Sherwood called its third pastor, Curtis Burge, who, from 1973 to 1976, led the "Together-We-Build" Campaign, a $1.3 million-plus program to construct a 1,000-seat sanctuary with bell tower, library, bridal and music suites, a pipe organ, and a completely furnished Sunday School department.

During the leadership of their fourth pastor, W.A. Smith (from 1979 to 1988), *Moody Monthly* honored Sherwood as having the "fastest growing Sunday School in Georgia." During this time, Sherwood began to invest in both radio and television ministry, airing their first video broadcast on a local cable network station in September of 1982. In 1983, they completed another $1 million-plus building project that included a Family Life Center with handball and basketball courts, a weight room, a pottery room, a running track, and educational space. In 1985, Sherwood opened its own primary school, Sherwood Baptist Christian School, serving grades K-3 through eighth. In 1993, Sherwood expanded its educational ministry, renaming it Sherwood Christian Academy and adding a high school in the process. Since 1986, Sherwood has ranked in the top one percent of Georgia Baptist churches in both baptisms and financial contributions to the Southern Baptist Convention's Cooperative Program, a cooperative financial effort on the part of all Southern Baptist churches to carry out the Great Commission.[2]

In 1989, Sherwood Baptist Church welcomed its fifth and current minister, Michael Catt, a graduate of Mississippi College, who has overseen Sherwood's most significant period of growth. Under his leadership, Sherwood undertook a new campaign, "The Decade of Destiny," that carried the church into the 21st century with the creation of a Christian Life Ministry Team, a ministry to widows, training for "decision" counselors, an Intercessory Prayer ministry, and a Long Range Planning Committee. Soon, Sherwood expanded its ministries to include divorce, cancer, and co-dependency support groups. In 1991, *Church Growth Today* listed Sherwood as one of the 210 fastest growing churches in North America in terms of worship attendance. In 1998, Michael Catt, his staff, and Sherwood's deacons unanimously approved plans for the construction of a 2,250-seat theater-seating-style worship center and a 300-seat chapel, both of which were completed in 2001. In 2000, Sherwood became the site of the New Orleans Baptist Theological Seminary's South Georgia Extension Center. Reverend Catt is also responsible for the creation of two evangelical conferences, Bridge Builders and ReFRESH. The former is a leadership training seminar for pastors, the latter a revival conference for ministers and laity alike. In 2004, the church built a massive sports park for church and community use and followed that up in 2005 with the creation of a Recreational Outreach center.

Though Sherwood may offer unique ministries and possess resources beyond the reach of many other Southern Baptist congregations, they are similar to their denominational peers in a most important way. The church website sums up its theology and doctrinal beliefs: "We are in agreement with the Baptist Faith and Message." The Baptist Faith and Message is, within some Baptist circles, a controversial document. Created in 1925 and revised in 1963 and 2000, it offers a Southern Baptist perspective on everything from the interpretation of scripture to marriage, all coupled with quotes from Scripture defending its perspective. Chief among these beliefs and doctrines are the infallibility and inerrancy of Scripture, the existence of the one, triune God who created and sustains all things, the virgin birth, the literal, visible return of Jesus, salvation through faith in Jesus Christ, and the necessity of evangelism.[3] Sherwood also affirms the depravity of humanity, limits leadership positions in the church to men, opposes homosexuality and abortion, and believes that marriage between one man and one woman is the foundational element of society. In this relationship, Sherwood affirms, "A husband is to love his wife as Christ loved the church. He has the God-given responsibility to provide for, to protect, and to lead his family. A wife is to submit herself graciously to the servant leadership of her husband even as the church willingly submits to the headship of Christ."[4] I highlight some of these beliefs because they repeatedly emerge as themes in their films that I analyze throughout this book.

In all things, Sherwood has remained focused on "reaching future generations for Christ so that 'a people yet to be created may praise the Lord' (Psalm 102:18)." In every ministry that they undertake and through every way in which they grow, it is Sherwood's desire to "touch the world from Albany, Georgia." Few things embody this desire more than Sherwood's commitment to multimedia and technology in the life of their church. As I mentioned above, Sherwood embraced both radio and television broadcasts to further the reach of their ministries. The church also features state-of-the-art video production and editing equipment that they use to create these broadcasts. In his book *Rapture Ready*, Daniel Radosh notes a feature of many evangelical congregations:

> It is commonplace for large churches these days to have in-house recording and editing studios where pastors can create polished videos to show during the service or in the rec room to the youth group. According to *Christianity Today*, 80 percent of all American churches have digital video projectors or display panels in their sanctuaries. High-tech sermons are meant for believers and have no direct impact on the world at large, but evangelicals frequently use the same media and marketing techniques to engage the culture in social and political conversation. The impact is often stronger and more lasting than when the same messages are transmitted through traditional intellectual argument.[5]

There might be some truth to Radosh's statement about the insularity of evangelical productions; however, over the past eight years, Sherwood Baptist Church has been challenging this assumption.

In 1999, Alex Kendrick joined Sherwood Baptist Church as their minister of media. Upon reading a survey that claimed that films had become more influential than churches, he set out to change the perception of movies in mainstream America. His brother Stephen joined Sherwood Baptist Church as an associate minister in 2001 and began to work with Alex on film projects. Unlike their evangelical counterparts that might simply complain about the negative effects of secular pop culture, the Kendrick brothers wanted to change an element of that pop culture. Reflecting on their encounter with that survey, Stephen recalls, "That really grieved us.... We said to our church, 'We can either curse the darkness or turn on a light.' I am a firm believer that we should not be overcome by evil but we should overcome evil with good."[6] As such, they are examples of what Lindvall and Quicke see as a "grassroots creative rebirth of media arts."[7] With absolutely no proper filmmaking training or experience, they approach their work with a total disregard for production costs and box office returns that often plague big-budget filmmakers and even their Christian counterparts. Stephen claims, "[We] are ministers first before we're movie makers, and our love for God has been the fuel to make movies that impact people. [... We] want to inspire in them a message of faith, hope, and love, and so that has been our reward to see the changed lives—the saved marriages. So, if the movie makes money, great—if it doesn't, we're ok."[8] As a result, their filmmaking and resulting films become the most recent example of what Lindvall describes as Christian filmmaking, "of, by, and for the people of the church, not aspiring to high aesthetic values nor aiming for economic profit, but seeking to renew, uplift, and propagate."[9]

With decreasing production costs and increasingly user-friendly production equipment, Stephen's financial carelessness is not irresponsible hubris but a reality of contemporary filmmaking. Working in something close to a megachurch with a wealth of volunteers further decreases producing costs. Soon Sherwood Baptist Church had a new ministry on its hands, Sherwood Pictures, which turned out four feature-length productions between 2003 and 2011. While Alex wrote Sherwood Pictures' first film by himself, Stephen took co-writing credits on the following three productions. Alex has directed all four films and, to varying degrees, acted in all of them as well. The films' gradual aesthetic improvements signify the ways in which the Kendrick brothers and their crew are growing as filmmakers while their success in the marketplace shows both their appeal to a conservative, evangelical audience hungry for wholesome entertainment and the changes taking place in the broader film industry that lets a team of inexperienced filmmakers provide this entertainment where trained, established filmmakers often fail. From their first production in 2003, Sherwood Pictures discovered a method for filmmaking that they utilized for each subsequent release. Most notably, they bathe every production in a "season of prayer," taking time to fervently

Ministers of movies and brothers Stephen (left) and Alex (right) Kendrick joined Sherwood Baptist Church in Albany, Georgia, and quickly breathed new life into church-based film production.

pray for a film's content, its pre-production, production, post-production, and theatrical release. Unlike any other religious production that I have discussed thus far, or will mention later, the cast and crew of a Sherwood Pictures film not only prays unceasingly while they work, but in reflecting on their work, they see prayer, and God's answer to it, as the reason for their success.

Producing *Flywheel*

Alex and Stephen Kendrick had a vision for faith-based filmmaking, but not everyone who shared their faith shared it. The church did not and could not (despite its size and financial assets) give them enough money to begin production, even though they only needed a relatively small sum. In the church's defense, this risky venture was compounded by the fact that they were currently undertaking a significant building campaign. So, as they have always done when faced with a controversy, the Kendrick brothers prayed for the financial and logistical resources necessary to start work on their first feature-length film. Alex determined that they would need $20,000 to produce *Flywheel*, a pitiful sum even by independent film standards. The Kendricks only ever wanted to show *Flywheel* in their local theater and to surrounding congregations. Fortunately, there were some Sherwood members who caught the Kendricks' vision and believed in it enough to pool some resources together, contributing $15,000, which allowed the cast and crew to move forward. With this seed money, the Kendricks purchased a key filmmaking ingredient, a digital Canon XL1s camera (the latest model of which retails for around $4,000), the only one they would use in the entire process of filming *Flywheel*. As he opened the packages containing the camera and its accessories, Alex joked, "With these pieces, we are going to revolutionize the way movies are made on video and shoot the first Sherwood Pictures movie." Prophetic hyperbole to be sure, but Alex had absolutely no idea just how close he was to accurately predicting their future.[10]

Production of *Flywheel* began in November 2002, and to describe the process as a learning experience for those involved is putting it lightly. While some of the key players in the film, Tracy Goode (actor and co-producer) and Alex (writer, director, producer, and actor), for example, worked in Sherwood Baptist Church's media ministry and television station, mostly editing shorter promo videos and prepping worship services for radio and television broadcasts, no one who worked on *Flywheel* had any formal film school or acting experience. Everyone involved in the production was either a member or employee of Sherwood. Only one member of the team, Lisa Arnold, who plays news reporter Hillary Vale, had any acting experience. Given her limited experience, Arnold also provided assistance behind the scenes with location scouting and other pre-production tasks.

As if their wealth of inexperience was not enough, Alex only received the camera a few days before shooting began. As filming progressed, he began to learn how to use the camera and exploit its potential, specifically its ability to create depth of field, a filmmaking technique that creates a stark contrast between foreground and background. In *Flywheel*, some scenes have a deeper depth of field than others, and Alex and Stephen point out that those

Learning as they go, director Alex Kendrick (left) and associate producer and co-star Tracy Goode (right) on the set of *Flywheel* (Sherwood Pictures, 2003).

scenes with a deeper depth of field were filmed later in the production process after they had learned how to better use the camera. *Flywheel*'s minuscule budget could not begin to cover the purchase of other production necessities like a camera dolly, tracks, a steadicam (equipment that allows for stable camera movement), or a camera crane (a device that allows for high-angle shots). Production manager Steve Dapper (the husband of lead actress Janet Lee Dapper) hand-made all of these accessories from supplies purchased at the local Home Depot. For example, to create the track and dolly, he glued segments of PVC pipe together and placed a wooden platform fitted with skateboard wheels on top of them. Dapper, a jack of all trades, also served as an assistant cameraman when needed.

It should go without saying, but *Flywheel* was shot entirely on location because the crew simply could not afford to build sets. For the lead family's house, the crew used a combination of two homes that belonged to church members, one for the exterior shots and the son's bedroom and another for all of the other interior shots. The film's primary setting, a used car lot, was an actual working used car lot owned by Mac Gordon, a member of Sherwood who supported the Kendrick brothers' vision. During production, the filmmakers replaced half of Mac's roadside sign with a prop sign that read JAY AUSTIN MOTORS. Mac's friends and acquaintances quickly wondered if Mac had sold his dealership. Far from it. Throughout production, he continued to sell used cars, and the cast and crew had to frequently break from shooting while customers browsed in the lot or closed a purchase in Mac's office. Alex points out in the DVD commentary that in some interior office scenes he speaks in a lower voice because Mac is actually working in the next room.

During production, Alex shared filming duties with actor and associate producer Tracy Goode. Because they used only one camera, Alex and Tracy often employed a common filmmaking technique known as shot/reverse-shot in which they filmed one character saying her lines, stopped filming, turned the camera 180 degrees to film another character saying his lines, and finally edited the shots together to form a seamless on-screen conversation. For scenes that required both Alex and Tracy's characters on screen, Steve Dapper operated the camera. In one scene, none of the cast or crew was available except Alex and the supporting actor in that scene. In order to not waste production time and money, Alex simply placed the camera on a tripod, framed the shot, started recording, stepped into the scene and acted out his part with the supporting actor. Briefly, a film with a skeleton crew actually became one with *no* crew at all.

Flywheel's minuscule budget affected two key ingredients in any film, sound and lighting. In terms of lighting, the crew, as in other matters, relied on God, settling for natural lighting in both exterior and interior scenes. When the crew created its own lighting, they used spotlights purchased at Home Depot to rid the scenes of unwanted shadows. With only one microphone and poorly insulated shooting locations, the crew frequently employed Automated Dialogue Replacement (ADR), the process of re-recording the original dialogue after filming to obtain a better sound quality version during post-production. The Kendricks re-recorded this dialogue in a homemade soundproof box in the AV room at Sherwood Baptist Church. Mark Willard, Senior Associate Pastor of Music at Sherwood, created and performed the music and score for the film, which included an original song, "Everything You Are," for the closing credits.

To edit *Flywheel*, Alex and co-editor Mark Mitchell employed Final Cut, an editing software that many mainstream, bigger budget films use. Sherwood Pictures' editing room looks less like a traditional editing studio and more like a computer geek's garage. Alex and Stephen recall how they often edited on the fly; if a day's shooting went well, they would edit the footage later that night. Given their lack of experience, the producers underestimated the length of time they would need to complete production for the April 9, 2003, release date. The *Flywheel* team quickly found themselves in the midst of a crisis when, just a few days before the film's release, they lost thirty minutes of final, edited footage. Alex and some of the crew stayed up around the clock to re-edit the lost footage and to complete other un-edited segments. Miraculously, they finalized the process and burned the film to DVD at 6:30 in the morning on the day of its release for a 1:30 P.M. screening at their local Carmike Cinema. Recalling the entire experience, Stephen pointed to Habakkuk 2:2–4 as a source of inspiration at that time:

> Then the LORD replied: "Write down the revelation and make it plain on tablets so that a herald may run with it. For the revelation awaits an appointed time; it speaks of the end and will not prove false. Though it linger, wait for it; it will certainly come and will not delay. See, the enemy is puffed up; his desires are not upright — but the righteous person will live by his faithfulness."

Distributing and Marketing *Flywheel*

Of course, that *Flywheel* could have ever premiered at Sherwood's local Carmike Cinema, a national theater chain, was never a sure thing. Even independent exhibitors have had difficulty maintaining any autonomy over what features screened at their theaters. For a significant portion of film history, studios owned their own theaters and exhibited their films. When this practice of vertical integration was ruled illegal, national theater chains rose to prominence. While the theaters were no longer explicitly connected to the studios, their owners still focused on the bottom line, gravitating toward the blockbusters and productions that appealed to the broader tastes of popular culture. Today, few, if any, theaters are willing to give up a screen to an unknown independent film and sacrifice box office receipts from screenings of much more lucrative blockbuster or mainstream films. Alex recalls their initial attempt to screen *Flywheel* at their local theater:

> We wanted to believe that we could show *Flywheel* in our local theater. It is a Carmike Theater and you can't walk into a movie theater and say, "Hey! Show my movie ... it's on video [...]." You can't just walk in and do that, but we believed that God could give us favor, and so we asked the Lord to open up our local theater, and He did. When we asked Carmike, they called their home office and said, "Look, a local church has made a two-hour movie and they want to show it in this theater. What do you think we should do?" And Carmike had favor on us, and they opened up this theater and allowed us to show it. They said [we could] have it [a screen] for a few days ... maybe a week.[11]

Carmike's decision paid off because, during its first week in their Albany theater, *Flywheel* was the second highest grossing film there. Carmike quickly asked Sherwood if they could screen the film for six weeks, during which Sherwood Pictures got a great start on recouping their $20,000 production budget by earning $37,000 on 4,200 tickets.

From the Carmike's Albany theater, *Flywheel* moved on to other theaters in nearby cities and towns. On August 13, 2003, it opened at Carmike Cinemas in Tifton, Georgia, and on October 17, 2003, it moved to the Hollywood Connection in Columbus, Georgia. Soon, churches started to contact Sherwood Pictures asking if they could show it to their congregations. As *Flywheel*'s fame spread, Inspiration Network hosted the world television premiere on Sky Angel; other Christian cable networks later aired it, including Christian

Network Television, Faith TV, Familynet, and Trinity Broadcasting Network. On October 22, 2003, Sherwood Pictures began work with Word Australia to distribute the film in Australia and New Zealand; in December 2003, they arranged to distribute the film in Canada through Crown Video; and from July to August 2004, they secured distribution in the United Kingdom.[12] When *Flywheel* was released on DVD, video rental chain Blockbuster bought 8,000 copies, and since its release, it has sold over 250,000 copies.[13] At an average of $10 per DVD, this makes for a potentially substantial boost to the film's financial performance.

Despite *Flywheel*'s surprising and overwhelming success, Alex and Steven still make apologies for their first film, treating it, in a way, like the black sheep of their cinematic family. Before the film begins on the DVD, Alex makes this opening statement to viewers:

> The movie you are about to see was the first project by Sherwood Pictures. We shot it in 2003 with a budget of $20,000 and with the help of some wonderful volunteers from Sherwood Baptist Church in Albany, Georgia. What we intended to be a local outreach turned into something that none of us expected. The movie found its way to video stores nationwide and on several television networks. Frankly, the response shocked us. Few of us had any experience making movies, and it's a wonder to me still today that the movie was ever finished. But it still holds a special place in our heart, and whereas we have improved the production quality in our recent movies, *Facing the Giants* and *Fireproof*, we hope that you will also be blessed by *Flywheel*. So thanks for watching it, and God bless you.

Of course, Alex's apology here is more veiled than explicit. Throughout the director's commentary on the DVD, Alex and Stephen laugh at their technical mistakes and point out where and how their filmmaking techniques improved during the production process. In the commentary, Alex even admits that he occasionally has the desire to go back and re-shoot *Flywheel* to improve its visual quality. Ultimately, Alex and Stephen argue that the fact that viewers can even watch the film on DVD is a testament to the work of God.

The Flywheel *Website*

Though *Flywheel* was released in 2003, the film did not have a website until the popularity of *Facing the Giants* and *Fireproof* brought their first film more recognition. The website, www.flywheelthemovie.com, features a variety of content. Visitors can follow a link to purchase the re-edited director's cut of the DVD from a list of Christian retailers and watch a trailer, clips from the film, and behind-the-scenes footage. The site includes a link to production notes that provide a brief history of how the film came to life. The resource page of the website includes the first session of the *Flywheel* study guide (clips and discussion packet) with the entire eight-part series available on the DVD. Visitors can also download desktop wallpaper and web banners to advertise, "*Flywheel* DVD, IN STORES NOW!!," on their own websites. Bloggers and journalists can access a press section and download press releases, biographies of the production team, artwork, video clips, more promo materials, and behind-the-scenes photos.

As we will see with numerous other films in this discussion, the site includes another option that is vital to the financial success of these films. Visitors to the *Flywheel* website can purchase the DVD in bulk (cases of 30) for a 40 percent discount through Provident Films. This allows buyers to give the DVDs away for free, re-sell them at a discounted rate, use them as promotional or outreach-focused gifts, or use them for fundraising campaigns by re-selling them at the retail price. Customers can also schedule group showings through

Outreach Marketing, where, for $199, they can purchase an Event Package that includes a DVD, screening license, promotional materials, and a study guide. Outreach Marketing suggests that potential audiences include churches, business ministries, Christian business owners, and schools. These bulk sales and Event Packages not only represent a significant revenue stream, but they also increase the size of the audience for a film that had virtually no broad theatrical release. As I will show later, many contemporary filmmakers and film historians regard such alternative exhibition sites (church-based screenings, for example) as important venues worthy of consideration when analyzing a film's popularity and financial performance.

Flywheel, the Film

In *Flywheel*, Alex creates a narrative to which he will return, with minor variations, over Sherwood Pictures' next two films. *Flywheel* tells the story of Jay Austin (Alex Kendrick), a used car salesman in Albany, Georgia, who is married to Judy (Janet Lee Dapper), with whom he has a young son, Todd (Richie Hunnewell). We quickly learn that Jay is a crooked dealer, overcharging all of his customers and lying about the condition of the cars that he sells. His co-salesmen, Bernie (Tracy Goode) and Vince (Treavor Lokey), have learned from the best, often competing to see who can make the best deal or gambling on how badly Jay will swindle his next customer. Jay has two other co-workers, Max (Walter Burnett), the dealership's older, wiser mechanic, and Sam (Marc Keenan), an African American car detailer, who provide the wholesome, morally upright foils to the underhanded dealers.

For unexplained reasons, Jay's home life is on the rocks. He has alienated himself from both his wife and son, and whenever Judy asks him about anything involving work, especially his financial transactions, he immediately becomes defensive and aggressive. After a few curt exchanges, he simply says, "We're not going to talk about this any more." Jay virtually ignores his son's attempts to connect with him and is completely ignorant of what is going on in the boy's life. The family occasionally attends church together (the producers use the interior of Sherwood Baptist Church for the one church-going scene). When we do see them attending morning worship service, Jay is sullen and even places an empty offering envelope in the plate to keep up a faithful appearance.

On the side, Jay and mechanic Max work to repair a broken-down Triumph TR-3 sports car. Max eventually learns that the car has a busted flywheel, the component that makes the engine run. Max tells Jay, "Without your flywheel, you're not going anywhere." When Jay expresses frustration that stretches beyond the difficulty of repairing a car, Max asks Jay if everything is all right. Jay tells him, "I cannot remember the last time I felt like my life was going right." Max suggests that Jay should pray, and Jay responds, "I don't think God would listen to me right now.... I mean, he knows I'm not an honest man. He knows I'm a lousy husband and father. He knows how selfish and prideful I am. I don't even like myself, Max. I've got friction with almost every person in my life. I owe money to the bank that I don't have." In this response to Max, Jay sums up everything that we have already learned about him thus far in the film. Two events in particular hang over him throughout the first half of the film: he overcharges a minister who buys a car for his daughter (the film regards this as the lowest form of behavior), and he has fallen behind on his mortgage and loan payments to the tune of $32,400.

After his discussion with Max, Jay sits alone in his living room, overcome with guilt.

Alex Kendrick stars in *Flywheel* (Sherwood Pictures, 2003) as Jay Austin, a crooked used car salesman who has both a soul and a classic sports car in need of repair.

He gets on his knees and prays, "Oh Lord, I don't want your face against me. I need you. I'm sorry. Help me, Lord. Help me get back in your will. I want to be a good man. Help me, Jesus. You're in charge now. You're the boss." With this, Jay's life is completely changed, as is the fate of his business and his finances. Over the last two-thirds of the film, Jay sets about righting wronged relationships, re-focusing his efforts to make honesty his business's policy, and atoning for past crooked deals. He begins at home by apologizing to his wife and son for his distance and anger and re-commits himself to being a better husband and father to them and their baby that is on the way.

However, Jay's changed life does not please or convince everyone. When he informs Bernie and Vince of his plans to sell cars at fair prices, Bernie erupts in angry disbelief, quits, and convinces Vince to leave with him. Jay then promotes Sam to salesman and hires a part-time salesman for the summer. Unbeknownst to Jay, this part-time salesman, Kevin Cantrell (Daniel Titus), is actually an undercover reporter conducting a study of used car dealerships across the country. Among a handful of used car dealerships, the report shows that only Jay Austin Motors deals fairly with its customers. After the report airs, customers flock to Jay's dealership, and he literally sells all of his cars in eight hours. The sales rush allows him to pay off his debts and to repay customers that he cheated over a period of two years.

Unfortunately, another reporter, Hillary Vale (Lisa Arnold), has spoken with Bernie and learned of Jay's past behavior. She exposes his fraudulent activity in an afternoon news report but has to quickly follow it up with a night-time report clearing his name after his customers step forward in his defense and tell how he repaid each of them the amount of money that he had originally swindled from them, and offered a heartfelt apology. Life is good for Jay as the final two scenes of the film reveal him lovingly reconnected with his family. In the next-to-last scene, he embraces his wife as they play with their new baby girl, Faith, so named because "that's what Daddy was learning when she was being born." In the final scene, the credits begin to roll as Jay and Todd cruise along country roads in his newly repaired Triumph sports car.

The Theology of *Flywheel*

Therefore, if anyone is in Christ, he is a new creation; the old has gone, the new has come!—2 Corinthians 5:17

Everyone who calls on the name of the Lord will be saved.—Romans 10:13

These two verses appear on screen before the final credits roll. As Alex establishes a narrative to which he will return in subsequent films, he mixes in religious and theological themes that find parallels in those films as well. A key feature of Sherwood Pictures films is the intensity, yet ambiguity, with which the Kendricks foreground theology and religion. In *Flywheel*, the religious element is ambiguous because although Jay is a religious person, he seems to have "fallen away" from "God's will." Though his wife attempts to bring him closer to God, her words and actions only frustrate and further alienate him. Comments like, "Does it not bother you that you don't keep your word," certainly do not endear Judy to Jay. A heated exchange between Jay and Judy implicitly reveals the theological worldview that animates, or frustrates, Jay's existence:

> JUDY: Your dad called. He wanted to know how we were.... Jay, your dad cares about you very much. He's never wanted anything but the best for you. You just need to talk to him.
>
> JAY: My dad is still disappointed in me and has been since I was eighteen years old.
>
> JUDY: Well, that's because you were stubborn, rebellious, and you never listened to him.
>
> JAY: If he gave me half the encouragement and support he gave Joey, things would be different.
>
> JUDY: But your brother honored your father. He at least showed him enough respect to listen to him.
>
> JAY: Okay. We're going to talk about something else.

This conversation establishes Jay as a mixture of both the prodigal son and the elder brother from parable fame. While Judy asserts that he was stubborn and rebellious in his youth, Jay expresses a thinly veiled jealousy of the love and support that his father showed to his brother. Furthermore, Jay clings to a particular vision of his heavenly and earthly fathers (to use evangelical Christian language) that may or may not be true.

Max the mechanic is a far more calming, reassuring presence in his boss's life. We know, although we never see it, that Max prays for Jay, and though he never confronts him directly, Max silently disapproves of the way Jay treats his customers. Despite his frustrations with Jay, Max cares about him and is there for him in his darkest moments. When Jay expresses frustration, Max responds, "I'm an old man, Jay. There's some things I wish I would have gotten right decades ago, but my pride got in the way. But when I let the Lord run my life, my life got a whole lot better. I don't mean to preach at you, but I just know I need Him. Frankly, I'd say that we all need Him." Even after Jay re-commits his life to the Lord, he must still face the consequences and public embarrassment of his past wrongs. When it seems as if everything is about to collapse around him, Max reassures Jay that the Lord will "fight your battles for you."

Another "pre-transformation" scene requires attention for its theological implications. After a particularly loud and angry exchange with Judy at the dinner table (Jay yells at her to shut up and only open her mouth to eat), Jay sits alone in the living room, switching the television channels. He lands on a televised sermon (actual video of Michael Catt, co-producer of Sherwood Pictures' films and senior minister of Sherwood Baptist Church). In the sermon, Catt preaches:

> Listen, folks, listen. You're in the shape you're in today because of the choices you've made. Your marriage is in the shape that it is in because of the choices you've made. Your relationship with your wife and with your children is in the shape it's in because of the choices you've made. You're in financial bondage because of the choices you've made. God's word would set you free if you'd read it, but you're in bondage, trapped, and you're under all the dirt and the stuff and you feel like you're a slave to your debt and to a relationship because you've not listened to the word of God. And until you listen to the word of God, you will make the wrong choices, go down the wrong road, lose your family, your home, your security, your investments, because God has a way to live life, and you and I cannot live life on our own terms and ask God to bless us. And the reason that many people that I'm talking to are in bondage and frustration and defeat is because you don't really want to know what God says, and you don't want to live it God's way.

Jay turns off the television, but when he tosses the remote on the couch, it actually turns the television back on. The preacher continues: "If any man is in Christ, he is a new creation. Old things have passed away ... all things ... not some things ... all things have become new." Jay turns off the television for good. This sermon does not turn Jay's life around immediately; however, combined with his wife's urging and Max's gentle prodding, it does plant the seeds for his eventual transformation.

While the more committed Christian characters in *Flywheel* see God at work and believe in His faithfulness throughout, Jay only awakens to it after his transformation. From that point on, he turns over his life and business to the Lord. He refers to God and Jesus as his boss, and tells his family that Jay Austin Motors no longer belongs to him but to God. At work the morning after he re-commits his life, Jay reads the Bible and tells God, "All right, Lord, this is your lot. I will honor you with it." Later, Jay tells Max, "If I go under, it's because God allowed it. I told Him it was His lot now." As the bank begins to breathe down Jay's neck and he loses his employees, Judy simply tells Jay to ask God for assistance. Shortly thereafter, the undercover reporter shows up, willing to sell cars for minimum wage. When Hillary Vale corners him on his former misdeeds, Jay prays for God's help, and the past customers with whom he has made amends confront the reporter and tell her their side of the story.

Some viewers might be convinced that God was working in Jay's life before he re-committed his life to Jesus. After he closes the deal with the minister whom he had overcharged, the minister asks Jay if he can pray with him. After praying for a blessing on the new car for his daughter and for her safety when driving it, he turns his attention to Jay, praying, "Lord, I ask for you to treat Jay just like he treated me today in this deal." Jay is startled but unwavering in his efforts to ensure the best deals for *his* business, not his customers. Shortly thereafter, Jay receives a phone call from the bank demanding his payment and threatening to repossess his cars and lot. God seems to be playing hardball here.

The cast and crew of *Flywheel* compare the process of making the film to the film's theme of gradually trusting God and of God being continually faithful to those who trust in Him. Just as Jay eventually gives his used car lot to God, actress Janet Lee Dapper commented, "It was not our set. It was God's set," and Alex Kendrick added, "The Lord knows how to make a better movie than anybody." With this in mind, the cast and crew began every day with prayer, asking God to bless their work and to give them creativity and discernment and to ensure that everything they did would bring honor and glory to God. Not only did they pray at the beginning of each shoot, they would often pause to pray together throughout the day's schedule. As rookie filmmakers and actors, they had few professional routines but made sure that prayer was one of them.

Due to their unceasing prayers and belief in an ever-present, active God, the cast and crew saw every coincidental occurrence, unexplainable event, or resolution of a difficult situation as an act of God. For instance, Alex needed a Miata for a humorous scene involving Bernie and Vince but could not find one on the car lot where they were shooting. Undeterred, Alex prayed about it that evening and, on the way to work the next day, stopped behind one at a red light. He followed the driver to his destination and asked if they could borrow his car for the shoot. The driver agreed, and God answered Alex's prayers. As the cast and crew reflected on the surprising success of their film and the simple fact that they had even completed production, Janet Lee Dapper spoke for everyone when she said, "Prayer made it work."

The more implicit theology on screen is brought to the forefront behind the scenes on the director's DVD commentary. Here, Alex and Steven give voice to the theology that undergirds *Flywheel* and characterizes the beliefs of Sherwood Baptist Church and much of the larger conservative evangelical Christian community of which it is a part. In their commentary, the brothers spend far more time sermonizing and quoting scripture than they do talking about the production process. Most of their comments center on Jay's wayward life and the ways in which he and others work to bring it into step with God's will for it. Though they recognize Judy's love for her husband, they are critical of the sarcastic ways in which she occasionally addresses her husband. As such, the film, along with its cast and crew, support the traditional, conservative notion of gender roles in the home and society that asserts the husband's role as the spiritual leader of the household. Throughout the commentary, the Kendricks reveal the depth to which this ideology reaches when they assert that the husband should wear a "mantle of leadership" that demands respect whether he acts like he deserves it or not.

In their commentary, the Kendrick brothers talk about one of the film's themes, one that they hope carries over in their future productions: "We wanted to show in all our movies that God is the hero, not man." In the making-of featurette, Alex adds, "God is the hero.... We're going to honor the painter over the painting. Rather than the triumph of the human spirit, and rather than honoring creation or people, let's honor our creator, the one who made us." *Flywheel* drives this point home as the characters consistently pray to God in times of trial and thank and acknowledge God when they make it through those difficult times. Yet the Kendrick brothers anticipate a popular critique of their films, one that I will address later in this book. Because God is so heroic in their films, some viewers might be left with the impression that a belief in or commitment to God will result in a life of ease.

The Kendrick brothers are quick to warn their audience that just because their characters may have re-committed their life to the Lord does not mean that everything will be smooth sailing thereafter. Although they stress this in commentaries and interviews (which many viewers will never hear), the content of their films remains, and it is difficult to ignore this implication.

Reception of *Flywheel*

As I have already indicated, the public reception of *Flywheel* came as a shock to everyone involved. Its distribution through cable television stations, theaters outside Albany, and DVDs for both sale and rental transcended the Kendrick brothers' original plans to just screen it at their local theater. The Dove Foundation, a non-profit organization designed to "encourage and promote the creation, production, distribution and consumption of wholesome family entertainment," gave the film five seals, its highest rating.[14] *Flywheel* even enjoyed international exposure, as festival attendees at the Sabaoth International Film Festival in Milan, Italy, awarded it Best Screenplay, the Parable Award, and Best Production. Yet despite its unexpected exposure and minor success, many viewers would not be aware of *Flywheel* until the release of Sherwood Pictures' subsequent films, *Facing the Giants* and *Fireproof*. In an interview, Alex remarked, "*Flywheel*, as most films, if left alone will slow down in its reach. But with each subsequent film that comes out, it gets another infusion of life."[15]

Even by most independent film standards, *Flywheel* had a limited theatrical release, and so finding critics' reviews of it can be difficult. Many reviews emerged after its DVD release, and again after the success of *Facing the Giants* and *Fireproof* encouraged critics and viewers to (re)discover Sherwood Pictures' first feature. As a result, I had to mine some rather unorthodox locations for critical reactions to the film. Far outweighing professional secular or Christian film critics, average viewers provide the majority of critical feedback to *Flywheel* through posts in discussion forums on movie websites like IMDb or through comments in customer review sections of retail websites like Amazon.com.

One of the few professional film websites to review *Flywheel* was HollywoodJesus.com, which did so only after the film was released on DVD. Greg Wright commented, "[Alex Kendrick] really does have a knack for telling stories that everyday people are likely to connect to. Here, the main issue is a father's desperate need for his son's and wife's respect, and Kendrick nails it. [... It] all rings true to the faith experience." In his review, however, Wright is slightly critical of all the piling-on of blessings in Jay's life after he re-commits it to the Lord.[16] Wright's review is important, because writing from a conservative, evangelical point of view, he still takes issue with the ways in which the film implies that maintaining a close relationship with God drastically improves one's life.

The viewers who posted comments about *Flywheel* online and who chatted with one another about the film set the stage for similar online discussions that take place around the reception of each of Sherwood Pictures' subsequent releases. Many self-professed Christian viewers heap praise on the film, citing it as a transformational or inspirational viewing experience. They praise the filmmakers for taking the initiative to create Christian films rather than waiting on Hollywood to answer their prayers. Other Christian viewers, who run the gamut from liberal to conservative, express frustration over yet another aesthetically and theologically poor Christian film. These viewers often cite other professional Christian filmmakers who make more visually appealing and morally and thematically complex films that accurately mirror real life. Finally, self-professed non–Christian viewers bash the film's poor aesthetic quality and lament yet another attempt on the part of evangelical Christians to infiltrate mainstream popular culture. One quickly wonders, however, why these viewers wanted to watch the film in the first place or why they did not turn the film off when they realized what they were seeing. As with most discussion forums, any "dialogue" that takes place between these different viewers often devolves into petty arguments or attacks on each other's beliefs or lack thereof. Here, I want to include a few comments that illustrate these various points of view. I will return to them for critical analysis later in the book.

I will begin with a couple of negative reviews of *Flywheel* before working my way "up" to some positive comments about it. Commenting on Amazon.com, M.J. Thomas from Lubbock, Texas, wrote:

> The only reason why I did not give it one star is because I do believe in faith and following Christ. The main character does a decent job acting but the rest are, well, not good at all. The plot is so elementary. I also think it gives young Christians the wrong message: that if you just pray hard enough and with enough sincerity, He will magically take care of your problems. As I said, I do believe in faith, but it doesn't work out like this movie.[17]

Thomas Johnston from the United States took a vehement approach to the film. He commented on the IMDb:

> I rented this movie by mistake and oh what a mistake it was! This movie is nothing but pure, unadulterated re-born Christian Bible-thumping. From a technical standpoint, the movie was even worse. It looked like someone ad-libbed the lines as they went and filmed it with a $200 home video camera. It actually looked like they were reading off of prompt cards at times! Absolutely awful! If you have little patience for Christian bigotry and holier-than-thou Bible thumping, this movie is guaranteed to raise your blood pressure.[18]

These two comments represent negative reviews of the film from two drastically different perspectives, one a self-professed Christian who takes issue with the film's theology and the other, an apparent non–Christian, who is deeply offended by what he believes is Christian propaganda.

On the completely opposite end of the critical spectrum, many viewers offer unending praise for *Flywheel*. On the IMDb, viewer allen808 from the United States wrote:

> This movie is truly one of the best movies ever produced. Hollywood CANNOT do what has been done with *Flywheel*. [...] The] heart of the movie is bigger than Hollywood's big budget box office flops and hits. I give this movie an all around "A" for its emotion, storyline, humor and drama. Thanks *Flywheel* for such a tremendous movie that shows us a world view that is much different than the usual Hollywood slant![19]

MotherLodeBeth from California commented on the film at Amazon.com, "Unlike so many low-budget religious theme movies, this movie is actually well made. [... It's] a great movie to remind those who profess a faith in the Lord, to be reminded that he wont [sic] let us down. That he will make sure that our enemies are shown to be who they really are."[20] These two reviews, characteristic of most of *Flywheel*'s supporters, praise not only the film's message but its visual qualities as well.

Some viewers keep the context from which *Flywheel* emerged (a church-based production created by an amateur cast and crew) at the forefront of their reflection on the film and offer more complex feedback that acknowledges both the film's shortcomings and its accomplishments. On the IMDb, shanghai777 from the United States wrote, "Okay, let's be honest. Low-budget, amateur actors, and a blatant agenda. All this has been commented on. Rather than 'getting past' all this, though, I think much of the charm in this movie is in constantly remembering these facts." The review continues:

> Part of what held my interest was my awareness that these are not professional filmmakers or actors; watching them grapple with these roles was a treat, and the result is surprisingly satisfying. Once you take it as a given that the goal is to present a particular message, I think you have to hand it to the Kendricks for handling it like they do. Just real enough to be effective; just sanitized enough to make it completely family-friendly.[21]

Another viewer, bRaDWeston from the United States, claimed that "getting past" the poor production quality is actually "when God starts working through the film."[22]

I want to conclude this section on *Flywheel* by referencing one of the first viewer comments about the film that I encountered when undertaking this "alternative" research. David A. Rivera of Millsburgh, Pennsylvania, makes a few statements that offer rich insight into the way many viewers approach not only *Flywheel*, but the rest of Sherwood Pictures' films as well.

> If you are going to judge it alongside Hollywood productions — yes, the quality is not on the same level; yes, the writing is not on the same level; yes, the acting is not on the same level; and yes, the production values are not on the same level. But it's still not bad — especially for a first-time effort by a group of amateurs. And believe me, I've seen plenty of larger-budget movies by Hollywood professionals that were much worse. You have to realize that although the intent of this movie is to entertain; the heart of it is to minister.... As a Christian, knowing that this is a message movie, *I watched it with "spiritual" eyes*, so I was able to overlook its inadequacies. There is such an anointing on this movie, and it is very apparent that Sherwood Baptist Church is yearning to bring glory to God and to lift up Christ.[23]

Rivera's comment about watching with "spiritual eyes" is an extremely interesting point to which I will return in my engagement with Sherwood Pictures' films as a whole and other films from the church film movement. For now, this seems to be a fitting way, if ambiguous, to understand how so many people have enjoyed a film that, by even their own aesthetic judgments, is quite poor. These viewers adjust their vision when watching these films, and in the process seem to lower their aesthetic standards and heighten their moral or spiritual perceptions and expectations.

Chapter 4

Facing the Giants, Facing an Industry

Producing *Facing the Giants*

On April 27, 2004, Sherwood Pictures began production of its second feature-length film, *Facing the Giants*. With a budget of $100,000 and over 500 volunteers and only five filmmaking professionals, this film would, like its predecessor *Flywheel*, achieve success beyond the cast and crew's wildest dreams and put Sherwood Pictures on the independent filmmaking map. Alex and Stephen Kendrick followed the same filmmaking recipe that they employed with *Flywheel*. At the end of the director's commentary on the *Flywheel* DVD, Stephen reflects on the filmmaking formula that they believe is the key to their success:

> Ask God for His ideas, trust Him to give you the discernment with the people involved ... that are involved for the right reasons, not just to further their career. And I'm not against someone furthering their career, but that can't be the main motive. The main motive here is to please the Lord and to seek His blessing and to allow Him to bring the fruit. So that is our strategy in how we make movies, and the formula that has worked for us. Please the Lord first, and allow him to bless it.[1]

Of course, making a film, despite their unwavering faith in God, is not as simple as that. In numerous public statements regarding the production of *Facing the Giants*, Alex and Stephen repeatedly claim that they had no money, few resources, and no experience and point to the blessings of God and answered prayers as the reason the film was completed in the first place. In fact, they often compare their experiences of making the film with the theme of the film itself, particularly that of facing the giants we all encounter in life. Such assertions would actually be more apt descriptions of their experience of making *Flywheel*. It seems as if the Kendrick brothers have forgotten just how valuable of a learning experience the production of *Flywheel* proved to be for them. Moreover, the above financial analysis of *Flywheel* shows that Sherwood Pictures was in a much healthier place, financially speaking, which enabled them to undertake a significantly more expensive, if still low-budget, production. While making *Facing the Giants*, the Kendrick brothers managed scenes with hundreds of extras, whereas *Flywheel*'s biggest scene might have included 30 extras. *Facing the Giants* included action sequences on the football field, while the most complex shot in *Flywheel* was the airplane shot of Jay and his son driving along country roads in their newly restored Triumph sports car. Moreover, director Alex Kendrick benefited from not only professional cinematographer Bob Scott, who joined Sherwood Pictures for *Facing the Giants*, but also the host of volunteers who reprise many of their roles from *Flywheel*.

With a professional grade camera and professional cinematographer, Bob Scott, Sherwood Pictures made a giant technical leap from *Flywheel* (2003) to *Facing the Giants* (2006).

Nevertheless, *Facing the Giants*, by most filmmaking standards, was a risky undertaking, even if the $100,000 budget gave them access to more professionals, like the aforementioned Scott, who has worked as a camera operator or second unit director on secular films like *Any Given Sunday* (Warner Bros., 1999), *The Replacements* (Warner Bros., 2000), and *Friday Night Lights* (Universal Pictures, 2004). From the opening shot, *Facing the Giants* proves to be visually superior to its predecessor. Where inconsistency characterized *Flywheel*'s visuals, consistency reigns in *Facing the Giants*. With Scott's help, the film retains an aesthetic on par with most made-for-television films and some mainstream theatrical releases.

Despite having a few professionals on hand, the Kendrick brothers relied heavily on volunteers ... over 500 of them. Alex and Stephen frequently comment on how blessed they felt to see their "church family" come together in support of this project and claim that the production team and process mirrors the way in which a congregation can and should work together. The closing credits list all of the volunteers with the credits for craft services and catering the most numerous of all ... not at all surprising, given the film's Southern Baptist church context. Steve Dapper reprises his role as production manager and the crew still uses the homemade equipment on which they relied in *Flywheel*. The filmmakers could either not afford or access a camera crane, so they borrowed a power company truck equipped with a bucket lift to light and film some of the football games. When the crew needed a crucial change in wind direction for one of the final football scenes, they used the same lift and pointed a leaf-blower at the flag in the direction they wanted the wind to blow. The crew still used only one camera for filming and, again, relied on shot/reverse-shot techniques for scenes that involved characters in conversation with one another. In the editing process, Alex and Stephen mixed staged football and crowd scenes with real footage from Sherwood Christian Academy's football games. In post-production, Alex again used Final Cut Pro to edit *Facing the Giants* and often digitally duplicated extras to enhance crowd scenes.

One line of the closing credits might surprise most viewers, the role of prayer coordinator. Yet with countless references to prayer, someone must have been organizing all those requests. Again, it seems difficult for the cast and crew to not see every event in the filmmaking process as answered prayer when they pray so fervently throughout the production. Shannen Fields, who plays the lead female role of Brooke Taylor, coach Grant Taylor's wife (Shannen also happens to be the wife of Sherwood Christian Academy's real head football coach), reflected on the production of *Facing the Giants*, "From day one, we dedicated [*Facing the Giants*] to God." Behind-the-scenes footage reveals the crew on their knees in prayer at the very first production meeting. Despite the uncertainty of the film's future, the cast and crew adopted a "prepare for rain" mentality that parallels one character's advice to Coach Taylor in the film. While I will say more about this later in my discussion of the film's theology, suffice it to say now that the producers prepared for success.

Distributing and Marketing *Facing the Giants*

With all of their attention on Divine providence and action, the cast and crew of *Facing the Giants* often ignore another form of providence at work, Provident Films. In looking for permission to use a song in *Facing the Giants*, Alex contacted Provident Music, a contemporary Christian music label who conveniently happened to be searching for Christian-themed films to release in theaters through their Provident Films label. Before Provident would grant Sherwood Pictures permission to use the song, they asked to view an early version of the film. They were so pleased with the film that they not only let Sherwood Pictures use the song, but aided in its theatrical release through their relationship with Sony Pictures, which was looking to make one final attempt to tap into the faith-based film market after two previous attempts had failed. The cast and crew saw this as yet another example of answered prayer and divine favor.

That Sherwood Pictures could ever connect with Provident in the first place was due to their relationship with Carmel Entertainment, a Christian company that "distributes motion pictures and television programming that tell engaging, entertaining and redemptive stories in which truth and hope prevail."[2] After an intense courtship, Sherwood Pictures finally agreed to sell the distribution rights to Carmel. Yet when Chris Bueno, director of Carmel, took the film to Lionsgate, the studio turned them down. When he took it to Fox Faith, they viewed the project as a direct-to-DVD release. Finally, when Bueno told the Kendricks that they would need to contact Provident Music for the rights to use one of their songs, the Provident Films/Sony Pictures relationship clicked.[3] Through these connections, *Facing the Giants* released to over 400 theaters across the country. The days of begging their local Carmike theater to screen their film were a thing of the past.

Facing the Giants *Website*

Accompanying the release of *Facing the Giants*, Sherwood Pictures launched a content-rich website, www.facingthegiants.com. Today, before one enters the site, he or she is offered

an opportunity to buy all of Sherwood Pictures' films in one package. Visitors must click another link to enter the *Facing the Giants* website. This website boasts a host of features and no doubt served as a model for the *Flywheel* and *Fireproof* websites as well. Here, visitors can purchase the special edition DVD, which includes a wealth of extra features. The DVD link takes visitors to another page with links to a variety of Christian retailers. Visitors can also purchase the DVD in bulk (cases of 30 discounted from $14.98 to $8.99 on DVD and from $28.99 to $17.34 on Blu-Ray) through Provident Films.

The *Facing the Giants* website also includes information for a "Movie Event Program" through which groups can screen the film in their church, school, or community, with proper licensing obtainable through Outreach Marketing. Based on a church's average weekly attendance, packages retail for either $99 or $199 and include a DVD, a screening license, promotional materials, a quick start guide, a message guide, discussion questions and more. Coaches, sports ministries, and Christian businesses can also play the film non-theatrically.

The "Faith & Football" section of the website includes "Inspiring Stories," brief accounts from coaches at all levels of sports and anonymous individuals about how the film impacted them, their families, their teams, or their faith communities. Visitors can listen to an interview with former professional football head coach Dan Reeves about the film and his coaching experiences. The website offers a downloadable letter from the "*Facing the Giants* Sports Advisory Council," a fictional group composed of famous coaches, their spouses, and their children. This letter, no doubt composed by the film's production and marketing team, puts *Facing the Giants* in the category of classic secular sports films like *Hoosiers* (De Haven Productions, 1986) and *Remember the Titans* (Walt Disney, 2000). The letter encourages readers to get out to their local theaters to support the film and concludes, "In our informal survey, 16 out of 16 coaches agree: this is one movie not to miss."[4]

The resources page of the *Facing the Giants* website includes links to purchase the DVD, downloadable banners and icons to advertise on websites, and desktop wallpapers of scenes from the film. Visitors can also download two different study guides. One booklet features an introduction by best-selling Christian author Max Lucado in which he notes the coincidence of the release of this film with the completion of his book *Facing Your Giants* (Thomas Nelson, 2008). The eight-page booklet is a summary of the film peppered with a series of theological, spiritual, and "action" questions and concludes with an advertisement for Lucado's latest book. Visitors can also download an excerpt of a longer study guide, but to download the entire version, they must register their e-mail address and other information through the *Facing the Giants* website.[5] The eight-session guide is an impressive resource that includes clips from the film in QuickTime format and a two-page-per-session discussion guide that includes a "Big Question," a description of the clip with background information, key study scriptures, discussion questions, a reflection, and suggestions for further study. Other resources include printouts like discussion questions, a pastor flyer, suggestions for making the most of film screenings, bulletin inserts, and activity pages for young children.

On the website, visitors can purchase the soundtrack or listen to it streaming over the Internet. Visitors can also launch a *Facing the Giants* media player that features a trailer,

Opposite: It is surprising that the poster for *Facing the Giants* (Sherwood Pictures, 2006) downplays the film's faith component. The phrase, "With God, all things are possible," echoes many athletes' post-victory speeches. The quote from former NFL coach Dan Reeves at the top of the poster implies that the film will be about football more than faith. Of course, all this parallels the film's own theological ambiguity.

clips, and production stills or follow a link to the IMDb message board devoted to discussions of the film. Next to this link is another request to join their team, which again sends visitors to the *Courageous* sign-up page where they can receive eBlasts about Sherwood Pictures' then soon-to-be-released film. Finally, website visitors can follow a link to the *Facing the Giants* page on Facebook where they can connect with other fans of the film.

Facing the Giants, the Film

Facing the Giants is essentially composed of three closely connected narratives that involve Shiloh Christian Academy head football coach Grant Taylor (Alex Kendrick) and his wife Brooke (Shannen Fields), Coach Taylor and the Shiloh Christian Academy Eagles High School football team, and David Childers (Bailey Cave), a walk-on member of the football team, and his wheelchair-bound father Larry (Steve Williams). Coach Taylor and his wife face a host of problems in their personal life together. Most notably, their inability to conceive (they have been trying to get pregnant for four years) dominates their marriage. Brooke is heartbroken, which in turn upsets Grant. She says, through a flood of tears, "How can I miss someone so much that I haven't even met yet?" A visit to her doctor reveals that nothing is "wrong" with her, but when Grant visits a specialist, he learns that their inability to conceive lies with him. The doctor attempts to encourage Grant by telling him that at least they now know the position they are in and can choose from the next steps of in vitro fertilization or adoption. Grant and Brooke also endure a host of other problems: They are in dire financial straits (Grant makes only $24,000 a year while Brooke makes only $6,000 working part time at the local florist), their only car constantly breaks down or refuses to start, their stove does not work, and their house leaks and, literally, stinks. They refuse to purchase another car because they cannot afford another bill, which begs the question of how they plan to afford children, especially if Brooke would have to temporarily quit her job.

Grant's life at work isn't much better than his home life. Along with assistant coaches Brady Owens (Tracy Goode, who also co-produced and co-starred in *Flywheel* and is an associate producer here) and J.T. Hawkins, Jr. (Chris Willis), he leads a team that has suffered through six losing seasons. To top it all off, they begin their seventh season by losing their best player when he transfers to a larger school for a better shot at a college scholarship. The team loses the first three games of the season and a group of men (some of the players' fathers) gather together and begin talking about firing Grant and promoting Brady, who remains undecided in his reactions to their offer.

The final story in *Facing the Giants* involves David Childers, a diminutive teenager who has great soccer skills but, unfortunately, nowhere to put them to use because Shiloh does not have a soccer team. His father, Larry, encourages him to try out for kicker on the football team, even though they already have one. David obviously serves as the central Biblical referent here, the high school David who will eventually face a Goliath of an opponent. Larry is unwaveringly confident in his son's abilities and tells him in one of their first scenes together, "David, I've asked God, since you were a baby, that He would show how strong He is in your life. And that, through you, people would see how good He is." David responds, "Then why would He make me so small and weak?" Larry counters, "To show how mighty He is."

After a particularly bad day of learning that their inability to conceive is his fault and accidentally spying on a meeting of the men who want to oust him, Grant arrives home late to find his wife anxiously waiting for him. He begins to break down as he tells her all that has happened that day and his frustrations over losing: "I've tried so hard ... why can't I win?.... Brooke, I can't provide you with a decent home or a working car. I'm a losing coach with a losing record. I can't give you the children you want.... What's God doing? Why is this so hard?" The scene fades out on them crying together at the kitchen table. In the next scene, Brooke wakes up at 3 A.M. to find Grant reading his Bible in the next room. She gets out of bed, kneels next to it, and begins praying for him. In the following scene, only a few hours later, Grant walks alone in a wooded field and reads aloud from the Psalms. He prays:

> Lord Jesus, would you help me? I need you. Lord, I feel like there's giants of fear and failure just staring down at me waiting to crush me, and I don't know how to beat them, Lord. I'm tired of being afraid. Lord, if you want me to do something else, show me. If you don't want me to have children, so be it. But you're my God. You're on the throne. You can have my hopes and my dreams. Lord give me something. Show me something.

After this, Brooke walks up to him, and he asks her, "If the Lord never gives us children, will you still love Him?" They embrace without saying anything else.

In two subsequent scenes, David's father criticizes his poor attitude on the football field after a missed field goal. David says he knew he was going to miss it even before he kicked it, to which his father replies, "Your actions will always follow your beliefs." He then shames his son by pointing to his own disability: "I can't walk. Should I stay home and pout about it?" In the next scene, Mr. Bridges (Ray Wood), an older gentleman who walks the halls of the school praying over the students' lockers for revival, brings a message from the Lord to Coach Taylor, telling him that God will not remove him from Shiloh until he is done with him there. Grant responds by saying that he just cannot see God at work in his current situation. Mr. Bridges tells him the story of two farmers who prayed for rain in the midst of a drought. However, only one of the farmers prepared his fields and farm as if rain was on its way. He asks Grant, "Which one are you?"

After this, Grant begins to re-think his approach and crafts a new team philosophy. Before the next practice, he gathers his team in the locker room and gives one of the film's central speeches. He offers a $10 reward if one of his players can name the state champion from several years ago. Their inability to recall past champions leads him to his point.

> COACH TAYLOR: What is the purpose of this team?
>
> MATT: To win ball games.
>
> COACH TAYLOR: Then what?
>
> MATT: We get a trophy and people talk about us.
>
> COACH TAYLOR: Maybe, for a while. Then what?
>
> MATT: I don't know. Get a scholarship, play for college, and coach little league.
>
> BRADY: What are you gettin' at, Grant? You think we're just wasting our time?
>
> COACH TAYLOR: If our main goal is to win football games, then yes.
>
> BROCK: You don't want us to win games?
>
> COACH TAYLOR: No, not if that's our main goal. Winning football games is too small a thing to live for, and I love football as much as anybody. But even championship trophies will one day collect dust and be forgotten. It's just that so far, all of this has been about us ... how we can look good ... how we can get the glory. The more I read this book [holds up the Bible], the more I realize life is not about us. We're not here just to get glory, make money, and die. The Bible says that God put us here for Him ... to

honor Him. Jesus said that the most important thing you can do with your life is to love God with everything that you are and to love others as yourself. So if we win every game and we miss that, we've done nothing. Football then means nothing. So I'm here to present you a new team philosophy. I think that football is just one of the tools we use to honor God.

BROCK: So you think God does care about football?

COACH TAYLOR: I think He cares about your faith. He cares about where your heart is, and if you can live your faith out on the football field, then yes, God cares about football because He cares about you. He sent His son Jesus to die for us so we could live for Him. That's why we're here. But, see, it's not just on the football field. We've got to honor Him in our relationships, in our respect for authority, in the classroom, and when you're at home alone surfing the Internet. I want God to bless this team so much that people talk about what He did. But it means we've got to give Him our best in every area. And if we win, we praise Him, and if we lose, we praise Him. Either way, we honor Him with our actions and our attitudes. So I'm asking you, what are you living for? I've resolved to give God everything I've got. Then I'll leave the results up to Him. I want to know if you'll join me.

As they make their way out onto the practice field, Coach Taylor challenges Brock (Jason McLeod), one of his best players, who remains skeptical of his new philosophy. He blindfolds Brock and forces him to perform the death crawl (a drill in which one player carries another player on his back while crawling on his hands and feet, keeping his knees off the ground). Brock guesses that he could crawl for about thirty yards, but Coach Taylor bets that he can make it to midfield (50 yards). As he starts out, Coach Taylor mildly cheers him on, but as Brock begins to wear down in the heat, Coach Taylor becomes louder and louder, encouraging him to not quit. Brock eventually collapses on the opposite end zone after having crawled the entire length of the football field, all 100 yards.

With this new philosophy and inspiration, the football team makes a miraculous run to the playoffs. Coach Taylor, along the way, receives a new truck from an unidentified

To prove a theological point, coach Grant Taylor (Alex Kendrick) challenges one of his players, Brock Kelley (Jason McLeod), to a blindfolded death crawl.

booster, along with a $6,000 raise from the school. He also finds the source of the odor that plagues his house, a decaying rat in one of the air conditioning vents. However, everything seems to come to a sudden halt when Shiloh loses in the first round of the playoffs to Princeton Heights. The coaches and players' high hopes come crashing down until Grant receives a phone call the next day. He quickly gathers his team on the field and tells them:

> I want you to know that I serve a big God, and He can do whatever He wants to do. He can open what He wants to open and shut what He wants to shut, and a team that plays for His honor and glory will have His blessings following that team, unlike those who try to cheat their way to the top, like Princeton Heights did in last Friday's game when they played two ineligible nineteen-year-olds. They have been disqualified, and we are advancing to the next round. Get your pads on for practice, boys! We're going to war with Tucker Friday night!

The team celebrates and wins every round leading up to a showdown with the Richland Giants in the final game of the state championship.

On the day of the big game, Brooke visits the doctor for a third time, believing that she might finally be pregnant. The initial report comes back negative, yet her nurse realizes minutes later that she had the wrong report and rushes out to tell Brooke the good news. Because Brooke has already agreed to meet Grant at home, she keeps the news of their pregnancy a secret until later that night.

The championship game starts off poorly as Shiloh falls to an early 14–0 deficit against their bigger (physically and numerically) and faster opponents. Yet they hang on and only trail by a touchdown at halftime. The Shiloh Eagles play hard throughout the second half and find the Giants only up by two points with the ball at the one-yard line with several seconds remaining. The opposing coach stubbornly refuses to kick a field goal, which would essentially seal the victory. On their fourth attempt to score a touchdown, the Giants fumble the ball and Shiloh returns it to their own 34-yard line with only a couple of seconds remaining. They can either attempt a Hail Mary pass or kick a field goal. Coach Taylor opts for the latter and sends David out to attempt a 51-yard field goal. David, doubtful and afraid, tells the coach that he cannot even kick a 35-yard field goal. Coach Taylor reminds him of their newfound commitment to honoring God and asks him if he believes that God can help him make the field goal. David reluctantly agrees, runs out onto the field and, with a sudden change in the wind direction to his back, kicks the winning field goal. The radio announcers are ecstatic, and one of them shouts, "A miracle has occurred here tonight!" Of course, Coach Taylor would agree. After the game, in the locker room, he asks each of his players individually, "What's impossible with God?" They all reply, "Nothing, coach!"

Grant arrives home later that night and tells his wife, "God did it, Brooke. He did it. He gave me this job. He provided for our needs ... took away my fear. He throws in a state championship just because He can." Brooke then tells him the good news of their pregnancy as they weep with joy in each other's arms. A final scene, two years later, shows Grant playing with their son as a pregnant Brooke looks on. The camera follows her into their living room as she walks by not one, but two, state championship trophies.

Reception of *Facing the Giants*

Facing the Giants wasn't released in theaters in the United States until September 29, 2006, but controversy began swirling around the film early in the summer of 2006 when the MPAA announced that it would be giving the film a PG rating. Numerous Christian organizations and publications expressed frustration over what they deemed religious discrimination because they felt that the Motion Picture Association of America (MPAA) was giving it that rating due to its religious content. The controversy even reached the halls of Congress where congressional leaders attacked the MPAA for religious discrimination. While this rating might have surprised some concerned Christians, it should not have come as a shock to anyone even remotely familiar with the MPAA's rating system. That the film contained numerous scenes of football violence and covered themes of infertility and depression always ensured the PG rating that it eventually earned. In fact, the producers anticipated a PG rating all along and did not appeal it. Some commentators observed that the uproar over the film's ratings was nothing more than an attempt to drum up free publicity for the film.[6]

Facing the Giants screened in over 56 countries and was translated into 13 languages. Along the way, it grossed $10,178,331 at domestic box offices, taking in $2.7 million of this within ten days of its release in 441 theaters and placing 13th in box office ratings in the first week of its release. Again, with its meager $100,000 production budget, the film approximated *The Passion*'s financial success. In fact, the film's promotional strategy of targeting ministers to help spread the word worked brilliantly. In my interview with Chris Bueno, he informed me that, based on exit polls that Sony conducted during the first days of the film's release, over 45 percent of participants said that they went to see the film because their pastor recommended it.[7] The film stretched its financial legs even further on DVD, raking in another $20,091,582 in sales and rentals to date.[8] As a result, given its broader theatrical release and impressive audience reaction to it, finding reviews of the film from professional critics, not just average viewers, is significantly easier than with its predecessor, *Flywheel*, as journalists and critics often focused as much or more on its box office returns than on the film itself. In fact, it seems as if many journalists and critics gravitated to the film because of the unexpected financial success that it enjoyed. Of course, if critics' reviews increased, so too did viewer feedback. At Amazon.com, viewers engaged in lengthy conversations about the film, and over 500 customers rated it, with 455 of them giving the film a five-star rating. Of course, many of those five-star ratings included numerous criticisms of the film's aesthetic shortcomings. Again, the reactions of both Christian and secular film critics and viewers reveal a diversity of opinions.

In terms of secular films critics, few were kind to *Facing the Giants*. While many of them gave scant attention to the fact that it was a church-based production, most of them quickly panned its script, direction, and action. The following are a few selections from negative reviews that also contain critiques of the film's religious and spiritual components, to which I will return later. In his review for *Variety*, film critic Joe Leydon wrote, "Technically polished but dramatically tepid, it might score in the niche market for Christian-themed entertainment. And yet, by preaching to the converted so heavy-handedly, the filmmakers fumble an opportunity to reach beyond their target demo of devout churchgoers."[9] Leydon also recognizes the film's troubling theological themes: "In the pic's early scenes, the Kendrick brothers do a fine job of vividly conveying the financial and emotional stresses that might beset someone in Grant's position. But after the coach decides to let God be his quarterback, the scripters run out of things to impede his uplift. Indeed, the rest of *Facing the Giants* is an unbroken string of triumphs for the born-again coach."[10] Josh Rosenblatt of the *Austin Chronicle* saw this unmistakable shift in the narrative and adds, "[Once] Taylor opens his heart to Jesus, all it takes is a little late-night Bible study, a few thoughtful walks through gauzy pastures, and a couple of well-placed prayers, and — presto! — he's got a winning football team, a brand-new truck and sperm of incomparable potency."[11]

Of course, not all negative criticisms came from the secular press. In his review for *Christianity Today*, Josh Hurst offers some compelling theological commentary that parallels Mara Einstein's critique of "programmatic conversions," which I will address later. Hurst writes, "[The] film glosses over Grant's change of heart — we briefly see him slip into despair, then, after a short sequence of walking in the woods and reading his Bible, he's suddenly a whole different person, all in a matter of minutes. One might not be looking for deep psychological drama here, but this transformation just feels cheap and tawdry."[12] Concluding his review, Hurst makes allowances for the low-budget amateur production but ultimately argues that, despite Sherwood's heart being in the right place, "when a film is as unintentionally corny as this one, it's anyone's guess as to how many viewers can stomach all the schmaltz for the positive message at the end."[13]

Reviewing the film for HollywoodJesus.com, Melinda Ledman glosses over bad acting and a predictable script to express her thanks that they did not prevent the film from enjoying a theatrical release. She ultimately praises the film for its "advanced spiritual truths" and its ability to "tell the truth about God and what he can do in our simple little lives. And that's something we all need to hear."[14] While she is initially skeptical of the ways in which Grant's life miraculously improves, she quickly reflects on how God has blessed her own life in similar ways and ultimately believes that these are indeed tenable points in the narrative. Paralleling Ledman's praise for the film, Melisa Pollock, reviewing the film for Christians Answers.net, gives the film an excellent moral rating (not too problematic) and a five-star rating for moviemaking quality (something with which the filmmakers themselves would perhaps disagree). Pollock's review is far less important for its insights into the film than it is for how she actually got to see the film. Because it was not playing at her local theater, she saw it at a local congregation that had purchased a screening license through the film's website. In the end, Pollock encourages her readers: "[If] you must drive for a bit to see the movie, it would be well worth the trip; take the whole family and enjoy the outing. You will find the film 'well-worth' [sic] the drive."[15] Another piece of viewer feedback reveals the effectiveness of Sherwood Pictures' marketing strategy and their encouragement of churches to screen the film. On the IMDb, Miked-61 from the United States wrote, "We need MORE movies like this! Buy some tickets and give them away ... you can affect a life or a family FOREVER!!! My church has committed to buy 1,000 tickets! WE are GIVING FREE tickets to every varsity football player and coach in our area! I challenge others to do the same in YOUR area. Spread the word! This film is a MUST-SEE!"[16]

The responses to Pollock's review are interesting as well. One reader, Chris, encouraged potential audience members to spend money on this film to "send a message to Hollywood that Christian films belong on the big screen."[17] Another reader, Meredith, found the film deeply problematic. She responded to Pollock's review, "I feel it gives a false impression of Christianity and God.... God is not a good fairy who fixes everything in your life because you believe in Him.... It wasn't morally offensive, but it was theologically offensive."[18] This is a fascinating comment because it reveals the tension that often arises in many of the films I will discuss and one that their producers often fail to realize, namely that a morally good, Christian film can be highly theologically offensive to many Christians. Another viewer, JM, responded to Pollock's article and offered a plea to Christian filmmakers:

> To all you future churches planning to make a movie: don't be afraid to show REAL life, even [if] you have to add some inconvenient truths into the mix. However much the baser

populace is wowed by this cotton candy treat, nobody has learned anything substantive from it. Give us the meat, the bones, the REAL stuff! True life applies to everyone, not just Christians, and that's one aspect *Facing the Giants* didn't manage to grasp.[19]

The diversity of these reviews yet again reveals the complexity of evangelical Christians in their approach to media and popular culture and leads us to a consideration of the film's theology.

The Theology of *Facing the Giants*

In many ways, the explicit and implicit theology both behind the scenes and on the screen of *Facing the Giants* mirrors much of what I discussed in the chapter on *Flywheel*. In conversations about the film, everyone in the cast and crew points to the power of prayer and God's faithful response to it as the key ingredients to their success. This echoes the message of *Flywheel* in which Jay turns his life over to God and everything works out positively in the end. However, as we saw in the previous chapter, even some Christian viewers took issue with these themes. If only hinted at in critiques of and reactions to *Flywheel*, accusations of prosperity gospel proselytizing become more prominent in reaction to *Facing the Giants*.

Unlike many proponents of the prosperity gospel, the Kendrick brothers, neither in interviews nor in their films, do not expressly say that God *wants* "His" followers to be wealthy here and now, nor do they particularly obsess over financial matters regarding their filmmaking or other church-based ministries.[20] Neither do they use their films to promote Sherwood Baptist Church in ways that Mara Einstein and other scholars argue that megachurch ministers like Joel Osteen or Rick Warren use their publications to promote their ministries and congregations.[21] Throughout their commentary on *Facing the Giants* and interviews about the film, they consistently claim that they do not support a prosperity gospel theology.

In an interview for *Christianity Today*, Alex talks about the film and theology: "That's always the first negative comment we get after our test screenings. I'm not a name-it-and-claim-it guy; I think God does allow us to struggle.... We ended up with our story for two reasons: number one, we had seen it happen around us, and number two, it's a movie, and we wanted people to leave inspired and encouraged."[22] In the *Facing the Giants* DVD commentary, they discuss one of the film's central themes: "[The film is] about taking the things you love and hope for the most and surrendering them to God.... And it's up to Him whether or not to fulfill them." They add, "Just because we surrender [to God] doesn't mean everything is peaches and sunshine." As the film concludes, so do they:

> ALEX: Look what God did. And that's a key ... is when God blesses us, a lot of times it's easy for us to take the success, but it's so important that we point out the one who has blessed us and enabled us to do what we can do in life.
>
> STEPHEN: It's not about that you'll always win the game and have the baby if you turn to God. It's what God wants to do, but He can give you those things, and He may choose not to give you those things if it's for His glory. But the point is getting to the place where you say, "God, I'll worship you ... I'll praise you either way."
>
> ALEX: And I'll love you more than anything else in life.[23]

Again, as with *Flywheel*, many viewers will not listen to these commentaries or read the interviews and, as a result, will be left with a narrative that suggests that turning one's life over to God can result in a wave of material and financial benefits.

Some viewers, Christian or not, might have problems with comments that the Kendrick brothers make in interviews and the DVD commentary. One might be the notion that "God allows us to suffer." The theodicy question rears its head again, but the evangelical inability to answer, or ask, why a good, loving, and omnipotent God would allow "His" followers to suffer will always necessitate the conversation. The Kendrick brothers' discussion with one another in the commentary hints at this theological problem. They do not really address the differences between the theology to which they adhere (a non-name-it-and-claim-it theology, if you will) and the theology implicit in *Facing the Giants*' narrative (a name-it-and-claim-it theology). The simple fact remains that everything ultimately ends up being "peaches and sunshine" for Coach Grant Taylor, much like it did for Jay Austin in *Flywheel*. Coach Taylor *does* win the big game, he *does* get out of financial crisis, he *does* receive a new truck, and to top it all off, despite the doctor's report, he and his wife Brooke *do* have a baby ... two, in fact! The Kendricks, or at least their film, leave us with no other recourse than to believe that Coach Taylor has only been blessed by his decision to follow God. Could not one of these blessings have been left out altogether or one need simply left unfulfilled? Would this not have lent an air of reality to the proceedings that many viewers find lacking now? Why did Shiloh *have* to win the state title? Was their progression further into the playoffs an act of God, as Coach Taylor seems to suggest? Did God force Princeton Heights to cheat? Why did Brooke have to get pregnant ... *twice*? Could the Taylors not have followed through with an adoption? Why did the new truck have to be so nice and shiny?

These are just a number of questions that might arise after a screening of *Facing the Giants*. Moreover, none of them demand that Coach Taylor's life *not* improve. They do, however, demand a complexity that mirrors real life that *Facing the Giants* ultimately does not deliver, as the comments from viewers listed above reveal. In the face of these continuing theological critiques, Alex and Stephen claim that every miracle in this film had real-world precedent. The two of them drew from their own experiences and stories from friends, family members, and church members in crafting the script. They modeled David's wheelchair-bound father after their own father, Larry Kendrick, who has multiple sclerosis. In a way, such claims are irrelevant because it is doubtful that their individual sources of inspiration experienced lives of uninterrupted blessing. Taking these true-life examples and cobbling them together to create a fictional narrative is simultaneously unfaithful to the source material and creates a highly idealized experience of the world that few, if any viewers, actually enjoy.

Secondly, their commentaries, and accompanying theologies, reveal a vision of a God who relates to humanity in ways that might be deeply problematic to many Christians. The Kendrick brothers speak of God choosing whether or not to fulfill our deepest hopes and dreams based on whether or not they are for "His" glory. Some Christians might argue that their deepest hopes and dreams are evidence of God moving in their lives. In the film, the Taylors' desire to have children could in no way be considered "evil," nor could having children in their situation be an act that would somehow *not* bring glory to God. In what way does their sorrow over not having children glorify God? How can simply praising and glorifying God in the face of infertility completely heal their broken hearts or allow proper space for grief? Taking this theology to the football field, some viewers might question how they are to perceive the members of the other teams. Are there no Christians on the other teams to whom Shiloh lays waste on its march to the championship? Is their defeat and experience of it a means to glorify God?

The cast and crew of Sherwood Pictures' films certainly hope that their films share a message and spark conversation. Yet for every theological claim that *Facing the Giants* explicitly or implicitly makes, it raises a host of more complex, unanswered questions that it and its producers often gloss over. The Kendrick brothers said that they made these narrative decisions because they were creating a movie and wanted audiences to leave uplifted and inspired. While there is nothing inherently wrong with wanting to uplift a movie audience, when this form of uplift and inspiration is couched in an explicitly Christian, theological context, it opens itself up to another level of critique from both secular and religious critics and audiences. Moreover, like *Flywheel*, *Facing the Giants* never gives attention to Jesus' warning to his followers that they will have troubles in this world because of Him.[24] Although the Kendrick brothers' next film would shy away from prosperity gospel implications, *Fireproof* would open the door to new theological critiques and retain the tacked-on feel of its spiritual themes.

Chapter 5

Fireproof ... A Foolproof Plan

Producing *Fireproof*

In December of 2005, while out jogging, Alex Kendrick had the idea for a movie about a husband who saves his crumbling marriage after he undertakes *The Love Dare*, a 40-day devotional challenge designed to teach the user how to better love their spouse through scriptural principles. Thus, Sherwood Pictures' third release, *Fireproof* (2008), was born. With a more sizable budget than they had worked with before, $500,000.00, the cast and crew began production on location in Albany. Working again with only a handful of professionals, most notably cinematographer Bob Scott returning behind the camera, Alex, who again co-wrote the film with Stephen, directed the film and has a small cameo role. Once again, the members of Sherwood Baptist Church and Albany citizens pitched in to cover the lion's share of the myriad jobs and tasks required to produce a feature-length film. At the conclusion of the director's commentary on the DVD, Alex and Stephen refer to the closing credits as a list of gratitude and speculate that about 1,200 church or community members volunteered throughout the production process. As with *Facing the Giants*, many of these volunteers put their culinary skills to use, contributing to catering and other food service roles. Prayer coordinators and assistants returned to organize the prayer requests and to assure that people were praying for the production almost around the clock. Babysitting coordinators ensured that key participants could do their jobs even with children in tow. Reflecting on all of this cooperation, Stephen reiterated his claim that a filmmaking crew is a perfect metaphor for what the church should be, a team working together towards a common purpose.[1]

Though Sherwood Pictures could have no doubt drawn more deeply from the profits from *Facing the Giants*, *Fireproof* remains a relatively low-budget film. On the other hand, the small increase in this production budget lends the film an even more impressive aesthetic quality, especially when compared to their previous productions. Moreover, the improvement that took place between their second and third films far surpasses the improvements that transpired between their first and second. It appears that every member of the cast and crew has continued to learn from their filmmaking experience and applied that knowledge to their work on *Fireproof*. Along with Scott's return, *Fireproof* benefits from the return of Steve Dapper for his third stint as production manager in a Sherwood Pictures film. Such continuity no doubt assists in the creation of a better product while providing volunteers with another opportunity for service and ministry.

Several features of the production of *Fireproof* signal Sherwood Pictures' commitment to low-budget independent filmmaking. For about 95 percent of the production, the crew only used one camera. Though the film focuses, to varying degrees, on four different couples, the crew only used one house for the interior shots of the three different homes that appear in the film, using different rooms or repainting the same room to stand in for a different house. The producers consider it a blessing that they were able to use all of the film's 16 locations, including an entire wing of a local hospital, for free. Conveniently, a member of Sherwood Baptist Church happened to be a captain of one of the fire stations in Albany, and on his days off he lent his expertise as a technical advisor. The cast of firemen also received training from real firefighters. For two days, a local railroad company gave the production team the use of a train for a suspenseful car wreck scene. As in *Facing the Giants*, when the crew could not access a camera crane, they used a telephone company's bucket truck to film the requisite high angle shots.

Unlike their previous productions, *Fireproof* stars a professional actor: Kirk Cameron, former child television star turned conservative, evangelical Christian celebrity, plays the lead role of fireman Caleb Holt. Cameron volunteered his services for free, commenting, "In terms of an acting role, I think that this is probably one of the most if not the most important role I have ever played because it is not only a role that contains a presentation of the Gospel but it is a part that is going to relate to so many men and women who have really blown it in their relationships and they need some help restoring it."[2] Given Alex's amateur performances as the male lead in *Flywheel* and *Facing the Giants*, Cameron's performance in *Fireproof* stands out. Cameron's on-screen partner, Erin Bathea (daughter of Sherwood Baptist Church's pastor Michael Catt), manages to hold her own as well. Along with bringing in a professional actor, the producers also hired an acting coach to work with many of the volunteer actors on their more emotional scenes.

Fireproof's score is noticeably better than that of its predecessors. While Mark Willard again contributes original music to the film, the producers recorded the score with a live orchestra, the Nashville String Machine, a group with extensive experience of recording scores for films. The soundtrack also features songs from popular contemporary Christian artists Third Day, Casting Crowns, and Warren Barfield.

In the behind-the-scenes footage of *Fireproof*, we again see the cast and crew on their knees in prayer on the very first day of shooting, dedicating the production to God. In a speech to the cast and crew, Alex says, "Today is the first day we go to war, and we're going to take some ground." Not only does this scene show the spiritual environment in which the cast and crew worked, it clearly reveals the notion of the culture war in which they see themselves participating. Although they never explicitly reveal from whom they are trying to take ground, one might assume that it is Satan and his secular minions in Hollywood. Reflecting on the differences between his experiences in secular filmmaking and his work with Sherwood Pictures, cinematographer Bob Scott said, "Never have I started a project where on the first day I was on my knees praying.... A Hollywood producer would melt."

Because the cast and crew continue to bathe every aspect of the film in prayer, they see every crisis resolved as an act of or the will of God. On the day of shooting a suspenseful car wreck scene, the crew realized they would have difficulty moving the wrecked car into position without further ruining it for the shot. They desperately needed a forklift to help get it into position. According to Alex and Stephen Kendrick, God provided: The man who lived in the house across the street from where they were shooting just happened to have a forklift. Not only does the crew see God at work behind the scenes during production, they actively seek to honor Him, beyond consistent, fervent prayer, on-screen as well.

For the first time in a Sherwood Pictures film, two characters would kiss. Even though their previous films featured married couples in the leads, their staunch commitment to monogamous marriage prohibited the lead actors from kissing one another. In order to remain faithful to the message of strengthening and honoring marriage in *Fireproof*, the producers also wanted to honor their lead actor's marriage. Instead of having the two actors act out a kiss for one of the concluding scenes, they flew in Cameron's wife from California to serve as the (un)official kissing double. As the two actors run to embrace in a concluding scene, the camera cuts to a silhouette shot of them embracing and kissing. Conveniently, Cameron's wife Chelsea had a similar build and could wear the same costume that Bathea used, and so Alex placed her in the shot and edited the scene to complete the kiss. Though they almost certainly seem trite, such actions and attitudes are prerequisites for participation in a Sherwood Pictures film. Alex and Stephen repeat over and over again that they want people involved in their films who want to honor God, not further their filmmaking career.

Distributing and Marketing *Fireproof*

Sherwood Pictures had a much easier time distributing *Fireproof* than they did *Facing the Giants*. In fact, their connection with Sony Pictures through *Facing the Giants* was simply the first of a three-film deal that the two companies worked out shortly after it made such a splash at the box office. At the very least, Sherwood Pictures got their foot in the door with this relationship. What they eventually did was establish themselves as a viable independent film voice in the Hollywood community.[3] With *Fireproof*, Sherwood Pictures embarked on a marketing and merchandising campaign that surpassed anything they had done before.

Fireproof Resources

Reflecting on his hopes for the effect of *Fireproof*, Stephen Kendrick claimed, "I would be thrilled if a *generation* of people would be able to raise a family where the children see their parents deeply in love and married."[4] Along with the film, he and his production team have given couples a variety of products to help strengthen those marriages. While it might be out of place to talk about a film's merchandise before talking about the film itself, I think it is appropriate here, because some of this merchandise was available to customers before they could see the film in their local theaters. As with *Flywheel* and *Facing the Giants*, Sherwood Pictures relied heavily on grassroots marketing to promote *Fireproof*. They again targeted churches, religious networks, and parachurch ministries like Focus on the Family and other Christian organizations that work to strengthen and preserve marriages and families. Such relationships were a win-win because the organizations gain a new tool that they can implement in their work, and Sherwood Pictures receives free publicity. Unlike their previous productions, however, with *Fireproof*, Sherwood Pictures embraces a favorite technique of mainstream secular filmmakers, the product tie-in.

In my introduction to the production of *Fireproof*, I mentioned that the lead character undertakes *The Love Dare*, a book of daily challenges accompanied by scripture that encourages the reader to be a better spouse. At first, Alex and Stephen only ever intended the book to be a simple plot device that helped the lead character turn his life around. However, response from preview audiences was so strong that they decided to write the book in full and publish it to "help readers learn each day about a unique aspect of love, the nature of love, and to offer a 'dare' to help implement that characteristic into their marriage." The

FROM THE CREATORS OF FACING THE GIANTS
KIRK CAMERON
ERIN BETHEA
FIREPROOF
NEVER LEAVE YOUR PARTNER BEHIND
IN THEATERS 9.26.08
www.FireproofTheMovie.com
AFFIRM FILMS

book was so popular that before the film's release on September 26, 2008, over 300,000 copies were already sold and a third round of printing was underway."[5] Those 300,000 pre-orders would eventually balloon into over four million copies sold, making it one of the best-selling inspirational books of the past three years. *The Love Dare* (2008, B & H Publishing) remained on the *New York Times* Paperback Advice Best-seller list for over 110 weeks and is still a popular seller.[6]

The original version of *The Love Dare* retailed for $14.99. The book is set up in a journal format and each day includes a quote from scripture, reflection on love ("Love is patient," "Love is kind," etc.), a challenge, and space to write a personal reflection as well as a place to check off when the daily dare has been completed. Dares include not saying anything negative to your spouse, purchasing a gift for your spouse, praying for your spouse, etc. From both a marketing standpoint and a spiritual or religious perspective, this ancillary product makes perfect sense. It gives the viewer-reader a greater investment in the film while also providing religious and spiritual meaning through the series of dares that strengthen his or her relationship.

However, *The Love Dare* crosses a line and seems to wander too far into blatant consumerism with subsequent releases and editions. In 2009, B & H Publishing released *The Love Dare Day by Day: A Year of Devotionals for Couples*, a "one-year devotional designed to challenge husbands and wives to understand and practice unconditional love." The book essentially follows the same format of its predecessor and includes 365 devotional readings on unique aspects of love, a year's worth of weekly dares to help couples express love in marriage, dozens of prayers, questions to encourage strategic thinking about marriage, and over 100 topics for Bible study. John Thompson, vice-president of marketing for B & H Publishing, defended the publication of the second book: "Many of our readers finished the 40 days [of *The Love Dare*] and began again. *Day by Day* takes them through an entire year."[7]

In 2009, B & H Publishing also released a daily calendar, *Living the Love Dare: A Year of Daily Reminders to Lead Your Heart* ($9.99), that featured brief copies of the reflections already included in the two *Love Dare* books. In January of 2009, they released the "Legacy Edition" of *The Love Dare*, which comes in a brown imitation leather cover for $22.99. Engaged couples can also purchase *The Love Dare: Wedding Edition* ($29.99) that has minor extended features, most notably an appendix entitled "Twenty Questions for Your Spouse." Stephen Kendrick said they "tried to include things [couples] can do to start their first year off right [including] a list of do's and don'ts during the first year of marriage."[8]

These individual ancillary products were just the tip of the iceberg for *Fireproof*'s marketing strategy. To accompany the theatrical and DVD releases, Alex, Stephen, and senior pastor Michael Catt created a study series. Viewers who wish to engage in the study series can do so on a number of levels. Published by Lifeway, the Southern Baptist Convention's in-house publisher, *The Love Dare Bible Study* comes in a variety of packages. For $68.29, viewers can purchase a Leader Kit that includes two DVDs and three paperback books. In 2008, before the release of the film, Outreach Inc. (also responsible for the movie event screening packages) published the *Fireproof Your Marriage* Couples Kit, the heart of the campaign surrounding the film. The study guide contains

Opposite: The lack of faith signifiers in a poster for another Sherwood Pictures film is puzzling. Only viewers of *Facing the Giants* (Sherwood Pictures, 2006) would suspect that this is a faith-baseed film. From all indications, *Fireproof* (Sherwood Pictures, 2008) seems to be a dramatic love story with firefighting action. As with *Facing the Giants*, potential viewers who look close enough will see a cross in the Sherwood Pictures logo.

everything you need to use the *Fireproof* film to help build strong, God-centered relationships. Couple's kit includes 6-session DVD with discussion-starting movie segments and two participants' guides that integrate scriptures and video clips with questions and devotions for individuals and couples. Also makes a great wedding or anniversary gift!.... Churches can purchase in bulk at www.outreach.com and save.[9]

Couples can also purchase the $59.95 *The Love Dare Study Bundle* which includes two copies of *The Love Dare*, a *Fireproof* DVD, and two study guides. The bundle "combines the power of *The Love Dare* with a *Fireproof* study on the biblical concepts of unconditional love, freedom from temptation, and the differences between men and women." — plus a free bumper sticker.[10]

While some of these product options might appeal to couples who would like to conduct the study series at home without the pressures or embarrassments of other couples, they are clearly intended to be undertaken in larger, congregational settings, as the opportunities for bulk orders suggest. Beyond the study bundles, customers have a variety of options to build their study series. They can also purchase single copies of the *Fireproof Your Marriage* Participants' Guide for only $8.95. For $24.95, customers can purchase the *Fireproof Your Marriage* Leader's Guide, which is "great for Sunday School class, small groups, or a weekend marriage workshop."[11]

As if these products were not enough, Michael Catt also wrote *Fireproof Your Life: Building a Faith That Survives the Flames* (2008, Christian Literature Crusade, $12.99). In the book, "[using] illustrations from his own life and from the movie *Fireproof* [...], Catt shows eight ways we can prepare our lives for the trials that will inevitably come our way. Discussing practical issues such as temptation, marriage and finances, he reminds us that in an eroding culture we are called to stand firm in our faith."[12] Christians who believe that even Christian movies are of the devil can also purchase *Fireproof* (2008, Thomas Nelson, $14.99), the novelization of Alex and Stephen Kendrick's script by Eric Wilson. Wilson also "novelized" both *Flywheel* and *Facing the Giants*. Christians on the go can purchase a *Love Dare* iPhone app that allows them to take the content of the books with them on their travels.

Lest we forget, there is an actual film at the heart of all this merchandising. Customers can choose from a number of versions of the DVD. The basic DVD retails for $14.49, while the Blu-Ray high definition version sells for $20.99. Customers can also purchase a special collector's edition with bonus features for $12.95. *Fireproof* is available in a Sherwood Pictures three-pack as well, along with *Flywheel* and *Facing the Giants*, for $52.99. As I was writing about the DVD options available to customers, I recalled that many negative reviews of the film came from people who felt like they had been duped into watching the film. They talked about having seen the film on the shelf at their local video rental store and giving it a shot. This made me take a closer look at the film's poster and DVD cover, the primary visual exposure most potential viewers would have of *Fireproof* since it did not have a traditional national advertising campaign.

Ironically, for such an overtly evangelical Christian film, there are no explicit Christian signifiers on the movie poster or the DVD. The cover of the DVD has the quote, "The #1 Inspirational Movie in America," but that is certainly an inoffensive description open to a variety of interpretations. On the back cover, Dr. Gary Smalley, author of *Change Your Heart, Change Your Life* (again not an explicitly religious-sounding publication), calls *Fireproof* "Amazing! Action-packed, heartwarming!" The description of the film reads:

> From the creators of *Facing the Giants* comes a powerful tale of triumph, honor and forgiveness. Kirk Cameron (*Left Behind*) stars as Caleb Holt, a heroic fire captain who values

dedication and service to others above all else. But the most important partnership in his life, his marriage, is about to go up in smoke. This gripping story follows one man's desire to transform his life and marriage through the healing power of faith and fully embrace the fireman's code: *Never Leave Your Partner Behind*.[13]

The back cover includes a few still shots from the film, but the only one that has any religious connotations is one of Catherine and Caleb renewing their wedding vows. If shoppers look closely, they will see a cross in the Sherwood Pictures logo. In the end, only three things give *Fireproof* away as a religious production: mention of *Facing the Giants*, *Left Behind*, and the "healing power of faith." Of course, familiarity with the first titles is necessary to make this connection, while the latter, again, could be open to interpretation. Faith in what? Furthermore, the mention of the "fireman's code" immediately after it draws shoppers' attention back down to earth, perhaps insinuating faith in this code. The lack of any explicitly evangelical Christian content on the film's poster and DVD case finds an interesting parallel in the film's ambiguous, diluted theology that I will discuss later.

Fireproof *Website*

Viewers, readers, and customers can visit the *Fireproof* website (www.fireproofyourmarriage.com) to access information on all of the products listed above. The website also advertises a "Special *Fireproof* Edition" of Safe Eyes Internet Protection, a filtering software "ideal for couples, families, teens, and recovery programs" that ties in with the issue of Internet pornography in the film. Website browsers can also purchase *Fireproof*-themed greeting cards from Dayspring.com, the online Christian greeting card company, T-shirts and hats, and the soundtrack to the film.[14]

Like its predecessors' websites, the *Fireproof* website is rich in content. It includes a trailer for and synopsis of the film; links to the merchandise described above; a link to Sherwood Baptist Church; a link to a marriage hotline and other resources for troubled marriages; plus several pages that target specific audiences for the film including couples, churches, communities, businesses, and firefighters. Each section contains information on how "Action Squads" can bring *Fireproof* to those intended audiences. While the business target audience might seem out of place, the website explains:

> If one of your employees' homes burned down, you'd immediately support them in every way possible. Thankfully, you might never have to deal with this situation. Unfortunately, your employees' emotional homes are burning down on a regular basis. Divorce statistics in this country are alarming, and companies are paying the toll. A study shows American businesses lose an estimated $6 billion annually due to decreased employee productivity stemming from marriage and relationship difficulties. What can you do to make a difference?[15]

While these community and business resources are free, they require the purchase of other materials like the film itself, a screening license, or study guides to get the full effect.

The couples and churches sections of the website include similar, brief resource guides that seem to be veiled advertisements for *Fireproof* merchandise as well as advertisements for non–*Fireproof* marriage and family therapy resources. Under the couples' page, visitors can find more specific links to resources for Dating or Engaged Couples. These links connect to pages with further diversified content specific to those stages, particularly books and brief PDF resource guides. The site also provides a link to a Couples Quiz "designed to start you thinking and talking about your relationship with your partner."[16] The website includes information about the film's "National Facilitating Partners," which include Association of Marriage and Family Ministries, Family Life, Focus on the Family, the Marriage Commission, Outreach, and Winshape, all of which are conservative, evangelical Christian movements engaged in the strengthening and preservation of marriages and families.

With the release of their third film and the accompanying ancillary products and more complex websites, Sherwood Pictures is rapidly becoming a recognizable brand that parallels the work of other participants in Christian pop culture. This is cyclical marketing at its finest: the film advertises the book which advertises the film (a label on the front of *The Love Dare* reads "As Featured in *Fireproof* the Movie"). The *Fireproof Your Marriage* study guides were released before the film, thus functioning as implicit advertisements for it in the process. While the resource guides provide opportunities for viewers to engage the film more deeply, it is impossible to ignore the fact that they simultaneously advertise the DVD version of the film as well. All of this turns Sherwood Pictures into what religion and popular culture scholar Mara Einstein calls a faith-brand. I will return to this notion in my discussion of the broader Christian pop culture context into which Sherwood Pictures has entered.

Fireproof, the Film

Fireproof opens with a prelude that involves a young girl talking to her mother about marriage, love, and husbands. We learn that the little girl loves her father and hopes to marry someone like him one day. In a picture on her nightstand, her father, a firefighter, kisses her on the cheek. We never see the little girl or her mother, but from the accompanying subtitle, "25 Years Earlier," we soon learn that it is a younger version of the lead female character, Catherine Holt (Erin Bathea). The next scene takes us back to the present day as a fire truck pulls into the station. We meet the lead male character, fire captain Caleb Holt (Kirk Cameron), as he reprimands a rookie firefighter for abandoning a partner on the job. He sternly reminds him, "You never leave your partner, especially in a fire."

When Caleb arrives home after his shift, we find that his relationship with wife Catherine is terribly strained. Their communication, what little there is, is fraught with tension and frustration. He complains about a lack of food in the house. She tells him that she is too busy with work to shop, and, after all, he has 48 hours off in between his 24-hour shifts during which to grocery shop. At their work places, the couple complains to their respective co-workers. Caleb asks his friend and fellow captain, Mike (Ken Bevel), "How is it that I get respect everywhere I go except in my own house?" This is Caleb's greatest frustration: his wife just will not respect him. He automatically expects his heroic deeds as a firefighter to influence his wife's interactions with him at home, regardless of how he treats her. Catherine, a public relations officer for the local hospital, complains to her nurse friends that Caleb is rude and selfish, and does not listen to her. She is also deeply disturbed by what she believes is his addiction to Internet pornography, which makes her feel unloved and unwanted.

Back at home, Caleb and Catherine lead fairly separate lives, which seems to be at Caleb's direction. They have separate bank accounts and clearly defined roles, most of which Caleb implicitly expects Catherine to fulfill. He has a sizable savings account that he hopes to use on a boat in the near future. Catherine feels like they could use that money to spruce up their solidly upper-middle class home or to assist in her ailing mother's medical bills.

In a particularly heated argument at the beginning of the film, Catherine calls out Caleb's "addiction" to pornography, although she never specifically calls it that. He becomes

I get no respect! From the beginning of *Fireproof* (Sherwood Pictures, 2008) Caleb Holt (Kirk Cameron) is angry with and verbally abusive to wife Catherine (Erin Bathea, daughter of Sherwood Pastor and executive producer Michael Catt). Photograph by Todd Stone.

enraged and yells at her, "Shut up! I'm sick of you! You disrespectful, ungrateful, selfish woman! How dare you say that to me? You constantly nag me and drain the life out of me! I'm tired of it! If you can't give me the respect I deserve ... look at me ... then what's the point of this marriage?!" She immediately begins to cry and, cowering against the wall, whispers, "I want out ... I just want out." He yells back, "Then that's fine by me!" This verbal confrontation sets the first half of the film in motion as the couple quickly grows further apart and eventually begins pursuing a divorce. They pass each other going to and coming from work like ships in the night and even begin to sleep in separate beds. At work, Catherine develops a close friendship with a doctor who is clearly interested in taking the relationship further. Caleb continues to sulk but does contact his father, John (Harris Malcom), to talk about his marriage difficulties. Throughout this tough time, Caleb's happily married friend Mike and his father provide God-centered advice and encourage him to avoid divorce and stick with his marriage.

When Caleb's father comes to visit him, he and Caleb go for a walk. During their conversation, his father tells him how he and his mother worked through a rough spot in their own marriage:

JOHN: The Lord did a work in us.

CALEB: The Lord? You're giving credit to God?

JOHN:: Why does that bother you? You've always believed in God.

CALEB: If there's a God out there somewhere, Dad, He's not interested in me and my problems.

JOHN: I disagree. I'd say He's very interested.

CALEB: Then where's He been in my life?

JOHN: I'd say He's been at work all around you. You just haven't realized it. You haven't exactly given Him an open invitation.

As John and Caleb continue their talk, they move through a wooded field that seems to have once served as a religious campground. After a few minutes, they come upon a wooden cross surrounded by some benches. Caleb, however, will not let his father preach to him and simply tells him that he wants peace in his life. His father asks him if there is any part of him that wants to save their marriage. When Caleb says yes, his father tells him to hold off on any plans for a divorce for another 40 days. He has something that he wants to share with Caleb ... something that saved *his* marriage.

In the meantime, Caleb and Catherine live their separate lives. Catherine struggles to care for her ailing mother, while her interest in her co-worker, Dr. Keller (Perry Revell), grows. Caleb continues to talk with Mike but is resigned to accept Catherine's desire for a divorce. This frustrates Mike, who tells him, "Caleb, man, I've seen you run into a building to save people you don't even know, but you're just going to let your marriage burn to the ground?" For some reason, this deeply offends Caleb, who shuts down and walks away from the conversation. In the next scene, Caleb receives a package form his father, a book called *The Love Dare.*

The Love Dare is a 40-day series of challenges, based in scripture, designed to make the reader a better partner. Caleb treats these challenges as a checklist and does just enough to get by, like ordering the cheapest bouquet of flowers on the day he is supposed to buy Catherine a gift. Unsurprisingly, none of these actions grab her attention or convince her that Caleb has made her a priority in his life. Soon, Catherine becomes suspicious of Caleb's actions and thinks that they are some kind of ploy to affect his standing in the divorce proceedings. Moreover, she still stews over his "addiction" to pornography and tells her mother, "He makes me feel so humiliated. When did I stop being good enough for him?"

After Catherine rejects a nice candlelit dinner that Caleb prepares for her (his first serious effort at reconnecting with her), he nears his breaking point and calls his father to vent his frustrations. His father schedules another visit, and their ensuing conversation forms the crux of the film. Because this scene is so integral to the film, I want to quote their conversation at length. Caleb complains about Catherine's lack of response to his completed dares, but his father sees through this and criticizes his lack of sincerity.

CALEB: Dad, if you're going to tell me I need Jesus, please don't. I don't need a crutch to get through life.

JOHN: Son, Jesus is much more than a crutch. He's become the most significant part of our lives.

CALEB: Dad, why do you keep saying that? He's the most significant part ... how ... how is that?

JOHN: When I realized who I was, and who He was, I realized my need for Him. I needed His forgiveness and salvation.

CALEB: See, I don't understand, Dad. Why do I need His salvation? What? Am I gonna be thrown into Hell? For what? 'Cause I got divorced?

JOHN: No, because you violated His standards.

CALEB: What? "Thou shall not kill"? Dad, I help people. I'm a good person.

JOHN: According to you, but God doesn't judge by your standards. He uses His.

CALEB: And what are His?

JOHN: Well ... truth.

CALEB: Okay?

JOHN: Love....

CALEB: I'm honest....

JOHN: Faithfulness....

CALEB: I care about people. I am those things.

JOHN: Sometimes, but have you loved God? The One who gave you life? His standards are so high that He considers hatred to be murder and lust to be adultery.

CALEB: Dad, what about all the good I've done?

JOHN: Son, saving someone from a fire does not make you right with God. You've broken his commandments and one day you'll answer for that. Caleb, if I were to ask you why you were so frustrated with Catherine, what would you say?

CALEB: She's stubborn, she makes everything difficult for me, she's ungrateful, she's constantly griping about something.

JOHN: Has she thanked you for anything you've done the last 20 days?

CALEB: No! And you'd think [...] that she would try to show me a little bit of gratitude, but she doesn't.... Dad, for the last three weeks, I have bent over backwards for her. I have tried to demonstrate that I still care about this relationship.... She does not deserve this, Dad. I'm not doing it any more. How am I supposed to show love to somebody over and over and over who constantly rejects me?

JOHN: [*who has now moved over to the same wooden cross from the previous scene and stands beneath it*]: That's a good question.

CALEB: Dad, that is not what I'm doing.

JOHN: Isn't it?

CALEB: No, Dad, this is not what this is about.

JOHN: Son, you just asked me how someone can show love over and over again when they are constantly rejected. Caleb, the answer is, you can't love her because you can't give her what you don't have. I couldn't truly love your mother until I understood what love really was. It's not because I get some reward out of it. I've now made a decision to love your mother whether she deserves it or not. Son, God loves you even though you don't deserve it, even though you've rejected Him, spat in His face. God sent Jesus to die on the cross and take the punishment for your sin because He loves you. The cross was offensive to me until I came to it. But when I did, Jesus Christ changed my life. That's when I truly began to love your mom. Son, I can't settle this for you. This is between you and the Lord. But I love you too much not to tell you the truth. Can't you see that you need him? [*Caleb slowly nods his head*]. Can't you see that you need his forgiveness? [*Caleb whispers, "yes."*] Will you trust him with your life? [*Caleb nods his head, they embrace and pray together.*]

In *Fireproof* (Sherwood Pictures, 2008), Caleb Holt (Kirk Cameron) believes that his heroism at work as a firefighter should automatically grant him respect at home. Photograph by Todd Stone.

The conclusion of this scene marks the halfway point of the film, both chronologically and thematically. Here, Caleb truly turns his life around by re-committing it to the Lord.

In the subsequent scene, Caleb tells Mike that he's now on "his team," metaphorically letting him know that he has become a fully committed Christian. Mike celebrates with him, but Caleb still expresses reservations about where his marriage is going. Mike warns him not to simply follow his heart but to lead his heart back into love with Catherine. Here, we also learn that Mike's current marriage is not his first and that before he became a Christian, he endured a painful divorce that still wounds him many years later. He says emphatically, "Man, God meant marriage to be for life!" Mike and Caleb are quickly called away to a house fire, and Caleb rescues a young girl trapped inside. During the rescue, he sustains minor burns and, while being treated at the hospital, runs into Catherine, who quickly walks away after seeing that he is going to be fine.

Catherine still resists Caleb's efforts to reconnect but, given his newfound faith, he is more committed to *The Love Dare* than ever. Day 23 tells him to beware of parasites that may destroy his marriage. According to the book, these parasites often come in the form of addictions to gambling or pornography. Caleb takes his computer outside and demolishes it with a baseball bat and replaces it with a dozen red roses and a note to Catherine that says, "I love you more." Unfortunately, despite his best intentions, he wakes up the next morning to find divorce papers on the kitchen table. On top of that, he later finds a love letter from Dr. Keller to Catherine and immediately confronts him at the hospital with a thinly veiled violent warning to keep away from his wife.

After a musical montage of the two going about their lives, Caleb sees that Catherine has stayed home sick from work. He goes out to get her lunch and returns to see that she has found his copy of *The Love Dare*. He tells her that he is on day 43. When she reminds him that there are only 40 days in the book, he asks, "Who says I have to stop?" When she questions this sudden change in him, he tearfully apologizes to her: "For the past seven years, I have trampled on you with my words and my actions. I have loved other things when I should have loved you." She tells him that she will need more time to process the change he has undertaken and to think things over.

During this time, Catherine learns that an anonymous donor has provided a much needed hospital bed and wheelchair for her mother. She assumes that Dr. Keller has made the donation, but when she visits the medical supply company to purchase sheets for the bed, she learns that Dr. Keller only paid $300 towards the equipment and that Caleb paid the $24,000 from his boat savings. Catherine rushes home in tears, puts on makeup and a dress, and goes to the fire station to meet Caleb and expresses her newfound love for him, telling him that she respects him and wants what happened to him to happen to her. The two embrace in the fire station with a kiss.

In the next montage, we see the happy couple together, getting in their car with Bibles in their hands, apparently going to church. In the following scene, another walk and talk between Caleb and his father, Caleb learns that his mother actually performed *The Love Dare* on his father and led him to Christ. This radically changes Caleb's opinion of his mother, who he always thought was a nagger. He runs home to embrace her and to ask her forgiveness for being consistently rude and alienating to her. In the final scene, Catherine and Caleb renew their vows to one another before a minister (director Alex Kendrick in a cameo) and their friends and family. Before the credits roll, a scripture verse, Romans 5:8, appears: "But God demonstrates his own love for us in this: while we were still sinners, Christ died for us." The credits conclude with advertisements for the *Love Dare* book, the statement "To God Be the Glory!," the question, "Are You Fireproof?," the address to the *Fireproof* website, and another verse of scripture, Romans 10:9, "If you confess with your mouth, 'Jesus Is Lord,' and believe in your heart that God raised Him from the dead, you will be saved."

The Reception of *Fireproof*

I could tell the story of Sherwood Pictures in one of two ways, as either a series of aesthetically improving films or a series of films that experience increasing financial success. *Fireproof* enjoyed an 18-week theatrical run that grossed $33,456,317 at domestic box offices. To date, its DVD sales total another $32,057,194.[17] If we take into consideration the sales of over four million copies of *The Love Dare* and perhaps the countless number of study guides, we could add another few million dollars to the financial performance of this franchise.[18] Clearly, *Fireproof* struck a chord, and reactions to it were similar to those of its predecessor, *Facing the Giants*, with some small exceptions and one significant one.

Given its release in over 800 theaters, *Fireproof* caught the attention of more mainstream movie critics than Sherwood Pictures' two previous releases did. Surprisingly, *Fireproof* received a 50 percent rating on Rotten Tomatoes (www.rottentomatoes.com), a website that aggregates reviews of a film from a variety of film critics to determine an overall opinion of the film, providing a snapshot of the wider culture's reaction to it. The reactions to *Fireproof* mirror the reactions to *Flywheel* and *Facing the Giants* with most secular film critics panning the film and Christian film critics and viewers offering diverse opinions.

In a somewhat surprising twist, Joe Leydon, who wrote a negative review of *Facing the Giants*, took a more favorable view of *Fireproof*. Writing for *Variety*, he quickly addressed the "notable uptick in tech values and narrative sturdiness of the filmmakers."[19] Though he regarded the film as "sincere, uncynical, and subtlety-free as a Sunday school lecture," he did foreground the context from which the film emerged, more so than he did with *Facing the Giants*. He added, "The faithful may flock to megaplexes to generate modestly impressive B.O. [box office revenue], but *Fireproof* likely will find its true calling as an instructional tool for moderators of faith-based marriage-counseling programs."

In his review for *The New York Times*, Neil Genzlinger also recognized the context of the audience toward which this movie is geared. He noted that *Fireproof* had a rare element to it that most films and television programs lack, "characters with a strong, conservative Christian faith who don't sound crazy."[20] In fact, he argued that the most appealing characters are "those nudging Caleb toward Christianity," specifically Mike and Caleb's father. Genzlinger recognized the appeal that *Fireproof* would have for its target audience but also found a deeper message that might have broader appeal. He wrote, "[This] is a decent attempt to combine faith and storytelling that will certainly register with its target audience. And maybe other folks as well: among those caring-for-marriage tips are some that anyone could use to improve any type of relationship, with or without the God part."

Another secular critic, Michael Hardy writing for the *Boston Globe*, pointed out an odd portrayal of marriage in one of the film's many contemporary Christian songs: "One of the film's songs advises couples who get married to 'lock the door and throw away the key.' That sounds more like prison than holy matrimony."[21] He situates this comment in an overall review that bemoans the Kendricks' greater concern for the lead characters' "religious fealty" than their actual relationship with one another. Hardy is definitely on to something here in his criticism of the film. Another song's lyrics talk about waiting on the Lord, and the film seems to suggest that Caleb and Catherine's marriage improved, not necessarily because Caleb became a better husband, but because they waited on the Lord.

Chris Willman, writing for *Entertainment Weekly*, was less concerned with or offended by the film's evangelical message than he was by the way the filmmakers treated it: "You probably can't blame pastors moonlighting as moviemakers for wanting to pack their film with multiple messages, but the conversion subplot feels shoehorned into the more crucial marital doings, as if coming to Jesus might be just one of a long checklist of steps to restore sizzle to your marriage, right between buying roses and preparing a candlelit dinner."[22] Willman also noted that its faith-based status and grassroots marketing lent it a certain invulnerability. "*Fireproof* is obviously critic-proof, though it hit theaters sans reviewer screenings, it had been heavily screened for pastors, who bought group tickets for their congregations, ensuring plenty of sold-out opening-weekend showings." On top of screenings for ministers, as we will see with Sherwood Pictures' latest production *Courageous*, the filmmakers invited numerous Christian media outlets to not only view previews of the film during production but to watch the filmmaking process itself. For example, in behind-the-scenes footage, we see that the crew invited two representatives from Focus on the Family to participate as prominent extras in one of the scenes. This type of preferential treatment could have resulted in greater positive word-of-mouth about the film among evangelical audiences.

In his review for *Christianity Today*, Peter T. Chattaway rehashes some of the scandals surrounding the release of *Facing the Giants* and his initial frustration with the film, which he ultimately set aside in encouraging the Kendrick brothers' "artistic" growth. His review of *Fireproof* notes the improved visual *and* theological qualities: "[The] Kendricks *earn* their resolution this time; instead of dropping miracles and messages from God on their characters, they keep the story focused on the Holts and driven by the choices that the Holts make. Put simply, it no longer feels like the filmmakers are 'cheating.'"[23] While Chattaway praises the Kendricks' desire to place the conversion moments in the middle, rather than the end, of their films, he still finds a problem with the way in which they present the evangelical message here in *Fireproof*. Chattaway parallels Willman's critique when he writes:

> However, in *Fireproof*, it is not quite clear how essential Caleb's conversion is to his efforts to save his marriage. *Flywheel* and *Facing the Giants* concerned men who already had some sort of connection to a church community, but Caleb only has his parents and a friend or two for spiritual support. The Kendricks have said that Caleb needs to know Christ if he is to love his wife as Christ loved the church — but by that same token, shouldn't he also be involved in an actual church? What if someone were to follow the steps outlined in *The Love Dare* without being a Christian? While the film works well enough as an extension of Sherwood Baptist's marriage ministry, it is hard to escape the feeling that the evangelistic element has been tacked on.

Another viewer critiqued the plot of the film, and its spiritual implications, from a different perspective. Hippiemama from Louisiana gave the film a one-star rating and titled her response, "from a modern female Christian point of view." She writes:

> [M]y number one problem with this "film"? [... Catherine's] main issue with him [Caleb] is his pornography problem. The director/writer ABSOLUTELY should have used the computer killing scene as a turning point. Having her "discover" what a good man he is because he spent $24,000 on a bed for her mom makes this about money. I was truly disgusted at that point. Those two scenes should have been switched, so she could say that she "can't be bought" and that he showed himself a changed man by replacing his computer with her.[24]

These are problematic elements of the film to which I will return in my analysis of its theology. I will also return to Chattaway's critique when I discuss the church film movement as a whole.

With few exceptions, viewer feedback on Amazon was overwhelmingly positive with 489 five-star reviews as opposed to 45 one-star reviews. Of course, people who enjoyed the film in the theaters are more likely to purchase the DVD online and leave positive reviews in the process. One reviewer, antsi from Indiana, gave a complex review that engaged not only the film but the people who both praised and hated it. He attempted to separate out the film's marriage and faith messages, even though he recognized that doing so would be difficult. He added:

> Anyone who has actually been married for a while and worked through problems will recognize the above themes as true to life — and, most emphatically, true to life in a way that Hollywood movie portrayals of love and romance are definitely not true to life. I believe that most of the people who liked this movie — certainly me and my wife — are resonating with FINALLY a movie that seems to understand what enduring marriage and love that grows over the years are really all about.[25]

Another viewer, Taraden Lyndaker, praised *Fireproof*'s writing, casting, and acting.[26] Harold Wolf, from Wells, Indiana, wrote, "It is an emotional roller coaster that will have you gasping, laughing, crying, holding your breath, wanting to scream a warning ... and perhaps, even a standing ovation at the end." He also encouraged people in both healthy and struggling marriages to go see it.[27]

I am intrigued, by viewers who left negative feedback and admitted that they did not know this was a religious film before watching it. Reluctant techie from Olympia, Washington, writes, "I can't believe I watched the whole thing ... it was like a slow train wreck. I didn't know it was a religious movie until I was about 15 minutes in, then it was like some 'church approved' movie that uses every chance it can get to weasel 'the word' in. Yeah. I've heard that before."[28] It would be interesting to learn what compelled reluctant techie, and viewers like him/her, to keep watching the film after those initial fifteen minutes.

Any consideration of the response to *Fireproof* would be incomplete without a reference to the reactions to the books that accompanied the film as well. As I have already indicated, a great number of viewers jumped at the chance to participate in *The Love Dare* that saved Caleb and Catherine's marriage. Not only did they take up *The Love Dare*'s challenges, some even started writing about them themselves, creating blogs and websites that chronicle their *Love Dare* journeys. The Association of Marriage and Family Ministries created a website, www.40daylovedare.com, where they encouraged couples to take the challenge. As of November 19, 2010, nearly 56,000 people had registered. The site hosted a blog by Eric and Jennifer Garcia in which they reflected on the dares in the book and their progress through them.[29] Furthermore, almost 800 people have submitted stories to the website about their relationship experiences and use of or plans to use *The Love Dare*. These stories range from accounts of relationships once broken but now healed to spouses in failed relationships waiting on their partner to return.[30]

The Paul Gustafson family and a handful of families from their community near Minneapolis started *The Love Dare* together and created "The Love Dare Blog" at http://paulgustafson.wordpress.com. Unlike the Association of Marriage and Family Ministries' site, this blog never picked up a full head of steam and appears to be nothing more than a repeat of each day's scripture and dare. Another blogger, Charlie T., began blogging about his *Love Dare* journey at http://doubledogdare2009.blogspot.com. Beginning on Monday, August 10, 2009, he never blogged past day 6 on Monday, August 17.

The Theology of *Fireproof*

The ironic ambiguity of Sherwood Pictures' theology is on full display in *Fireproof* in three areas: the character of Caleb, Caleb's salvation, and the lack of a congregational or communal setting in which that salvation takes place, all of which are closely intertwined. First, Caleb, like his Sherwood Pictures predecessors Jay Austin and Grant Taylor, is an ambiguously religious character. Recall this exchange between Caleb and his father:

JOHN: The Lord did a work in us.
CALEB: The Lord? You're giving credit to God?
JOHN: Why does that bother you? You've always believed in God

If Caleb has always believed in God, then why does he ridicule or dismiss his father's faith? What has hardened his heart against the faith? Why has he turned to Internet pornography for "fulfillment"? Why is he so verbally abusive to his wife? Why has their marriage so quickly fallen apart? These are questions that the filmmakers leave unanswered. As viewers, we simply take it at face value that Caleb is a jerk to his wife. As in *Flywheel*, the Kendricks never really explain the source of tension and anger in the lead characters' marriage. Ironically, this is not because such information did not exist or that the filmmakers did not think this through themselves. In an interview, Alex comments, "[We] gave [Cameron and Bathea] a back story to draw emotionally from. We make up more than what you seen on the screen. We told them, 'One time, she did this to him and he did this to her.'"[31] The inclusion of such information in a montage or a short establishing scene could have given the characters greater depth and added clarity to the plot.

As it stands, Caleb's ambiguous religious identity leads to an ambiguous salvation experience. A few critics, both secular and Christian, noted the problematic ways in which the filmmakers handle Caleb's spiritual transformation. It is difficult to disagree with them, especially when we recall the conversation between Caleb and John. It is unclear why Caleb needs to give his life to Jesus, but as Willman suggests in his *Entertainment Weekly* review, one of those might be to get his wife back. Consider this advice from John to Caleb: "Caleb, the answer is, you can't love her because you can't give her what you don't have." The implication here is that Caleb needs to embrace the love of Jesus so he can be a better husband. As such, the creators of Sherwood Pictures' films inadvertently turn faith into exactly what Caleb says he doesn't need ... a crutch to get through life. Another reason that Caleb needs Jesus in his life is to prevent him from going to Hell. Recall this exchange:

> CALEB: See, I don't understand, Dad. Why do I need His salvation? What? Am I gonna be thrown into Hell? For what? 'Cause I got divorced?
>
> JOHN: No, because you violated His standards.

Finally, the ambiguity of Caleb's salvation experience is due in large part to its detachment from any visible congregation or community of faith.

In his *Christianity Today* review, Chattaway mentions that the lead male characters in both *Flywheel* and *Facing the Giants* had attachments to communities of faith. However, as I have shown, these attachments were tenuous at best. He does rightly point out that in *Fireproof*, all attachments to such membership have been broken. Recall his critique: "The Kendricks have said that Caleb needs to know Christ if he is to love his wife as Christ loved the church — but by that same token, shouldn't he also be involved in an actual church?" Again, there are no scenes of Caleb or Catherine participating in a community of faith before or after their reconciliation. There is one shot of them getting into their car and both holding a black book, but only the most perceptive and religious viewers will recognize that the two are going to church together. This absence is deeply ironic given the fact that this film is a church-based production. To be set in a small Southern town and produced by ministers, *Fireproof*'s lack of institutionally religious elements (aside from the renewal of marriage vows, which even non-religious couples do) is disingenuous at best and suspect at worst. The absence of such features is all the more puzzling given the filmmakers' desire to present a clear theological-religious-spiritual message.

Of course, all of this was never the filmmakers' intention. In the director's commentary, Stephen said, "We wanted the Gospel presentation to be clear and strong, not over the top, not forced. We didn't want to stop the story line in order to preach at the audience and then re-start it again. It really is integral to what's going on here. It is a part of this journey." Later, he asserted that they did not want to force themselves on people. Unfortunately, they are not as successful at this as they had probably hoped. The scenes in which Caleb's father presents the Gospel to him are the longest scenes (around six minutes long) in the film, so it does feel as if the film stops and re-starts around them. On top of that, Caleb's life does the exact thing. Ironically, Stephen and Alex seem aware of some of the film's theological ambiguity, particularly in the scene in which Caleb hints to Mike that he is now a committed Christian ("I'm on your team"). The Kendricks recognize that they have employed "Christianese" here, something of a coded language between evangelical Christians. Unfortunately, this simultaneously undercuts their desire to be clear and strong in the presentation of their message. Catering to insiders in such a way limits the film's appeal and reach to outsiders.

On the other hand, there is a positive theological element implied in *Fireproof*. Sherwood Pictures' third film is interesting, especially when compared to its predecessors, because, unlike them, it focuses less on acts of God and more on human agency and responsibility. Its characters do not constantly harp on how everything that has gone right (or wrong) in their lives is a result of God's action. Caleb, especially, does not simply turn his life over to God and experience immediate blessings beyond his wildest imaginations, like Coach Grant Taylor in *Facing the Giants*. Unlike Jay Austin in *Fireproof*, Caleb never says, "Okay, God, this is your marriage now. If it succeeds or fails, it's because you wanted it to." The only character who speaks of God boldly acting in this world is Caleb's father when he says that God "did a work" in his marriage and that God is at work all around Caleb, whether he sees it or not. Caleb not only has to begin to make right choices, but he has to do so with the proper attitude in order to save his marriage and improve his own life. God will not simply mend the wounded relationship overnight because Caleb trusts his life to Christ. Yet even in what I find to be a highlight of Sherwood Pictures' third release, there are some problems.

Any ambiguity that might define *Fireproof*'s theology rapidly falls away in consideration of its cultural worldview. The film, and its producers' reflections on it, are crystal clear examples of three key points in the Baptist Faith and Message to which Sherwood Baptist Church adheres, namely the identity of marriage as a union between one man and one woman, the family as the foundation of society, and the gender hierarchy in that relationship. Of course these have grave theological implications as well.

Throughout production, the cast and crew knew that the film could be an effective marriage ministry tool. In one of the making-of featurettes, Jim McBride, an associate minister at Sherwood Baptist Church and a co-producer of the film, talks about marriage being under attack. While he never asserts who or what is attacking marriage, I believe it is safe to assume that he is referring to sexual promiscuity in secular pop culture, the high divorce rate among couples in the United States, and, of course, gay marriage. Stephen's assertion that "God is in the business of resurrecting dead marriages" no doubt greatly appealed to marriage ministries and family organizations like the Association of Marriage and Family Ministries, Focus on the Family, FamilyLife, and the Marriage Commission to whom they targeted the film. The film and the producers' statements about it fall directly in line with Sherwood's commitment to the identity of marriage between one man and one woman as expressed in the Baptist Faith and Message. Even though a marriage, in Sherwood Baptist Church's mind, is between a man *and* a woman, their films always place emphasis on the former. Throughout Sherwood Pictures' films, but especially in *Fireproof*, the wife seems to be a foil for her husband's spiritual and emotional development. Moreover, when Caleb listens to his father talking about God doing a work in their marriage, he automatically assumes that his father led his mother to Jesus. He is visibly shocked at the film's conclusion to learn that his mother actually brought his father into a relationship with Christ.

As a result, the film's view of marriage has drastic implications for the gender roles in that relationship. The notion of the man being the head of the household and the woman submitting to him, so controversially outlined in the Baptist Faith and Message for example, forms the framework for the relationships in *Fireproof*. Caleb *demands* respect from Catherine even though he acts in ways that simply do not merit that respect. Moreover, the Kendrick brothers' assertion that the husband should wear the mantle of leadership whether or not he deserves it further problematizes this hierarchy. They never explicitly question or critique Caleb's chauvinistic attitude and assumptions that dominate the beginning of the film (i.e., he expects Catherine to buy groceries and wash clothes even though she works long hours every day). They also establish a simplistic male-female dichotomy drawn along emotional and spiritual boundaries, repeatedly asserting that "men long for respect and women long to be loved." While they attempt to backpedal and say that men also want to be loved, their initial dualism prevails throughout the commentary.

Women are not often portrayed favorably in Sherwood Pictures' films, nor are they ever their main focus. Unfortunately, their lowest representation might be in *Fireproof*. At one point in the commentary, the Kendrick brothers refer to Catherine, and by extension all women, in objectionable terms when they comment on her intensifying friendship-relationship with Dr. Keller, "Her rose needs water and she'll get it wherever it is available." With each repeated viewing of the film, it struck me just how shallow the filmmakers' presentation of Catherine is and how shallow the male characters' views of her are. Throughout the film, Catherine is presented as a passive object to be won or lost with little emphasis on her own hopes, dreams, or desires. The scene in which Caleb confronts Dr. Keller smacks of primitive male behavior. He accuses Dr. Keller of trying to "steal" Catherine's heart and threatens to beat him up if he does not cease his advances. Moreover, Caleb must run an obstacle course, albeit highly spiritual, to "win" her back. Catherine's behavior and ultimate decision to be "taken back" is highly problematic. Perhaps the film's most touching scene is when Caleb smashes his computer to pieces and puts a dozen roses in its place with the note that reads, "I Love You More!" Yet this is not enough for Catherine, who only returns to Caleb after realizing that he spent $24,000 on her mother's medical needs, thus implicitly and simultaneously placing a price tag on her love. This did not go unnoticed among some female viewers, as hippiemamma's comment on Amazon indicates.

Again, the Kendrick brothers' desire to tell a story that helps minister to Christians and strengthen marriages is commendable. However, they fail to see how the criticisms that reviewers and I have raised might undercut those attempts. I will return to many of these critiques later in my discussion of the church film movement as a whole. For now, I want to turn to an analysis of Sherwood Pictures' most recent production, *Courageous*, which has turned out to be not only their best production and one of the best Christian films ever made, but a fine film in general.

Chapter 6

A *Courageous* Future

With the money that *Fireproof* generated through box office receipts, DVD sales, and ancillary products, Sherwood Pictures planted its flag as the leading producer of independent Christian films, setting a mark for which all subsequent church-based production studios now aim. Not content to rest on their laurels, the Sherwood Pictures team (Alex and Stephen Kendrick, Michael Catt, and Jim McBride) announced the title and theme of their fourth feature-length film at an evening church service on November 15, 2009.[1] The film, *Courageous*, with the tagline "Honor Begins at Home," would focus on the theme of fatherhood through a story about a group of law enforcement officers who "willingly stand up to the worst the world can offer [yet] at the end of the day [...] face a challenge that none of them are truly prepared to tackle: fatherhood." A synopsis included this teaser: "When tragedy hits home, these men are left wrestling with their hopes, their fears, their faith, and their fathering. Can a newfound urgency help these dads draw closer to God ... and to their children?"[2]

Co-writers and brothers Stephen (left) and Alex (right) Kendrick announce the title and theme of their fourth feature-length film, *Courageous* (Sherwood Pictures, 2011), at a service at Sherwood Baptist Church on November 15, 2010. Photograph by Travis Hatfield.

Many elements of *Courageous*' production, marketing, and advertising speak volumes about Sherwood Pictures' engagement with potential audiences, their awareness of changes in communication, their evolution as the preeminent Christian independent film studio, and, more broadly speaking, the future of independent filmmaking. Perhaps the most significant change that took place between the production of *Fireproof* and *Courageous* had less to do with filmmaking technology or Sherwood's know-how than with the growing influences of digital communication and the establishment of social network sites as a dominant form of communication and social interaction.

A Note on Social Network Sites

In their article "Social Network Sites: Definition, History, and Scholarship," Danah M. Boyd and Nicole B. Ellison offer a brief definition of social network sites that is fitting for our discussion here. They write:

> We define social network sites as web-based services that allow individuals to (1) construct a public or semi-public profile within a bounded system, (2) articulate a list of other users with whom they share a connection, and (3) view and traverse their list of connections and those made by others within the system. The nature and nomenclature of these connections may vary from site to site.[3]

While this is only a portion of their in-depth definition, the ability to share profiles, connect with other users, and move through other lists of connections are the most important features for our discussion of Sherwood Pictures' increasing use of social network sites. As Boyd and Ellison point out, there are numerous social network sites that cater to a variety of interests. For the sake of brevity and to pinpoint Sherwood Pictures' reliance on them, I will briefly focus on the importance of Facebook and Twitter.

I could write a chapter-length introduction to Facebook, but I will try to be brief. Facebook is, perhaps, the most successful social network site to date. With a reported 500 million–plus users, the site was once valued at over $100 billion. Facebook's slogan, "Facebook helps you connect and share with the people in your life," is a deceptively simple description of what can be a complex network.[4] Through the site, users create a profile page on which they post personal information like date of birth, gender, relationship status, school affiliation, employment history, etc. Users can also share photos and videos on their profile pages. On Facebook, users connect with each other by "friending" one another, allowing them to see one another's profile and to potentially connect with new friends through expanding networks. At any time, users can update their status, which lets their friends (followers) know what they are presently doing, eating, thinking, watching, etc. As Facebook has grown in popularity, companies and products (including films) have created Facebook pages that users can visit and "like" in order to both keep up with the company, organization, or product and to share it with their friends.

Sherwood Pictures created a Facebook page for *Courageous*, which has, thus far, 291,406 followers. I think that it is important to note that if every fan of the Facebook page purchased a movie ticket to the film at an average cost of $10 per ticket, the box office receipts would surpass the film's production budget. This does not mean that Sherwood Pictures would break even on these sales alone (far from it), but it is a great start. The ease with which Facebook users could express their anticipation of *Courageous*' impending release or their appreciation for the film after having seen it to a potentially broad section of Facebook's over 500 million users is stunning. The effectiveness of *Courageous*' Facebook page on advertising and marketing is difficult to estimate. Here, users can view and comment on the same videos and photos featured on the film's website and talk about the film with other Facebook users who follow, or like, the *Courageous* page. When a user follows the *Courageous* Facebook page, Facebook alerts that user's friends, implicitly encouraging them to like, or at least view, it too. Unfortunately, the number of page views that the *Courageous* Facebook account receives is only available to Sherwood Pictures.

Twitter is, in a way, a downsized version of Facebook. It is "a real-time information network that connects you to the latest information about what you find interesting."[5] Twitter users send 140-characters-long messages known as "tweets," which are displayed in the user's "feed." These tweets, like Facebook status updates, allow users to share what they are doing or to upload pictures and videos or links to other media. Users can follow other accounts to keep up with their tweets and "re-tweet" or share them with their own followers. Evan Williams, co-founder and CEO of Twitter said, "We think of Twitter [...] not as a social network, but [as] an information network. It tells people what they care about as it is happening in the world."[6] What started as a simple social networking interface that allowed people to stay in constant contact has quickly become an essential business tool because it provides business with free advertising and marketing to a network of, potentially, millions of customers. The effectiveness of Twitter is hard to measure; yet a leading business user, Dell Computers, said that $9 million of its 2009 sales came directly through Twitter and Facebook combined.[7] Such financial reports are not hard to fathom given Twitter's over 100 million users and growing.

As I wrote this chapter, the *Courageous* Twitter account, @CourageousMovie, had 7,930 followers and had sent out 1,868 tweets. Yet the number of followers a single account has does not tell the complete story. A user's followers also have their own followers, so when @CourageousMovie posts an update on the film's shooting schedule or a prayer request, the number of people who see it is inestimable because its followers can share it with hundreds or thousands of their own followers. At the very least, Twitter allows Sherwood Pictures to get their film in the public eye without spending thousands of dollars on traditional print advertising or trailer spots on national television. Moreover, it contributes to the sense of community that has begun to develop around Sherwood Pictures' releases. As Marian Salzman wrote in her article "Why You Need to Twitter," "[Twitter] allows users a global social networking capability that texting doesn't.... The short-messaging format brings far-flung people together around a shared interest."[8] While I will say more on Sherwood Pictures' use of Facebook and Twitter in my discussion of their production and marketing of *Courageous* and the film's subsequent reception, suffice it to say that these social network sites now provide valuable insight into the production of a film and its filmmakers' intentions for it, information all once reserved for DVD featurettes or director's commentaries only available months after a film's initial release.

Producing *Courageous*

The most notable difference between *Courageous* and its predecessors is its reported production budget of $2 million, which shows both behind the scenes and on the screen. Obviously, as is the case with previous productions, Sherwood Pictures invested some of *Fireproof*'s profits into *Courageous*' production. Reflecting on the output of Sherwood Pictures as a whole and audience response to the films, Alex Kendrick said, "It's been the Bible's story of Jesus multiplying the boy's fish and loaves.... God has multiplied these movies beyond our wildest dreams."⁹ However, the multiplied fish and loaves, or increasing box office receipts and DVD sales, should not fool observers. *Courageous*' producers still relied heavily on an army of volunteers for much of the production, especially for extras, production design, locations, and craft services. The credits list a battalion of day-care providers, food donations (both local restaurants and Sunday School classes), and the ever-present prayer coordinator. No doubt, many of the volunteers from *Flywheel*, *Facing the Giants*, and *Fireproof* returned to lend a hand in their respective fields.

On the other hand, from behind-the-scenes footage and photos available on *Courageous*' website, it is apparent that Sherwood has put their financial resources to good use. Returning cinematographer Bob Scott filmed with a RED digital camera, the body of which costs $17,500, almost as much as the entire production budget for *Flywheel*. Additional accessories can even increase the cost of the camera to almost half the total production budget of *Facing the Giants*. Behind-the-scenes photos reveal a significantly larger crew than any Sherwood Pictures has used before. The *Courageous* production team featured construction crews, a second unit, and Hollywood-style lighting and sound equipment. Long gone are the days of the homemade dolly and camera crane, both of which are now professional grade.

Courageous' producers relied on Facebook and Twitter to drive potential audiences to the film's website (www.courageousmovie.com; more on it below). A banner at the top of the site said it all: "EXPERIENCE THE MAKING OF *COURAGEOUS* LIVE FROM THE SET." Here, Sherwood Pictures gave visitors behind-the-scenes glimpses into the production process via brief videos and interviews with cast and crew. Through video and blog posts, future audience members could keep up to date on the production of the film. On April 26, @CourageousMovie posted, "Production of #CourageousMovie begins at 8 am (EDT) today! Please be praying for the first day of shooting in Albany, Ga." A few hours later, they checked back in with, "The first scene has been shot! Lots of moving parts coming together, but it sure looks great." Throughout the production, the producers continued to keep future audiences up to speed on major events as they happened through daily Twitter posts.¹⁰

More important than shot updates was another consistent feature of a Sherwood Pictures productions, faith and prayer. As their blog, Twitter, Facebook, and video updates showed, the cast and crew bathed yet another Sherwood Pictures release in prayer. Once again, they began each day of shooting with prayer and a devotional led by a member of the cast and crew or, occasionally, a visiting minister. The producers also assigned a scripture verse to each day. On April 29, 2010, for example, @CourageousMovie posted, "Verse to pray from #CourageousMovie prayer team: 'I know that You are our Defender and You will fight for us' (Ps 7:10)." On May 6, 2010, they added, "'The LORD does not look at the things man looks at. Man looks at the outward appearance but the LORD looks at the heart' (1 Sam 16:7)." Again, while opening of a film shoot with prayer is not unprecedented, even in the history of Hollywood, the frequency of organized and spontaneous prayer sessions seems to be a unique feature of Sherwood Pictures' production schedules.

Throughout numerous interviews, the Kendrick brothers echo their filmmaking desires to which they have remained faithful from *Flywheel* to their most recent production. These include the glorification of God, spreading the Gospel message, challenging and uplifting believers, and countering godless Hollywood productions. These are all present in Sherwood Pictures' intentions for *Courageous*, but Stephen Kendrick provides further insight into their hopes for *Courageous*. Stephen said:

> I heard a statement years ago that we don't have godly nations because we don't have godly churches, and we don't have godly churches because we don't have godly families, and we don't have godly families because we don't have godly fathers.... This movie is going after the jugular in calling men in the body of Christ around the world to step up to spiritual leadership over their own lives and their wives and their kids. What would happen around the world if men stepped up and grabbed the steering wheel again and said, "As for me and my house, we will serve the Lord?" It would impact the next generation in a huge way.[11]

Marketing *Courageous*

Sherwood Pictures' reliance on the social network sites Facebook and Twitter formed a significant part of its marketing strategy and no doubt helped it reach a broader audience, but the studio also relied on traditional avenues of marketing like a robust website and ancillary products.

The Courageous *Website*[12]

The *Courageous* website is Sherwood Pictures' most robust and inviting Internet presence yet. Unlike their previous films' websites, *Courageous*' site allowed viewers to watch making-of videos almost as soon as they were shot. Each day, a production member chronicled the day's events with a two-minute video that (s)he then posted to YouTube and the *Courageous* site. In these videos, a host usually describes the work that is taking place behind her or summarizes what the cast and crew did or would do that day. By the time shooting wrapped, the site boasted 70 videos and nearly as many blog posts. Many of these videos feature interviews with the cast and crew or visitors to the sets, all of whom praised the work of Sherwood Pictures and encouraged viewers to support the film in theaters when it released.

Videos that did not focus solely on the work of the cast and crew often included conversations with ministers, members of the press, or other "religious celebrities" who happened to be visiting the set. Frequently, the conversations in these videos covered the theme of fatherhood and the importance of being a godly father. Such interviews were a relatively inexpensive means to spread positive word of mouth as Sherwood Pictures began to grow its pre-release network of potential audiences. One blog post informed viewers, "The Provident Films team invited key ministry leaders and media members to the set to get a feel for what *Courageous* and Sherwood Pictures is all about."[13] These leaders could then take their on-set experiences back to their congregations and organizations to build excitement about the upcoming release.

As they did with *Fireproof*, Sherwood Pictures targeted potential audience members through an emphasis on *Courageous*' central theme. Whereas marriage was the central theme of *Fireproof*, the themes of fatherhood and the necessity of families having strong fathers forms the center of *Courageous*' message. As a result, the film's website is full of videos with members of and references to organizations like All Pro Dad, Fathers.com, and National Fatherhood Initiative. The site features a section entitled "Courageous Dads" with videos and sound-bites from stars in the film and celebrities like former NFL head coach Tony Dungy, former NFL wide receiver Eddie Kennison, Mark Teixeira of the New York Yankees, and Yankees manager Joe Girardi. A strong commitment to family values, broadly speaking, obviously follows close behind the desire for stronger fathers. To that end, Sherwood Pictures also partnered with Family Life and Focus on the Family. All of this is Sherwood's (both church and film studio) attempt to present an alternative to so many families' experiences of overworked, distant, or absentee fathers, and other single parent homes, and, though unspoken, children with gay and lesbian parents. That law enforcement officers are the film's central characters gives *Courageous* another, although by no means mutually exclusive, target audience.

Courageous' website allowed viewers to purchase tickets to the film through a variety of third-party providers like Fandango.com, MovieTickets.com, and MovieFone.com. The site also offers a synopsis of the film and information about the cast and crew and provides visitors the ability to share their excitement for and love of the film through downloadable trailers, posters, web banners, flyers, digital wallpaper, a Facebook profile image, and bookmarks. Perhaps of more importance to the producers is the "Take Action" section where potential viewers can do just that. Here, the marketing teams asks: "Who in your church or community needs to see this movie and discover what families and fatherhood should be? Who is willing to step up and make that happen?" The section goes on to list a few other ways in which fans can take action:

- Will you gather a group of influential churches and leaders together to bring the movie to your town if it's not scheduled to open there by committing to buying 500 tickets?
- Will your church step up and buy out a show time, providing 200–250 tickets for your congregation and the people they influence?
- Will your ministry or business purchase 50–150 tickets to hand to people you reach out to every day?
- Will you personally purchase 25 tickets for the people in your neighborhood, Sunday school class, or couples small group?[14]

This portion of the site had been "Liked" through Facebook over 5,000 times, Tweeted 134 times, or otherwise shared 333 times. When I first saw the film at a Regal Cinemas theater, a table in the lobby had flyers for the film along with an eye-catching bright orange paper that provided contact information for group sales staff and encouraged audiences to book groups of 25 or more for a "*Courageous* Event" by offering them a free $25 Movie Gift Card if booked by October 13.

Courageous *Resources*

Most importantly, and of longer-lasting value, the homepage of the *Courageous* website features a link to a separate website where viewers can access *Courageous* Resources, www.courageousresources.com. Well before the release of the film, Sherwood Pictures made it known that *Courageous* would have book tie-ins like *Fireproof*. The website, UrbanChristianNews.com, reported:

> *Courageous* will be twinned with a new title from B & H Books [...] that will center on the film's theme of fatherhood. It will be accompanied by a book on the same topic by Michael Catt [...]. The Kendricks' new book [will] not be as closely linked to the film as had been the case with their best-selling *The Love Dare* [...], which was featured as a plot device in *Fireproof*, said B & H President and Publisher Brad Waggoner. The brothers were concerned "to avoid anything that would seem contrived or opportunistic," he said.[15]

Regarding opportunism, while the film's September 30, 2011 release did not coincide with the celebration of Father's Day, it will most likely experience new life when Father's Day 2012 rolls around as Sherwood Pictures can encourage customers to purchase the DVD as a gift for their dads.

The *Courageous* Resources website opens with a welcoming message from Michael Catt, who tells visitors that these resources exist to help people apply biblical principles of fatherhood to their daily lives and to have God help make them (dads?) a "hero to your family." These *Courageous* resources are all text-based and are designed for churches and individuals or their families. Most closely linked to the film is the novelization of *Courageous* by Randy Alcorn, available from Tyndale House Publishers for $14.99. Aside from this book and its audio version, all of the other resources are devotional or study material. Reminiscent of their publication of *The Love Dare* alongside the release of *Fireproof*, the Kendrick brothers have released *The Resolution for Men* (B & H Publishing, $14.99) alongside *Courageous*. Not leaving their better halves out of the spiritual equation, Sherwood Pictures and B & H Publishing invited author Priscilla Shirer to write *The Resolution for Women* (B & H Publishing, $14.99). Based on a Resolution that the main characters in the film sign (more on this below), the two are devotional books that encourage men to be "the bold and intentional leaders of their homes, marriages, and children as they strategically create a Godly legacy" and women "to embrace and thrive in God's beautiful and eternal call on their lives [...] to live with grace and create a Godly legacy with [their lives]."[16] Coinciding with the film's release, Michael Catt wrote *Courageous Living: Dare to Take a Stand* (B & H Publishing Group, $12.99), in which he "brings fresh insight to stories of people in the Bible who displayed great courage when it would have been easier to play it safe ... [and who] challenge me to keep moving forward [... and] demand that I examine my priorities and deal with anything that brings fear to my heart."[17] Shortly before the film's release, associate producer and pastor Jim McBride published *Rite of Passage: A Father's Blessing* (Moody Publishers, $13.99), in which he offers parents advice on how to lead their children into adulthood with purpose.

Churches also have the opportunity to employ *Courageous* in their worshipping life by purchasing a *Courageous* Church Campaign Kit for $34.99. It includes a planning guide, supportive sermon outlines, a four-week small-group study (with member book and supporting film clip DVD), evangelism outreach materials, a DVD-ROM with promotional trailers and worship helps, a copy of Catt's *Courageous Living* book, plus "branded products featuring official art to create an exciting campaign suitable for your church or ministry needs."[18] All of this, of course, is part of Sherwood's efforts to help churches strengthen their fathers and families. For $19.99, church leaders can purchase a *Courageous Living* Bible Study that "provides leader resources for this four-week Bible study to help strengthen families and fathers. The kit includes a 64-page member book and a DVD-ROM featuring *Courageous* film clips to support each week's lesson." The series focuses on four areas:

- Responsibility — serving, protecting, and casting a vision for the family.
- Priorities — focusing on eternal things rather than what is temporary.
- Legacy — recognizing a father's potential impact as a godly role model.
- Faith — increasing in wisdom and strengthening a father's identity in Christ.[19]

For $7.99, congregants can purchase *Honor Begins at Home: The* Courageous *Bible Study Member Book* that guides them on a longer eight-week study that takes participants "deeper into biblical truths for a godly family, exploring topics such as redeeming your history, walking with integrity, winning and blessing the hearts of your children, and more."[20] These studies employ clips from the film and even reading selections from *The Resolution for Men* and *The Resolution for Women*.

Through DaySpring, fans of the film can purchase inspirational greeting cards for and from men, a calendar, and three versions of the Resolution featured in the film. Men can choose from a framed, family-portrait-ready version for $79.99, a framed resolution for $59.99, and an unframed version for $9.99. For an additional $10, fans can personalize their copy of the Resolution. They can also purchase hats and t-shirts with a *Courageous* logo, and churches can purchase display cases in which to stock and sell these products. All of these *Courageous* resources, but especially the devotional and educational materials, serve a greater purpose. According to Jason Ellerbrook, LifeWay's director of Training and Events Production and Adult Ministry, all of these resources represent Sherwood (Pictures and Church) and their partners' hope that "God will lead us to experience more than a ministry, but a movement and a miracle among men."[21]

Courageous' E-mail and Twitter Campaign

As the film's theatrical release date approached, Sherwood Pictures ramped up their Twitter posts and, in partnership with Provident Pictures, engaged in an intense e-mail campaign to spread the word. Provident Films sent numerous e-mails encouraging viewers to purchase tickets in advance. They also notified fans of opportunities to get early glimpses of the movie through behind-the-scenes shows like "The Making of *Courageous*" on GMC TV or through interviews with Alex Kendrick and Ken Bevel on FoxNews. Provident Films used these early e-mails to allay conservative viewers' fears of the film's PG-13 rating (more on that below). Through e-mails, fans of Sherwood Pictures were even alerted to the way they could watch the Internet broadcast of *Courageous'* red carpet premiere in Atlanta, Georgia, on August 26.

A month before the film's release, Provident informed potential audiences that they could obtain group tickets through Sony Group Sales. As early as August 25, Provident began reporting that some theaters had already sold out their Friday and Saturday prime time screenings for *Courageous'* opening weekend. During the week of the film's release, Provident asked viewers, "Who's ready to be Courageous this weekend?" These e-mails also contained blurb-length reviews of the film from audience members who had already seen it and reflections on it from key figures like Tony Dungy, Beth Moore, and Raleigh Washington, president of Promise Keepers. After the film was released, Provident continued to e-mail viewers each week encouraging them to go see the film again and to take friends and family members with them.

Along with Provident Films' e-mails, the @CourageousMovie Twitter feed lit up in the months leading up to the film's release. Posts encouraged viewers to see the film multiple times and to return with friends. Sherwood Pictures' knowledge of the inner workings of Hollywood is on display in many of these tweets as they ask viewers to make a special effort to see *Courageous* on opening weekend in order to boost its box office performance and send a message to Hollywood. A list of @CourageousMovie tweets provides valuable insight into Sherwood's thoughts of and hopes for the film.

- July 26, 2011: "Make an impact when #CourageousMovie opens Sept. 30. Lead the way in your town with an Action Squad. [link to action page]"
- Later on July 26, 2011: "3 typical R-rated films sked [scheduled] to open Sept. 30. One atypical film challenging men to step up as dads: #CourageousMovie."

- August 3, 2011: "The movie industry's bellwether is a film's Opening Weekend. See #CourageousMovie Sept. 30–Oct. 1. [link to ticket page of *Courageous* website]" To emphasize the point, @CourageousMovie re-posted this later that day.
- August 8, 2011: "Know a law enforcement officer? Share #CourageousMovie with them by passing along this great video clip. [Link to a scene from the film.]"
- August 12, 2011: "Two best ways to support #CourageousMovie: (1) pray for the impact of the film (2) see it opening weekend, Sept. 30–Oct. 2."

On August 22, 2011, @CourageousMovie announced a movement, of sorts, around the film: "40 days of prayer for #CourageousMovie begins today on the Blog. Pray for movie's impact on families and more. [Link to prayer campaign]" The prayer movement featured daily blog posts with a brief reflection, a daily scripture verse, and two prayer suggestions, one for families and one for the film. Day four of the prayer campaign provides a succinct summary of the daily prayer requests:

> Thank you for your commitment to pray daily for *Courageous* and the impact it can have when it plays in theaters. Please take time to pray today for the following....
> **Today's Key Verse:** *Have I not commanded you? Be strong and courageous! Do not tremble or be dismayed, for the LORD your God is with you wherever you go. (Joshua 1:9)*
> **Pray for Families:** Pray for men to reject passivity and become strong leaders in their homes and not allow the fear of failure, fear of rejection, or the fear of the culture to stop them from doing what God has called them to do.
> **Pray for** *Courageous*: Pray for *Courageous* to have favor with theater chains and that they will support the movie with great show times and a long theatrical run beginning September 30.[22]

@CourageousMovie also shared what other people were saying about the film who had had the opportunity to see it at advance screenings.

- August 1, 2011: "RT @jordangreene I have bought OTHERS tickets to go see #CourageousMovie. // Awesome ministry tool coming Sept. 30!"
- Later on August 1, 2011: "RT @DrBrentTaylor I hope my pastor friends will do what @fbccarrollton is doing: rent out a theater for opening weekend of #Courageous-Movie."
- September 13, 2011: "Meagan says: 'Attention movie industry: This is the kind of movie I like.' Vote for #CourageousMovie at the box office. [Link to list of theaters screening the film]"

Finally, on the day of the film's release, September 20, 2011, @CourageousMovie re-tweeted a post from Jim McBride: "2 yrs. ago *Courageous* began in prayer. Today we share it with the world. The movie is the Lord's Yesterday, Today, and Forever. Praise God." In the days and weeks since the film's theatrical release, @CourageousMovie has continued to link to reviews (all positive) of the film and re-tweeted positive audience reactions to it. I will highlight some of these later in this chapter.

Opposite: Again, aside from the Sherwood Pictures logo and the references to *Fireproof* (Sherwood Pictures, 2008), there is nothing in the poster for *Courageous* (Sherwood Pictures, 2011) that signifies its faith-based themes. The marketers seem to be content to rely on potential audiences' prior knowledge and experiences of Sherwood Pictures' films. The poster reflects the film's expanded storyline but none of the images show the characters in church or engaged in Bible study, which they frequently do in the film.

Courageous, the Film

The plot of *Courageous* differs slightly from its Sherwood Pictures predecessors in that writers Alex and Stephen Kendrick broaden their focus from one family (couple) to five. Four of the main characters, Adam Mitchell (Alex Kendrick), Shane Fuller (Kevin Downes), Nathan Hayes (Ken Bevel), and David Thomson (Ben Davies), are law enforcement officers of varying levels of experience (David is the rookie) with varying levels of family dysfunction. David has an illegitimate daughter with whom he has never had a relationship (he left her mother before she was born). Shane is divorced and up to his neck in alimony payments. Adam seems to have the best family life of the three but is distant from his children as his work keeps him busy and tires him out. Nathan, a veteran officer new to the Albany police force, is the moral compass of the group and enjoys a strong family life now but suffers from past family trauma.

In the opening scene, Nathan saves his infant child from a gang member who attempts to steal Nathan's truck. After he meets his fellow officers who respond on the scene, we see the four officers, along with their co-workers, gathered for their daily briefing. The sheriff delegates assignments and partners veteran Nathan with rookie David, then shares some statistics about the criminals they are likely to face. He claims that statistics show that many criminals either come from single parent homes, most without a father, or do not live with their parents. Acknowledging that their jobs are tough, he ends with a bit of friendly advice: "Go home and love your families."

In a subsequent scene, we finally meet the fifth character, Javier Martinez (Robert Amaya), a Latino construction worker who has just lost his job. Life is a struggle for Javier and his family, wife Carmen (Angelita Nelson) and children Isabel (Ellie Zapata) and Marcos (Evan Zapata), as they barely have enough money to pay rent and put food on the table. The family only has one car so Javier must walk to work or to any job openings that arise. One of these openings closes just before he arrives, and on his walk home, he stops in the middle of the street and cries out to God for help. Suddenly, he hears his name. Adam, who lives on the same street, has been yelling at Javier to come help him. Unbeknownst to Javier, Shane had hooked Adam up with a friend of his named Javier to help him build a shed. Unbeknownst to Adam, our Javier is not Shane's Javier. This case of mistaken identity provides Javier with temporary employment until Adam finds him a more permanent job through a friend at the local string factory. All of this draws Javier further into the circle of police officer friends.

Tragedy strikes this group of friends as Adam's daughter Emily (Lauren Etchells) is hit by a drunk driver and killed. Adam, his wife Victoria (Renee Jewell), and son Dylan (Rusty Martin) are thrust into a place of great confusion and grief. Adam visits his pastor for counseling and receives some helpful advice. The pastor tells him he can either be thankful for the time he had with Emily or angry for the time he no longer has with her. When the pastor asks Adam what he wants, he tells him that he wants to be a better husband and father and to help his wife and son heal. Adam enters into a six-week study period where he turns to Scripture to find inspiration to be a better husband and father. As a result, he crafts The Resolution, a document that reads:

> I do solemnly resolve before God to take full responsibility for myself, my wife, and my children.
> I WILL love them, protect them, serve them, and teach them the Word of God as the spiritual leader of my home.

I WILL be faithful to my wife, to love and honor her, and be willing to lay down my life for her as Jesus Christ did for me.

I WILL bless my children and teach them to love God with all of their hearts, all of their minds, and all of their strength.

I WILL train them to honor authority and live responsibly.

I WILL confront evil, pursue justice, and love mercy.

I WILL pray for others and treat them with kindness, respect, and compassion.

I WILL work diligently to provide for the needs of my family.

I WILL forgive those who have wronged me and reconcile with those I have wronged.

I WILL learn from my mistakes, repent of my sins, and walk with integrity as a man answerable to God.

I WILL seek to honor God, be faithful to His church, obey His Word, and do His will.

I WILL courageously work with the strength God provides to fulfill this resolution for the rest of my life and for His glory.

"As for me and my house, we will serve the Lord."—Joshua 24:15

Adam presents it to David, Shane, Nathan, and Javier, all of whom agree to sign it and hold each other to its standards. When Nathan shows it to his wife Kayla (Eleanor Brown), she tells him that they need to make it official, because something this special requires a ceremony. The four men put on their Sunday best and participate in a ceremony officiated by William Barrett (Daniel Simmons), reciting the vows in their Resolution before God, their families, and each other.

Various trials and tests face each of the men throughout the second half of the film. David takes the necessary steps to begin reconnecting with his daughter and her mother. Nathan strives to effectively parent his teenage daughter, "protecting" her from the advances of an unwelcome suitor (who we know to be a member of a gang that the Albany Police are tracking). Javier's boss offers him a promotion—but asks him to lie on a shipping report

As director and actor, Alex Kendrick ratchets up the action in *Courageous* (Sherwood Pictures, 2001). Here, Officer Adam Mitchell engages in a climactic shootout with two gang leaders. Photograph by Todd Stone.

in order to get it. When Javier refuses to lie, his boss reveals that it was just a test to see if he could trust him. Adam still grieves the loss of his daughter while also working to establish a stronger relationship with his son. Of this group of resolute friends, Shane is the only one who fails to live up to his side of the bargain. When Adam learns that evidence (drugs) has gone missing from some of their casework, he initially suspects Shane. His suspicions are confirmed when he catches Shane in the act. Shane's defense is that he needed extra money to pay alimony and child support. Committed to justice, Adam has Shane arrested and put in jail, but he does visit him and promises to look after his son while he is in prison.

In a climactic shootout, Adam, David, and Nathan finally corner and capture the two leaders of the gang they have been tracking. The young man who wanted to date Nathan's daughter is also caught. The film ends in a rare church scene in which Adam stands before a large congregation to share their Resolution and challenges the men in the church to take a stand and be better fathers and husbands. As Adam loudly asks, "Where are you, men of courage?!" the title *Courageous* blasts onto the screen. Joshua 24:15, which reads in part, "But as for me and my household, we will serve the Lord," fades in and out, and the credits begin to roll.

Reception of *Courageous*

At the time of printing, *Courageous* had ended its theatrical run with a box office tally of just over $34.5 million. DVD sales of the film currently total just over $15 million. With only a $2 million production budget, Sherwood Pictures had a fourth financial hit on their hands. Both the Sherwood Pictures team and Provident Films were thrilled by *Courageous'* opening weekend performance where it finished #1 among new releases that weekend and fourth overall, even though it played in less than half the theaters (1,161) of its competitors. *Courageous* earned $9.1 million in its opening weekend, but experienced a significant drop-off to $4.8 million in its second weekend of release and $3.3 million the following weekend, not great signs for analysts who take a broader look at a film's box office performance and lasting appeal.[23]

Provident Films and Sherwood Pictures touted *Courageous'* A+ rating on CinemaScore, a market research firm that passes out cards before screenings on which audiences can write their reactions to the film. We must take into account the fact that this A+ CinemaScore is a bit skewed because many of the people attending *Courageous* screenings were already fans of Sherwood's work and Christian films in general. Given its comparatively limited theatrical release, audience members had to seek out screenings or were forced to lobby for them in the first place.[24] The CinemaScore ballot does ask why viewers attended, but audience responses to this question were not reported. We could assume that popular choices were "Director," "Subject Matter, Characters or Plot," or "Type of Movie."

While audiences loved *Courageous*, critics, both mainstream and Christian, were divided. *Courageous* is, without a doubt, Sherwood Pictures' most technically accomplished film to date with impressive cinematography and several truly inspired action and dramatic sequences. On the whole, the performances are solid and the dialogue feels far less stiff or forced than in most of Sherwood Pictures' previous films. Unlike those films, *Courageous* also benefits from several genuinely funny moments that provide welcome relief from what is, at heart, an emotional and, at times, depressing film. The Kendrick brothers also imbue the film with greater diversity, both economic and racial, than their previous films, a feature that will no doubt help *Courageous* resonate with a larger audience. While many viewers and critics have praised this feature, others, like Gary Goldstein, took issue. Reviewing the film for *The Los Angeles Times*, Goldstein wrote:

> Also troublesome is the movie's doubtlessly inadvertent racial stereotyping. Yes, Nathan is seen as the near-perfect family man and an upright law enforcer, but otherwise, almost every criminal in town is also African American. In addition, the retro portrayal of Latinos — of the sing-songy, "have a tortilla" variety — like so much else presented here, is more cringe-worthy than authentically, well, courageous.[25]

No doubt Goldstein also found much of the characters' faith cringe-worthy as well. This is unfortunate because for the first time, the Kendrick brothers give us main characters that genuinely elicit viewer sympathy. Like Adam, we grieve death, feel disconnected from family members, and long to be better parents and spouses. While I will say more about this below, suffice it to say that the faith of these characters feels more real, more natural, because it is something that gives them meaning and purpose, not *simply* something to which they turn when times get tough — although they do that too.

In nearly every review of *Courageous*, be they mainstream or Christian, critics first note the aesthetic improvements in cinematography, acting, and in the action sequences that open and close the film. On the other hand, these critics were divided over the film's direction, plot, and script. Few mainstream critics gave the film overwhelmingly positive reviews. Most, like Paul Brunick of *The New York Times*, criticize Alex Kendrick for "preaching to the choir." As I will discuss later, this critique is rather shortsighted, because this is exactly what Sherwood Pictures hopes to do, in part, with their films. Nevertheless, Brunick argues, "*Courageous* contains enough parables, 'are you there, God?' monologues and tearful affirmations of faith-based fatherhood to furnish a dozen megachurch services. To sweeten the sermon there is also some light gunplay."[26] Paralleling Goldstein's critique of the way *Courageous* portrays racial diversity, Brunick is critical of the ways in which Sherwood Pictures approaches many of its central themes. Goldstein also adds, "Despite the story's earnest emotional core, actions and reactions can prove overly simplistic; black-and-white when gray is so clearly called for. The many topics raised — gangs, drugs, immigration, absentee parents, poverty — are examined with didacticism and platitudes instead of by mining their inherent complexities."[27]

Like Brunick, Frank Scheck of *The Hollywood Reporter* claims that *Courageous* suffers from a storyline that often feels bogged down. However, Scheck commends the film for featuring characters that are "complex and well-drawn, struggling with various personal issues that test their faith and character in believable ways."[28] Unfortunately, these complex characters are all men, a consistent focus in Sherwood Pictures' films. This male-dominated film lead Goldstein to write, "And what of the importance of mothers here? It often feels like a case of '"Oh, them."'"[29]

As has been with most of Sherwood Pictures' releases, Joe Leydon, writing for *Variety*, is dubious about *Courageous*' crossover appeal but does believe that its message of responsible parenting could reach beyond its core Christian audience. Leydon affirms the believability of its religious elements and conversations, but claims that it is too long-winded and could have benefited from a few well-placed cuts. Leydon notes that the Kendricks brothers' turn to more serious subject matter strengthens the effectiveness and appeal of their film. He writes, "It should be noted that the underlying message of *Courageous* is all the more compelling because of its context. Time and again, the [film] effectively emphasizes how the deputies are reminded on a daily basis what eventually can happen to at-risk children who don't have fathers involved in their lives."[30]

Baptist Press covered *Courageous*' progress and theatrical release and published a handful of reviews. While Michael Foust claimed, in his article's title, that *Courageous* was better than *Fireproof*, he went on to add, "*Courageous*," though, isn't just better than *Fireproof*. It's in another league. Gone are the weaknesses you saw in *Fireproof*. I struggled to come up with a serious critical comment watching *Courageous*."[31] That a writer for *Baptist Press* would love the film is hardly surprising given its family- and faith-affirming message. In his review of the film for HollywoodJesus.com, Greg Wright compares *Courageous* to Sherwood Pictures' previous releases and notices an important difference. He writes:

> I'd have to say that, of Sherwood's four feature-film efforts, *Courageous* is the most pointedly aimed at a church audience. Yes — the other films have had more conspicuous "come to Jesus" moments than does *Courageous*; but the values espoused by this last film are less universally applicable, I'd say. Why? Because *Courageous* has the guts to tell the whole Christian story about how men (and women) can transcend human frailty. We can't do it on our own, and it's more than just Jesus-flavored positive thinking. It's God and the power of His Spirit that pull us through. Past Sherwood films have left themselves more open to a generically American "bootstrap" mentality. *Courageous* displays more "Kingdom thinking" than its siblings.[32]

Wright's point here is worth quoting in full because it begins to get at some of the theological implications of the film that I will discuss later and highlights the continuing appeal of Sherwood Pictures to a particular audience. Wright adds:

> [The film connects] solidly to men (and women alike) who are tired of the conventional pop culture approach to mainstream entertainment, which consistently makes men the butt of every joke. And, of course, Sherwood's films resonate deeply with what's loosely defined as the "faith audience:" millions of average small-town and middle–Americans who still believe in the power of God and religion.

Of all the reviews of Sherwood Pictures' films, both mainstream and Christian, the reviews from *Christianity Today* have been the most consistently complex and even-handed. Their contributors and critics consider both the context from which these films emerge and the targeted context into which they release. The same holds true for Steven D. Greydanus' review of *Courageous*. He echoes Sherwood's concern about the effects of fatherlessness and single parent homes on children and society at large. He recognizes that the film is Sherwood's attempt to address, on a personal level, the issue and provide a model for a better way. Greydanus argues that they are well-equipped, financially and experientially, to make a broader impact: "With each outing, the brothers not only enjoy a bigger budget and better production values, but become more adept in their handling of characters, relationships, and the difficult theme underlying all their films: conversion."[33] As Greydanus points out, and as I will discuss below, Sherwood still wrestles with how to integrate conversion into their narratives as it still comes off as didactic and schematic. Greydanus appropriately notes that Sherwood has yet to attain the Hollywood aesthetic for which they are aiming but that they have gotten close. This is interesting because even as Sherwood rejects or critiques "Hollywood's message" (or function), the improved cinematography evidences a desire for or commitment to a particular form or aesthetic dictated by mainstream Hollywood productions.

Of course, critics are only one barometer with which to determine a film's appeal. A more accurate assessment of *Courageous*' impact will include responses from individual viewers as well. As a relatively new release at the time of this writing, *Courageous* had fewer audience responses posted on the IMDb. What early viewer posts were available at the IMDb generally praised the film. There was only one one-star review among over 50 posts at the time of this writing. Self-identifying Christians or not, most commenters praise its faith- and family-friendly inspirational messages. Those that are aware of Sherwood Pictures' previous releases often comment on the cinematic improvements evident in *Courageous*. IMDb reviewer, jwrowe3 from Tampa, Florida, argues:

> Yes, it's a "Christian movie" ... and yes, there's a "happy ending" and yes, there's a "message." So what? [...] It's nice to see a movie where there's a strong message of family unity. Even Disney movies have taken to trying to tell us that your average family is a broken one. That may be factual, but why can't we have some entertainment that focuses on people trying to be strong fathers? And that leads to strong mothers, and then stronger children. And in the end, a stronger community.[34]

No doubt in agreement with jwrowe3, petersonmlp, from the United States, found the film more satisfying than other Hollywood productions and welcomed its deeper message: "My time and money is too valuable to just be 'amused.'"[35]

In his IMDb post, zack_wall, from the United States, excuses the film's slow pace and its predictability. Yet in a surprising turn, he argues against pigeonholing it as a "Christian" production: "While this movie was produced by Christians, and had Christian actors, it should not be designated a 'Christian movie,' but rather an inspirational tale of faith, courage, family, and honor[....] Don't think of it as a 'religious' film, but as an informational and educational story of faith and [...] courage."[36] Most viewers, sympathetic with the film or not, will disagree with zack_wall. It was extremely difficult to find a completely negative review of the film, but one eventually emerged on the IMDb. Fredkins, from the United States, called *Courageous* "another lackluster Christian fest," and encouraged potential viewers to "run a mile from this mess of a film" and to "save your money from the church — it doesn't need it anyway."[37]

If Sherwood Pictures employed Twitter to spread the word about *Courageous* and to encourage viewers to go see it, those same viewers returned the favor and used the social network to share their love of and reactions to the film. The following Twitter posts sum up much of the positive responses from fans of the film.

- @seanmillsh2o #CourageousMovie. INCREDIBLE!!! Every man needs to see this movie and especially all Dads. Challenged me as a man & Dad.
- @saragodsgirl Went and saw #CourageousMovie. praying my future husband will be a Man of Courage!!!
- @chris_r_stevens Just watched #CourageousMovie and can't quit thinking about my legacy as a dad #BeStrongAndCourageous
- @FluffySushi #CourageousMovie will make you cry your eyes out, warm your heart, and then make you laugh till your sides hurt! #ilovedit!
- @DavidBurtonEv My neighbor said "every man ought to be MADE to see #Courageous" I agree! Im taking more for third time. Keep believing!
- @tbcchildren Don't miss Courageous! Amazing movie! Better than Fireproof and Facing the Giants (both were great) dld.bz/afmZx
- @MaryStarrCarter Did I tell you how good the movie Courageous is yet? IT ROCKS. We have brought 7 people to see it so far. #courageous
- @kbcogop If I have ever felt God at a movie I just did.... Courageous is POWERFUL

In the days and weeks following *Courageous*' release, fans of the film echoed similar praise. While Sherwood Pictures definitely appreciates and benefits from such feedback, they are also looking for deeper impact. Fans and communities did not disappoint.

Recall the section on *Courageous* Resources. Churches began using them even before the film opened in theaters. On August 4, 2011, over a month before the film's release, Emmanuel Baptist Church in Tuscaloosa, Alabama, tweeted, "Courageous series (based on #CourageousMovie) — Sermons & groups begin Sept. 11." A *Baptist Press* article highlighted the work of another church in Alabama and one in Indiana that are using the film to minister to fathers and families. Heritage Baptist Church in Montgomery, Alabama, used the *Courageous* Church Campaign Kit that I highlighted above. (The church also used *Facing the Giants* for a "men's movie night" in 2008.) Scott Overby, a men's ministry leader at Heritage, talked about the church's plans for the film and the study: "We plan to use the eight-week follow-up study and complete it with a ceremony service, including the Resolution from the film.... We hope to host a Courageous breakfast and use this to group our men for further accountability." Other churches across the country are following alongside Heritage including Gasburg Baptist Church in Mooresville, Indiana. Jim Shields, Gasburg's men's ministry leader, spoke of a need in contemporary society: "If we want to see revival in this country, it will only happen if the men who call themselves Christian start responding to God's call on their lives." He claimed that the film will be a source of inspiration for that revival because it shows that "disobedience can cause repercussions and consequences, that redemption and forgiveness are possible, and that we cannot go it alone."[38] Via Twitter, Clay Hallmark (@clayhallmark), pastor of First Baptist Church in Marion, Arkansas, wrote about a *Courageous* movie event at his church: "Great night for @firstmarion folks at #CourageousMovie. People being saved, others enlisting in *Courageous* Living LifeGroup." The church began its *Courageous* Living LifeGroup on October 12, 2011.

Churches are using the film and accompanying small group studies to minister to their congregants, and to reach out to and evangelize first responders in their communities. Numerous reports of churches buying tickets in bulk and giving them out to police officers and EMTs circulated on the Internet around the time of the film's release. In another article for *Baptist Press*, Mickey Noah spotlighted a group of churches in Richmond, Virginia, that had purchased tickets for first responders as a show of appreciation and admiration: "To date, some 500 first responders — sworn law enforcement officers, certified firefighters and emergency medical personnel — from 16 Richmond metro jurisdictions have claimed their pair of free tickets to see the movie at any of four local movie theaters."[39] Fans of the film posted via Twitter that they had taken or purchased tickets for neighbors who work in law enforcement. In his article, Noah tells the story of a funeral for a local firefighter in which his widowed wife took the opportunity to encourage mourners to go see *Courageous*. She also allowed flyers and free tickets to be placed in the notice at his funeral.

At the time of this writing, there can be little doubt that *Courageous* has had an impact on its audience. How diverse that audience has been is more difficult to determine, and how long that impact will last remains to be seen. Sherwood Pictures' assertion that they have once again shocked Hollywood with *Courageous*' box office performance is saying far too much. The film was released during a down period in the industry as studios and theaters geared up for awards-worthy and holiday releases. Their obsession with Hollywood's opinion or reaction is ironic given their clear opposition to it. Do they want Hollywood to take the burden off of them? Do they think Hollywood should try to beat them at their own game? Nevertheless, a certain Christian audience remains pleased with and moved by Sherwood Pictures' work. And with their fourth release, Sherwood seems to have embraced some small but significant theological shifts that will go a long way towards broadening that Christian audience and, perhaps, granting them some crossover appeal.

Courageous Theology

The behind-the-scenes and on-screen theology of *Courageous* is in line with that of *Flywheel*, *Facing the Giants*, and *Fireproof*. From my discussion of Sherwood Pictures' production and marketing, much of *Courageous'* behind-the-scenes theology should already be clear. In constant prayer for production and subsequent success and impact, Sherwood Pictures saw good things as gifts from God and impediments as the work of "the enemy" to be overcome through prayer and faithfulness. Through Twitter and Facebook, the production team shared applicable Scripture verses that resonated with the themes of the film. Sherwood Pictures hopes that *Courageous* sparks a revival in fathers' and men's lives that will influence families and communities with the end result of bringing the wider culture "back" in line with basic, conservative Christian principles. As a result, the film is both a tool for evangelism and discipleship. That much of *Courageous'* audience will already be committed Christians does not concern Sherwood Pictures, who embraces the opportunity to strengthen their faith and families. If early reports are accurate, many people are responding to the call. As I mentioned above, the film ends with an inspirational challenge from Adam to a packed sanctuary. When he asks, "Where are you, men of courage?" some moviegoers have said that many men in the theater stood up as a way of signaling their response to the cinematic challenge. Through Twitter, @leahbellej wrote on October 9, 2011, "Was thrilled to see men stand in the theater as a way of saying 'I will be courageous' at the end of #CourageousMovie."

Though the message of *Courageous* is far from subtle, the film does contain some thematic and theological subtleties that call for a closer look. As I mentioned earlier, the characters here, particularly Adam, are far more sympathetic than the leads in *Flywheel*, *Facing the Giants*, and *Fireproof*. Much of this has to do with their approach to their Christian faith, which is clearly an integral part of their lives (at least for Nathan, Adam, and Javier) rather than something to which they turn to get out of a jam or to get their life in order. Although, there is a sense that this is what David does, but more on that later. These characters do not expect God to do everything for them. They take initiative in their lives. Javier may pray to God for help in finding a job, but that does not stop him from pounding the pavement in search of one. Adam cries out to God in anguish over the death of his daughter, but he also searches scripture for inspiration to be a better husband and father in order to help Victoria and Dylan heal. Nathan, who seems to have it all together, takes an active role in his daughter's life, raising her in the way he believes she should go. Even when his daughter's suitor, of which he disapproves, lands in jail, we see Nathan mentoring him in the faith towards the end of the film. These men put their faith in action rather than passively waiting for God to solve everything. This echoes the subtle shift that took place between *Facing the Giants* and *Fireproof* that I discussed in the previous chapter.

Contributors to *Christianity Today* often detect an ironic theological ambiguity from creators who are anything but ambiguous about their faith and beliefs off-screen. In *Courageous*, the Sherwood team is far more direct with its faith (salvation) message as Wright pointed out above. Although Greydanus argues that the Kendrick brothers have become more adept at dealing with conversion in their films, the theme feels more forced here than it has in previous releases. Apropos of nothing, around halfway through the film, we are taken to a scene with Nathan and David finishing up target practice at a shooting range. Out of the blue, David expresses his skepticism of Nathan and Adam's faith, which presents an opportunity for Nathan (and by extension the Kendrick brothers and Sherwood Baptist

"Where are you men of courage?!" A man of action, Officer Adam Mitchell (Alex Kendrick), calls his congregation to action as Javier (Robert Amaya), David (Ben Davies), and Nathan (Ken Bevel) look on at the conclusion of *Courageous* (Sherwood Pictures, 2011). Photograph by Todd Stone.

Church) to share the gospel message. When David says that he hopes his good actions outweigh his bad, Nathan uses it as an entryway to talk about God being a good and perfect judge. He presents a scenario in which David's mother has been brutally attacked, but when the attacker is put on trial, the judge lets him go because the good deeds in his life outweighed this one bad action. When David agrees that this would not be a good judge, Nathan tells him that God does not operate that way either. God punishes evildoers, but Jesus died to take away that punishment and bear that burden. However, Nathan tells him, it will only work if he accepts it. The filmmakers imply that David understands what Nathan is telling him, but the scene transitions before we see David make a profession of faith.

The type of theology here, substitutionary atonement, that promotes a vision of an angry, vengeful God more than ready to dole out just deserts, except for the fact that his son died to take that away, is far from unusual in conservative, evangelical Christian circles, even if it makes other Christians squirm. What is interesting about this attempt at a "moment of salvation" scene is the characters involved and the positioning of the scene in the film. That Nathan gives David the "come to Jesus" speech is hardly surprising given his solid moral standing among this group of friends. David was skeptical of faith earlier in the film so, as expected, Nathan targets him. However, situating this scene in David's broader situation of being disconnected from his daughter and her mother brings about a subtle but important implication. After what we assume is David's conversion, he begins to reconnect with his daughter and her mother, an effort only strengthened by his participation in the Resolution ceremony. The implication here is that good, ethical, or moral behavior is somehow more difficult (or impossible) to engage in apart from a Christian commitment. Furthermore, that Shane is never gung-ho about his faith like Nathan, Adam, and Javier sets him up to be the bad cop and signals that it is also not just a Christian commitment but a certain type that is necessary for a good, moral, or ethical life. In a world where extremely vocal conservative ministers and leaders are frequently found guilty of the very sins against which they preach, had Shane been portrayed as a more committed Christian, perhaps his transgression would have carried more weight.

On the other hand, an explicit theological or religious highlight of *Courageous* is the scene in which Adam visits his pastor for counseling after the death of his daughter. Pastor Hunt (Ed Litton, the pastor of First Baptist North Monroe in Alabama) provides some welcome Christian advice, certainly the least offensive in nearly all of Christian cinema. Pastor Hunt gives Adam space to grieve and refuses to gloss over the tragedy of Emily's death by chalking it up to God's will or by promising that God would work something good out of her death. He does, however, claim that this loss might open up a closer relationship to God because Adam, and his family, will need to rely on God for comfort and healing more than ever before. Though Pastor Hunt says that Adam can either be thankful for time spent with Emily or angry about time lost, he does not imply that Adam does not have a right to be angry. Rather, Pastor Hunt does not want Adam to become so mired in anger that he begins to alienate himself from his wife and son even as he is trying to help guide them through the grieving process.

A significant portion of *Courageous*' theology is implied in its social, cultural worldview. The most significant feature of that worldview is the belief in an ideal household composed of a father, mother, and children. Moreover, as Sherwood stresses, the father must be an emotionally, physically, and spiritually strong household leader who takes an active role in the lives of his wife and children. Although Sherwood Pictures and fans of *Courageous* stress that this is a film for the entire family, it really is geared towards parents (adults), but particularly men. The film's intense focus on fathers and fatherhood promotes a patriarchal system that has long been a point of contention for more moderate to liberal Christians. Adam's Resolution insists that men stand up and *take* their *rightful* place as head (spiritual, financial, and emotional) of their household. There is no room for a stay-at-home dad here, as *Courageous* men go out into the world and provide for their families.

Of course, all of this has implications for women. Foust reports that Stephen Kendrick believes that many women have been waiting for a movie like this as well because their husbands have not been the type of godly leaders that they need to be.[40] This is exactly how women are portrayed in the film too, as passive subjects waiting for their husbands to get their lives in order. Throughout the film, the women seem like so much window dressing, only present to prod their husbands into better behavior or to feed them when they are hungry. There is no sense that these women have lives outside of the home. While we do see a woman on the police force, the wives of three of the main characters (Nathan, Adam, and Javier) seem to exist solely for the sake of their husbands, children, and the domestic space. The mother of David's daughter works, but the filmmakers strongly imply that this situation is far from ideal. The $500 check that David eventually sends as he begins to set his life in order is only a stepping stone to what is, or should be, their necessary reconciliation. There is no affirmation of single mothers here, which is ironic and potentially offensive given the fact that many of them so boldly shoulder the burden of raising children in a single-parent home. The only option here for single women seems to be to find a good man. If posts on Twitter are any indication, many women are picking up the message. On August

19, 2011, @CourageousMovie shared a comment from an early viewer: "I prayed DURING the film for my future husband to take this stand!"

Despite its (mis)treatment of women, Sherwood Pictures is right to be concerned about the effects of divorce on families and the broader society. That divorce is rampant in contemporary American society is undeniable. That couples who lose children often divorce is also not surprising. As a result, *Courageous*' representation of a couple who "toughs it out" is a welcome vision of healing through loss and grief and the ability of love and faith to guide them through that. Of course, the implication here that faith can save marriages ignores the very real presence of a significant divorce rate among Christians (even with comparisons to divorce rates among non-believers aside).

Rightfully concerned about the negative effects of divorce, Sherwood might still be leaning too heavily on its insistence that families *must* have a father present. The filmmakers telegraph their point in an opening scene when the sheriff tells his officers about fatherless statistics, a scene that feels about as forced as Nathan's evangelization of David. The sheriff cites statistics about fatherless homes contributing to children's turn to a life of crime, Nathan repeatedly says that the absence of his father scarred him in so many ways he cannot number them, and David fears that his absence from his daughter's life will do her irreparable harm. In none of these cases do the filmmakers consider the socio-economic conditions that contribute to both single parent homes and the difficulties that often make life harder for single women, especially in lower income situations. There can be no doubt that single-parent homes are difficult on both the child and the parent. However, it is increasingly the case that two-parent homes are far less ideal than Sherwood makes them out to be as both parents must work to support the family, leaving the children in the care of (one hopes) loving relatives or competent childcare givers. The insistence on fathers, or gender diverse parents, skews research that simply claims that children benefit from two parents, regardless of their gender or sexual orientation.

In terms of sexuality and marriage in *Courageous*, it is worth noting that a key absence in the film again signals Sherwood's commitment to family values. Three loving, seemingly happy married couples are at the center of the film, but not once do any of them make intimate physical contact beyond hugging one another. When Emily dies, Adam and Victoria briefly embrace. Nathan and Kayla barely ever touch each other. Most "explicit," however, are two scenes with Javier and Carmen. In the first, when Javier returns from his surprise job working for Adam, Carmen tells him that she is so happy that she could kiss him. As he moves in to receive his kiss, she cuts him off, telling him that he is too hot and sweaty. Later, when Javier leaves in the morning for his new job at the string factory, he tells Carmen that he is so happy that he could kiss her. As she moves in to receive her kiss, he cuts her off, telling her that she has bad breath. While these are moments of comic relief for the filmmakers, they serve another function as well. These scenes allow the filmmakers to imply physical contact between actors who are not married to one another in real life without actually having them forsake their vows to their respective real-life spouses. (This is all a continuation of the silhouetted kiss scene between Kirk Cameron and his real-world wife in *Fireproof*.)

Ironically, the most "romantic" scene in *Courageous* involves Nathan and his daughter, Jade (Taylor Hutcherson). As I have mentioned earlier, Nathan thwarts the advances of a young man who is interested in Jade. While on a father-daughter date at a nice restaurant, Nathan explains to Jade why he is so strict. He tells her that there will be many boys who will try to "win her heart," but that they will not know how to "treasure" it. He goes on to tell her, "One day, I will give you away to another man, and I want that man to love God more than anything, because if he does, then he will love you." He promises her that if she will let him guard her heart until she is 17, he will approve of a boyfriend who is acceptable to him and her mother. To make his vow official, he places a diamond heart-shaped ring on her left ring finger and tells her it should stay there until her future husband replaces it with a wedding ring. While this scene might seem creepy to some viewers, it will be familiar to many evangelical parents and teens who engage in such commitment, chastity ceremonies like True Love Waits.[41] While a chief form of abstinence education in evangelical circles, this also portrays young women as property to be guarded and given away at the father's discretion. It can be little wonder, with this foundation, that young women grow up to be the passive subjects we see married to the men in the film.

Finally, *Courageous*' setting is worth noting. As with all of their films, the Kendrick brothers set the action in their small town of Albany, Georgia. In each of their films, Albany could be a stand-in for Anywhere, USA, except for big cities. That their films primarily play in smaller towns and avoid larger cities says something about the audience to which they want to speak. The events that take place in *Courageous* are more dangerous than anything Sherwood Pictures has depicted thus far. Film and religion scholar Richard Lindsay notes some implications of the small town setting and the events that take place there:

> The world [Sherwood Pictures] portrays in the film is highly dangerous, and it's up to this group of dedicated, "Godly" men to stand against it. Think about it: in this small town in Georgia, within a small circle of friends, they had a child killed by a drunk driver, a gang member [attempting to date] a daughter, a carjacking that could have led to [a] child's death, a drug dealer, and a deadbeat dad. [...For] the primarily white, suburban or small-town audience this film is going to resonate most strongly with, there seems to be an irrational fear of what can happen to them in the world, and a strong sense that this is due to the "increased sinfulness" of society. The darker side of that is outright xenophobia — this belief that when you mix races and religions and classes and people in different family structures in "diverse" settings like big coastal cities, this kind of crime and disarray is bound to happen, and will then "spill over" into their quaint exurban communities.[42]

At the same time, however, *Courageous* does present an interracial community (both social and congregational) that, in its own way, works for the betterment of the broader culture and works against Lindsay's critiques of possible xenophobia. Yet an environment of fear, from Nathan's protection of Jade to drug dealers plaguing an idyllic community, does present itself as an undercurrent in the film.

From *Flywheel* to *Courageous*, Sherwood Pictures has made leaps and bounds in technical and aesthetic improvements in filmmaking. They have cornered a market and grabbed an industry's attention. In the previous four chapters, I have shown how they have accomplished all of this evolving from an up-start production studio to an industry leader. Yet the Kendrick brothers did not invent independent filmmaking, and in the next chapter, I want to outline the rich history and fertile *secular* filmmaking soil from which Sherwood Pictures emerged and further situate them in the evangelical Christian pop culture of which they are a part.

Chapter 7

How Did We Get Here?

At first glance, two Baptist ministers without proper film training believing they could revolutionize the filmmaking industry seems to be the type of hubris that such Christians are divinely commanded to avoid. However, the work of Sherwood Pictures and the church film movement that it has inspired is both the culmination of a history of technological evolution and changing industry practices as well as an embodiment of the current and future states of independent filmmaking. With limited crossover appeal, these films rely heavily on consumers in the evangelical pop culture market to ensure their success, thus blurring the lines between the secular and the sacred and providing further insight into the relationship between evangelical Christians and pop culture.

If Chapter One offered a "sacred" history of cinema, recounting the ways in which Christianity was portrayed in or involved with film production, then this chapter is a secular version of that history. Here, I want to consider some of the technological developments and changes in industry practices that allowed alternative voices to emerge into the mainstream. I will also say a bit about the state of the industry into which Sherwood Pictures' films release, giving consideration to exhibition sites, the importance of DVD and digital download versions of their films, and niche marketing and broadcasting. I will conclude this chapter with a brief discussion of the evangelical pop culture market, a field in which Sherwood Pictures has no cinematic equal, and the ways in which "faith brands" have become the sacred equal to their secular counterparts.

An Evolutionary History of Filmmaking

The history of American cinema can be told in a variety of ways. In fact, I have already presented one avenue in the first chapter of this book through an examination of the history of religious films and the relationship between cinema and American Christianity. Another, more popular avenue of film history considers the changes in technology and filmmaking practices throughout the last century. Here, historians traditionally follow a series of phases, the advent of motion pictures in the late 1800s, the establishment of a silent art form throughout the teens and early twenties, the transition to sound in the late twenties, the dominance of the studio system of film production from the mid-thirties to the early sixties, the rise of "the movie brats" in the seventies, the emergence of the Hollywood blockbuster from the mid-seventies through the eighties, and finally the digital revolution and independent filmmaking in the nineties. Throughout all these inventions and transitions, we can see the entrance of new voices into the world of cinema, oftentimes made possible by cheaper and more accessible equipment.

As I have already shown in Chapter One, even in its humble beginnings, everyone had grandiose views of the cinema. Again, its supporters saw the emergence of a new language, a new art form that could transcend cultural and language barriers and perhaps even bring about world peace. Its opponents saw the cinema as a handmaiden of the devil, poison for the minds of youth, immigrants, and the infirm. Rather than a tool for moral uplift, these critics saw an effective educational tool for a life of crime, illicit sexual behavior, and other forms of cultural deviancy. These hopes and fears may seem quite odd to viewers today. After all, we are only talking about a little bit of light, shadow, and motion. However, the youthfulness of this medium and the rather simple technology that it involved allowed almost anyone to participate in film production and exhibition. This new medium attracted a host of immigrants, which, no doubt, contributed to the cultural elite's fear of and disdain for it.

The early history of film producers and exhibitors is a story of a bunch of nobodies rapidly becoming an influential group of somebodies. Hungarian, Russian, German, and Canadian immigrants, nearly all of Jewish descent, emerged from businesses as diverse as the fur trade, shoe repair, scrap metal, and vaudeville, and took the medium by storm. They helped transition cinema from its Silent Era (1894–1929) to its Golden Age (1929–1949) and, in the process, took an "anything goes," free-wheeling enterprise and turned it into an industry that, in many ways, still dominates the world of filmmaking today. Their names, and the names of their creations, are with us yet: Fox, Warner Brothers, MGM, Columbia, and Paramount.[1]

The most significant change that these film pioneers brought to this new enterprise was the creation of film studios, factories that turned out films on a conveyor belt–like system that mirrored the means of production dominating industry at that time.[2] While everyone had their own role to play in the conveyor belt, a successful production relied on effective communication and cooperation between departments. Breaking into the studio on one of the lower levels, as a writer or costume designer for example, was far less difficult than working one's way up that ladder. This was a rapid departure from the Silent Era when almost anyone could direct if they had the ambition and the opportunity arose. In fact, Hollywood soon began to exhibit a level of self-awareness as evidenced by the emergence of film characters like the gruff studio executive obsessed with nothing but financial profit. Perhaps one of Hollywood's greatest moments of self-awareness of this style of production came in *Singin' in the Rain* (MGM, 1952) in which the lead characters, Don Lockwood (Gene Kelly) and Cosmo Brown (Donald O'Connor), walk through a sound stage and, within just a few steps, pass in front of scenes from a football game, a wild west shootout, and a tribal dance. Cosmo later tells Don, much to his chagrin, that Kathy (Debbie Reynolds) does not particularly care about movies because, "If you've seen one, you've seen them all."

This means of production not only impacted the *way* films were made but *what* they contained as well. Under the watchful eye of the studio boss and, as we have seen, the Catholic church, film representations of sex, gender, violence, and religion were greatly restricted. Of course, writers, producers, and directors found ways to subvert these restrictions but, for the most part, a conservative ethos prevailed. While many harsh critics of censorship are quick to bemoan such an "oppressive" filmmaking environment, we must consider the cinematic treasures created in that system. Films like *Gone with the Wind* (MGM, 1939), *The Wizard of Oz* (MGM, 1939), *Citizen Kane* (RKO, 1941), and *It Happened One Night* (Columbia, 1934) still entertain, uplift, and inspire discussion.

Though the studio system would dominate film production worldwide, it was not without its fair share of difficulties. Filmmaking's greatest ally, technology, soon became its greatest enemy. The invention of the television and its increasing conspicuousness in American homes struck a significant blow to movie attendance, which had already begun to decrease with the invention of the automobile and then the financial crisis of the Great Depression. Studios scrambled to provide movie-going experiences that television could not replicate and began experimenting with a host of new technologies like 3D, Cinerama, and CinemaScope. Although 3D is attempting to mount a comeback, the latter two are perhaps the lasting legacy of this era. Both provided a more immersive viewing experience by employing larger, wider screens. As I mentioned in the first chapter, these screens were soon filled with Hollywood religious epics like *The Robe*.

Of course, the challenges to the studio system transcended competing technologies, economic crises, and declining audiences. Changes in the surrounding culture, to which few institutions had any effective responses, shook the filmmaking industry, and its studio center could not hold. Cultural revolution and political upheaval in the '60s and '70s were direct attacks on the established social mores that Hollywood films embodied and propagated.[3] Audiences were growing disaffected with the conservatism and predictability of much of Hollywood's output. Moreover, an influx of foreign films with more liberal perspectives on topics like sex and religion whetted many viewers' appetites for an American cinematic revolution. At the same time, the increase in film studies programs in colleges and universities across the country not only lent an air of respectability to the medium, but inspired a generation of new filmmakers. Changes in technology would help fuel this revolution and simultaneously breathe new life into the world of American cinema. The creation of smaller and cheaper hand-held cameras allowed filmmakers to shoot on the streets. Aspiring directors no longer needed to break into the studio or work their way up the industry ladder. Other inventions like Garrett Brown's steadicam in 1976 helped strengthen the aesthetic qualities of this guerrilla style of filmmaking.[4]

Soon, new filmmaking "bosses" emerged like Roger Corman and Russ Meyer, whose films sexually or violently (and most often simultaneously) challenged the status quo. With just a few thousand dollars per project, Corman began to invest in young filmmakers who had similarly fresh visions. Thanks to his faith in a handful of young filmmakers, he is directly responsible for the beginnings of the careers of Francis Ford Coppola, Martin Scorsese, Ron Howard, and James Cameron, to name a few. At the same time, however, filmmakers like George Lucas and Steven Spielberg undertook what was fast becoming a more traditional path into the business, film school. Both filmmakers embraced recent changes in technology and, with their special effects crews, advanced the field by leaps and bounds. Their unprecedented success with blockbusters like *Jaws* (Universal, 1975) and *Star Wars* (Lucasfilm, 1977) signaled a new era in the history of American cinema, the Hollywood blockbuster, which would eventually, rightly or wrongly, characterize American film from then on, overshadowing the more intimate, personal projects of other filmmakers.

The history of the Hollywood blockbuster since the late 1970s and early 1980s is, with a few rare exceptions, one of both great originality and banality.[5] Filmmakers and technicians made leaps and bounds in the area of special effects, which allowed them to envision the invisible in ways unmatched in the history of American cinema. However, these effects were often put to use in the service of films that lacked any compelling plots. For example, the ability of filmmakers to craft scenes of great devastation and loss outpaced their ability or willingness to convey the emotions that (should) accompany those experiences. Soon, the power and influence of the studios returned as they recognized the value of the blockbuster and, especially, its sequel(s). Another Hollywood ethic and aesthetic gradually emerged with its own social, economic, and political implications. Critics of the blockbuster genre bemoan the ways in which studios began to exploit films with sequels, product tie-ins, and franchises, but these studios simply responded to the desire of a younger generation of moviegoers to connect with the narrative. Nevertheless, an audience remained that wanted more original productions, and one filmmaker eventually obliged.

Enter Quentin Tarantino, an untrained filmmaker whose film school consisted of endless hours watching films and working at a video rental store. His first independent feature, *Reservoir Dogs* (Dog Eat Dog Productions, 1992), breathed fresh life into American cinema and energized independent filmmaking in ways that few filmmakers had ever done. Soon studios and producers began to emerge that specialized in the production of independent films. This led to the creation of cable television networks like the Independent Film Channel and Sundance, which served as a showcase for these films. While avenues to showcase independent productions increased, the changes in filmmaking technology made it possible for aspiring filmmakers to create the films they wanted to make. The digitalization of filmmaking made it more affordable for amateur filmmakers and low-budget visionaries to get their productions into the mainstream. The growth of the Internet in the mid to late '90s provided independent filmmakers with both a venue to eventually screen their work and a network of free, inexpensive, word-of-mouth digital publicity. *The Blair Witch Project* (Haxan Films, 1999) is perhaps the first commercially successful film that embodied the technological and communication changes impacting the industry with word of the film spreading across the Internet. *Blair Witch* cost only $60,000 to produce yet it earned over $140.5 million at domestic box offices.[6] More recently, *Paranormal Activity* (Blumhouse Productions, 2007), with a budget of only $12,000, earned $107.9 at domestic box offices.[7]

The first decade of twenty-first century American film history can be defined, in part, as the democratization of filmmaking. More sophisticated cameras have become cheaper and easier to use while computers come pre-packaged with film editing software that, only two decades ago, would have been unthinkable for first-time filmmakers. Avenues of film exhibition have diversified with theatrical releases no longer the ultimate goal for independent filmmakers. On-demand cable services, download services from iTunes, and on-line streaming allow filmmakers to place their films in tens of millions of households instantaneously. Of course, YouTube remains a popular video hosting service but is no longer the only game in town as other video hosting sites like Vimeo have given filmmakers places to showcase their films with less restrictions.

In his essay "Film Production in the Digital Age — What Do We Know About the Past and the Future," S. Abraham Ravid provides invaluable insight into the current state of the filmmaking industry. One of his observations is worth quoting in full:

> [Independent filmmakers] are now able to produce technically more accomplished films for less money than ever before. Digital cameras enable the independent filmmaker to repeat shots without budget constraints. Lighting, which is costly and complicated, is less of an issue in the digitally alterable film, and shots can be viewed in real time. One day, a writer with the right software will be able to create a theatrical quality movie, animate actors or other digitally created images, and costlessly and instantaneously deliver the finished product to theaters and to home projection devices around the world.[8]

Ravid claims that this will result in two changes: (1) filmmaking will become more like writing a book, and (2) movies that appeal to smaller audiences will become financially viable. As a result, Ravid argues, the identity of major studios will transition from production entities to marketing and distribution entities, much like book publishers. That is, a filmmaker will bring a completed project to a studio for them to handle the particulars of marketing and distribution. In fact, some filmmakers like Ed Burns are bypassing the studios altogether, producing their own films and working out deals with alternative distribution sources like iTunes and On-Demand cable services.[9]

Just as filmmakers are realizing the changing nature of production, they have also begun to consider alternative exhibition sites as well. Documentarian Jon Reiss recently published *Think Outside the Box Office: The Ultimate Guide to Film Distribution and Marketing for the Digital Era*. While this book is targeted to filmmakers and producers, film scholars will also gain valuable insight into the industry. Unlike many filmmakers and film scholars, Reiss takes non-theatrical film venues seriously, specifically their potential for financial impact and audience exposure. Theatrical exhibition is self-explanatory, conventional theaters where admission is charged. On the other hand, non-theatrical and semi-theatrical venues include a broader range of exhibition sites. Semi-theatrical venues include "all non-conventional theatrical venues in which a fee is charged for admission," while non-theatrical screenings include "free viewings on school campuses, libraries, or any other venue where *admission is not charged*."[10] Reiss also claims that burgeoning exhibition sites include grassroots or community screenings, an "exploding field of individuals and organizations obtaining films to screen for their community."[11] These might be more issue-driven films that speak to an organization's political or social interests. Reiss also reveals that, along with a diversity of exhibition sites, filmmakers must consider the location of those sites. He asks filmmakers to reconsider the traditional practice of sinking money into two or three large markets and to consider using those resources to screen their films in several smaller markets. Reiss adds, "Your film might have strong audiences in a specific region of the country, so it will be easier to perform well and build word of mouth out of those areas."[12]

Reiss also encourages filmmakers to be intentional about determining their target audience(s) and how they will market their films to them. He asks aspiring filmmakers to consider several key questions, including what they want from their film (to impact the world, create a long-term fan base, etc.) and who their audiences are (core, secondary, etc.). He encourages aspiring filmmakers to think about the marketability of their films from several perspectives including type of genre, use of stars, and type of stories. Reiss even explicitly references the rise in Christian-themed films that attempt to serve that underserved audience. While stars obviously help sell films, Reiss also encourages filmmakers to have a "marketing hook or sellable story about the creation of the film" and to "strive to find a compelling hook about your film that reviewers and bloggers can write about."[13]

As would be expected, Reiss embraces the power of the Internet to market films. He argues that it is the most cost-effective way for filmmakers to promote their films and that a filmmakers' website is "the frontline in your sales to the outside world."[14] He also encourages filmmakers to use social networks like Facebook and Twitter to not only post updates on their films' progress, but to ask questions and listen to the answers that might impact the production process.[15] As important as these resources are, Reiss still sees marketing value in traditional press outlets as well. However, it is media's ever-compartmentalizing nature that will help filmmakers reach their target audience. As a result, filmmakers should seek out "press about the issue/subject of your film [which] makes people want to see the film because they are concerned about the underlying issue."[16]

All of this contributes to a paradigm shift that Reiss sees taking place, particularly among many independent filmmakers. In this new paradigm, "filmmakers move from a project-to-project model to a career development model [where they] are not 'marketing,' rather they are developing a relationship with their audience, which in turn builds a long-term support structure."[17] Filmmakers will go a long way toward developing this relationship if they follow Reiss' advice: he argues that keeping costs low obviously means that filmmakers can quickly recoup their production budget through their own distribution entities rather than relying on outside help (and investment).[18] Filmmakers who do this can move on to new productions faster rather than obsessing over the financial performance of one expensive production.

Filmmakers can maintain the relationships they make with their audiences through DVD and digital releases. Conveniently, these are also key sources of revenue for filmmakers. In her essay "Critiquing Hollywood: The Political Economy of Motion Pictures," Janet Wasko discusses ancillary markets that accompany, or follow, a film's theatrical release. She notes that one of the most financially viable ancillary products has been DVD sales which "have provided especially lucrative rewards for films that do well in theaters, as well as giving 'legs' to films that have not performed well in theatrical release."[19] In fact, as Ravid points out, income from TV, video, and DVD sales exceeds domestic box office receipts for the average American movie.[20] In his essay "Profits Out of the Picture: Research Issues and Revenue Sources Beyond the North American Box Office," Charles R. Winberg notes, "In 1997, the MPAA estimates there were only six hundred movie titles available on DVD, by 2002, that number exceeded twenty thousand."[21] According to the MPAA's Theatrical Market Statistics, worldwide box office revenue totaled $29.9 billion in 2990 with $10.6 billion of that coming from domestic box offices.[22] The Entertainment Merchant Association reports, "Consumers spent $22.4 billion buying and renting DVDs and Blu-Ray Discs in 2008."[23] They also show that consumer Internet movie spending totaled $141.8 million in 2008 and that online subscription rental services (like Netflix) for example, which allow online streaming of movies, was responsible for 25 percent of the rental business in 2008 with chains like Blockbuster still holding to 69 percent of the market. Although DVD sales might be declining, it does not spell the end for home entertainment as consumers are simply shifting their consumption to downloadable or streaming formats that will provide an increasing amount of revenue for filmmakers. These on-demand versions are more susceptible to impulse buyers because customers do not have to leave their home to purchase a disc or wait for a delivery.

As helpful as it is, the world of secular filmmaking is not the only arena that demands our attention to help understand the success of Sherwood Pictures and other participants in the church film movement. Although many of these films enjoy mainstream theatrical releases, they are far more at home in the world of evangelical Christian pop culture than they are secular pop culture. The multi-billion dollar Christian pop culture industry depends on niche marketing and broadcasting like its secular counterparts and draws from them to market itself in some confounding ways.

The Evangelical Christian Pop Culture Industry

Sherwood Baptist Church and the other congregations that participate in the church film movement that I will discuss in the next chapter have not been the first evangelicals to benefit from changes in technology. In his essay "Technological Changes and Monetary

Advantages," Barry Gardner examines the growth of evangelical funding from 1945 to 2000. He argues that while the growth of evangelicals certainly depended on demographic shifts (more people expressing or converting to evangelical denominations), changes in technology account for much of that growth as well because it improved their fund-raising and organizational strategies. He writes, "I think that developments in communications technology, the widespread adoption of computers, the development of direct mail, and the expanded use of the telephone have had profound impact on evangelical organizations and their funding."[24] Gardner illustrates the rapidity with which evangelicals adapted to radio and television, echoing the shift in broadcasting that doomed the church film movement of the 1920s. Evangelicals used radio and television to get their message out, whether through simple church service broadcasts or elaborate televangelist productions that offered salvation but also proved to be big business.

Despite this ease that evangelicals have exhibited towards technology, they have a more ambiguous relationship with the broader secular culture of which it is a part. Lindvall's discussion of the schizophrenic relationship that Christianity had with art and culture is no more apparent than in evangelical Christians' relationship with popular culture.[25] For decades, they have struggled to be in but not of pop culture even as the latter becomes more and more encompassing. The church film movement is just the latest chapter in this broader ongoing history. As such, consideration of the evangelical Christian pop culture world into which these films are released and the ways in which other artists navigate this space will provide further insight into the production, marketing, and reception of these films.

Religious expression never exists in a vacuum. Religion and culture scholar Lynn Schofield Clark notes, "Religion has always taken place within cultural contexts largely shaped by both the culture's storytellers and the expectations of the marketplace of the day." She argues that the "logic of the marketplace" transforms religious meaning and experience and that these transformations often carry with them deep cultural and political conflicts.[26] For two contemporary commentators on religion, Heather Hendershot and Daniel Radosh, this cultural context is primarily the world of popular culture (film, television, publishing, merchandise, music, etc.). They both research the ways in which evangelical Christians navigate this world and the ways in which many evangelicals have created their own pop culture (what Radosh calls a "parallel universe") in response. They take similar approaches to evangelical Christian pop culture as well, considering a variety of avenues in this multibillion dollar industry from book publishing to filmmaking to the Contemporary Christian Music industry. Radosh even uncovers evangelical Christian versions of sex advice, wrestling, superheroes, and theme parks, to name a few.

In *Shaking the World for Jesus*, Hendershot notes just how difficult it is for evangelicals to be in the world but not of it. While they may have created their own pop culture artifacts (books, films, clothing, etc.), evangelicals have borrowed from secular pop culture trends to do so. Thus, the relationship becomes far more complex than many evangelicals would like to consider, affecting both the culture from which these evangelicals borrow and the evangelicals themselves. Across publishing, music, film, and the rest of the evangelical pop culture spectrum, Hendershot argues that one key question faces the producers of these artifacts: how explicitly will they prese nt their gospel message? Those artists who want to have greater crossover appeal into the mainstream will choose to, or be forced to, tone down or mask this message. For those artists or producers content to thrive in the Christian industry, they can be as explicit as they want to be. From her analysis of these various media, Hendershot concludes, "I would argue, however, that over the course of the past thirty years, Christian media have become not more secular but more ambiguous."[27] This is ironic because, Hendershot points out, "a culture that shuns 'moral relativism' and favors literal Biblical interpretation is increasingly producing cultural artifacts with messages that are hard to pin down."[28]

Though this may be the case, Hendershot argues that even these theologically diluted products serve an important function for evangelicals. She writes:

> Beyond providing clean-cut entertainment, such media can also help people deal with emotional crises, teach them political lessons, instruct them in chastity and other Christian modes of behavior, or provide inspirational models for praise and worship. In short, such media both reflect and construct evangelical understandings of the sacred and the profane, of the saved individual and his or her place in the wider world."[29]

In other words, they attempt to minister to their Christian audiences. Unfortunately, it seems as if evangelicals cannot agree on the best way to do this. Although Radosh seems to be working with a looser definition of crossover success, he does help clarify the different approaches that evangelicals take to navigating pop culture.[30]

Radosh draws heavily from Jay R. Howard and John M. Streck's *Apostles of Rock: The Splintered World of Contemporary Christian Music* to understand the broader realm of evangelical popular culture. These different approaches will help us critique and understand the criticisms of the church film movement later in Chapter 9. Howard and Streck outline three approaches, separational, integrational, and transformational.[31] Artists "choose" their approach based largely on different opinions of the proper relationship between Christianity and the broader culture. Separational contemporary Christian media "takes the viewpoint that the surrounding culture is evil. So therefore, what Christians are called on to do is to come out and be separate, and then to convert other people so they can come out and be separate.'"[32] This media has an overt evangelical agenda to convert non-believers. Ironically, however, it often mirrors the styles most popular in the surrounding mainstream culture to do so. For these artists, music, filmmaking, art, or performance are all just tools to help convert non-believers.

Integrational Christian media do not see the surrounding culture as completely evil and even believe that they can, at their highest potential, embody Christian ideals. These media are not necessarily about conversion, but about providing a wholesome alternative to potentially offensive secular pop culture creations. Integrational media are negatively Christian ... that is to say, they are Christian by virtue of what is *not* there (nudity, sex, drugs, violence, foul language, etc.). Because these media are less propositional, separational artists view their integrational counterparts as sell-outs who prioritize profit over message. Radosh counters, "[What] separational fans call selling out is really *engagement*, which is what evangelicals are called to do; that in fact one should make sacrifices to be part of the larger culture, because if Christianity is strident but separate, it is essentially sterile."[33]

The third type of media, transformational, are much more sophisticated and, therefore, rare. These artists see a much more intimate relationship between art and the divine. Here art does not so much serve God but manifests something of the divine through its aesthetic qualities. Far from propositional, these media are all about exploring questions and searching for answers rather than leaning on pre-packaged statements. Brokenness, failure, alienation, trauma of the human experience are much more prevalent themes here. Radosh adds, "[When] transformational Christian artists sing songs that are not explicitly religious, it is not because they are trying to fit in with the world — as integrational artists are — but because all songs are religious to them."[34]

No matter the approach that evangelicals take to the creation of media, they all contribute to the growth of the industry. In fact, evangelical Christian pop culture has grown to such a degree that it has mirrored the practices of its secular counterparts. There are awards ceremonies, stars, and, perhaps most importantly, brands. Though they are not writing specifically about pop culture, the research of Lynn Schofield Clark and Mara Einstein has important implications for it. They survey the broader religion and culture landscape and arrive at a similar conclusion: religion has become a brand among brands.

In "Identity, Belonging, and Religious Lifestyle Branding (Fashion Bibles, Bhangra Parties, and Muslim Pop)," Schofield Clark defines the process of imbuing the things we pay for — goods, activities, and artifacts — with meaning in a religious culture as "religious lifestyle branding."[35] While Schofield Clark emphasizes the personal nature of religious lifestyle branding, for example the way in which an individual might embrace a piece of media and make religious meaning out of it, Einstein sees another side to the coin. She observes how organizations and business have recognized the tendency for individual believers to do this and have embraced the process for its potential market value. The results are faith brands, "religious organizations that have taken on names, logos or personalities, and slogans that allow them to be heard in a cluttered, increasingly competitive marketplace."[36] She explains:

> Branding also occurs through the creation of stories or myths surrounding a product or service.... Another aspect of branding is that over time consumers don't have to intentionally think about a product's attributes. The name on the logo appears and everything that is associated with that brand comes to mind.... Brands also assist in creating personal identities.... Branding faith becomes shorthand for reaching the new religious consumer.[37]

Einstein sees a bottom-line mentality to faith branding: growth.[38] Unfortunately, it often comes at a steep theological, religious, or spiritual price.

Throughout her book, Einstein consistently points to the danger that faith brands offer a corrupted religious message at worst or a watered-down version of the faith at best. This mirrors Hendershot's discussion of the ways in which Christian artists must negotiate the severity of their gospel message. Clark is much more ambiguous about the effects of branding, recognizing that the process can go in one of two directions: "[In] some cases the commercial realm may facilitate rather than undermine, authentic practices of faith. But such items also may be marshaled for political ends in ways that the original producers never intended, thus making them less a distraction from faith than an accomplice in a larger political project."[39]

Of course, there are numerous other features of pop culture, be it evangelical Christian or secular, that could help provide insight into the work of Sherwood Pictures and their filmmaking peers. However, the brief discussion here of the evangelical use of technology, different approaches to the creation of media, and resulting faith brands will help us see the effectiveness of Sherwood Pictures' ministry. Combined with the discussion of the secular filmmaking industry at the beginning of this chapter, we see that Sherwood Pictures straddles two worlds in ways that few other Christian production companies have been able to do. One might even begin to question whether or not Sherwood Pictures has become a faith brand itself, because it too has seen a host of knock-offs and imitators in its wake. Their success has not gone unnoticed by other congregations. We now turn to other churches and production companies that have emerged to join Sherwood and thus create a new church film movement.

Chapter 8

A New Church Film Movement

There are several ways to determine the success or significance of Sherwood Pictures and their films. We have already explored some of these: box office returns, DVD sales, critical reaction, and audience feedback. However, to limit an analysis to these few areas is to miss another important influence that this studio has had in the world of independent filmmaking. Sherwood Baptist Church and Sherwood Pictures represent a highly replicable model for Christian filmmaking in the twenty-first century for other faith communities interested in film production. In fact, with the production of *Fireproof*, Sherwood Pictures released a CD-ROM of its movie production files that include advice on choosing the ingredients (script, cast, crew, etc.), a prayer strategy, call sheets, a detailed shooting schedule, legal documents, and even a babysitting schedule. Since *Fireproof*'s release, Alex has visited other congregations to give talks and workshops on film production. As a result, I want to briefly consider the churches and film production companies that have already followed in Sherwood's footsteps as another way of understanding the significance of their impact on independent and Christian filmmaking. Taken together, these congregations and their film production ministers make up a twenty-first century revitalization of the church film movement that finally brings to fruition many of the hopes and dreams that Protestant ministers had for film in the early 1900s. In the rest of this chapter, I will discuss some of these new church-based production companies, highlighting either key aspects of their production, marketing, reception, or content.

New Song Community Church, New Song Pictures, and *To Save a Life*

Hal and Lori Seed founded New Song Community Church in their home on January 9, 1992, as an "externally focused church, [one that] invites people far from God to find out how life-changing a relationship with Him can be."[1] They drew the name of their new church from Psalm 40:3, "He put a new song in my mouth, a hymn of praise to our God. Many will see and fear the Lord and put their trust in him." Throughout the mid to late '90s, New Song experienced rapid growth and worshipped in a variety of locations until they closed escrow on their own building on August 18, 2000. Currently, their facilities include an auditorium that only seats 500 people, which, due to their size, necessitates three identical weekend services. Like many growing megachurches, they are currently in the process of increasing their space.

Though New Song itself is a multi-racial church of over 1,000 members, it counts a much larger family: "We have seen over 5,000 come to Christ in the last 16 years, planted seven daughter churches, helped launch four parachurch organizations [and] are watching the birth of our fifth and sixth parachurch groups." Like Sherwood Baptist Church, New Song's main focus of ministry and evangelism is on "the next generation." To reach that goal, they hope to be a combination of "The Church Next Door" and "A Great Serving Core." For New Song, the former means being an effective welcoming and entertaining neighbor in the community while the latter focuses on "teams of people serving together in life-changing and people-changing ministries both inside and outside of the church." To be "The Church Next Door," New Song recognizes the importance of "awesome artists, whose ministry touches hearts [and] can sponsor God-moments and experiences during each service."[2]

Signaling its commitment to the arts and the next generation, New Song Community Church established New Song Pictures to make films "that tell relevant stories while being encouraging and uplifting."[3] Jim Britts, the Youth Pastor at New Song Community Church, wanted to write a film after he and his wife Rachel, a high school English teacher, continually encountered teens in great depression and pain. They both wanted to create a film that would address that pain and provide hope to suffering teenagers. The result was *To Save a Life* (2010), the first feature-length production of New Song Pictures. Jim Britts claims that the film "offers an uplifting message and alternative to the hopelessness teens may face as they struggle with challenges including violence, suicide, and unplanned pregnancy."[4] Steve Foster, an executive pastor at New Song Community Church, joined the project as a producer along with Nicole Franco, an independent filmmaker whose "goal is to be involved in filmmaking and entertainment that makes the world a better place."[5] The team hired Brian Baugh to direct; although *To Save a Life* was Brian's directorial debut, he had worked as cinematographer on other films like the aforementioned *The Ultimate Gift* (2006) and *An American Carol* (2008, Mpower Pictures). In an interview with Hollywood Jesus, Baugh claimed that Foster "had seen some movies that other churches had done and wanted to raise the bar—but more so, just to do something for youth that youth would like." Ultimately, Baugh admits that Steve told him that he wanted to "make a movie that doesn't suck."[6] Given the popularity of Sherwood Pictures at this time, it is difficult to ignore the possibility that Stephen was referring to films like *Facing the Giants* and *Fireproof*.

New Song Pictures, like Sherwood Pictures, benefits greatly from being a ministry of a megachurch. It too can draw from a wealth of members who donate time, money, and/or other resources. Though the production team depended on these volunteers for most of the less glamorous tasks of filmmaking, New Song Pictures employed experienced Hollywood actors for the film's major roles. On screen, volunteers or ministers at New Song Community Church are limited to brief supporting roles or extras. The professionalism of *To Save a Life*'s actors lends the film a quality not often found in many of its Christian film counterparts. Furthermore, its visual qualities are significantly better than nearly every other faith-based production discussed here and are even on par with many mainstream Hollywood films. Furthermore, it benefits from a less theologically rigid script than most other Christian films, a feature that characterizes slight differences between New Song and the other faith communities participating in the church film movement.

To Save a Life *Website*

Like Sherwood Pictures' films, *To Save a Life* boasts a content-rich website. Visitors can connect to the website and each other via Facebook, MySpace, and Twitter. Plenty of

Anything you can do, I can do better. New Song Community Church formed New Song Pictures to release *To Save a Life* in 2009 in an attempt to produce better church-based productions. The poster's darker aesthetic hints at the more mature themes and events on which the film focuses.

them have done so as over 273,000 have become members of the film's Facebook fan page. The website also advertises National *To Save a Life* Week (September 6–12, 2010), the campaign that the producers created to align with the DVD release. In over 10,000 locations, communities gathered together to watch the film and to "help those viewers put its life-changing principles to work in the world around them."[7] As with Sherwood Pictures' films, communities can screen *To Save a Life* by applying for movie license packages that range from $129 (audiences of less than 100 people) to $229 (audiences of 100 to 1,000 people) to $339 (audiences of more than 1,000 people). The package includes two versions of the film (the full-length version and a church-friendly version), a screening license, a movie event planning guide, tickets, mailers, posters, bracelets, buttons, digital resources, and other promotional products. The site includes free downloadable materials to help publicize the event; most are digital, e-mail, or social network–based. Visitors to the site can also purchase ancillary products including clothing, the soundtrack to the film, audio and print devotionals, and church-based curriculum for youth and family discussion series.

To Save a Life's website includes an area where viewers can share their own stories of how the film impacted their life and how they endured hardships or experiences similar to those it depicted. As of January 2011, over 1,900 visitors had posted their own stories to the site.[8] Nearly all of these stories are from teenagers who feel or have felt alienated at home or at school and then found insight or encouragement from the film. To further assist visitors in need, the website provides a wealth of information on other organizations that provide services for some of the crises featured in the film including suicide prevention, self-injury (cutting), substance abuse, and depression.

To Save a Life, *the Film*

This high school drama tells the story of Jake Taylor (Randy Wayne), a golden boy, all-star basketball player with a bright future ahead of him (he has a basketball scholarship to the University of Louisville). The film opens at a funeral for Roger Dawson (Robert Bailey, Jr.), Jake's childhood friend. As Jake's popularity grew throughout junior high and high school, thanks to his basketball skills and good looks, his new high school friends drew him away from Roger, whose physical handicap makes him something of an outcast (when they were kids, Roger was hit by a car after pushing Jake out of the way and has walked with a limp ever since). Early in the film, Roger commits suicide in one of the school hallways directly in front of Jake and many other students. This tragedy sends Jake on a search for answers as to why this happened and simultaneously causes him to reevaluate his life. Jake begins to grow apart from his high school friends who obsess over drinking, partying, and hooking up. A youth minister at a local church, Chris Vaughn (Joshua Weigel), reaches out to Jake and invites him to the youth group. Jake gradually becomes more interested in what this community of faith has to offer, but he soon realizes that the experiences at school that led to Roger's suicide also exist in the church.

Jake remains committed to the community of faith and begins to grow closer to some of its members and, in the process, God. His life does not miraculously improve: he still faces challenges and consequences based on poor decisions that he made earlier, especially with his girlfriend Amy (Deja Kreutzberg), who is now pregnant after they slept together at one of the last parties Jake attended. On top of that, his parents are constantly fighting and eventually separate because his mom discovers that his father is cheating on her. These

Jake Taylor (Randy Wayne), Amy Briggs (Deja Kreutzberg), and Andrea Stevens (Kim Hidalgo) must navigate a tragedy at school and their spiritual journeys in *To Save a Life* (New Song Pictures, 2009).

pressures strain his newfound faith and friendships, particularly with Johnny Garcia (Sean Michael Afable), a quiet, troubled teen. Jake quickly develops a close friendship with Johnny; however, when his own troubles distract him from that friendship, Johnny begins to revert to old, dangerous habits. Along the way, youth pastor Chris is a constant presence beside Jake, faithfully listening to him, providing him with encouragement and good advice, and standing by him no matter what.

Reception of To Save a Life

To Save a Life premiered on January 24, 2010, and screened in 441 theaters nationwide. With a production budget of $500,000, the film grossed $3,773,863 at the box office.[9] The DVD was released on August 3, 2010, but I have yet to find sales figures for it. Samuel Goldwyn Films, one of the companies that also handled Sherwood Pictures' films, was in charge of theatrical distribution for *To Save a Life*. For the most part, secular critics gave the film negative reviews that bemoaned its bland acting, boring, predictable, and lengthy plot, and hokey faith-based message. On the other hand, Christian critics and viewers loved the film, which makes its comparatively poor box office performance all the more ironic.

Though it is slightly more even-handed than most, Ian Buckwalter's review for NPR ultimately took a negative approach. He writes, "[It] is miles ahead in terms of production values and a conscious avoidance of overt proselytizing. It will likely be an enormous success with the evangelical communities at which it's targeted. That doesn't save it from being an utter failure outside that narrow context."[10] He concludes, "To its credit, *To Save a Life* can be as critical of hypocrisy within the church as it is of the emptiness of a life outside of it

[...]. But the film only pays lip service to the severity of the problems teens can face, offering up little in the way of tangible solutions."[11] Writing for *The New York Times*, Andy Webster claims that the film "would be a mere nuisance if not for its shameless exploitation of school shootings to advance its agenda."[12] Webster concludes, "But forget the lame performances and arch, preachy sentiment; the movie's sham hip-hop and spurious alternative music alone should keep teenagers away. Thank goodness."[13]

Though he cites its strong production quality and the ways it effectively captures youth culture, *Christianity Today* reviewer Todd Hertz had problems with some of the film's messages and the ways in which they were presented: "[While] it talks a lot about living differently, living for God and being transformed, it never says *why* or *how*. I wish there had been more focus on showing *what* changed Jake.... The youth group becomes a place of acceptance and caring for misfits and sinners, but it seems that their reason is to make sure others don't feel lonely — not because of the gospel of Jesus Christ."[14] Writing for Beliefnet.com, Nell Minow takes a far more positive approach to the film. She also praises the production quality and argues that its realistic portrayal of youth culture is one that its targeted teenage audience will most likely appreciate. Moreover, as a religious critic, she appreciates the portrayal of the youth minister "who walks the walk, making his leadership about meaning and values and most of all kindness. He does not try to make God the explanation for everything, just the beginning of the answer."[15]

To Save a Life generated far less viewer feedback on the IMDb than its Sherwood counterparts; however, the comments that viewers posted about it were overwhelmingly more positive. Reduxinflux_1 from Orange County, California, a self-professed Christian viewer, praised its message but understood that non-religious viewers might not appreciate the film. He writes, "Primarily — it's a film exhorting Christians to BE followers of Jesus rather than passive egocentric judgmental consumers. Secondarily — it's a powerful listening ear to the hurt, depressed and marginalized among us who may feel invisible to the cold world around them. It also empathizes with those who wrestle with fundamental questions of purpose and meaning."[16] Another viewer, CeilingofStars from Athens, Georgia, claims that (s)he has experienced similar feelings of loss and alienation and that the film does not deal with them maturely enough. (S)he writes, "My hunch is that the screenwriter, who is a youth pastor, has had personal experiences with parent trouble, how troubled teens act, etc. What he does NOT understand is how it actually feels to be a troubled teen. [A]ll of their diatribes were along the lines of, 'Nobody understands me. I feel so alone.' It never went much deeper than that."[17] Numerous viewers posted comments on the IMDb and Amazon.com that argued that the film perfectly captured high school life and accompanying feelings of loneliness and alienation.

As I hinted in my discussion of Sherwood Pictures' films, the cast and crew who participate in the church film movement are well aware of their detractors and often politely address common criticisms of their films. However, none of them have responded to their critics as vehemently as actor Steven Crowder, who played Doug, Jake's hard-partying, womanizing best friend in *To Save a Life*. In reaction to the film's negative publicity, he wrote an opinion piece for FoxNews.com entitled "Why Does Hollywood Hate *To Save a Life*?" in which he expresses frustrations with Hollywood that many of his Christian filmmaking peers share. In it, he rails against the "media elites" who bashed his film and, after quoting a couple of negative reviews, speculates as to why these critics took such an approach: "So, why the hatred? There's really only one answer. The movie's message of salvation is decidedly Christian.... Preaching Christian salvation is to preach moral absolutes. Hollywood no likey. It seems that the snobs at *The New York Times* would rather see more teens go ahead and off themselves than find salvation through the Christian faith."[18]

It is tempting to simply dismiss Crowder's article as nothing more than an attempt to voice his disappointment in critics' negative reaction to his film, and ordinarily I would, but his arguments mirror much of the evangelical Christian responses to criticisms of *To Save a Life* and other films like it. First, to call the film "decidedly Christian" is too simplistic as the debates about the film's message *within Christian* communities evidences. Second, the film contains none of the "moral absolutes" that Crowder asserts are essential to preaching Christian salvation. Youth Pastor Chris' exchanges with Jake contain none of the strict guidelines in which Sherwood Pictures' films traffic. In fact, it seems that this is exactly the type of rigid Christianity that the folks at New Song Community Church and New Song Pictures want to avoid.

Furthermore, Crowder and his evangelical Christian peers often fail to identify just whom they are critiquing and, by extension, who is critiquing them and how they do it. He asks why Hollywood hates *To Save a Life*, but the two reviews he engages are from NPR and *The New York Times*, hardly model representatives of Hollywood. What Crowder fails to see is that *he*, and the production in which he stars, *is* Hollywood. Samuel Goldwyn handled theatrical distribution of his film while Sony handled its DVD and Blu-Ray distribution. With articles on new faith-based production companies and films appearing in the trade press on an almost monthly basis, it is clear that Hollywood does not hate, but rather loves (or at least loves to exploit) Christian productions. Finally, Crowder reads too much into these critiques. None of them evidence a hatred of Christianity. Precious few, if any, negative reviews of his film, or films like it, ever embody a *hatred* of Christianity itself. What critics often attack are the ways in which these filmmakers seem to use Christianity for personal or professional gain.

The Theology of To Save a Life

The high production quality of *To Save a Life* initially struck me as one of its key strengths. However, far more interesting for the purposes of this discussion is the theology behind *To Save a Life* and the ways in which both it, and some of the film's content, differs from other films in the church film movement. *To Save a Life* includes scenes of teenagers cursing, drinking, and doing drugs. While the filmmakers do glamorize this behavior, they do not advocate it. More importantly, however, at least they do not pretend it does not exist, unlike most other Christian filmmakers. Though the film refrains from showing sex, it strongly hints at teens engaging in pre-marital sex, which, not surprisingly in this genre, results in teen pregnancy. Rather than dwelling on the abortion-birth dichotomy as an answer to this dilemma, the film sets up adoption as a positive alternative that blesses both the birth and adopting parents. Yet even more interesting than these features is the film's theology and the ways in which it differs from other films in the church film movement.

While *To Save a Life* does embody a conservative theological and cultural worldview, it tones down any explicit evangelical Christian salvation message, much to the chagrin of some Christian critics and viewers. That Jake's transformation seems to be more culturally than theologically based will perhaps appeal to the more "I'm spiritual but not religious" set. When they first meet, youth pastor Chris gives Jake his business card and tells him to come "check us out." Jake tells Chris that he's not a religious person, to which Chris responds, "That's okay, I'm not either." Such an exchange would simply never find its way into any of the Christian films that I have discussed or will discuss in this book. As Jake further wrestles with whether or not to more fully commit to "accepting God," he tells Chris, "I don't want to be just another Christian," and Chris responds, "I don't want you to." Of course, the implication here is that Jake and Chris long for a deeper faith that transcends labels, but some viewers could miss this and find the exchange confusing.

Unlike other Christian films, *To Save a Life* is highly critical of the hypocrisy of the church. Jake challenges the teenagers in the youth group who apparently only attend for show. He is the impetus for a communal lunchtime gathering of diverse students at school every day. When the church's senior pastor learns of Jake and Amy's pregnancy and implies that they do not belong there, Chris comes to their defense and argues that the church could learn a lot about following Jesus from Jake and Amy. Even the senior pastor has difficulty getting through to his own teenage son, who does not believe in the message that Chris preaches and prefers to smoke weed with his friends from school.

Ironically, *To Save a Life* presents a rather progressive vision for how newcomers can become part of communities of faith. A more conservative or traditional way of thinking about church membership might be a believing, behaving, and belonging paradigm whereby new members only fully belong to a community of faith after their beliefs and behavior align with those of that community. This is, perhaps, the paradigm that most religious outsiders envision, one that most likely turns them off to the idea of joining a particular congregation. On the other hand, another paradigm exists for thinking about belonging to a community of faith. We might think of it as the belonging, behaving, and believing paradigm. Here, the community of faith invites the newcomer to belong to the community and participate in it regardless of their beliefs or behavior (within reason, of course). As the newcomer experiences loving and welcoming community, it will (one hopes) mold and shape her behaviors which in turn will lead her to share in the beliefs of that community. *To Save a Life* seems to advocate the latter paradigm as Chris invites Jake to join in his community of faith, even as Jake wrestles with a host of questions, gets drunk, and gets his girlfriend pregnant. As Chris and other teens reach out to Jake, their hospitality gradually affects his behavior, particularly how he treats outsiders at school, which ultimately shapes his ideas about the meaning and purpose of life in general and his experiences in particular. This welcoming paradigm finds biblical precedent as Jesus simply asks his disciples to follow him before he ever asks them to believe in anything or behave in a particular way.[19]

One of the final scenes of the film features Chris preaching at church. The audio from this scene carries over to a shot of Amy who has just given birth and is surrounded by Jake, his mom, and the adopting parents. Again, it would be hard to envision this shot, or Chris' sermon in many contemporary Christian films. Chris preaches:

> Life is a journey, not so much to a destination but a transformation. Looking back, doesn't it sometimes feel that our richest times come right in the midst of our hardest? But God made us to live in community, to laugh and cry, to hurt and celebrate with each other no matter what we're going through. And transformation is tough, and we don't always end up where we think we will, but we have to remember that even when we struggle to believe in Him, He always believes in us. He fills our lives with purpose and passion if we just let Him. And, you know, the best part of the journey is that the God of the universe sometimes allows us to play a part in changing the world. Isn't that a trip?

Although many viewers might hear this as preachy (Chris is preaching, after all!), it is far less dogmatic than most similar occurrences in Sherwood Pictures' films, particularly the televised sermon that prompts Jay Austin's transformation in *Flywheel* or the exchange between Caleb and his father in *Fireproof*.

Possibility Pictures and *Letters to God*

While not explicitly church-based, Possibility Pictures is an important part of the current state of contemporary Christian cinema. In a way, however, it does have ties to the church film movement as its founder, David Nixon, was one of the producers on *Facing the Giants* and *Fireproof*. Nixon has had an extensive career in producing and directing documentary films throughout Russia, India, and Europe. He has also produced and directed national commercials for major fast food restaurant chains and businesses. However, during those experiences, he felt a call to use his talents in other ways. Nixon says:

> Twenty-seven years ago, I had a dream. I dreamed to use motion pictures to spread the Gospel, but unfortunately, twenty-seven years ago, Hollywood didn't want to have anything to do with faith-based films. Until about six years ago when something extraordinary happened. A religious film made $600 million. That was *The Passion*, and it opened the door for theatrical distribution of faith-based films."[20]

With the timing suddenly right for the production of faith-based films, Nixon partnered with Sherwood Pictures, and with this new relationship, his dream and calling became a reality. It is clear, however, that the time Nixon spent toiling away at documentary films and commercials provided him with the skills necessary to produce feature-length narrative films. His presence and experience no doubt contributes to the improved quality of Sherwood Pictures' films.

Nixon has big plans for the future and wants to make Orlando, Florida, a hub of independent Christian filmmaking. With resources like Universal Studios and a wealth of large denominational and non-denominational megachurches nearby, his dreams could come true. His new production company, Possibility Pictures, represents a first step towards making that dream a reality. Recognizing the power of films to "touch hearts, change perceptions, and renew lives," Possibility Pictures was "formed from God's will to reach out and spread His word through film [by presenting] stories that uplift the spirit and spread the word of hope and love."[21] The Possibility Pictures team also includes producer Kim Dawson, executive producer Tom Swanson, and writer Sandra Thrift, all of whom have extensive experience in the filmmaking industry or in marketing. Both Dawson and Swanson claim that God had placed in their hearts a desire to produce Christian movies and that Nixon's creation of Possibility Pictures and invitation to join him were answers to their prayers. Swanson says, "Our big audacious goal is to be the category leader in faith-based films, media, television, publishing, and social networking to grow the Kingdom."[22]

Letters to God, the Film

On April 9, 2010, Possibility Pictures released *Letters to God*, its first feature-length film. *Letters to God* is based on the true story of Tyler Doherty (played by Tanner Maguire), a young child who died of brain cancer. In the film, we meet Tyler after he returns home from surgery and his first round of treatment. We see him writing and mailing one of his many letters to God, which we soon learn are his prayers for his family, friends, and himself. He addresses them TO: GOD, FROM: TYLER and faithfully places them in the mail every day. The new mailman on Tyler's route, Brady McDaniels (Jeffrey S. S. Johnson), like his predecessor, does not know what to do with the letters. Jeffrey's life is in shambles, particularly from a D.U.I. conviction that has separated him from his wife and their young son. He lives in a disheveled one-room apartment in town and gets drunk every night. Late one

Letters to God (Possibility Pictures, 2010) had many viewers, Christian or not, asking God for better Christian movies. This child-like poster reflects the film's child-like theology that had most viewers cringing throughout.

night, drunk, Brady drops into a local church where he plans to leave Tyler's letters, but before he can leave, the minister confronts him and suggests that he keep the letters because God might have something in store for him through them.

As the film progresses, Tyler deals with the complications of his disease, both the physical (his treatments make him sick) and the emotional (kids pick on him at school and he sees the strain his disease places on his mother Maddy [Robyn Lively] and brother Ben [Michael Christopher Bolten]). Through it all, his grandmother Olivia (Maree Cheatham) remains a faithful presence in their lives, reassuring them that God cares and has a plan for them through all of this. However, given their own struggles with Tyler's illness, Maddy and Ben find it difficult to simply accept Olivia's perspective.

Along the way, Tyler also draws comfort from his best friend Sam (Bailee Madison) and her grandfather, Mr. Perryfield (Ralph Waite). Mr. Perryfield assures Tyler that God has chosen him to be His special warrior, and that through his battle with his disease, Tyler will prove that God is truth and thus lead others to Him. This is indeed what happens as his perseverance and boundless joy inspire Brady to get his own life in order. He stops drinking and becomes a close friend and supporter of Tyler and his family. As Tyler's condition worsens, Brady finally reads the letters and is inspired to give them to the people about whom and for whom Tyler prayed as a way of inspiring and encouraging them. Though Tyler passes away, he leaves a legacy behind as he inspires countless people of all ages to write their own letters to God.

Brady McDaniels (Jeffrey Johnson, left) stars as a disgruntled postal worker who is transformed by his relationship with Tyler Doherty (Tanner Maguire), a cancer patient with a heart and faith of gold, in *Letters to God* (Possibility Pictures, 2010).

Marketing Letters to God

The producers of *Letters to God* have a marketable product on their hands from two perspectives, faith and cancer. As a faith-based film full of specific references to God and Jesus and constant scenes of prayer, it clearly appeals to the evangelical Christian market. On another level, it appeals to people suffering from cancer and to their family members and friends as well. In fact, the producers have created movements around the film to offer hope and encouragement for these viewers and their family and friends. The film's website contains a link to "The Movement of Hope," an effort on the part of Possibility Pictures to extend the impact of the film beyond the initial viewing experience to "ignite the hope for a deeper, more meaningful life" and to seek and develop "partnerships and resources that will help and encourage people in challenging and difficult circumstances."[23] Through the site, they promote "Communities of Hope," which encourage individuals and congregations to practice care, compassion, and acceptance for people and communities in need. Churches can purchase a Contagious Hope Movie Resource Kit (prices differ according to potential audience size: 0–100 equals $179, 101–1000 for $279, and more than 1,000 equals $379) that includes a copy of the film, an annual screening license, a movie planning guide, a six-part sermon series, a Power Point presentation with movie clips, a six-part small group series integrated with the sermons, music videos, posters, tickets, and postcards.

Reception of Letters to God

It will be important for such kits and DVDs to sell well because with a $3 million production budget, *Letters to God* only made $2.8 million at the box office. Thus far, the film has made just over $6 million from DVD sales.[24] Most critics, even religious ones, gave the film overwhelmingly negative reviews. For *Christianity Today*, Carolyn Arends wrote, "A more unique difficulty with *Letters* is its expressly protestant, Christian, evangelical perspective [...] because the language *will* be foreign to non-churched viewers and mostly because films thrive on action and it is very hard to depict quiet, introspective prayer with dramatic impact." Arends' desire for the creators of *Letters to God* has broader implications for all would-be or current Christian filmmakers: "I'd also ask them, next time, to explain a little less and trust their story (and their audience, and the Spirit of God for that matter) a little more."[25] Roger Moore, writing for *The Orlando Sentinel*, was not particularly kind to the local production. He argues that only lip service is paid to cynicism and skepticism and that the blast of doubt and anger that Maddy exhibits at one point in the film is "out of place in this altar-call of a drama."[26] He adds, "[Whatever] flashes of conflict turn up in the four-writers-script are quickly rubbed off in some misguided attempt to render everything and everyone 'nice.'"[27]

Few viewers offered feedback on the film at either Amazon.com or the IMDb. This could be due to the film's limited theatrical release and its recent DVD release at the time of this writing. The positive reviews all praised it as a faith-affirming, uplifting film. One reviewer, Robert S. Arnold from Spring, Texas, wrote, "This is probably the best movie I've seen in a long, long time! I was thrilled to see a movie that totally smashed the modern non-religious mentality. Thank God that this story has been told! I hope and pray to see more like it."[28] Another viewer, Mary Brown from Georgia, wrote, "After watching this film I am even more moved than ever to spread my faith to others. I think this film completely achieves what it was made for. A must see."[29] Still another viewer admitted that the film had an even more profound affect on her: twilightmomforever (location not specified) wrote, "It made me want to have faith in God again. Which I have been struggling with."[30] Finally, one viewer, Jeffery Shoell (location not specified), wrote his review as a letter to God, praying:

> Dear God, would you please inspire film-makers to make more movies like *Letters to God* that I just watched. The world you created for us has become a very cold place with hate, greed and violence everywhere. Hollywood adds to this by continuing to make movies and Reality Shows that depict the worst in our society. This movie gave me a renewed hope that there are still good people and values on our Planet Earth and hopefully with your help, Writers, Directors and Producers will create more films like this one.... Thank you God for the people that made this movie.[31]

The negative reviews on both Amazon.com and the IMDb either bemoaned the inability of Christian filmmakers to produce anything of aesthetic value or simply attacked their beliefs.

The Theology of Letters to God

The theological foundation of *Letters to God* is perhaps the most explicit of all the films I will discuss here. Olivia and Mr. Perryfield's advice for and encouragement of Tyler basically sum up the film's theology. They both see Tyler's illness as, at best, an opportunity or, at worst, a test from God for Tyler to show others that God can work in and through him. This theology will no doubt resonate with a significant portion of an evangelical audience who views God as being in control of everything that happens in their lives. On the other hand, some Christian viewers (even evangelicals) will find this theology deeply troubling and question why God had to make a young child like Tyler suffer so painfully to make "Himself" known to others.

This theological certainty hamstrings the rest of the film. To be sure, people encounter trials and tribulations on a daily basis in life and, no doubt, often do so with a smile or at least a stiff upper lip. At the same time, these experiences often cause individuals to have moments of deep doubt and despair as well. While it attempts to include those moments, *Letters to God* ultimately only pays lip service to them, as Moore pointed out in his review. When Ben becomes jealous of all the attention that Tyler receives and begins to express his feelings of anger and loneliness, Olivia essentially sweeps them under the rug by literally forcing him to pray with her. That he retains these feelings later in the film might signal the ineffectiveness of such an approach. Later in the film, as Tyler's condition worsens, Maddie is inconsolable. As her mother tries to be encouraging by quoting scripture to her, Maddie screams at her to stop quoting the Bible because it is not healing her son. This would be one of the more effective scenes in the film were it not sandwiched in between scenes of irrepressible happiness and joy that overshadow it. That the film cannot linger over Maddie's emotions perhaps suggests an unwillingness to stray from the faithful assurance that God controls everything.

Jenkins Entertainment, *What If...*, and Harvest Bible Chapel

Most people are less familiar with Dallas Jenkins than they are with his father, Jerry Jenkins, the co-creator of the wildly popular *Left Behind* series of apocalyptic novels. Along with his father, Dallas represents one-half of Jenkins Entertainment, a production company that specializes in faith-based, family friendly films. In 2002 they released their first feature-length film, *Hometown Legend*, at a cost of $2 million. They followed this with the films *Though None Go with Me* (2005) and *Midnight Clear* (2006), and while I have been unable to find detailed records of their box office receipts and DVD sales, *Hometown Legend*'s box office return of just under $112,000 does not bode well for the rest of their productions. However, their presence on DVD, combined with television broadcasts, no doubt makes up some of the financial difference.

In 2010, Jenkins Entertainment produced its fourth feature-length film, *What If...*, in partnership with 10 West Studios, "an award-winning independent motion picture production company and production facility dedicated to crafting cinematic narratives that challenge and inspire."[32] This most recent production, which enjoyed a wider theatrical release than its predecessors, attracted the attention of Harvest Bible Chapel, a megachurch with 13,000 members spread out over five "campuses" in and around Chicago. Like other churches, Harvest clings to a conservative Christian doctrine that mirrors that of Sherwood Baptist Church and other evangelical communities. Unlike Sherwood Pictures, who grew their film production ministry from within by nurturing the Kendrick brothers' vision, Harvest Bible Chapel signaled another level of commitment to church-based filmmaking when they hired Jenkins to be their Director of Visual Media. Starting in 2011, he began producing and directing feature-length films for Harvest Bible Chapel for theatrical release.

The crew of *What If...* (Jenkins Entertainment, 2010) looks on as Dallas Jenkins (center) gives direction. As far as I know, Jenkins is the first minister to be hired by a church solely for the purpose of writing and directing faith-based films. His hiring finally brings the early 20th century Protestant hopes of ordaining moviemaking ministers to fruition.

There can be no doubt that his hiring is a direct reaction to the popularity and success of Sherwood Pictures. In a recent *New York Times* article, Dallas refers to *Facing the Giants* and *Fireproof* and Harvest's reaction to them. He commented, "They weren't any good ... but *Fireproof* made $33 million; it was the biggest independent film of 2008. So the pastor [of Harvest] said, "We can do that, but let's do it well, use a real director, real actors.'"[33]

Marketing and Distributing What If...

The marketing and exhibition of *What If...* provide interesting insight into the current and future states of the church film movement and will no doubt provide an interesting lesson for future filmmakers. The producers only planned a two-city theatrical release for the film; however, it quickly expanded to 100 screens in 20 or 30 locations with more to follow. Their theatrical release strategy is instructive for would-be faith-based filmmakers and reveals the state of the industry that Reiss highlights in *Think Outside the Box Office*, particularly the benefits of releasing a film in a larger number of smaller markets as opposed to a small number of larger markets. Jenkins surveyed the theatrical landscape and argued, "We don't go into a market unless we already know in advance that it has a decent chance of opening [and] that there are local churches, local radio stations, local sponsors on board who will buy 400 tickets and then sell them, or give them to a local youth group or whatever. So we have some idea of how it's going to do."[34] This is obviously beneficial for everyone involved because it gives theater owners something of a guaranteed, if much smaller, audience that only big-time blockbusters can provide while ensuring a low-budget film a theatrical release that it might not otherwise have enjoyed. Like Mel Gibson and the Kendrick brothers, Jenkins took a grassroots approach to marketing and targeted ministers with advanced screenings to spread word-of-mouth among their congregations.

This targeted marketing also acknowledges the religious landscape in the United States or, at least, a particular perspective on it. Ted Mundroff, chief executive of Landmark Theaters, adds, "The reason that there are more theaters playing a film in the heartland may be the result of more churches or organizations in that particular area and where the majority of the people living there will resonate with the film's particular message."[35] Unfortunately, this viewpoint and marketing strategy ignores the presence of churches and other religious organizations in larger cities and implies that they might not be worth the trouble. Nevertheless, Hollywood has begun to take a page from the Christian film marketing manual and embraced a similar grassroots marketing campaign. Bob Berney, president of Newmarket Films who also helped orchestrate the release of *The Passion*, argues that churches "want to be talked to."[36] Now, movie marketing organizations like Motive Entertainment and Grace Hill Media are on the rise, helping facilitate conversations between churches and Hollywood by promoting religious productions and highlighting secular films that, while not explicitly touting a Christian message, might appeal to congregations.

What If..., *the Film*

Ben Walker (Kevin Sorbo) is an aspiring minister with a girlfriend, Wendy (Kristy Swanson), whom he leaves behind in their small midwestern town in order to get in on the ground level of a new business in the big city. He justifies his decision to leave by telling Wendy that the more money they have, the more effective their future ministry will be. Wendy's worst fears come true as they grow apart as Ben pursues an investment banking

Ben Walker (Kevin Sorbo, left), a once-promising minister, is at the height of his business career as competitor Joel Muller (Stelio Savante) looks on during a meeting in *What If...* (Jenkins Entertainment, 2010).

career in which he strikes it very rich. Fifteen years later, he has just been made partner, has bought a $250,000 Mercedes Benz, and is about to fly off to a weekend in Paris with his new fiancée. Everything seems perfect for Ben until he takes his new car out for a quick joy ride and it breaks down. The mechanic who shows up to help is more than he seems. In fact, Mike (John Ratzenberger) the mechanic quickly tells Ben that he is an angel sent to help him figure out his life. But Ben does not necessarily think he has anything left to figure out. Mike, and by extension God, disagree.

For the rest of the film, Mike and God force Ben into an alternate reality in which he lives the life that he could have had with Wendy had he not gone down his successful business path. In that life, Ben and Wendy are a lower middle class family with two daughters, Kimberly (Debby Ryan) and Megan (Taylor Groothuis). In this alternate world, Ben graduated with a Ph.D. from Moody Bible Institute and took a job as the pastor of the small hometown church in which he grew up. Though Ben initially fights this alternate universe kicking and screaming, he gradually realizes that the "simple" life he could have had with Wendy was God's will for him all along and thus preferable to the life he lived before.

Reception of What If...

While I could not locate the production cost for *What If...*, given the similar production quality to the rest of Jenkins Entertainment's films, it probably cost between $2–$3 million. However, with its widest theatrical release in only 82 theaters, it has only made $756,545 from box office receipts. Given that limited theatrical release and a yet-to-be-

Back in the pulpit, Ben Walker (Kevin Sorbo) is a bit out of practice having worked in the business world for so long in *What If...* (Jenkins Entertainment, 2010).

released DVD, both critics' reviews and viewer feedback were in short supply at the time of this writing. The few reviews and little feedback offer perspectives similar to those of other films I have discussed. In her review for *Christianity Today*, Annie Young Frisbie notes the film's confusing theology, most notably its weird tension between divine providence and free will, its limited understanding of vocation, its twisted take on redemption, and its disdain for non–Christians.[37] Only a few readers responded to Frisbie's review, two of whom disagreed vehemently with it and praised the film for its uplifting Christian message, which, one of them claimed, was a nice alternative to all the "Hollywood trash." Writing for the *Memphis Commercial Appeal*, John Beifuss bemoaned the fact that the film seemed to prefer a life of career ministry over a business career.[38]

The Theology of What If...

What If... takes the alternate reality premise of *It's a Wonderful Life* (1946, Liberty Films) and twists it in some confounding ways. In director Frank Capra's classic, Clarence the angel employs it to show a depressed, suicidal character the value of his life as a businessman who thinks that he has failed the people of his small town. It shows the countless ways in which the lives we lead can bless others without us knowing it, even when we are not specifically "trying" to help others. *What If...* takes a businessman and forces him into a life that he didn't choose and makes him feel guilty about not choosing it. Though Mike tells Ben that he will always have the choice to go back to his former life, he can only do so after he fully commits to this alternate reality. He may face a choice at the end of the film, but it is perfectly clear that the die have been cast.

In the process, this forced alternate existence simultaneously devalues the successful life that he has lived thus far, privileging, as Beifuss argued, a career in ministry over a career in business. Mike stubbornly argues that Ben's banking career was never the life that God intended for him. Yet we are left to wonder why Ben is so extremely good at it. On top of that, compared to his co-workers, he is even magnanimous in his work, allowing heads of corporations that his company takes over to remain in power, an act of "charity" that angers his more cutthroat co-workers. Ben even remembers his secretary's birthday and brings her roses. Though Ben might like his toys and a pretty woman, there is no sense that he is evil. Moreover, if we are expected to identify with Ben, as the filmmakers no doubt intend, then the implication of the film is that God would have us all be career ministers instead of successful lawyers, doctors, or businesspeople. In response to my review of the film for my website, Pop Theology, Dallas Jenkins responded:

> For the record, there was no implication or intent to say that you have to be a minister to be truly happy, or that ministers are better than businessmen. The implication was that BEN was called to be a minister and father and husband of Wendy, and he was living outside his calling. Any larger or broad statements about ministers or businessmen in general were not being made by this film. The film was about finding your specific calling, period.[39]

Again, like many directors' comments about their films that I have discussed thus far, this statement will not reach many viewers; audiences are simply left with the film before them. Here, the filmmakers could have clarified this point by allowing us to see Ben serving as a minister before he left Wendy so that we could know he was betraying something

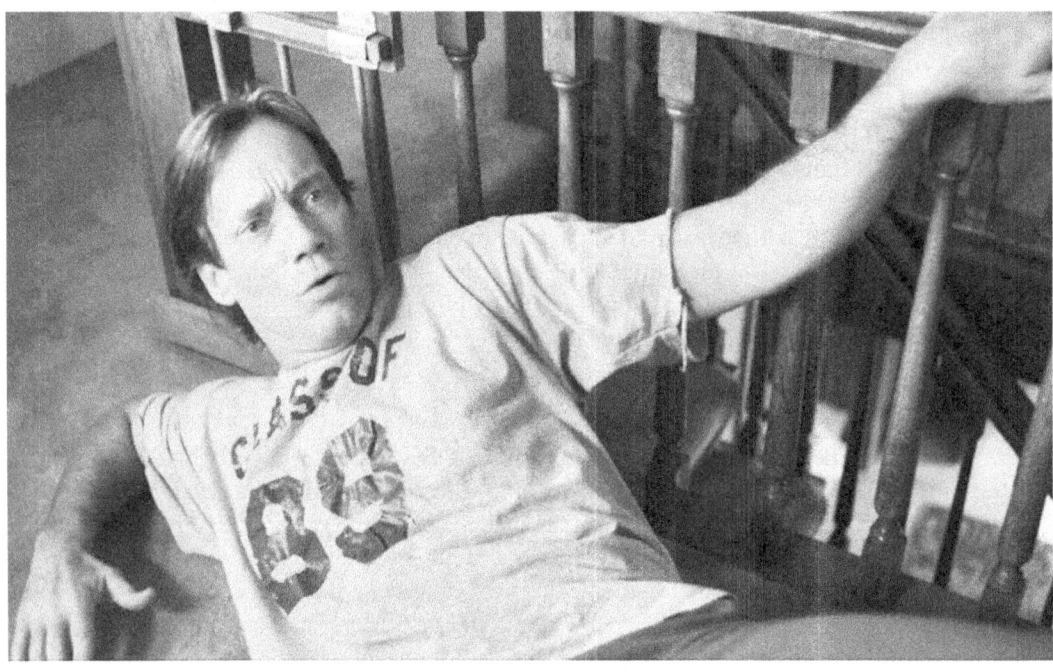

Ben Walker (Kevin Sorbo) is just as confused as the audience is upon being thrust by an angel into an alternate universe where he follows his potential as a minister in *What If...* (Jenkins Entertainment, 2010).

that he was gifted to do. On the other hand, another interesting move would have been to have Mike "force" Ben to put his business talents to use for the good of others. In fact, the film seems to betray itself when Ben invests his alternate family's meager checking account into stock from a company that he knows is about to be overtaken by his former employer. The money he makes from this wise investment (insider trading?) helps repair both the church and his house, thus revealing that secular talents can be put to sacred use.

Finally, *What If...* embodies the kind of cultural and theological homogeneity characteristic of much of contemporary Christian cinema that even many evangelicals are beginning to bemoan. I will turn to their criticisms in my conclusion, but suffice it to say that evangelical media scholars Quentin J. Schultz and Robert H. Woods would continue to be frustrated by the white, solidly middle-class context of yet another evangelical Christian film. *What If...* explicitly spells out its cultural homogeneity in the name of the church that Ben pastors, the Little White Church.

Calvary Church of the Nazarene, Graceworks Pictures, and *The Grace Card*

Few congregations have responded as strongly to the success of Sherwood Pictures as Calvary Church of the Nazarene in Cordova, Tennessee, a suburb of Memphis. Like a growing number of churches in the United States, Calvary is technologically well equipped to undertake film production. Under their list of ministries on the church website, they list Worship and Creative Arts, which boasts both a Media Team and a Media Lab. Calvary believes that "there is no more important place of service in Worship & Arts" than the media team which provides "a real opportunity for a host of non-musicians" to serve in worship.[40] With the Media Lab, Calvary has the capability to "create and edit all of [their] own audio and video projects, [many of which] find their way into worship services as commercials for events and support for worship and Pastor's sermons."[41]

Chief among Calvary's worship productions has been its annual Passion play. For years, Dr. David Evans, a Memphis-based optometrist, has been in charge of this production as writer, producer, and director. He has overseen casts as large as 250 people and massive sets that feature hydraulic lifts, computerized lighting, and exotic animals. Each year, Dr. Evans spends up to three months in pre-production work, assembling the staging and crafting the choreography required for the performances. Whether he knows it or not, Dr. Evans follows in DeMille's footsteps by creating Passion plays with "a new, modern-day story to parallel the story of Christ [that require] a new script and new characters year after year," rather than simply retelling the same story over and over again. Dr. Evans' work on these Passion plays brings "people together in a unified effort to share the message of the gospel with the community."[42]

In 2008, Dr. Evans' creative world was turned upside down after watching a film that inspired him to make the transition from stage to screen. The account of this experience is worth quoting in full:

> In September 2008, David and his wife, Esther, joined a large group from Calvary Church to watch *Fireproof* on opening night. "I realized during that movie that God had been putting us through training during the fifteen years of our passion play," he says. He committed

the next few months to turning his newest passion play story into a full-length screenplay. David used the "blue-print" for faith-based filmmaking created by Sherwood Pictures in Albany, Georgia.[43]

Dr. Evans immediately formed Gracework Pictures and began writing the script for *The Grace Card*, his first feature-length film, which he also financed to the tune of $450,000 of his own money. Evans hired Howard Klausner, a Hollywood veteran, who co-wrote *Space Cowboys* (Warner Bros., 2000), to assist with a rewrite of the script. Evans describes his motivation for writing this film: "I wanted a modern script that gives people something to grab hold of when they leave the theater. Hollywood misses out because it is not giving people something deeper to digest."[44]

Filming for *The Grace Card* began on October 14, 2009, and wrapped after an intense 30-day shooting schedule. Like Sherwood Pictures, Graceworks Pictures relied on an army of volunteers to bring the film to completion. The producers also depended on the generosity of the Memphis community. The fire and police departments donated uniforms, squad cars, and time to train the actors who played police officers. Local restaurants catered the production for free while other businesses allowed the producers to shoot on location at no cost. Graceworks also benefited from the use of an entire hospital wing that was under renovation at the time. The Rev. Lynn Holmes, pastor of Calvary Church, estimates that volunteers collectively logged 15,000 hours during the film's production.[45] Holmes and Evans regarded the work of these volunteers as an act of great sacrifice. That few, if any, of these volunteers had any experience in filmmaking was a positive for Evans and producer John Nasraway. They claimed that, due to this inexperience, the volunteers worked extremely hard because they were simultaneously learning *and* doing.

While most of the volunteers worked behind the scenes, many stepped in front of the camera as rookie actors as well. If experience, or lack thereof, did not concern the producers, faith did. Evans required every actor with a speaking role to be a Christian. Such employment restrictions harken back to the restrictions that Christian Herald Motion Picture Bureau employed in the early 1920s. For the two lead roles, Evans cast Michael Joiner, a popular conservative Christian comedian, and Mike Higgenbottom, a newcomer to the screen. In a supporting role, Evans was able to land Oscar-winning actor Louis Gossett, Jr., who also starred in Christian films like *Left Behind: World at War* (Cloud Ten Pictures, 2005) and *The Least Among You* (Witenuckle Films, 2009). Gossett participated in the picture because its message of overcoming racism resonated with his Eracism Foundation, "a nonprofit designed to create a 'conscious offensive against racism, violence and ignorance.'"[46] Its Christian theme of forgiveness and redemption also spoke to his own faith. Banking on the popularity of *Fireproof*, Dr. Evans cast one of its most beloved actors, Stephen Dervan, who played the hot sauce–drinking firefighter, the film's main source of comic relief. In the end, however, Dervan would not play a major role in the film.

Whether volunteers or Oscar-winning actors, everyone who participated in the making of *The Grace Card* viewed their work as ministry. The cast and crew saw the film and their participation in it as a way to spread the Gospel message, uplift believers, and inspire audiences to combat racism in their communities. Like Sherwood Pictures' productions, Grace-

Opposite: In February 2011, Graceworks Pictures released *The Grace Card*, which featured a plot device similar to that of The Love Dare in *Fireproof* (Sherwood Pictures, 2008). Unlike Sherwood Pictures posters, this one centers its faith components both in its title and the image of a church in a prominent place.

WITNESS THE POWER OF FORGIVENESS

MICHAEL JOINER   MICHAEL HIGGENBOTTOM   AND LOUIS GOSSETT JR.

THE GRACE CARD

IN THEATERS 2-25-11
TheGraceCardMovie.com

works bathed their filmmaking in prayer, beginning every day with a devotional and a prayer. Evans' wife Esther, also one of the film's producers, claimed that the project was "meant to be" and that "God had His hands on it." To make it official, Calvary Church even conducted a commissioning service for the participants in the film in which congregants laid hands on and prayed for the cast and crew before production began. With this theological and spiritual framework in place, the Graceworks team saw any hindrance during filmmaking as the work of "the enemy" and any good thing that happened as "a miracle" or the "work of God."

Marketing The Grace Card

With a limited budget (only $500,000 for production), Graceworks Pictures relied on viral marketing in partnership with Affirm Films and Provident Films, two companies that helped make Sherwood Pictures' films a success. First and foremost, Provident Films reached out to, in large part, its built-in Sherwood Pictures fan-base through e-mail blasts that repeatedly directed potential viewers to the film's website, reminded them of the film's release date, and provided screening locations. With a less robust Facebook and Twitter presence, *The Grace Card*'s website (www.thegracecardmovie.com) was the chief source of information for audiences and fans. Here potential viewers and subsequent fans could watch a trailer, read more about the film and its cast and crew, watch clips and interviews with cast and crew, discover books on the film's themes, order ministry resources and download Bible study curriculum. Through Outreach Marketing, the company that also partnered with Sherwood Pictures, churches could schedule movie events ranging in price from $99 to $299. The package includes a DVD of the film, an annual screening license, an event planning guide, posters, bulletin inserts, and invitation tickets. Through this licensed event, Outreach encouraged ministers to "Create a Grace Awakening in Your Church and Community."[47]

The Grace Card, *the Film*

Somewhat similar to Sherwood Pictures' *Courageous*, *The Grace Card* tells the story of two Memphis police officers who are polar opposites in almost every area of their lives. Bill "Mac" McDonald (Michael Joiner) is a middle-aged white man who, for nearly two decades, has been trapped in grief and despair over the tragic death of his first son when he was a toddler. This unresolved grief has polluted his relationship with his wife Sara (Joy Moore) and his surviving, now teenage, son Blake (Rob Erickson) and has made him something of a pariah on the police force. Frequently passed over for promotions, he becomes even angrier when he is partnered with the recently promoted Sam Wright (Michael Higgenbottom), an African American bi-vocational officer and pastor. Sam's joyous spirit and evangelical Christian worldview clash with Michael's negative, reclusive demeanor. Sam senses that Mac harbors deep-seated racism as well. This strained relationship begins to have an effect on Sam's faith as he struggles to love and witness to Mac and to share this experience with his family and congregation. Sam even begins to question why God put the two of them together if their partnership is having such a negative effect on him.

As Mac and his family continue to grow further apart, Blake begins to run with the wrong crowd. When Mac and Sam respond to reports of suspicious activity at a warehouse, the two officers disrupt a burglary. Believing that one of the thieves has a gun, Mac fires his weapon. When he approaches the thief to remove his mask, he realizes that it is his son

"Mac" McDonald (Michael Joiner, left) and Sam Wright (Michael Higgenbottom, right) are racial and spiritual opposites in *The Grace Card* (Graceworks Pictures, 2011).

Blake. Though Blake will recover from the gunshot wound, the doctors learn that he has a rare kidney condition and that, without a transplant, he will not survive. With Blake's life in the balance, Mac is in emotional shambles and afraid that he will lose his son and that his wife will leave him. In the midst of this crisis, Sam not only leads Mac to Christ but donates one of his kidneys so that Blake can make a full recovery.

In the final scene, Mac and his family worship at Sam's church. In the middle of the service, an African American man makes his way down the aisle and interrupts the service. He tells the congregation that as a teenager he killed a young child while fleeing a drug bust. While in prison, he committed his life to Christ and, upon his release, entered the mission field. He turns to Mac and begs his forgiveness. Victim and violator embrace, and Sam looks on in tears as the congregation celebrates and the credits begin to roll, preceded by the verse from Ephesians 2:8, "For it is by grace you have been saved."

Reception of The Grace Card

The Grace Card was released in 352 theaters across the United States on February 25, 2011, and after remaining in some of these theaters for up to eight weeks, eventually earned $2,430,735 in box office receipts, $1,010,299 of which came on opening weekend.[48] The DVD was released on August 16, 2011, and at the time of this writing, I was unable to locate any sales or rental figures for it. Reflecting on his hopes for the film, Holmes said, "We don't want people to leave saying, 'What a great movie,' but 'What a great God!'" He got his wish. Most mainstream and some Christian critics were not kind to the film.

Reviewing the film for *The Washington Post*, Sean O'Connell critiqued the heavy-handed way in which Evans presents its message, a common criticism. He bemoans the lack of subtlety, writing, "Suffice it to say, Mac's a damaged soul in need of saving. Can you guess if the subtly named Mr. Wright is the right man for the job?"[49] O'Connell praises the lead actors' performances but has trouble with the film's sudden, major plot twist that intensifies its preachiness. In the end, he argues, "[The] film's shortcomings show how far the Christian genre has to go if it someday hopes to preach to anyone but the choir."

Writing for *Christianity Today*, Todd Hertz gives perhaps the most even-handed assessment of the film. He too praises Joiner's and Higgenbottom's performances and regrets that the film did not feature more scenes of the two of them interacting with each other. Hertz adds:

> It has moments of feeling like a current era Clint Eastwood–directed film like *Million Dollar Baby* or *Gran Torino*. But *The Grace Card* gets bogged down in cliché, coincidence, and corniness as it heaps big plot point onto big plot point. There are such strong hints of a hard-hitting, smarter character study that I was disappointed by the candy-coated, tie-all-ends, over-manipulative plotting. Part of that may be due to trying to write the film for both those in and out of the church — to be all things to all people, instead of just telling a story.[50]

Like a handful of critics, Hertz recognizes that this is the latest entry in a "tide shift" of church-based filmmaking. Of course, his final point here could also apply to many of the church-based productions discussed in this book. When these studios figure out how to effectively navigate that tension, they will take a bigger step towards reaching a broader audience.

Finally, Joe Leydon of *Variety*, seemingly the publication's go-to critic for church-based productions, praises *The Grace Card*'s technical aspects and writes that it has "fine performances, credible dialogue, and slick production values that belie a reportedly paltry budget."[51] Leydon also notes that the script and plot are "edgier" than other contemporary faith-based productions as they address racism and prejudice.

With its limited theatrical run and recent DVD release, viewer feedback had yet to accumulate as it had for Sherwood Pictures' films at the time of this writing. Almost universally positive reviews populate the feedback sections of both the IMDb and Amazon.com. On the IMDb, Jaimi Thomsen called *The Grace Card* "The Best 'Christian' Film I Have Seen." Thomsen added:

> When they had the pre-screening I was reluctant to go because as an avid movie watcher I was afrid that as a church produced movie the quality would not be what I wanted. Boy was I wrong!!..... It was as if it was produced and filmed by Warner Brothers.... I saw the film at the Trevecca Nazarene University pre-screening and on February 25th I WILL pay the $10.50 to go see it again. And maybe even again after that.[52]

If enough viewers saw the film multiple times, then these repeat attendees and an underwhelming box office performance speaks to a comparatively limited impact for the film.

Clearly disagreeing with critics like O'Connell, dhenry68 from Sydney, Australia, argued that the film was, in fact, not preachy. He wrote on the IMDb, "[It] uses a good storyline to teach a valuable lesson. Mainly we learn to put things in context, and that many people out there who are mean, or horrible to others are themselves hurt.... If we can see the other person's hurt, we can understand where they are coming from and possibly meet them half way."[53] Some viewers valued the film's message and tone. Joswircz responded on Amazon.com with a five-star review and posted, "This movie is so God-filled!.... Thank you! I wish more movies had God-filled messages."[54]

Other Christian viewers were disappointed with *The Grace Card*. These negative responses continue to reflect the diversity of even conservative Christian reactions to conservative Christian films. A couple of viewers turned to the IMDb and Amazon.com to express their frustrations over what they found to be the film's theological shortcomings. Chestnutyouth from the United States pointed out two weaknesses in the film that are worth quoting at length:

> First, while I like the portrayal of the pastor I really was taken back by the fact that neither of the times he is shown preaching does he actually read or quote the Word of God. He talks about experience and says some fine things but unless it comes from the Scriptures it isn't preaching it is just motivational speaking.[...] Second, my biggest fault with this film was the lack of God-centered grace. The theme of the entire film was grace, but the whole time they speak of grace to fellow man and never grace from God. The only reason we can give grace to one another is because it has so freely been given to us on the cross. It is a fundamental point that I felt this movie just lacked. They mentioned Jesus plenty of times, but never explained the gospel and while that is not something necessary in Christian film I just don't get how you have a movie about grace and never show that.[55]

With a significant majority of five-star reviews on Amazon.com, one of its two two-star reviews is important. Echoing the theological concerns above, Steve Montgomery from Atotonilco, Mexico, writes:

> *The Grace Card* presents a Christless, crossless Christianity. I counted the name of Jesus five times in an hour and a half: once when the protagonist is half humming, half singing "Jesus Loves Me" and the name Jesus slips out; twice in a background song by Third Day (not totally sure of the artists) and (only) twice spoken in conversation [...]. Was the omission of the Name above every name intentional?[56]

He concludes, "Dr. Evans, you can do better! Calvary Church, don't lose the Gospel in your desire to put out a Christian film. Come on, guys! Do it better!" For viewers like chestnutyouth and Steve Montgomery, *The Grace Card* was clearly not Christian enough. These diverse Christian reactions to the film bring us to a brief discussion of its theology.

The Theology of The Grace Card

The Grace Card's audiences were divided over the message, or theology, of the film. Many mainstream critics felt that the producers laid the message on too thick. Many Christian viewers felt that the message was just right while others claimed it was not strong enough. As a Christian film, *The Grace Card* is about as preachy as its contemporaries. It avoids the prosperity gospel pitfalls that plague Sherwood Pictures' earlier productions. As the title informs us, the film's central theme is grace and, by extension, forgiveness. However, while Sam's character does testify to the grace and love of God, on the whole, the film seems to be less concerned with God's grace than it is with the grace and forgiveness humans extend toward one another. Despite some Christian viewers' frustrations with this, this thematic shift is a welcome feature in faith-based filmmaking.

As Hertz pointed out, *The Grace Card* shines brightest in its scenes between Mac and Sam. These scenes also form the film's theological core. Sam is, perhaps, the most believable, likable Christian character in any film, faith-based or not. The film focuses on his ability to be gracious with, forgiving of, and loving towards Mac, one of the more *un*lovable characters to be found in Christian film. Sam's struggles with Mac and his personal faith are sincere and reveal not only the power of grace, love, and forgiveness, but also the very real difficulty of living them day in and day out. Of course, the film is not all about Sam. Mac is in need of grace to break the prison of anger and hatred in which he has trapped himself. Mac's situation reveals the destructive power of unresolved grief and the unwillingness to forgive and embrace those who hurt us. That Mac would find this grace was always a given, which is part of many critics' frustrations with faith-based films like this. That Mac's conversion is theologically murky frustrates many Christian viewers at the same time. What motivates Mac's turn to God and Jesus other than fear and despair? From what and to what is Mac being saved? Is his salvation merely a desperate attempt to preserve his son's life and his marriage? As long as evangelical Christian filmmakers are bound by plot and narrative yet determined to include a "message of salvation," such theological questions will arise.

Perhaps drawing from the Kendrick brothers' creation of *The Love Dare* for *Fireproof*, Evans and his team include a device in the film that viewers can employ in their daily lives. Here, it is the titular grace card, a mantra of sorts that Sam's grandfather (Gossett, Jr.) gives him when he counsels him on his struggles with Mac. The card reads, "I promise to pray for you every day, ask your forgiveness, grant you the same, and be your friend always." That this is from the hand of one of Sam's ancestors, a slave, who writes it to his former owner, complicates both the film and the device. Some viewers might take issue with the implication that the burden of reconciliation is placed on the victim rather than the violator. Why should a young slave ask for his owner's forgiveness? Why should Sam, a victim of Mac's anger and racism, ask Mac's forgiveness or give his kidney to Blake?

Rookie actor Michael Higgenbottom (left) holds his own with Oscar-winning veteran Louis Gossett, Jr., in *The Grace Card* (Graceworks Pictures, 2011).

On the other hand, such graceful positioning breaks the cycles of violence that enslave all of humanity and reveals the power of grace and forgiveness to be that catalyst. Sam's willingness to love and give of himself shows that grace and forgiveness are not always easy and often require great sacrifice. At the same time, Mac's acceptance of this love, grace, and forgiveness is not part of a smooth life transformation. He embraces it, in a sense, kicking and screaming. But, wisely, Evans and Klausner do not paint a picture-perfect life for Mac after his moment of salvation as so many other Christian films do. While Blake is healed, the filmmakers do not take the extra steps of including lifted financial burdens, Blake's reinstatement into private school, or a promotion for Mac.

Mac's experiences of tragedy through the loss of his first son and his shooting of Blake raise the theodicy question. In the hospital chapel as Blake's life hangs in the balance, Mac asks Sam, "Why would [God] let two little boys die and a miserable wretch [like me] go on?" Sam has no easy answer and seems to let the question hang in the air; however, he reassures Mac that his son's death and Blake's situation are not something that God caused. At the same time, Sam refuses to blame God for the difficulties of this world, adding, "We brought suffering on ourselves." Of course, this too begs the question of what Mac "did" to cause or deserve his child's death or, more pointedly, what Sam did to deserve Mac's racism and the broader racism of the film's Southern setting.

While some critics have praised *The Grace Card* for tackling a more mature topic like racism, the film does not address the issue in as mature a fashion as one might hope. The chief example of taking an easy way out in regards to race takes place in the hospital as Sam gives Blake his kidney. As Sam's wife and children wait in the lobby, his youngest daughter timidly asks her mother, "How do they know a black kidney will work in a white boy?" Her mother responds, "Because, honey, on the inside, we're all pretty much the same." She glances over at an older white man sitting across the way who smiles at her and gives her a wink of approval. The implication in the film (and, by extension, for the members of Graceworks and Calvary Church) is that racism is a personal issue best addressed by a change of heart or attitude. While this is true, the film fails to consider the ways in which these individual forms of racism have become institutionalized into racist systems (police forces are often accused of being such), which in turn shape and inform individual racist opinions. In fact, at one point in the film, Sam even accuses Mac of pulling over a car that was only going five miles over the speed limit because the passengers were Latino.

This individualistic approach to racism or, as members of Calvary Church would rightfully call it, sin evidences a particular theological worldview. In the director's commentary, Evans and Holmes critique what they see to be a contemporary obsession with (social?) justice. They argue that any pursuit of justice apart from grace and forgiveness (from God?) is empty and fails to satisfy. Grace and forgiveness, asked of and received from God, must precede justice. As an example, they point to the character who accidentally killed Mac's son. Prison (justice) did not fully heal him, but God's grace and forgiveness did, they argue. Ironically, even as this assertion comes from a theologically conservative place, audiences could see this as a liberal critique of the contemporary justice system in that the practice of simple punishment, often primarily through imprisonment, is an insufficient approach to rectifying the ills that plague our society.

Finally, further signaling their commitment to the Sherwood Pictures filmmaking model, Dr. Evans and the rest of the Graceworks Pictures team are currently in a "season of prayer" for their next project.

Yorba Linda Friends Church, Ocean Avenue Entertainment, and *Not Today*

Perhaps the most surprising participants in this emerging church film movement are the Quakers, specifically Yorba Linda Friends Church in Southern California. Like Calvary, Yorba Linda also has a Worship and Creative Arts ministry. They offer several options for volunteer service, which include assisting with PowerPoint presentations and other visual media during worship or serving as stage managers, moving and setting up equipment for the band and other participants in worship. The Worship and Creative Arts ministry relies on one of the church's foundational values, innovation. Yorba Linda states, "We encourage and value new, creative ways of serving God. While our vision will remain unchanged, our methods need to always stay fresh and relevant."[57] Their Worship and Creative Arts ministry also has its own set of core values including authenticity, diversity, excellence, intentionality, sacrality, and relationality.[58]

In 2008, the church produced a documentary short film entitled *Deletes*, which was directed by Jon Van Dyke, the church's Media Director. It focused on the Dalits, an oppressed, enslaved group of outcasts in India. The project seems to have emerged out of lead pastor Matthew Cork's experiences in India and conviction of the importance of education in improving the lives of the Dalits there.[59] Yorba Linda has since partnered with Ocean Avenue Entertainment, a Christian organization "committed to developing, producing, and distributing films and television programs that are engaging and redemptive," to produce their first feature-length film, *Not Today*, which expands their work with *Deletes*.[60] Ocean Avenue was founded by Chris Bueno, the director of Carmel Entertainment who was responsible for ensuring distribution for Sherwood Pictures' films. Bueno's experiences have provided Ocean Avenue with "key relationships with major studios and smaller niche distributors, making it possible for producers to fully realize their potential to successfully reach their target audience," which they are currently putting to use in their work with Yorba Linda Friends Church.[61] Ocean Avenue has also developed WingCinema, a company that "offers redemptive values-based, entertaining feature films, enlightening, faith-based documentaries, and compelling short films to churches and other organizations for licensed public showing," which mirrors much of the work that OutReach and Provident Films did for Sherwood Pictures.[62] WingCinema will enable individuals and groups to purchase DVD copies of the film in bulk at discounted rates for a variety of outreach and fundraising options.

Jon Van Dyke is reprising his role as writer and director, while Brent Martz, the Pastor of Creative Ministries at Yorba Linda, is also assisting in production. Pre-production began in May 2009 and production began on location in India in mid–2010. Like Sherwood Pictures has done with *Courageous*, the producers of *Not Today* have kept up an extensive blog detailing the film's production. The site includes blog posts and behind-the scenes-footage of production and interviews with the cast and crew. The film (still far from complete) will tell the story of a group of college students who travel to India for a summer vacation. The poverty that they encounter there impacts one student who develops a close friendship with an Indian man and her daughter, Dalits by birth. After he returns home, the images of poverty haunt him and force him to return to help. When he does, he learns that the young girl has become a victim of sex trafficking. He and her father set out on a journey across India to rescue her.[63]

From early reports about the production of the film, it sounds like *Not Today* might focus less on the Christian faith of its characters and more on the troubled world in which they live. Bueno said, "We won't shrink from using the name of Jesus, but it's part of the story [...]. Some Christians want very overtly Christian messages. Others want to see gritty truthful stories of people struggling with faith, who may or may not lead perfect lives but are genuinely seeking."[64] To leverage the impact of their film, the producers are partnering with groups like International Freedom, Dalit Freedom Network, and Operation Mercy India, organizations geared toward the education of and service to the Dalit people in India. Such relationships will be mutually beneficial as they increase *Not Today*'s potential audience while providing a campaign tool for these organizations to increase awareness and affect positive change around this issue.

It is fitting to conclude this chapter with a discussion of the work of Yorba Linda Friends Church and *Not Today*, because it appears to be drastically different from any of the other films I have discussed thus far. First and foremost, it has been shot on location in the slums of India, a far remove from the comfortable middle-class settings of its Christian film counterparts. Second, its subject matter is sex trafficking, a topic far more scandalous than any that these other films have addressed. As a result, *Not Today* is poised to be a welcome voice in the church film movement, one that might address the shortcomings that many critics find in the genre. I will now turn to those criticisms.

Chapter 9

Critiquing the Films ... and Their Critics

Throughout this book, I have provided examples of both positive and negative criticisms of films from the church film movement, and as we have seen, a criticism of one of them is likely to apply to all of them. I have delayed my engagement with the responses to these films for a couple of reasons. First, I wanted to paint a picture of the movement itself, the secular and Christian filmmaking past from which it emerged, and the state of the secular filmmaking and evangelical pop culture industries in which it moves. Second, I felt that it was important to show how, by and large, the movement's harshest critics fail to take this broader context into consideration when analyzing these films. On the other hand, perhaps the movement's most ardent supporters emphasize this context too much, allowing it to blind them to its films' aesthetic and even theological problems. In this chapter, I want to engage the reactions to these films through religious aesthetician Frank Burch Brown's notion of kitsch. Perhaps doing so will help provide a clearer, more level-headed way to analyze and talk about these films.

Make no mistake about it, the majority of the films from the church film movement discussed here qualify as kitsch. While this may seem like an insult, it is in fact a more complex analysis if we employ Burch Brown's definition of the term. In his book *Good Taste, Bad Taste, and Christian Taste: Aesthetics in Religious Life*, Burch Brown argues that if we simply equate kitsch with art that is trashy or worthless, then we had better not use the word in religious circles, because to do so will immediately ignore the "people whose hearts have truly been touched and whose spirits have genuinely been moved, at one time or another, by the supposed 'kitsch' that one is dismissing as worthless." He argues for a much more complex understanding of kitsch, and while lengthy, it is worth highlighting a few of Burch Brown's points to better understand the weaknesses of these films, their fans' praise of them, and their opponents' critiques.

He claims that kitsch is art that is designed to "tap into highly predictable responses in the viewer — responses not so deep as those tapped by artfully rendered archetypal symbols and the like, but more like emotional reflexes. Those reflexes are very real — rather like basic sexual responses.... Kitsch and erotic art are both primed to take advantage of such responses." Fans of kitsch often mistake these automatic responses for more mature experiences. Burch Brown adds, "The aims of a work of kitsch, and the emotions it elicits, can be genuine, so far as they go. But, from the vantage point of most educated and disciplined artists, and of their institutions and clients, kitsch succeeds to an embarrassing extent. Its effects outrun its causes."[1]

Despite these shortcomings, kitsch can have a positive effect by "releasing and exercising sentiments that otherwise might be so protected as to atrophy through disuse." However, lingering too long here can lead to sentimentality, which truncates religious development. It does so, he argues, because "kitsch is forever immature — and often in a way that cries out to be counteracted and reformed at a more mature level. In and of itself, kitsch ordinarily conveys a distorted impression of the higher goals to which it typically alludes or aspires. And it cannot often carry one very far toward those goals." Finally, however, Burch Brown is also open to the possibility that kitsch might also engender religious experiences in viewers that "can at times be something entirely genuine and beyond reproach."[2] As a result, critical assessment of art that we might deem as kitsch must be done on a hospitable level, practicing and embracing what Burch Brown refers to as ecumenical aesthetics.

The foundation of Burch Brown's notion of ecumenical aesthetics is the recognition that all matters of taste are not individual but communal. Assessments of and conversations of taste must therefore take this communal context into account. As he writes, "When it comes to appraising quality in the realm of religious art, therefore, we need to take into account (among other things) the context of the individual viewer (or listener or reader), the context of the maker, and the context of the community — the various possible publics."[3] In short, such awareness must lead to a highly "open" critical posture that keeps three key activities in mind:

> (1) to recognize and indeed relish certain aesthetic and religious differences without regarding them as inevitably and permanently alienating; (2) to learn to discern, as an act of love, what others find delightful and meaningful in art that has little appeal to one-self or one's group; and (3) to notice, both more precisely and more generally, points in life and worship where aesthetic aims and religious aspirations (or aversions) are wedded to one another, and thus to see how spiritual growth can have a properly artistic and aesthetic dimension subject to criticism, cultivation, and education.[4]

This is indeed a daunting task, one that requires much patience, reflection, and magnanimity. Unfortunately, few film critics take the time to embrace this approach, failing to fully consider the theological and cultural contexts from which these films emerge or to simply admit and appreciate the fact that other viewers value films they find ridiculous. At the same time, however, the producers of these films and their staunchest supporters often fail to carefully consider their critics and the potential that their criticism has to inspire further reflection or self-criticism.

Returning to some of the positive and negative reactions to these films will show how they qualify as kitsch. Taken in their entirety, supporters of these films rarely discuss them *as films*. While they do make mention of their weaknesses in plot, acting, direction, or cinematography, for example, they quickly dismiss them in order to discuss how the films ministered to them or conveyed a deeper theological or spiritual truth. On the other hand, critics who take a negative view of these films often fail to think about the contexts or intentions of these filmmakers at any great length. They foreground their critiques of the films' aesthetic weaknesses and seem to view them as insurmountable roadblocks that prevent the filmmakers from ever attaining the goals to which they aspire. These critics fail to see that thousands, maybe millions of viewers simply do not care about cinematography or direction. For these critics, aesthetic differences are, as Burch Brown puts it, "permanently alienating."

One of Sherwood Pictures,' and by extension much of the church film movement's, harshest critics has been Barbara Nicolosi, a former nun turned scriptwriter and film educator. In October 2006, she wrote a scathing response to *Facing the Giants* on her website in which she attacked both the filmmakers and the members of Hollywood who have attempted to exploit these films. Nicolosi gets at Burch Brown's understanding of the automatic responses that kitsch engenders when she writes, "Adult Evangelical Christians watching *Facing the Giants* are like sex addicts watching the Spice Channel."[5] Paralleling Nicolosi's critique of audience reaction to *Facing the Giants*, Radosh offered a similar reaction to *Fireproof*. Referencing the film's Internet pornography subplot, he writes, "Indeed, it's possible *Fireproof* is so obsessed with stamping out pornography because it recognizes the competition. *Fireproof* is a porn version of Christianity — a ludicrously contorted, heavily airbrushed fantasy of the real thing, and ultimately every bit as unsatisfying."[6] At first, these comments seemed like snarky attacks on films they disliked, until I recalled Burch Brown's discussion of kitsch. Burch Brown might well agree with Nicolosi and Radosh that there is something pornographic about these films, but, unlike them, his criticism is not that these responses exist, but that the people who experience them do not adequately reflect on them or think through or beyond them. Unfortunately, critics like Nicolosi also fall victim to kitsch because she does not think beyond her initial revulsion to the films and how other Christians might have genuine spiritual experiences through viewing these films, as so many viewer feedback posts evidence.

On the other hand, Nicolosi does have a keen awareness of the context of some of the producers of these films. She sees a dichotomy that exists in the world of Christian filmmakers between those who, simply put, value the message over the medium and those who realize that the medium and the message are inseparable, that they shape and influence each other. Nicolosi would place much of the church film movement in the former camp, and, indeed, many of these filmmakers would embrace that identification. After all, the Kendrick brothers are fond of saying, "We don't want to make a good movie, we want to make a God movie." Nicolosi claims that she and others like her are "Abel Christians," those who value creativity and want to present the "first fruits" of their creativity to God. Nicolosi and her colleagues would argue, against the Kendricks, that serving God and furthering a filmmaking career do not have to be mutually exclusive. This is one of the stronger points of her argument because it has the potential to inspire greater creativity on the part of these filmmakers and encourage them to think more fully about how the style of their films enhances or distracts from their message.

Finally, Nicolosi is highly critical of the broader industry that has rushed to capitalize on the church film movement and thus inspired a host of followers. This is another strong point in her argument because she speaks truth to power. Her criticisms of the industry should force the larger companies that distribute, and occasionally produce, these films to think more clearly about their relationship with filmmakers and audiences. At the same time, evangelical Christians need to know when they, and the Christian message they value, are being exploited. Indeed, many of them do as their responses to some of these films show. Nicolosi writes, "So am I saying that the Fox Faith thing will be bad for the whole God in Hollywood thing? I don't know yet. I do know that green-lighting two movies for what one regular studio picture usually costs says that FOX believes that believers can be had on the cheap. And they are probably right. Pathetic and sad." She concludes by stating, "Making a movie that is beautiful is damn hard. Damn hard. Expecting to be able to produce a film with no experience or training is arrogant and as absurd as someone thinking they could just build a building with no training or experience in architecture."[7] While this criticism might apply to larger established studios like Fox, who have greater financial resources, it is a moot point regarding participants in the church film movement. Producing a film with no experience or training is no longer either arrogant or absurd. It is, quite simply, a reality of the world in which we now live. Sherwood Pictures, New Song Pictures, Graceworks Pictures, and the other participants in the church film movement have taken matters into their own hands and made their voices heard when no one else could or would speak for them.

Far more interesting and helpful are the comments from critics who actually do consider the context from which these films emerge. In fact, their recognition of this context makes their criticisms even more valid and poignant. Like Burch Brown, these critics seem to recognize both the promises and the limitations of these films (kitsch). Joe Leydon, a film critic for *Variety*, and Terry Mattingly, a Christian pop culture blogger, have been critical of what they see as Sherwood Pictures' missed opportunities. Leydon writes of *Facing the Giants*, "[By] preaching to the converted so heavy-handedly, the filmmakers fumble an opportunity to reach beyond their target demo of devout churchgoers."[8] Terry Mattingly adds, "Do you see the irony? This is a solid niche market. But it will not help shape the mainstream. Also, it is hard to imagine how contemporary Christian cinema will reach many people who do not already believe. This is evangelism for the already evangelized."[9] I will say more about this later in this chapter, but for now, a weakness of these criticisms is that they fail to recognize that preaching to the choir *is* one of Sherwood's goals. Nevertheless, these critics' arguments that films from the church film movement fail to convert non-believers or minister to believers are still valid.

In terms of converting non-believers, these films often fail to present a clear Gospel message, as both Christian and secular critics have pointed out. I find it utterly confusing that there seems to be a conscious avoidance of any specific religious context to most of these films. In terms of Sherwood Pictures' films, it is certainly ironic that in three feature-length films the church-based production studio only provides one scene that takes place in a church. Moreover, this scene does not provide any specific religious or theological framework for the narrative but simply highlights a character's poor moral standing. Perhaps the inclusion of religious institutions or a more specific religious or theological setting would go a long way towards clearing up the religious, spiritual, or theological ambiguity that both secular and Christian viewers find in these films. Recall both Willman and Chattaway's reviews of *Fireproof* for publications as diverse as *Entertainment Weekly* and *Christianity Today*. They both argue that the "evangelical component" (Caleb's spiritual transformation) feels like an unnecessary addition to the narrative rather than a foundational element of it.

Willman and Chattaway's critiques are some of the more levelheaded reactions to these films. At the same time, their remarks are not without precedent, as their skepticism of *Fireproof*'s "evangelical component" finds its source in a broader critique of evangelical conversion narratives. Evangelical spiritual programs like the Alpha Course and the Purpose Driven Life, which essentially promise changed lives through the completion of them, parallel Christian filmmakers' aspirations for their films, namely that people's lives would be changed by watching them. Religion and culture scholar Mara Einstein is highly skeptical of these promises. She writes, "But what we can and should question is whether the product delivers on the marketed message, which as presented suggests that changing your life can be simple. I would argue that no life can be fundamentally turned around in 40 Days of Purpose or 10 weeks of Alpha."[10] She would also, no doubt, be skeptical of Caleb's transformation through *The Love Dare*. However, such skepticism ignores a key characteristic of the evangelical Christian experience. In his book *American Evangelicals: A Contemporary History of a Mainstream Religious Movement*, Barry Hankins discusses the character and history of evangelical conversion experiences. He writes,

> [The] evangelical form of conversion took a distinct shape in the eighteenth century. The experience was more immediate than Puritans and many other English-speaking Protestants had known. Moreover, the conversion experience was non-institutional—that is, it usually came outside of the sacramental institutions of the established churches and often even outside of church buildings.... While there might not be much of a change in one's head knowledge of religion, ... real conversion would result in a profound change in feelings and passions that would reorient one's entire life.[11]

Hankins even claims that this type of conversion experience would be necessary even for people who already had knowledge of theology and valued the Bible as an authoritative text. He continues, "In terms of revivalist evangelicalism, however, they were unconverted until they had an inward and supernatural experience of forgiveness of sins that was possible because of Christ's death on the cross."[12]

Hankins' discussion of evangelical conversion experiences might help explain the spiritual transformation that characters in films from the church film movement often undergo. At the same time, it might help us understand both the experiences that Christian filmmakers want audiences to have and the fact that some viewers have them. It is not difficult to imagine that, through their combination of dramatic images and music, Sherwood Pictures' films could lead to a type of transformation in feelings and passions like Hankins describes above. However, it is necessary to question how long that transformation will last beyond the initial viewing experience. I am reminded of Burch Brown's critique of kitsch's message that "ordinarily conveys a distorted impression of the higher goals to which it typically alludes or aspires. And it cannot often carry one very far toward those goals."[13] Perhaps the inclusion of a community of faith, institutional or otherwise, that will nourish the lead characters' transformation or provide a place for spiritual growth through education and service might lengthen the spiritual experiences that many viewers have while watching these films. What better way to minister to Christians than by showing ministry in action?

However, there might be something else at work here with the lack of a more defined conversion experience or an explicit religious context in which that conversion takes place. While thinking about these particular criticisms of Sherwood Pictures' films, I recalled the early silent religious films that I discussed in the first chapter. Many of them featured only a few intertitles mixed in with their moving images. For example, an early silent film that depicted the life of Jesus would contain scenes that reenacted gospel stories. In between these scenes, intertitles would quote a verse or two of scripture from that story. Yet the action on screen would go well beyond the few quoted verses, thus signifying the filmmaker's expectation that their audiences would be familiar with the biblical narrative. Perhaps the Kendricks, and other Christian filmmakers, craft their stories with the assumption that their audiences are already familiar with narratives of spiritual transformation. Maybe their evangelical audiences know the implications of the characters' conversations with one another, like the lengthy dialogue in *Fireproof* between Caleb and his father that abruptly ends in prayer, Caleb's quick "insider" exchange with Michael, or Nathan and David's conversation in *Courageous* because they have experienced them themselves.

Yet when we think about individual experience, this might be the very factor that stands in the way of these filmmakers reaching their goal of ministering to other Christians. The most significant, recurring critique of Sherwood Pictures' films, for example, is that they do not operate in the realm of reality. While this is certainly a harsh criticism, it is one to which I am increasingly inclined to agree. The lack of a more specific religious setting in these films not only creates an ambiguous theological or spiritual message, but quite simply betrays the reality that all of these filmmakers experience on a daily basis. The only films that feature extended scenes in a community of faith are *To Save a Life* and *What If...*, both of which present church membership as an integral part of their characters' lives, not an oddity for audiences to puzzle over. While these films' avoidance of scenes of gratuitous sex and violence or glamorized scenes of alcohol and drug use is understandable, it seems that their extreme piety has swung the pendulum too far in the opposite direction. Recall Sherwood Pictures' decision to fly in a kissing double for Erin Bathea or the inability of Javier and Carmen to kiss one another because he is sweaty or her breath stinks. Their desire to "preserve" their lead actors' marriages is commendable, but this reveals a deeper problem with their films. In three movies, all of which feature a married couple in the lead role, this is the first time we ever see a husband and wife kiss. In the process of avoiding offensive content, Sherwood Pictures simultaneously handcuffs its own portrayals of reality.

Another example of these films' unfaithfulness to reality is the way in which blessings pour down on the lead characters, particularly in *Flywheel* and *Facing the Giants*. The Kendrick brothers, however, are quick to point out that their films are grounded in reality, that they have seen these blessings and miracles take place in their personal lives or in the lives of friends and family. However, the films that they construct from these real-life experiences simply cannot be considered true-to-life accounts. Nicolosi strikes at the heart of the matter when she writes, "The goal of these folks seems to be to create fantasy movies for Christians, made by Christians, and paid for by Christians. *Facing the Giants* from any serious perspective is a fantasy film. Its message is very dangerous for Christians, and scandalous for pagans."[14] Though the events in *Flywheel* and *Facing the Giants* may have real-world parallels, they are still fantasies because, in the case of the Kendricks, they draw from a variety of miraculous sources. Rather than faithfully presenting life as it is, this amalgamation of experiences presents a world that is in no way similar to our own experiences and one that viewers may hope to attain, but never can.

Radosh also questions the ability of contemporary Christian cinema to effectively minister to the saved or unsaved. Though he is commenting on *Fireproof*, his criticism could equally apply to many of the films discussed here. He writes:

> [In] making evangelism — and acceptability to the most insular Christian audiences — a priority, Christianese films all but guarantee artistic failure. Art demands an honesty that the evangelical bubble would find intolerable. Committed to promoting an unambiguous message that god solves all problems, *Fireproof* never portrays Christians doing anything untoward, or even experiencing any sorrow.[15]

Though a film like *Letters to God* steers clear of the prosperity gospel implications that plague *Facing the Giants* (Tyler is not miraculously cured of cancer, for example), it does not make space for any real sorrow, as Tyler's grandmother simply tries to brush it all away. *Facing the Giants* wipes away any pain or difficulty by "blessing" the Taylors with not one but two babies and state championships. Could the Kendricks have left one of the Taylors' needs unfulfilled? Moreover, this evangelical filmmaking philosophy betrays the very theological tradition from which it emerges. Nicolosi adds, "It is icky to tell people that they should be Christian because of the career and health benefits. We have the problem on the team of that embarrassingly unsuccessful crucified coach of ours."[16] Or as I mentioned earlier, there is never any indication that Christians might experience difficulties, and not just blessings, because of their decision to follow Jesus. As a result, these films' messages of faith and hope often come at a deeper theological price. The problem with nearly all of the films in this new church film movement is that without honest depictions of darkness against which to shine, the light of their messages becomes blinding rather than illuminating.

While critics like Nicolosi and Radosh argue that Sherwood Pictures' films fail to portray reality, these and other films from the church movement are characteristic of the broader context of contemporary evangelical media of which they are a part. Radosh recalls a conversation with Andy Buchter, editor of *Christian Retailing*, in which he claimed that much of contemporary Christian pop culture reflects "the culture of contemporary middle America even as it presented itself as the timeless message of Jesus." Buchter responded, "This is definitely American Christianity. There is a very individualistic emphasis on a lot of the material. It's *me and my God*; *me and my life*.... Some people would question too the emphasis on prosperity."[17] Even critics from within the evangelical Christian community, like Schultze and Woods, Jr., bemoan the homogeneity of much of the evangelical Christian creative output. They ask, "What would evangelical media say to church and society if they welcomed the stories of the people who are living on the margins of social respectability?"[18] While they do not have a definitive answer to this question, they argue that it would look drastically different than the solidly middle-class, white output of Sherwood Pictures and much of the rest of the church film movement's releases. Again, let us recall the name of Ben's church in *What If...*: the Little White Church.

Critiques such as these notwithstanding, the world that makes up the settings of Sherwood Pictures' films may be true to the experiences of many viewers who watch and enjoy these films. After seeing *Courageous*, film and religion scholar Richard Lindsay wrote:

> [Watching] this film, I can see with more clarity [Sherwood Pictures'] claim that Hollywood does not reflect the values of a large segment of the American population. The kind of characters and actors in this film would never be in Hollywood films. They look like normal people.... People pray all the time in real life. They go to church. They struggle over personal morality. Hollywood rarely depicts any of this. When they do, it's always the stereotype of the hypocritical religious leader or mindless followers. It strikes me that to some extent Hollywood claims to reflect America, and in some ways claims to "invent" America. To the extent that they ignore white, or even more diverse, "Red Staters" that go to church, it fails to reflect real life in America. What Sherwood is doing in making this kind of independent film is the same thing small-time gay, or ethnic, or women filmmakers have been trying to do in countering the dominant narrative that Hollywood creates.

Lindsay's critique here is spot on, even if most of the films from the church film movement do not foreground church participation in their narratives. Though Lindsay sees striking similarities between Sherwood Pictures' productions and gay cinema (which parallels my argument that Sherwood Pictures owes its existence to, in part, the likes of Roger Corman and Russ Meyers), he also notes a key difference between Sherwood Pictures and the other genres of film to which he compares them. He adds, "The difference, I would think, is that Sherwood probably sees themselves as the 'real' America, rather than one perspective among many, which is what they really are. They are really a kind of ethnic cinema."[19]

Given the middle class comfort reflected in the content of these films and the congregational contexts from which they emerge, their producers' defense of them and evangelical Christianity sounds much too defensive. Schultze and Woods write, "The idea that particular media are Christian and others are merely secular, however, does not work very well for understanding the real world. It simplistically suggests that Christian media are entirely godly while secular media are entirely godless."[20] This, however, is the type of strategy that participants in the church film movement and their staunchest supporters employ. They set up Hollywood as a godless, more powerful opponent that turns out a stream of offensive trash. On the other hand, they present themselves as the weaker, more wholesome alternative. This David vs. Goliath narrative appeals to many American evangelical Christians who often feel marginalized in contemporary pop culture. Radosh is attentive to the political atmosphere that surrounds Christian pop culture when he writes, "Somehow the more powerful the religious right grows, the more desperately Christians cling to the fantasy that they are only one act of Congress away from being herded into concentration camps."[21] Joel A. Carpenter echoes this sentiment in his essay "Contemporary Evangelicalism and Mammon: Some Thoughts" when he writes, "For all the tendency to complain about outsiderhood and disadvantage, and some leaders' outraged thumping on the 'Christian American theme,' American evangelicals have no idea what marginality really means."[22]

However, this defensive posture is yet another key ingredient to Sherwood Pictures' success and the growing influence of the church film movement. Hendershot draws from religious historian Christian Smith's study of American evangelical Christians, whom he defines as "embattled and thriving."[23] She echoes his findings that

> American evangelicalism has remained strong "not because it is shielded against, but because it is — or at least perceives itself to be — embattled with forces that seem to oppose or threaten it ... the evangelical movement's vitality is not a product of its protected isolation from, but of its vigorous engagement with pluralistic modernity." In other words, American evangelicalism is not weakened by its differences from and conflicts with the wider culture. In fact, one might say that evangelical identity is shored up by such conflicts.[24]

So it should come as no surprise that the team at Sherwood Pictures continues to claim cultural marginalization even as they increasingly turn to the culture's resources in an effort to assert their presence and rally their members. As a result, Schultze and Woods conclude, "Perhaps the most significant impact of evangelical media has been to make various tribes more internally cohesive with shared identities and common understandings of who they are and how they should relate to mainstream culture."[25] The church film movement also illustrates Leslie E. Smith's argument that mastering media "has been a task that evangelicals have taken seriously as they mobilize to fight cultural and spiritual corruption."[26] Yet Smith also picks up on the irony of this task: "Although evangelicalism readily adapts itself to and is fueled by postmodern consumerist popular culture, paradoxically it simultaneously sees itself as the victim of that very culture."[27]

Participants in the church film movement are unlikely to tone down this defensiveness, given its appeal to their target audience. However, it might be in their best interest to do so if they hope to appeal to a broader audience. As Mattingly writes, changing the culture from an evangelical cinematic perspective is difficult work that "takes talent, patience, skill, and teamwork — teamwork that almost always is going to include seeking excellence among unbelievers as well as believers."[28] Even if filmmakers like the Kendrick brothers do not want to work with non–Christians and remain skeptical of Hollywood, they need to recognize that Christians are working there too. Both Lindvall and Mattingly point out a wealth of Christian talent producing good work in the mainstream film industry. Rather than alienating themselves from Hollywood, perhaps members of the church film movement should seek out their fellow Christians doing good work there in an effort to partner together to create better films.

All of these criticisms, from the lack of a clear theology to unrealistic narratives to homogenous settings, work against the Kendrick brothers' goals for filmmaking, which are both evangelical and ministerial. Alex Kendrick re-emphasizes their motivation: "Are we preaching to the choir? Sure, but the choir needs it if they are not singing on key. We also have a second audience of people who need clarity about who Christ is and why they need him. Yes, we know we get mixed responses, and some people roll their eyes. But we're clear: We are here to present the Gospel, but not to ram it down people's throats."[29] I could go on and on about the criticisms of the church film movement and whether or not the Kendrick brothers and their filmmaking peers have reached their goals. One thing is for certain, the numbers do not lie. Of all the films listed here, Sherwood has experienced financial success in ways that most of their church-based filmmaking peers have yet to attain. As a result, we cannot ignore the fact that these criticisms have fallen on a host of deaf ears. What do we make of the positive reactions to these films?

We would do well to recall Burch Brown's emphasis on the twofold reactions that kitsch can bring about. He recognizes that kitsch can lead to both cheap and easy religious experiences and religious experiences that "can at times be something entirely genuine and beyond reproach."[30] It seems to me that as I conclude this chapter on the reactions to these films, I must acknowledge that countless viewers of Sherwood Pictures' films have had genuine religious experiences that are beyond reproach. It also seems far less important for me to understand *how* this happens than it is to be respectful of the times when it *does* happen. To simply dismiss fans of the genre as nothing better than porn addicts, as Nicolosi seems to do, will simply not do. A respect for and appreciation of these experiences is in order, even if we do not share them, if we are to fully understand the appeal of these films and the effectiveness with which Sherwood Pictures, at least, has won over an evangelical Christian audience. To the extent that viewers have these genuine experiences, then Sherwood has, in part, reached their goal of ministering to their Christian viewers.

I am well aware, however, that for the purposes of this book, an acknowledgment and appreciation of these genuine experiences is not enough. I am compelled to question *why* and *how* these experiences occur, even among viewers who express frustration over these films' poor visual qualities. While reading about these experiences occasionally confounds me, I am aware that I have already highlighted a few reasons for their existence. We can trace the explanation all the way back to the first chapter and my discussion of religious expectations for motion pictures in the early 1900s. From the birth of the cinema, countless Christian viewers demanded "cleaner" motion pictures, "morally uplifting" alternatives to all of the filth that flooded the nickelodeons and eventually the theaters. A sizable Christian public still bemoans Hollywood filth and the prevalence of gratuitous images of sex, violence, and profanity. Starved for inoffensive content, these viewers will watch whatever they can get, even if it is not the most visually appealing option on the menu. As I have suggested in my discussion of *Fireproof*, Sherwood Pictures has become a recognizable brand to many moviegoers and, as a result, an easy choice when deciding what to watch.

Second, these films speak to many evangelical Christians' theology and experience of the world. The Kendrick brothers, for example, are not alone in thinking that God works the way they believe God does. Many viewers offered feedback on Amazon.com, the IMDb, or Beliefnet.com that they, or people they knew, had similar experiences to those depicted in the films. As I suggested in my discussions of the production of Sherwood Pictures' films, they are faithful to the world from which they come. In my conversation with Chris Bueno, he suggested that this faithfulness makes them, in a way, beyond reproach. He likened their ability to capture the world in which they live on film to the ways in which Spike Lee captures his urban experiences. Of course, he bemoaned the fact that many people are quick to criticize the Kendrick brothers but not Spike Lee.[31]

Leaders of the brand. The leadership of Sherwood Baptist Church *and* Sherwood Pictures. Seated, Michael Catt (senior pastor and executive producer). Back from left: Alex Kendrick (associate pastor, writer, producer, director, and actor), Jim McBride (executive producer and executive pastor), and Stephen Kendrick (senior associate pastor and writer-producer). Photograph by Todd Stone.

At the same time, the narratives that the Kendrick brothers and their filmmaking peers build around the production of their films appeal to evangelicals as well. The notion of an "us vs. them" relationship between participants in the church film movement and Hollywood fuels the "embattled and thriving" aspects of evangelical Christian identity. Furthermore, the underdog status of a low-budget, independent film outperforming its larger budget, big studio counterparts not only adds to their embattled feelings but echoes the David vs. Goliath narrative that appeals to so many Christians. In feedback posts, many viewers encouraged people to go see Sherwood Pictures' films or to buy the DVDs to "send Hollywood a message." Most of the films discussed here and the viewers who flock to them are of the "separational" brand of evangelical Christian media, even as they walk a fine line between it and "transformational" media by using the tools of the very culture apart from which they hope to stand.

Third, setting aside the tension between the sacred and the secular, many evangelical Christians find Sherwood Pictures' films so appealing because they genuinely feel ministered to through them. Recall Hendershot's discussion of the functions of evangelical media: "Beyond providing clean-cut entertainment, such media can also help people deal with emotional crises, teach them political lessons, instruct them in chastity and other Christian modes of behavior, or provide inspirational models for praise and worship."[32] Numerous stories that viewers posted on the *To Save a Life* website tell of younger viewers with suicidal thoughts managing to work through them after watching the film. On both the *Fireproof* website and blogs devoted to *The Love Dare*, viewers recount their experiences with both the film and the book and how they saved their marriages. Dozens of men posted on Twitter that they had been inspired to be better husbands and fathers after having seen *Courageous*. While we may question their ability to miraculously transform non-believers into believers, these films seem to be, as Hendershot puts it, instructing viewers in Christian modes of behavior.

Finally, I believe that there is a fourth reason behind the appeal of these films to so many evangelical Christian viewers, even if it is a tenuous one. I am still fascinated by the statements in which viewers acknowledge and quickly dismiss a particular film's poor aesthetic qualities and then talk about how great it is. In his definition of kitsch, Burch Brown says that it is art that many people "enjoy in God." While this is a rather nebulous idea, I believe it helps explain many viewers' reactions to these films. Recall David A. Rivera's assertion that he had to watch *Fireproof* with "spiritual eyes" in order to fully appreciate it. Or consider the countless other viewers who talked about "getting past" *Flywheel*'s or *Facing the Giants*' aesthetic weaknesses in order for God to work through those films. Perhaps the act of watching these films, for some viewers, is akin to a devotional practice as they lower their visual expectations, so to speak, while heightening their spiritual or theological awareness. This seems to be a fitting parallel to the ways in which the filmmakers themselves approach their work, sacrificing a concern for their films' visual qualities for their devotion to the films' messages.

Unfortunately, as I have suggested, this altered vision also creates blind spots to aspects of the films that might work against the very spiritual experience viewers hope to have while watching them. These viewers' inability or unwillingness to be more critical of these films allow some of them to make the bold claim that these are the best films ever made or that Hollywood simply cannot compare to these productions. Such hyperbolic statements are further examples of kitsch, particularly of Burch Brown's assertion that kitsch's "effects outrun its causes." The Kendrick brothers' hope that their films will change lives and save marriages is a lofty goal for the cast and crew of Sherwood Pictures, but one that is certainly admirable. On the other hand, viewers who assert that these are the best films ever made either do not watch many films or have been swept up in the throes of kitsch.

Conclusion

The wisdom of Ecclesiastes holds true yet again: there is nothing new under the sun. In my conversation with Chris Bueno, I told him about the efforts of Protestant ministers to establish film production, distribution, and exhibition networks in the early 1900s. He was shocked, having had no idea that such a history existed. For all their excitement over film production and theatrical releases, the members of the church film movement in the twenty-first century are just the latest chapter in the ongoing story of film and American religion. Lindvall has uncovered a vibrant history with both *The Silents of God* and *Sanctuary Cinema*. No doubt, other historians of both film and religion will continue to mine his discoveries and follow unexplored paths to new insights into the relationship between religion and popular culture and the histories of American film and religious experience.

We have seen that a vibrant church film movement existed from the late 1800s to the mid-1920s. Unfortunately, it was beset by a host of problems from within and without. A lack of internal support from other ministers, poor financial and logistical planning, delayed communications, the advent of radio and sound motion pictures, and, of course, the Depression cut short the life of church-based film production, distribution, and exhibition. Church-based filmmaking would go underground for decades as mainstream, secular Hollywood became, as Lindvall puts it, a religion of its own.[1] In doing so, as we have seen, it also co-opted Christianity's texts to create biblical epics that attracted significant crowds. As secular filmmaking hit its stride in the Studio Era, independent, avant-garde filmmaking would always fly well below the radar. The cultural revolutions of the '60s and '70s, however, begged for fresh cinematic voices. Evolutions in filmmaking technology made it easier and more affordable for those alternative voices to make their way into the mainstream. The digitalization of filmmaking two decades later soon shifted the balance of production power away from the studios and into the hands of independent, maverick filmmakers. As Ravid pointed out, soon aspiring filmmakers will be able to control every phase of a film's life, from production to exhibition. Today, the ability of an individual filmmaker to reach a mass audience has grown to unimaginable heights.

Sherwood Pictures and the rest of the church film movement are beneficiaries of these past and current changes in filmmaking technology and industry practices. The roadblocks that stalled the early church film movement in the mid-1920s no longer plague congregations attracted to film production. The Kendrick brothers pieced together $20,000 for their first production, which they only ever intended to exhibit locally. However, the wired culture in which we live enhanced word-of-mouth publicity and took the film through avenues and to locations beyond their wildest imaginations. It brought them connections with mainstream Hollywood companies who, rather than helping them produce their second film, simply helped distribute it in ways that Ravid highlighted in his essay. Given time, perhaps, Sherwood Pictures could one day handle this aspect of the business themselves. By keeping their budgets extremely low, seeing a return on their investments has never been a problem for Sherwood Pictures like it has been for other independent Christian studios like Gener8xion Films or Cloud Ten Pictures, for example, who spend anywhere between $2 and $11 million on productions that make a fraction of Sherwood's profit. Moreover, these low budgets allow the Kendricks to remain faithful to their message unlike other Christian filmmakers who accept financial contributions from outside sources that carry with them restrictions on their film's content.[2]

Even though they have enjoyed wider exposure with each subsequent theatrical release, Sherwood Pictures still employs a smart release strategy that embodies Reiss' notion of exhibiting in a variety of smaller markets rather than trying to win over a few larger ones. The websites for each of Sherwood's films are evidence that they grasp the importance of this, practically free, marketing tool. The websites for their first three films are all similar in appearance and functionality, but as I mentioned, the *Courageous* site has many more features that draw visitors further into the film and the production process. The *Courageous* Twitter account also fulfills Reiss' call for filmmakers to use such social networking features as both a way to advertise their film and establish a relationship with their audience. It is clear from the websites of their respective films and their partnership with Outreach Marketing that Sherwood is actively targeting the non-theatrical market as they sell event licenses for churches and encourage screenings at schools, businesses, and community organizations.

Such marketing allows them to focus less on their films' theatrical performances. While even the briefest of theatrical runs will ensure those involved with the distribution of Sherwood Pictures' films a return on their investment, like the wider filmmaking industry, Sherwood itself no doubt sees huge revenue streams from DVD and ancillary product sales. Though I have already listed the figures, they are worth highlighting again in this context. DVD sales of *Facing the Giants* are almost double that of box office returns. This should not be surprising given its limited theatrical release (441 theaters) and the ease of obtaining the DVD. *Fireproof* was released on almost double the number of theaters (839) and, along with increased visibility, had a box office take that tripled its predecessor. DVD sales almost equaled its box office performance. Yet more revenue poured in through sales of the *Fireproof Your Marriage* group kits and millions of copies of *The Love Dare*. *Flywheel* did not have a proper theatrical release, but we have seen what kind of business it did on DVD.

Of course, any success they have at the box office or through DVD sales is due to generous, free publicity. As it has grown, Sherwood Pictures has been featured in both mainstream and niche press articles from sources as diverse as *USA Today* and *Baptist Press* that focus on not just the films, but the production process as well. Sherwood Pictures has exploited the themes of their films, marriage and fatherhood for example, to great effect by connecting with organizations that make them the center of their ministries. Finally, as I suggested in the discussion of the supporters of the church film movement, Sherwood Pictures has one of the most marketable hooks of any evangelical Christian media ministry, namely their "little-studio-that-could" mentality. This speaks to both Reiss' encouragement to filmmakers to have a hook to sell their films as well as Einstein's recognition of the necessity of myth and story to build a faith brand.

In fact, all of these factors working together, from cheaper technology to changing means of communication, seem to be turning Sherwood Pictures into another faith brand.

Of course, one would be hard-pressed to accuse Sherwood Pictures of being in the business of faith branding with their initial release of *Flywheel* in 2003. As the Kendrick brothers frequently asserted, they only wanted to show their first film in their small town and, maybe, in theaters in surrounding towns. One never gets the sense, in listening to their DVD commentaries or reading interviews in the press, that the Kendrick brothers created *Flywheel* to promote Sherwood Pictures or Sherwood Baptist Church as a brand, especially not in the ways in which the representatives of Possibility Pictures say they want to be the "category leader" in faith-based filmmaking. While the Sherwood Pictures team consistently talks about their hopes that their films will change viewers' hearts and lead them to a relationship, or enhance their existing relationship, with Christ, there is no sense that they believe these relationships should be lived out in Sherwood Baptist Church or that other churches should follow a Sherwood Baptist Church model (like, for example, Saddleback or Willow Creek churches).[3] Nevertheless, the seeds of a faith brand seemed to be planted with this film and would come to fruition with their subsequent releases.

Though it was more financially successful and popular than *Flywheel*, *Facing the Giants* still does not qualify as a faith brand in the way Einstein envisions it. True, it was more extensively marketed than its predecessor and benefited from a wider, initial theatrical release and enjoyed a successful DVD release. While these realities fit in with much of Einstein's discussion of marketing religion, they are only a small part of Sherwood's success. Far more important are the producers' efforts to create stories about the productions of both *Flywheel* and *Facing the Giants*, which highlighted their low-budget, underdog status. The constant emphasis on low-budget, rough-around-the-edges productions endears audiences to Sherwood Pictures' output. Just as important as a wide theatrical release, a tiered DVD marketing strategy, and an engaging website, these stories no doubt drive consumers to purchase tickets and DVDs and to visit their films' websites to learn more about them. By the time Sherwood Pictures released its third feature, it was impossible for them to claim a lack of experience, even as they clung to a cheap production budget. Yet as this part of their story fades, they make up for it in new ways, particularly through ancillary products.

With the release of their third feature-length film, *Fireproof*, Sherwood Pictures becomes a full-blown faith brand, perhaps a cinematic equivalent to Joel Osteen or Rick Warren's ministries, if only on a smaller scale. Whereas Osteen and Warren can market themselves, and by extension their ministries, it is much more difficult for filmmakers to establish themselves as a brand. In their essay "Theatrical Release and the Launching of Motion Pictures," Charles C. Moul and Steven M. Shugan discuss the difficulty of branding motion pictures:

> Branding is conspicuously absent from both production and distribution in the motion picture industry. With a few exceptions (e.g., Pixar and Disney movies for children and families), most motion pictures fail to create significant links to the studios, distributors, and exhibitors who promote the movies. The only reputations that seem to be at work are those of the cast, the property (e.g., the book, play, or comic book), and, to a lesser extent, the director.[4]

However, we have seen that Sherwood Pictures has built a connection between their studio and a devoted fan-consumer base. The studio itself, based out of a church, creates a link not only between the producers and the promoters, but between the producers and the consumers as well. For a sizable audience, the name Sherwood Pictures has begun to speak volumes in ways that Pixar or Disney do for other viewers.

Sherwood Pictures' success in the evangelical Christian pop culture market depends heavily on their consistent self-identification as ministers, even as their films contain ambiguous spiritual, religious, or theological messages. As openly and unashamedly Christian, they do not have to play the marketing games that Disney and other mainstream Hollywood corporations do. In fact, the Kendrick brothers appeal to the culture war that Gibson helped fuel in the defense of his film. Such tactics not only attract, but solidify their audience. This "cross-cultural" tension aside, their films also appeal to a wide group of evangelical Christians because of their content. Sherwood Pictures, unlike Cloud Ten Pictures or Gener8xion Entertainment, tackles less "theologically problematic" subject matter. It is one thing to talk about a championship run from an undersized football team, but it is quite another to speculate about bodies suddenly disappearing or global warfare. Despite their lingering theological and religious ambiguity, this avoidance of controversial content also affects the tone of their films. As Chris Bueno told me, "[Sherwood Pictures'] films were the first Christian films that weren't either exploitation or bait-and-switch."[5]

Like Sherwood Pictures, much of the church film movement benefits, at least financially, from insularity. That is, given the size of their target audience, they can take evangelicals' money at the box office and through DVD sales without having to worry about breaking out of that conservative bubble. Unfortunately, this will not influence the broader culture in ways they feel divinely mandated to do. As we have seen, even some evangelicals have begun to complain about the banality of these films. This insularity might also be dangerous from a cultural perspective. Radosh argues, "[It] is precisely insularity that breeds intolerance.... When their only audience is other Christians, though, the feedback loop amplifies narrow-mindedness and inhibits self-examination."[6] This is unfortunate because Radosh, and other scholars like Schultze and Woods, Jr., know that evangelical Christian media can be a force for good in the broader popular culture.

Even as he is highly critical of it, Radosh recognizes the contributions that evangelical Christian pop culture can make to society at large. In his discussion of its proximity to secular pop culture, he argues that the former can be a force for moderation against the excesses of the latter. He continues:

> I loved American pop culture [...], and for the most part I still do. But the best aspects of Christian culture — the unabashed celebration of the transcendent, the challenge to crass materialism, the commitment to personal responsibility — helped me see more clearly what is too often lacking in secular entertainment and media. Jesus' radical message of brotherhood, selflessness, and dignity may be just the antidote to our contemporary ethos of shamelessness and overindulgence.[7]

Unfortunately, most participants in the church film movement are sacrificing their ability to think creatively about how to do this in exchange for well-worn narratives that they know will appeal to their base. This lack of imagination parallels the ways in which the church film movement of the 1920s largely chose criticism over creation. Most of the films discussed here might be wholesome alternatives to the excesses of popular culture, but they fail to speak creatively and effectively to the very brokenness that leads to those excesses.

In the conclusion to his chapter on kitsch, Burch Brown argues that the very future of a long-term viable Christianity depends on "a new and renewed artistry." He continues:

> That means recovering and developing diverse modes of artistic creativity and discernment that are popular without being kitsch. It also means cultivating in a serious and sustained manner religiously significant art that is not afraid at certain points to be extraordinarily disciplined, theologically searching, and profoundly imaginative — even if that means being unpopular.[8]

While films from the church film movement might minister to countless numbers of viewers, it is difficult to consider them as either disciplined, theologically searching, or profoundly imaginative. As a result, the genre is in desperate need of new voices, and fortunately, we can already see avenues through which those voices might come.

It should be clear from my preceding discussion of the church film movement that many of the congregations involved in it are communities with financial resources to spare. Moreover, they are often communities of early adopters, congregations who have been quicker to embrace technology and media and therefore more able to exploit them for their religious and socio-political effects. Yet they also all share, beyond financial resources and technical know-how, common conservative theological and cultural worldviews. Unfortunately, mainline or more liberal or progressive communities of faith, whose voices the movement desperately needs, often lack both the financial resources and technological know-how to enter into film production. If they happen to have these resources at hand, they are often unfamiliar with how changes in film production, distribution, and exhibition have made it possible for them to share their productions with a wider audience. I want to conclude this book by looking at both an organization and the production of an upcoming film and the implications that they have for the future of the church film movement.

Nicolosi may be one of the staunchest critics of the church film movement in its current form. However, she has not been content to simply sit back and let them have all the fun. In 1999, she founded the Act One Program (www.actoneprogram.com), an organization that trains aspiring Christian film executives, producers, directors, and writers. Unlike much of the church film movement, the founders of and participants in Act One seem to be more concerned with the style of their medium than with proselytizing. More accurately, they believe that the value of the medium and the message are inseparable. Act One focuses on four themes:

1. Artistry: "Mastering the craft of storytelling to move audiences through the radiance, wholeness, and harmony of beauty."
2. Professionalism: "Exceeding the best practices of the industry in excellence, honesty, trustworthiness, hard work, and a 'no excuses' mentality."
3. Meaning: "Telling stories of substance to beckon audiences toward truth, goodness, and even faith."
4. Prayer: "Sustaining a soul-nourishing spiritual journey of holiness and love made possible by individual and community prayer."[9]

Nicolosi and the other "Abel Christians" that make up Act One talk about "excellence [...] and 'the demands of beauty' [...] and of professionalism and the rigors of the craft."[10] In short, they believe that the beauty of a film can communicate the Gospel just as effectively as heavy-handed dialogue, and perhaps more so. Nicolosi's vision for Christians in Hollywood is that they basically be there as "artists and professionals of integrity and probity and nobility and skill" and that they be there "as presences of prayer and charity in the heart of every studio lot, office, set and writers room."[11] Individuals interested in participating in Act One can sign up for a variety of certificate programs that feature night and weekend courses as well as internships at mainstream Hollywood studios. While the courses help provide the know-how, the professional connections will no doubt enhance future productions that participants undertake.

Even if a community benefits from a member who has the ability and vision to begin film production, the problem of adequate finances still exists. But, this too is becoming less of an issue. While I agree with Nicolosi that making a good film is damn hard, it does not have to be damn expensive. In 2008, filmmaker Steve Taylor began raising money to make a film adaptation of Donald Miller's popular spiritual memoir *Blue Like Jazz*. Fundraising seemed to be progressing smoothly until one investor backed out, leaving the production team over $125,000 short of their necessary budget. When two fans of the project, Zach Pritchard and Jonathan Frazier, heard that the production might not move forward, they set up a website, www.savebluelikejazz.com, and organized a grassroots campaign to raise the necessary funds to continue production. Within ten days, they reached their goal of raising $125,000, and after 30 days, they had raised over $300,000. To fuel their fundraising campaign, Pritchard and Frazier used Kick Starter (www.kickstarter.com), a website that allows aspiring filmmakers to create an account, upload information about their project, set a target fundraising goal, and provide a place where supporters can make donations.[12]

This is the best example of the growing practice of crowd-funding, a phenomenon that exchanges a few big financial contributions for many smaller ones, much like the financial campaign that fueled Barack Obama's run to the White House. The film's supporters claim that it is one of the largest crowd-funded projects ever created. Like most crowd-funded projects, donors to the *Blue Like Jazz* production will not see a return on their investment. However, they will be "rewarded" in other ways. Everyone who helped fund the production will receive a T-shirt and a phone call from Donald Miller thanking them for their participation and keeping them up to date on production. Larger donors will receive a credit for "associate producer," which will no doubt make for a lengthy credit roll at the end of the film. Of course, for larger, more commercial projects, filmmakers and their donors can work out any number of financial arrangements. Large donors could demand a return on their investment from box office receipts or, more likely, DVD sales. Donors who give enough money could also exercise a measure of creative control during production, while smaller donors might be content to see their name at the end of the film.

While faith-based filmmakers might obtain enough money through crowd-funding, they still need people and equipment on which to spend it. As I have suggested throughout this book, equipment has consistently become cheaper and more user-friendly. Good high-definition cameras only cost a few thousand dollars while sophisticated editing software only costs a few hundred. Finding people to exploit that hardware and software to its full potential is even more important. Communities can take their crowd-funded budget and crowd-source their production. Thorough websites like craigslist.com, showbizjobs.com, entertainmentcareers.net, and mandy.com, communities can connect with aspiring directors, cinematographers, editors, designers, and actors. Producers can contact potential team members to see samples of their previous work and then make their choices based on need and budget. Some up-and-coming filmmakers might even be looking to expand their résumé while others might be looking to engage new material or donate their talents to non-profit work or work at a discounted rate. The possibilities truly are limitless.

Through this book, I have attempted to highlight what I believe is a growing, significant independent film movement taking place in the United States. At times, it has felt like wrestling a wild bull to get a handle on this material as new production companies, consulting groups, and films emerge that must be included in the conversation. Nevertheless, I believe that this book has provided a vision of the movement as it exists now, the history from which it has emerged, and the future that lies before it. Just as there is a limitless future for would-be participants in the church film movement, there are countless possibilities for scholarly research into it. To consider a few, scholars would do well to consider the work

No money? No problem. Fans of the upcoming film *Blue Like Jazz* rallied together and raised money through Kickstarter.com to continue production.

of African American religious filmmakers and networks like BlackChristianMovies.com and the African American Christian film list on ChristianCinema.com. Research into the religious aspects of Tyler Perry's film empire and its reception among black and white audiences, both secular and religious, is well past due. Finally, further research into the movement that I have begun to explore will most certainly benefit from interviews with its participants, not only to clarify lingering questions that I have about logistics of production, sources of finances, and revenue and profit division, but to also explicitly consider the ways in which the participants in the church film movement view their work as spiritual practice. Across all church-based film production studios, a common bond exists. Everyone who participates in the production of one of these films, from the executive producer down to the babysitting volunteer, views their work as a ministry, an attempt to spread the love of God and the message of salvation through film.

In the 1920s, Rev. James K. Shields had a vision that the church would commission filmmakers who would be more effective at spreading the gospel than their preaching and singing evangelist peers. Over eighty years later, his vision seems to be coming to fruition. Across the country, churches are making space for ministers of media, either by hiring outsiders or nurturing the cinematic visions of their members. These filmmaking ministers are taking up both their crosses and their camcorders to spread the Gospel message and are moving out of the sanctuary and into the Cineplex to share it.

Appendix: Internet Resources

Films

Amazing Grace: www.amazinggracemovie.com
The Chronicles of Narnia: Prince Caspian: http://adisney.go.com/disneyvideos/liveaction/princecaspian/
The Chronicles of Narnia: The Lion, the Witch and the Wardrobe: http://disney.go.com/disneypictures/narnia/
The Chronicles of Narnia: Prince Caspian: http://adisney.go.com/disneyvideos/liveaction/princecaspian/
Courageous: http://www.courageousmovie.com
End of the Spear: http://www.endofthespear.com
Facing the Giants: http://www.facingthegiants.com
Fireproof: http://www.fireproofthemovie.com
Flywheel: http://www.flywheelthemovie.com
The Grace Card: http://www.gracecardmovie.com
Letters to God: http://letterstogodthemovie.com
The Nativity Story: http://www.thenativitystory.com
Not Today: http://nottodaythemovie.wordpress.com/
One Night with the King: http://www.8x.com/onenight
To Save a Life: http://www.tosavealifemovie.com
The Ultimate Gift: http://www.theultimategift.com
What If...: http://www.thewhatifmovie.com/

Churches

Calvary Church of the Nazarene: http://www.memphiscalvary.org
Harvest Bible Chapel: http://www.harvestbiblechapel.org/
New Song Community Church: http://www.newsongchurch.com/
Sherwood Baptist Church: http://www.sherwoodbaptist.net
Yorba Linda Friends Church: http://www.ylfc.org

Production, Distribution and Marketing Companies

Act One Program: http://www.actoneprogram.com
Affirm Films: http://www.sonypictures.com/homevideo/affirmfilms/guides/
Anschutz Film Group: http://www.aegworldwide.com/05_affiliates/afg.html
Bristol Bay Productions: http://www.bristolbayproductions.com
Carmel Entertainment: http://www.carmelentertainmentgroup.com/
Fox Faith: http://www.foxfaith.com

Grace Hill Media: http://www.gracehillmedia.com
Graceworks Pictures: http://www.graceworkspictures.com
Jenkins Entertainment: http://jenkins-entertainment.com/
Ocean Avenue Entertainment: http://web.me.com/criscobueno/Ocean_Avenue_Entertainment/Ocean_Ave.html
Possibility Picutres: http://possibilitypicturesllc.com/
Provident Films: http://www.providentfilms.org
Sherwood Pictures: http://www.sherwoodpictures.com
10 West Studios: http://www.10weststudios.com
Walden Media: http://www.walden.com
WingCinema: http://web.me.com/criscobueno/Ocean_Avenue_Entertainment/WingCinema.html

Box Office Receipts and DVD Sales

Box Office Mojo: http://www.boxofficemojo.com
The Numbers: http://www.the-numbers.com

Film Reviews

Christian Answers: http://www.christiananswers.net
Hollywood Jesus: http://www.hollywoodjesus.com
Internet Movie Database: http://www.imdb.com
Rotten Tomatoes: http://www.rottentomatoes.com

Chapter Notes

Introduction

1. Alva Johnston, "Pictures Which Have Discarded Satan for Mother Church," *Vanity Fair* 27 (October 1931), 55, 84. Cited in Terry Lindvall, *Sanctuary Cinema: Origins of the Christian Film Industry* (New York: New York University Press, 2007), 218.

2. Texts include Richard Abel, *Americanizing the Movies and "Movie-Mad" Audiences, 1910–1914* (Berkeley: University of California Press, 2006), Larry May, *Screening Out the Past: The Birth of Mass Culture and the Motion Picture Industry* (Chicago: The University of Chicago Press, 1983), Robert Sklar, *Movie-Made America: A Cultural History of American Movies* (New York: Vintage Books, 1994), and Francis G. Couvares, ed., *Movie Censorship and American Culture* (Amherst: University of Massachusetts Press, 2006).

3. The out-of-control budget (its original $2 million budget ballooned to over $44 million) and behind-the-scenes scandals during the production of *Cleopatra* (1963, 20th Century-Fox) epitomized the demise of studio epics.

4. Timothy K. Beal and Tod Linafelt, Introduction, *Mel Gibson's Bible: Religion, Popular Culture, and The Passion of the Christ*, ed. Beal and Linafelt (Chicago: The University of Chicago Press, 2006), 2.

5. Hanna Rosin, "Can Jesus Save Hollywood?," *The Atlantic.com*, December 2005, http://www.theatlantic.com/magazine/archive/2005/12/can-jesus-save-hollywood/4398/ (accessed on January 4, 2011).

6. Box Office Mojo, http://boxofficemojo.com/movies/?id=facingthegiants.htm (accessed November 4, 2010).

7. Terry Lindvall, "Hollywood Chronicles: Toward an Intersection of Church History and Film History," in *Reframing Theology and Film: New Focus for an Emerging Discipline*, ed. Robert K. Johnston (Grand Rapids: Baker Academic), 126–42.

8. Craig Detweiler, *Into the Dark: Seeing the Sacred in the Top Films of the 21st Century* (Grand Rapids: Baker Academic), 26.

9. Ibid., 27, 28.

10. Lindvall, "Hollywood Chronicles," 127, 128.

11. Ibid., 134.

12. Ibid., 134.

13. Ibid., 137.

Chapter 1

1. Lindvall, *Sanctuary Cinema*, 19.

2. Ibid., 107.

3. Michael Morris, Class Lecture, "Religion and the Cinema," Fall 2006, The Graduate Theological Union, Berkeley, California.

4. Adele Reinhartz, *Jesus of Hollywood* (New York: Oxford University Press, 2007), 252.

5. Morris, Class Lecture.

6. Simon Louvish, *Cecil B. DeMille: A Life in Art* (New York: Thomas Dunne Books, 2007), 258.

7. Michael Morris, Class Lecture.

8. See Judith Weisenfeld, *Hollywood Be Thy Name: African American Religion in American Film, 1929–1949* (Berkeley: University of California Press, 2007), 52–87.

9. Peter E. Dans, *Christians in the Movies: A Century of Saints and Sinners* (Lanham, Maryland: Rowman & Littlefield Publishers, 2009), xvii.

10. See Weisenfeld, 19–51.

11. Thomas Doherty, *Pre-Code Hollywood: Sex, Immorality, and Insurrection in American Cinema* (New York: Columbia University Press, 1999), 321.

12. Lee Grieveson, *Policing Cinema: Movies and Censorship in Early-Twentieth-Century America* (Berkeley: University of California Press, 2004), 67, 68.

13. Lindvall, *Sanctuary Cinema*, 46.

14. Ibid., 6.

15. Ibid., 52.

16. Ibid., 111, 112–13.

17. Tom Gunning, "The Cinema of Attractions: Early Film, Its Spectator and the Avant-Garde," in *Early Film: Space, Frame, Narrative*, ed. Thomas Elsaesser and Adam Barker (London: British Film Institute, 1989), 56–62.

18. Lindvall, *Sanctuary Cinema*, 184, 185.

19. Ibid., 185.

20. Ibid., 186.

21. These Protestant ministers contribute to a rich history of the relationship between Protestantism and the visual arts as illustrated most notably by David Morgan, *Protestants and Pictures: Religion, Visual Culture, and the Age of American Mass Production* (New York: Oxford University Press, 1999).

22. Lindvall, *Sanctuary Cinema*, 118–19.
23. Ibid., 130.
24. Ibid., 131–32.
25. Ibid., 140–41.
26. Ibid., 143.
27. Ibid., 147.
28. Ibid., 163.
29. Ibid., 170.
30. Ibid., 173–74.
31. At a raucous, three-day party in 1921, a young starlet became severely ill and died four days later. Newspapers went wild with the story, alleging that popular silent screen comedian Roscoe "Fatty" Arbuckle had killed Virginia Rappe with while savagely raping her. Though the newspapers of the day reveled in gory rumors, juries found little evidence that Arbuckle was in any way connected with Rappe's death.
32. Lindvall, *Sanctuary Cinema*, 148.
33. Ibid., 148.
34. Lindvall, *Sanctuary Cinema*, 219–20.
35. The Jesus Film Project, "History," http://www.jesusfilm.org/aboutus/history (accessed January 4, 2011).
36. Hendershot, 185.
37. Ibid., 188.
38. "Plans for Big Budget *Left Behind* Remake," October 13, 2010, http://www.cloudtenpictures.com/site2/news_article.php?id=42 (accessed November 11, 2010).
39. Ibid.
40. Hendershot, 198.
41. Box Office Mojo, http://boxofficemojo.com/movies/?id=omegacode2.htm (accessed January 10, 2011).
42. Hendershot, 198.
43. Ibid., 202.
44. Ibid., 204.
45. See Barbara Rossing, *The Rapture Exposed: The Message of Hope in the Book of Revelation* (New York: Basic Books, 2004).
46. Terry Lindvall and Andrew Quicke, *Celluloid Cinema: The Emergence of the Christian Film Industry* (New York: New York University Press, 2011).

Chapter 2

1. Box Office Mojo, http://boxofficemojo.com/movies/?id=passionofthechrist.htm (accessed November 10, 2010).
2. Timothy K. Beal and Tod Linafelt, Introduction, *Mel Gibson's Bible: Religion, Popular Culture, and The Passion of the Christ*, ed. Beal and Linafelt (Chicago: The University of Chicago Press, 2006), 2.
3. Jose Marquez, "Lights! Camera! Action!," in *Mel Gibson's Bible: Religion, Popular Culture, and The Passion of the Christ*, ed. Timothy K. Beal and Tod Linafelt (Chicago: The University of Chicago Press, 2006), 177–86.
4. William G. Little, "Jesus's Extreme Makeover," in *Mel Gibson's Bible: Religion, Popular Culture, and The Passion of the Christ*, ed. Timothy K. Beal and Tod Linafelt (Chicago: The University of Chicago Press, 2006), 169–76.
5. See Parts II and III of J. Shawn Landres and Michael Berenbaum, eds., *After The Passion Is Gone: American Religious Consequences* (Walnut Creek, California: AltaMira Press, 2004), and Parts I and II of S. Brent Plate, ed., *Re-Viewing The Passion: Mel Gibson's Film and Its Critics* (New York: Palgrave Macmillan, 2004).
6. See Part III of Plate.
7. Beal and Linafelt, 7.
8. Sharon Waxman, "Hollywood Rethinking Films of Faith After *"Passion,"* *The New York Times*, March 15, 2004, http://query.nytimes.com/gst/fullpage.html?res=9906E7DC1F3EF936A25750C0A9629C8B63&sec=&spon=&pagewanted=2 (accessed November 10, 2010).
9. Charles Laurence, "After *The Passion*, Hollywood Asks: What About the Sequel?," *The Telegraph*, March 20, 2004, http://www.telegraph.co.uk/news/worldnews/northamerica/usa/1457429/After-The-Passion,-Hollywood-asks-what-about-the-sequel.html (accessed November 10, 2010).
10. Ibid., italics mine.
11. Filmmakers as diverse as Cecil B. DeMille and Rev. James K. Shields offered advance screenings of their religious productions to audiences of ministers.
12. Peter A. Maresco, "Mel Gibson's *The Passion of the Christ*: Market Segmentation, Mass Marketing and Promotion, and the Internet," *Journal of Religion and Popular Culture* 8 (Fall 2004), http://www.usask.ca/relst/jrpc/art8-melgibsonmarketing.html (accessed November 10, 2010).
13. Mark Silk, "Almost a Culture War: The Making of *The Passion* Controversy," in *After The Passion Is Gone: American Religious Consequences*, ed. J. Shawn Landres and Michael Berenbaum (Walnut Creek, California: AltaMira Press, 2004), 29.
14. J. Shawn Landres and Michael Berenbaum, Introduction, *After The Passion Is Gone: American Religious Consequences*, ed. Landres and Berenbaum (Walnut Creek: California: AltaMira Press, 2004), 3.
15. Maresco, "Mel Gibson's The Passion…."
16. William J. Cork, "Passionate Blogging: Interfaith Controversy and the Internet," in *After The Passion Is Gone: American Religious Consequences*, ed. J. Shawn Landres and Michael Berenbaum (Walnut Creek, California: AltaMira Press, 2004), 35–46.
17. Terry Lindvall, William J. Brown, and John D. Keeler, "Audience Responses to *The Passion of the Christ*," *Journal of Religion and Media* 6 (2007): 87–107.
18. Lindvall, Brown, and Keeler, 102.
19. Ibid., 103, 104.
20. Terry Lindvall and Andrew Quicke, "Moving from Films to Digital Movies," in *Understanding Evangelical Media*, ed. Quentin J. Schultze and Robert H. Woods, Jr. (Downers Grove, Illinois: Intervarsity Press, 2008), 68.
21. Sharon Waxman, "Hollywood's Newfound Passion for Christ," *International Herald Tribune*, July

20, 2005, http://www.iht.com/articles/2005/07/19/business/christians.php?page=1 (accessed November 10, 2010).

22. Laura Coverson, "Fox Pursues the Flock," ABC News, September 21, 2006,http://abcnews.go.com/Entertainment/story?id=2472082&page=1 (accessed November 14, 2010).

23. Mark Moring, "Fox Feeds the Flock," *Christianity Today.com*, October 3, 2006, http://www.christianitytoday.com/movies/interviews/2006/foxfaith.html?start=1 (accessed November 10, 2010).

24. Steven Zeitchik, "Weinsteins Put Faith in Film: Company Forms Christian-based Distribution Label," *Variety*, December 6, 2006, http://www.variety.com/article/VR1117955243.html?categoryid=13&cs=1 (accessed November 10, 2010).

25. Ibid.

26. Affirm Films, http://www.sonypictures.com/homevideo/affirmfilms/guides/, (accessed November 10, 2010).

27. AEG Worldwide, http://www.aegworldwide.com/05_affiliates/afg.html (accessed November 10, 2010). For information on early twentieth-century views of cinema as moral and educational uplift, see Grieveson, *Policing Cinema: Movies and Censorship in Early-Twentieth-Century America*.

28. Ibid.

29. Kathy Bruner, "Thinking Outside the Tribal TV Box," in *Understanding Evangelical Media*, ed. Quentin J. Schultze and Robert H. Woods, Jr. (Downers Grove, Illinois: Intervarsity Press, 2008), 302 n. 6.

30. AEG Worldwide, http://www.aegworldwide.com.

31. BBC News, "Profile: Tycoon Philip Anschutz," July 5, 2006, http://news.bbc.co.uk/2/hi/uk_news/5150192.stm (accessed November 10, 2010).

32. Provident Films, http://www.providentfilms.org/about.php, accessed July 6, 2010.

33. Lindvall and Quicke, 63.

34. Grace Hill Media, http://www.gracehillmedia.com/aboutus/ (accessed November 10, 2010).

35. Ted Baehr founded Movieguide (www.movieguide.org), a conservative religious website that provides film reviews and commentary on the industry.

36. http://www.the-numbers.com/movies/2005/LWWRB.php (accessed November 13, 2010).

37. Mick LaSalle, "Children Open a Door and Step into an Enchanted World of Good and Evil — the Name of the Place is *Narnia*," *The San Francisco Chronicle*, December 9, 2005, http://www.sfgate.com/cgi-bin/article.cgi?f=/c/a/2005/12/09/DDG9QG4FJS1.DTL&type=movies (accessed November 10, 2010).

38. Roger Ebert, Review of *The Chronicles of Narnia: The Lion, the Witch, and the Wardrobe*, *Chicago Sun Times*, December 8, 2005, http://rogerebert.suntimes.com/apps/pbcs.dll/article?AID=/20051207/REVIEWS/51203001/1023 (accessed November 10, 2010).

39. http://www.the-numbers.com/movies/2008/NARN2.php (accessed May 10, 2009).

40. Peter T. Chattaway, Review of *The Chronicles of Narnia: Prince Caspian*, Christianity Today, May 16, 2008, http://www.christianitytoday.com/movies/reviews/2008/princecaspian.html (accessed November 10, 2010).

41. Kenneth Turan, Review of *The Chronicles of Narnia: Prince Caspian*, *The Los Angeles Times*, May 16, 2008, http://www.latimes.com/entertainment/news/reviews/la-et-narnia16-2008may16,0,1410930.story (accessed November 10, 2010).

42. David Criswell, Review of *The Chronicles of Narnia: Prince Caspian*, Christian Answers, http://christiananswers.net/spotlight/movies/2008/chroniclesofnarnia2008.html?zoom_highlight=prince+caspian (accessed November 10, 2010).

43. http://www.the-numbers.com/movies/2006/NATVT.php (accessed November 10, 2010).

44. A.O. Scott, "The Virgin Mary as a Teenager with Worries," *The New York Times*, December 1, 2006, http://movies2.nytimes.com/2006/12/01/movies/01nati.html (accessed November 10, 2010).

45. The Numbers, http://www.the-numbers.com/movies/2006/ONWTK.php (accessed November 10, 2010).

46. Russ Breimeier, Review of *One Night with the King*, Christianity Today, October 13, 2006, http://www.christianitytoday.com/movies/reviews/2006/onenightwiththeking.html (accessed November 10, 2010).

47. *One Night with the King* Press Release, http://www.8x.com/onenight/epk.html (accessed November 10, 2010).

48. http://www.the-numbers.com/movies/2006/ENDSP.php (accessed November 10, 2010).

49. Greg Wright, Review of *End of the Spear*, Hollywood Jesus, December 13, 2005, http://www.hollywoodjesus.com/comments/greg/2005/12/end-of-spear.html (accessed January 5, 2011).

50. http://www.the-numbers.com/movies/2007/AMGRC.php (accessed January 5, 2011).

51. http://www.the-numbers.com/movies/2007/ULGFT.php (accessed November 10, 2010).

52. Mark Moring, "Fox Faith: Is It Working?," *Christianity Today*, October 9, 2007, http://www.christianitytoday.com/movies/news/2007/foxfaithworking.html (accessed November 10, 2010).

53. Joe Leydon, Review of *The Ultimate Gift*, *Variety*, March 8, 2007, http://www.variety.com/review/VE1117933023.html?categoryid=31&cs=1 (accessed November 10, 2010).

54. Mark Olsen, Review of *The Ultimate Gift*, *The Los Angeles Times*, March 9, 2007, http://www.calendarlive.com/printedition/calendar/cl-et-gift9mar09,0,7711662.story (accessed November 10, 2010).

55. Scott, "The Virgin Mary as a Teenager with Worries."

56. Carlyle Ellis, "The Parson Who Believed in Pictures," *Everybody's Magazine* 36 (February 1917): 140–43. Reprinted in *The Silents of God: Selected Issues and Documents in Silent American Film and Religion, 1908–1925*, ed. Terry Lindvall (Lanham, Maryland: Scarecrow Press, 2001), 166.

57. Michael Morris, e-mail message to author, May 6, 2009.

58. Criswell, "Review of *The Chronicles of Narnia: Prince Caspian*," on-line article.
59. Wright, Review of *End of the Spear*, on-line article.
60. Ruth Vasey, *The World According to Hollywood, 1918–1939* (Madison: The University of Wisconsin Press, 1997), 136.
61. Mark I. Pinsky, "The Reader, the Evangelists, and the Wardrobe," *Harvard Divinity Bulletin* 34 (Winter 2006), http://www.hds.harvard.edu/news/bulletin_mag/articles/34-1_pinsky.html (accessed November 10, 2010).
62. Ibid.
63. Mark Moring, "Amazing Abolitionist," *Christianity Today*, February 22, 2007, http://www.christianitytoday.com/ct/2007/march/18.34.html (accessed November 10, 2010).
64. Michael Foust, "Amazing Grace Film About Wilberforce Called Inspirational," *BaptistPress.com*, February 2, 2007, http://www.bpnews.net/bpnews.asp?ID=24883 (accessed November 10, 2010).
65. Charles Colson and Anne Morse, "The Wilberforce Strategy," *Christianity Today*, February 19, 2007, http://www.christianitytoday.com/ct/2007/february/45.132.html (accessed November 10, 2010).
66. Waxman, "Hollywood's Newfound Passion for Christ."
67. Ibid.
68. Quentin J. Schultze, Introduction, *Understanding Evangelical Media: The Changing Face of Christian Communication*, ed. Schultze and Robert H. Woods, Jr. (Downers Grove, Illinois: InterVarsity Press, 2008), 295 n. 1.
69. Quentin J. Schultze and Robert H. Woods, Jr., "Being Fairly Self-Critical About Evangelical Media," in *Understanding Evangelical Media: The Changing Face of Christian Communication*, ed. Schultze and Woods, Jr. (Downers Grove, Illinois: InterVarsity Press, 2008), 282.
70. Lindvall, *Sanctuary Cinema*, 176.
71. Waxman, "Hollywood's Newfound Passion for Christ."
72. Waxman, "Hollywood Rethinking Films of Faith After *Passion*."
73. Ibid.
74. Suzanne Goldenberg, "Hollywood Finds Christ as Fox Faith Plans Series of Religious Movies," *The Guardian*, September 20, 2006, http://www.guardian.co.uk/world/2006/sep/20/religion.media (accessed January 6, 2011).
75. Landres and Berenbaum, 14, italics mine.
76. Hendershot, 79.

Chapter 3

1. All information on the history of Sherwood Baptist Church available from http://www.sherwoodbaptist.net/templates/cussherwoodbc/details.asp?id=33770&PID=326931 (accessed November 15, 2010).
2. The Southern Baptist Convention Cooperative Program, http://www.cpmissions.net/2003/what%20is%20cp.asp (accessed January 5, 2011).
3. "Baptist Faith and Message," http://www.sbc.net/bfm/bfm2000.asp (accessed November 14, 2010).
4. Ibid.
5. Daniel Radosh, *Rapture Ready: Adventures in the Parallel Universe of Christian Pop Culture* (New York: Soft Skull Press, 2010), 249.
6. Chris Carpenter, "Facing New Giants: On the Set of *Fireproof*," ChristianBroadcastingNetwork.com, February 2008, http://www.cbn.com/entertainment/screen/carpenter-FireproofSet_0208.aspx (accessed November 16, 2010).
7. Lindvall and Quicke, "Moving from Films to Digital Movies," 88.
8. Richard Rogers, "Special Assignment: *Fireproof*," WRDW.com, November 5, 2008, http://www.wrdw.com/entertainment/headlines/33800894.html (accessed November 14, 2010).
9. Lindvall, *Sanctuary Cinema*, 1.
10. Unless otherwise noted, all information on the making of *Flywheel* comes from the directors' commentary track and behind-the-scenes featurettes on the DVD edition of the film.
11. Alex Kendrick, *Flywheel* DVD Director's Commentary.
12. *Flywheel* Press Release, "The *Flywheel* Time Line," http://www.flywheelthemovie.com (accessed July 22, 2010).
13. Rebecca Easterling, "The Making of *Flywheel*, *Facing the Giants*, and *Fireproof*," ChristianWebNews.com, February 12, 2009, http://www.cwnewz.com/content/view/589/2/ (accessed July 22, 2010).
14. For more information on the Dove Foundation and its rating system, visit www.dove.org.
15. "Fireproof: Discussing Filmmaking with Brothers, Writers, Producers, and Director Alex and Stephen Kendrick," ChristianCinema.com, September 1, 2008, www.christiancinema.com/catalog/newsdesk_info.php?newsdesk_id=747 (accessed November 15, 2010).
16. Greg Wright, "Low Budget, Big Heart," Hollywood Jesus, http://www.hollywoodjesus.com/DVDDetail.cfm/i/396174A5-B867-6858-42CD4CDF67950CA2/ia/396390CE-EF59-A215-C81DA47F232B19CF (accessed November 8, 2010).
17. M.J. Thomas, "The worst acting ever…I'd rather have been doing dishes," Amazon, February 22, 2008, http://www.amazon.com/Flywheel-Directors-Rosetta-Harris-Armstrong/product-reviews/B000VECADK/ref=cm_cr_pr_hist_2?ie=UTF8&showViewpoints=0&filterBy=addTwoStar (accessed November 15, 2010).
18. Thomas Johnston, "What can I say? Pure trash!," IMDb, May 28, 2005, http://www.imdb.com/title/tt0425027/usercomments?start=30 (accessed November 15, 2010).
19. allen808, "Awesome movie; Excellent story; A must see!!," IMDb, December 27, 2004, http://www.imdb.com/title/tt0425027/usercomments?start=0 (accessed November 15, 2010).
20. MotherLodeBeth, "Great Story," Amazon, May

4, 2008, http://www.amazon.com/Flywheel-Directors-Rosetta-Harris-Armstrong/product-reviews/B000VECADK/ref=cm_cr_pr_hist_5?ie=UTF8&showViewpoints=0&filterBy=addFiveStar (accessed November 15, 2010).

21. shanghai777, "Surprisingly good," IMDb, February 25, 2005, http://www.imdb.com/title/tt0425027/usercomments (accessed November 15, 2010).

22. bRaDWeston, "Heartwarming...story triumphs low budget!," IMDb, December 22, 2004, http://www.imdb.com/title/tt0425027/usercomments (accessed November 15, 2010).

23. David A. Rivera, "The Establishment of a Ministry," Amazon, February 13, 2009, http://www.amazon.com/Flywheel-Directors-Rosetta-Harris-Armstrong/product-reviews/ B000VECADK (accessed November 15, 2010), italics mine.

Chapter 4

1. Unless otherwise noted, all information on the making of *Facing the Giants* comes from the director's commentary and behind-the-scenes featurettes on the DVD edition of the film.

2. Carmel Entertainment, http://www.carmelentertainmentgroup.com/Home.html (accessed January 5, 2011).

3. All distribution information on *Facing the Giants* from personal interview with Chris Bueno, October 8, 2010.

4. "*Facing the Giants* Sports Advisory Letter," Portable Document Format (PDF), http://www.facingthegiants.com/dvdfaith.php (accessed November 15, 2010).

5. The link now takes visitors to the website for *Courageous* where they can enter their email address at the *Facing the Giants* site to access the complete study guide.

6. For articles on the controversy, see Mark Moring, "Facing the Critics," *Christianity Today*, September 26, 2006, http://www.christianitytoday.com/ct/movies/interviews/2006/alexkendrick.html (accessed November 15, 2010), John Jalsevac, "*Facing the Giants* Rated PG for 'Mature Themes' Not Christianity: MPAA," Life Site News, June 20, 2006, http://www.lifesitenews.com/ldn/2006/jun/06062001.html (accessed November 15, 2010), and Sam Hananel, "Lawmakers concerned about Christian film's PG rating," FredericksburgStar.com, July 15, 2006, http://fredericksburg.com/News/FLS/2006/072006/07152006/203756?rss=local (accessed November 15, 2010).

7. Chris Bueno, personal interview.

8. Box Office Mojo, http://www.boxofficemojo.com/movies/?id=facingthegiants.htm (accessed November 4, 2010) and The Numbers, http://www.the-numbers.com/movies/2006/FCGNT.php (accessed November 4, 2010).

9. Joe Leydon, Review of *Facing the Giants*, *Variety*, October 1, 2005, http://www.variety.com/review/VE1117931756.html?categoryid=31&cs=1 (accessed January 5, 2011).

10. Leydon, "*Facing the Giants*," on-line article.

11. Josh Rosenblatt, "*Facing the Giants*," *Austin Chronicle*, November 16, 2006, http://www.austinchronicle.com/gyrobase/Calendar/Film?Film=oid%3a417777 (accessed January 6, 2011).

12. Josh Hurst, "*Facing the Giants*," *Christianity Today*, September 29, 2006, http://www.christianitytoday.com/ct/movies/reviews/2006/facingthegiants.html (accessed January 6, 2011).

13. Ibid.

14. Melinda Ledman, "Heavy-Handed Messages, But True," Hollywood Jesus, 2006, http://www.hollywoodjesus.com/DVDDetail.cfm/i/2EDA8C02-B003-0230-EB9644DF13B91C59/ia/2EE18AB8-E6AB-A9B4-1(ED520603F1EF70 (accessed January 6, 2011).

15. Melisa Pollock, "*Facing the Giants*," Christian Answers, http://christiananswers.net/spotlight/movies/2006/facingthegiants2006.html?zoom_highlight=facing+the+giants (accessed January 6, 2011).

16. Miked-61, "Absolutely incredible!," IMDb, September 15, 2006, http://www.imdb.com/title/tt0805526/usercomments (accessed November 16, 2010).

17. Pollock, "*Facing the Giants*," viewer comments.

18. Ibid.

19. Ibid.

20. For discussions and critiques of the prosperity gospel, see Michael S. Hamilton, "More Money, More Ministry: The Financing of American Evangelicalism Since 1945," in *More Money, More Ministry: Money and Evangelicals in Recent North American History*, ed. Larry Eskridge and Mark A. Noll (Grand Rapids: Wm. B. Eerdmans Publishing Co., 2000), 104–38.

21. Mara Einstein points this out quite insightfully in her discussion of Joel Osteen Ministries in her book *Brands of Faith*. She shows how his televised sermons are spiritual advertisements for his books, CDs, and tours, "An Evening with Joel."

22. Mark Moring, "Facing the Critics," article on-line.

23. Alex and Stephen Kendrick, *Facing the Giants* DVD Director's Commentary.

24. Matthew 5:10–12.

Chapter 5

1. Unless otherwise noted, all information about the production of *Fireproof* comes from either the director's commentary or behind-the-scenes featurettes on the DVD version of the film.

2. Carpenter, "Facing New Giants: On the Set of *Fireproof*."

3. Information on the distribution of *Fireproof* from Chris Bueno, personal interview, October 8, 2010.

4. Ricki Barker, "The Love Dare Wedding Edition is now available," *Albany Herald*, April 4, 2010, http://www.albanyherald.com/home/headlines/89854892.html (accessed November 17, 2010).

5. Josh Kimball, "*Love Dare* Racks Up Big Num-

bers Ahead of *Fireproof* Release," *The Christian Post*, September 15, 2008, http://www.christianpost.com/article/20080915/-love-dare-racks-up-big-numbers-ahead-of-fireproof-release/ (accessed November 17, 2010).

6. Paperback Advice Best-seller List, *The New York Times*, January 9, 2011, http://www.nytimes.com/best-sellers-books/2011-01-09/paperback-advice/list.html (accessed January 6, 2011).

7. Monique Sondag, "The Love Dare — New Book and #1 iPhone App," Christian News Wire, September 29, 2009, http://www.christiannewswire.com/news/9031711687.html (accessed November 17, 2010).

8. Barker, "The Love Dare Wedding Edition is now available."

9. Amazon product description, http://www.amazon.com/Fireproof-Your-Marriage-Couples-Kit/dp/0978715373/ref=sr_1_2?ie=UTF8&qid=1290098120&sr=8-2 (accessed November 17, 2010).

10. Amazon product description, http://www.amazon.com/Couples-Study-Bundle-Books-Guides/dp/0978715349 (accessed November 17, 2010).

11. Amazon product description, http://www.amazon.com/Fireproof-Your-Marriage-Leaders-Participants/dp/0978715381 (accessed November 17, 2010).

12. Amazon product description, http://www.amazon.com/Fireproof-Your-Life-Michael-Catt/dp/0875089844/ref=sr_1_1?ie=UTF8&s=books&qid=1290098753&sr=1-1 (accessed November 17, 2010).

13. *Fireproof* DVD cover.

14. *Fireproof* resources, http://www.fireproofthemovie.com/resources/ (accessed November 17, 2010).

15. *Fireproof* business resources, http://www.fireproofmymarriage.com/businesses.php (accessed November 17, 2010).

16. *Fireproof* couples resources, www.fireproofyourmarriage.com/couplesquiz/ (accessed November 17, 2010).

17. http://www.the-numbers.com/movies/2008/FRPRF.php (accessed November 18, 2010).

18. As I wrote this, I had yet to gain access to financial reports regarding those ancillary products.

19. Joe Leydon, Review of *Fireproof*, *Variety*, September 26, 2008, http://www.variety.com/review/VE1117938520.html?categoryid=31&cs=1 (accessed November 15, 2010).

20. Neil Genzlinger, "Putting Out Fires, Reigniting Passions," *The New York Times*, September 27, 2008, http://movies.nytimes.com/2008/09/27/movies/27proof.html?ref=movies (accessed January 6, 2011).

21. Michael Hardy, Review of *Fireproof*, *Boston Globe*, September 27, 2008, http://www.boston.com/movies/display?disaply=movie&id=12208 (accessed June 11, 2010).

22. Chris Willman, Review of *Fireproof*, *Entertainment Weekly*, October 10, 2008, http://www.ew.com/wearticle/0..20229911,00.html (accessed June 11, 2010).

23. Peter Chattaway, Review of *Fireproof*, *Christianity Today*, September 26, 2008, http://www.christianitytoday.com/ct/movies/reviews/2008/fireproof.html (accessed June 11, 2010).

24. hippiemama, "From a modern female Christian point of view," Amazon, March 14, 2010, http://www.amazon.com/Fireproof-Kirk-Cameron/product-reviews/B001KEHAFI/ref=cm_cr_dp_hist_1?ie=UTF8&showViewpoints=0&filterBy=addOneStar (accessed November 15, 2010).

25. antsi, "+ and — reviews reflect the reviewers more than the movie," Amazon, February 3, 2009, http://www.amazon.com/Fireproof-Kirk-Cameron/dp/B001KEHAFI//ref=sr_1_1?ie=UTF8&qid=1290108996&sr=8-1 (accessed November 15, 2010).

26. Taraden Lyndaker, "Fireproof — Awesome," Amazon, November 24, 2008, http://www.amazon.com/Fireproof-Kirk-Cameron/product-reviews/B001KEHAFI/ref=cm_cr_pr_hist_5?ie=UTF8&showViewpoints=0&filterBy=addFiveStar (accessed November 18, 2010).

27. Harold Wolf, "If You Buy Only One DVD This Year — Make This Your Choice," Amazon.com, October 16, 2008, http://www.amazon.com/Fireproof-Kirk-Cameron/product-reviews/B001KEHAFI/ref=cm_cr_pr_hist_5?ie=UTF8&showViewpoints=0&filterBy=addFiveStar (accessed November 18, 2010).

28. reluctant techie, "Jesus approved video for the non-secular," Amazon, June 1, 2010, http://www.amazon.com/Fireproof-Kirk-Cameron/product-reviews/B001KEHAFI/ref=cm_cr_dp_hist_1?ie=UTF8&showViewpoints=0&filterBy=addOneStar (accessed November 15, 2010).

29. http://40daylovedare.blogspot.com/ (accessed November 18, 2010).

30. http://www.40daylovedare.com/stories.asp (accessed November 18, 2010).

31. "*Fireproof*: Discussing Filmmaking With Brothers, Writers, Producers, and Director Alex and Stephen Kendrick."

Chapter 6

1. "Sherwood Pictures Announces *Courageous*," Coming Soon, November 15, 2009, http://www.comingsoon.net/news/movienews.php?id=60921 (accessed October 21, 2011).

2. http://www.courageousmovie.com (accessed October 21, 2011).

3. Danah M. Boyd and Nicole B. Ellison, "Social Network Sites: Definition, History, and Scholarship," *Journal of Computer-Mediated Communication* (13) 1 2007 http://jcmc.indiana.edu/vol13/issue1/boyd.ellison.html (accessed October 21, 2011).

4. http://www.facebook.com/facebook?sk=info (accessed October 21, 2011).

5. http://www.twitter.com/about (accessed October 21, 2011).

6. "A Conversation with Evan Williams," Web 2.0 Summit 2009: Evan Williams and John Battelle, O'Reilly Media, October 21, 2009, www.youtube.com/watch?v=p5jXcgZnEaO&fmt=18 (accessed May 28, 2010).

7. Stuart Tunton, "Twitter Earned Dell $9 Million," *PC Pro*, March 3, 2010, http://www.pcpro.co.

uk/news/enterprise/356044/twitter-earned-dell-9-million, (accessed May 28, 2010).

8. Marian Salzman, "Why You Need to Twitter," CNBC, February 12, 2009, http://www.cnbc.com/id/29163055/salman_why_you_need_to_twitter (accessed January 7, 2011).

9. "Sherwood Pictures Announces *Courageous*," article on-line.

10. All references to Twitter posts from @CourageousMovie in this chapter can be found on-line at http://www.twitter.com/courageousmovie. If you have the time and patience, you can trace your way all the way back to their earliest posts.

11. Michael Foust, "*Courageous* is amazing (& better than *Fireproof*)," *Baptist Press*, June 20, 2011, http://www.bpnews.net/BPFirstPerson.asp?ID=35579 (accessed October 21, 2011).

12. With the inclusion of Latino characters, the site is also available in Spanish in a trimmed-down format.

13. "Watching the Film Develop," *Courageous* Blog Post, May 17, 2010, www.courageousthemovie.com/blog/ (accessed May 27, 2010).

14. http://www.courageousmovie.com/takeaction (accessed October 21, 2011).

15. "*Courageous* Movie to Feature Related Books," UrbanChristianNews.com, May 24, 2010, http://www.urbanchristiannews.com/ucn/2010/05/courageous-movie-to-feature-related-books.html (accessed May 28, 2010).

16. http://www.bhpublishinggroup.com/books/products.asp?p=9781433671227 and www.bhpublishinggroup.com/books/products.asp?p=9781433674013 (accessed October 21, 2011).

17. http://www.bhpublishinggroup.com/books/products.asp?p=9781433671210 (accessed October 21, 2011).

18. http://www.lifeway.com/Product/courageous-church-campaign-kit-P005371570 (accessed October 21, 2011).

19. http://www.lifeway.com/Product/courageous-living-bible-study-leader-kit-P005371695 (accessed October 21, 2011).

20. http://www.lifeway.com/Product/honor-begins-at-home-the-courageous-bible-study-member-book-P005371686 (accessed October 21, 2011).

21. "*Courageous* could spark nationwide men's movement," *Baptist Press*, September 30, 2011, http://www.bpnews.net/BPnews.asp?ID=36234 (accessed October 21, 2011).

22. "Continuing to Pray for *Courageous*," Courageous Movie Blog, August 25, 2011, http://www.courageousthemovie.com/blog/2011/08/continuing-to-pray-for-courageous%E2%80%94day-4/ (accessed October 24, 2011).

23. http://boxofficemojo.com/movies/?id=courageous.htm (accessed October 24, 2011).

24. Jessica Clark, "Grass Roots Effort Brings *Courageous* Movie to St. Augustine," FirstCoast News.com, September 26, 2011, http://www.firstcoastnews.com/news/article/220413/3/Grass-Roots-Effort-Brings-Courageous-Movie-to-St-Augustine (accessed October 24, 2011).

25. Gary Goldstein, "Review: *Courageous*, from Alex Kendrick," *The Los Angeles Times*, October 3, 2011, http://www.latimes.com/entertainment/news/reviews/la-et-courageous-20111003,0,5984643.story?track=rss (accessed October 24, 2011).

26. Paul Brunick, "Fathers Who Tend to Their Flocks," *The New York Times*, October 2, 2011, http://movies.nytimes.com/2011/10/03/movies/courageous-directed-by-alex-kendrick-review.html?partner=rss&emc=rss (accessed October 24, 2011).

27. Goldstein, "Review: *Courageous*, from Alex Kendrick."

28. Frank Scheck, Review of *Courageous*, *Hollywood Reporter*, September 30, 2011, http://www.hollywoodreporter.com/review/courageous-film-review-242705 (accessed October 24, 2011).

29. Goldstein, "Review: *Courageous*, from Alex Kendrick."

30. Joe Leydon, Review of *Courageous*, *Variety*, October 1, 2011, http://www.variety.com/review/VE1117946281?refcatid=31 (accessed October 24, 2011).

31. Foust, "*Courageous* is amazing (& better than *Fireproof*)."

32. Greg Wright, "Bold Indeed," Hollywood Jesus, 2011, http://www.hollywoodjesus.com/movieDetail.cfm/i/3AAC4D32-98DA-7BC2-098899A8615930B0/ia/BA7E59D7-FF24-D026-B5D3D56F91B6F16D (accessed October 24, 2011).

33. Steven D. Greydanus, Review of *Courageous*, *Christianity Today*, September 30, 2011, http://www.christianitytoday.com/ct/movies/reviews/2011/courageous.html (accessed October 24, 2011).

34. jwrowe3, "Another Excellent Effort," IMDb, September 30, 2011, http://www.imdb.com/title/tt1630036/reviews?start=0 (accessed October 24, 2011).

35. petersonmlp, "Exciting," IMDb, October 1, 2011, http://www.imdb.com/title/tt1630036/reviews?start=0 (accessed October 24, 2011).

36. zack_wall, "Predictable movie with a great message," IMDb, September 30, 2011, http://www.imdb.com/title/tt1630036/reviews?start=0 (accessed October 24, 2011).

37. fredkins, "Another lackluster Christian fest," IMDb, October 8, 2011, http://www.imdb.com/title/tt1630036/reviews?start=60 (accessed October 24, 2011).

38. "*Courageous* could spark nationwide men's movement."

39. Mickey Noah, "*Courageous* used to reach first responders," *Baptist Press*, October 10, 2011, http://www.bpnews.net/BPnews.asp?ID=36307 (accessed October 24, 2011).

40. Foust, "*Courageous* is amazing (& better than *Fireproof*)."

41. For an interesting take on abstinence movements like this, see *The Education of Shelby Knox* (2005, Incite Pictures).

42. Richard Lindsay, e-mail message to the author, October 8, 2011.

Chapter 7

1. See, for example, Neal Gabler, *An Empire of Their Own: How the Jews Invented Hollywood* (New York: Anchor Books, 1988), Scott Eyman, *Lion of Hollywood: The Life and Legend of Louis B. Mayer* (New York: Simon & Schuster, 2005), and A. Scott Berg, *Goldwyn: A Biography* (New York: Riverhead Books, 1989).

2. See, for example, Thomas Schatz, *The Genius of the System: Hollywood Filmmaking in the Studio Era* (New York: Metropolitan Books, 1996), Douglas Gomery, *The Hollywood Studio System: A History* (London: British Film Institute, 2008), Richard B. Jewell, *The Golden Age of Cinema: Hollywood 1929–1945* (Malden, Massachusettes: Blackwell Publishing, 2007), and Jeanine Basinger, *The Star System* (New York: Vintage Books, 2007).

3. See, for example, Barry K. Grant, *American Cinema of the 1960s: Themes and Variations* (Piscataway: Rutgers University Press, 2008), J. Hoberman, *The Dream Life: Movies, Media, and the Mythology of the Sixties* (New York: The New Press, 2007), and Peter Biskind, *Easy Riders, Raging Bulls: How the Sex-Drugs-and-Rock 'n Roll Generation Saved Hollywood* (New York: Simon & Schuster, 1998).

4. This device stabilized the camera as a mount attached to the cameraman mechanically isolated the operator's movement from the camera, allowing a very smooth shot even when the operator moved quickly over an uneven surface.

5. See, for example, Tom Shone, *Blockbuster: How Hollywood Learned to Stop Worrying and Love the Summer* (London: Simon & Schuster, 1997).

6. Box Office Mojo, http://boxofficemojo.com/movies/?id=blairwitchproject.htm (accessed January 10, 2011).

7. Box Office Mojo, http://boxofficemojo.com/movies/?id=paranormalactivity.htm (accessed January 10, 2011). For more on the history of American independent film, see Greg Merritt, *Celluloid Mavericks: A History of American Independent Filmmaking* (New York: Thunder's Mouth Press, 2000), Emanuel Levy, *Cinema of Outsiders: The Rise of American Independent Film* (New York: New York University Press, 2001), and Jim Hillier, ed., *American Independent Cinema: A Sight and Sound Reader* (London: British Film Institute, 2001).

8. S. Abraham Ravid, "Film Production in the Digital Age — What Do We Know About the Past and the Future," in *A Concise Handbook of Movie Industry Economics*, ed. Charles C. Moul (New York: Cambridge University Press, 2006), 53–54.

9. For information on the production and distribution of Ed Burns' latest independent feature, *Nice Guy Johnny*, see Monte Burke, "Landing the Big One," Forbes.com, August 9, 2010, http://www.forbes.com/forbes/2010/0809/life-ed-burns-filmmaking-independent-film-landing-big-one.html (accessed January 6, 2010), and Burke, "Ed Burns, *Nice Guy Johnny*, and a New Way of Distributing Films," Forbes.com, October 20, 2010, http://blogs.forbes.com/monteburke/2010/10/20/ed-burns-nice-guy-johnny-and-a-new-way-of-distributing-films/ (accessed January 6, 2010).

10. Jon Reiss, *Think Outside the Box Office: The Ultimate Guide to Film Distribution and Marketing for the Digital Era* (New York: Hybrid Cinema Publishing, 2009), 47.

11. Ibid., 47.
12. Ibid., 168.
13. Ibid., 81.
14. Ibid., 93.
15. Ibid., 119–21.
16. Ibid., 213, 214.
17. Ibid., 343.
18. Ibid., 344.

19. Janet Wasko, "Critiquing Hollywood: The Political Economy of Motion Pictures," in *A Concise Handbook of Movie Industry Economics* ed. Charles C. Moul (New York: Cambridge University Press, 2006), 16.

20. Ravid, 53.

21. Charles R. Winberg, "Profits Out of the Picture: Research Issues and Revenue Sources Beyond the North American Box Office," in *A Concise Handbook of Movie Industry Economics*, ed. Charles C. Moul (New York: Cambridge University Press, 2006), 173.

22. Motion Picture Association of America, http://mpaa.org/ (accessed January 6, 2011).

23. The Entertainment Merchants Association, http://www.entmerch.org/annual_reports.html (accessed January 6, 2011).

24. Barry Gardner, "Technological Changes and Monetary Advantages," in *More Money, More Ministry: Money and Evangelicals in Recent North American History*, ed. Larry Eskridge and Mark A. Noll (Grand Rapids: Wm. B. Eerdmans Publishing, 2000), 300.

25. Lindvall, *Sanctuary Cinema*, 36.

26. Lynn Schofield Clark, Preface to *Religion, Media, and the Marketplace* (Piscataway: Rutgers University Press, 2007), ix-x.

27. Hendershot, 7.
28. Ibid., 71.
29. Ibid., 8.

30. He seems to suggest that Christian products' availability in secular retailers like Barnes & Noble and Wal-Mart is a key marker of crossover success.

31. Jay R. Howard and John M. Streck, *Apostles of Rock: The Splintered World of Contemporary Christian Music* (Lexington: The University Press of Kentucky, 1999). Howard and Streck are highly influenced by H. Richard Niebuhr's classic *Christ and Culture* (New York: Harper and Row, 1951).

32. Radosh, 164.
33. Ibid., 165–66.
34. Ibid., 168.

35. Lynn Schofield Clark, "Identity, Belonging, and Religious Lifestyle Branding (Fashion Bibles, Bhangra Parties, and Muslim Pop)," in *Religion, Media, and the Marketplace*, ed. Schofield Clark (Piscataway: Rutgers University Press, 2007), 3.

36. Mara Einstein, *Brands of Faith: Marketing Religion in a Commercial Age* (New York: Routledge, 2008), xi.

37. Ibid., 12–13.
38. Ibid., 93.
39. Clark, "Identity, Belonging, and Religious Lifestyle Branding," 7.

Chapter 8

1. Information on the history of New Song Community Church is available from http://www.newsongchurch.com/app/w_page.php?id=54&type=section (accessed November 20, 2010).
2. Information on the ministries of New Song Community Church is available from http://www.newsongchurch.com/app/w_page.php?id=53&type=section (accessed November 20, 2010).
3. "*To Save a Life* Coming to Blu-ray and DVD August 3," *To Save a Life* website, May 17, 2010, http://www.tosavealifemovie.com/latestnews/ (accessed November 20, 2010).
4. Josh Kimball, "Southern Calif. Church Enters Movie-Making Business," Christian Post, July 23, 2008, http://www.christianpost.com/article/20080723/southern-calif-church-enters-movie-making-business/index.html (accessed November 21, 2010).
5. Monica Unhold, "Youth pastor draws from life for screenplay," Sign on San Diego, July 18, 2008, http://legacy.signonsandiego.com/news/northcounty/20080718-9999-1mcl8movie.html (accessed November 21, 2010).
6. Greg Wright, "A Film That Doesn't Suck," Hollywood Jesus, 2010, http://www.hollywoodjesus.com/dvddetail.cfm/i/05A963E1-A3C5-1FDF-6FD94DCF973D2FC9/ia/570B0657-CAE9-7E5F-55086E9A3DDCA17E (accessed November 21, 2010).
7. http://www.tosavealifemovie.com/tsalweek/ (accessed January 6, 2011). Information on the 2010 event has been removed, and the webpage now encourages visitors to stay tuned for information on the 2011 event.
8. http://www.tosavealifemovie.com/stories (accessed January 6, 2011).
9. http://boxofficemojo.com/movies/?id=tosavealife.htm (accessed November 20, 2010).
10. Ian Buckwalter, "*To Save a Life*: A Sermon Aimed Right at the Choir," NPR.com, January 21, 2010, http://www.npr.com/templates/story/story.php?storyid=122784345 (accessed on November 20, 2010).
11. Ibid.
12. Andy Webster, "An Athlete in Search of Redemption," *The New York Times*, January 22, 2010, http://movies.nytimes.com/2010/01/22/movies/22tosave.html?partner:RottenTomatoes&ei=5083 (accessed November 20, 2010).
13. Ibid.
14. Todd Hertz, "*To Save a Life*," *Christianity Today*, January 22, 2010, http://www.christianitytoday.com/ct/movies/reviews/2010/tosavelife.html (accessed November 20, 2010).
15. Nell Minow, "*To Save a Life*," Beliefnet, August 2, 2010, http://blog.beliefnet.com/moviemom/2010/08/to-save-a-life.html (accessed November 20, 2010).
16. Reduxinflux_1, "Authentic," IMDb, January 23, 2010, http://www.imdb.com/title/tt1270286/usercomments (accessed November 20, 2010).
17. CeilingofsStars, "Good intentions, but falls very flat," IMDb.com, January 31, 2010, http://www.imdb.com/title/tt1270286/usercomments?start=20 (accessed November 20, 2010).
18. Steven Crowder, "Why Does Hollywood Hate *To Save a Life*?," FoxNews.com, August 17, 2010, http://www.foxnews.com/opinion/2010/08/17/steven-crowder-save-life-jesus-movie-film-hollywood-critics-npr-new-york-times/ (accessed November 20, 2010).
19. For more on this paradigm, see Chapter 5, "Postmodern Believing," of Philip Clayton, *Transforming Christian Theology for Church and Society* (Minneapolis: Fortress Press, 2010), 34–42.
20. http://letterstogodthemovie.com/possibilitypictures (accessed November 20, 2010).
21. http://www.possibilitypicturesllc.com/ (accessed November 20, 2010)
22. http://letterstogodthemovie.com/possibilitypictures (accessed November 20, 2010).
23. http://www.letterstogodthemovie.com/the-movement-of-hope/movement-of-hope/ (accessed November 20, 2010).
24. http://www.the-numbers.com/movies/2010/LTGOD.php (accessed November 20, 2010).
25. Carolyn Arends, "*Letters to God*," *Christianity Today*, April 9, 2010, http://www.christianitytoday.com/ct/movies/reviews/2010/letterstogod.html (accessed November 21, 2010).
26. Roger Moore, "Movie Review: *Letters to God*," *Orlando Sentinel*, April 7, 2010, http://blogs.orlandosentinel.com/entertainment_movies_blog/2010/04/movie-review-letters-to-god.html (accessed November 20, 2010).
27. Moore, "Movie Review: *Letters to God*," article on-line.
28. Robert S. Arnold, "Definately [sic] a Movie to See!," Amazon, May 31, 2010, http://www.amazon.com/Letters-God-Jeffrey-Johnson/dp/B003NKU9AK/ (accessed November 20, 2010).
29. Mary Brown, "Wonderful spiritual film very moving," Amazon, August 21, 2010, http://www.amazon.com/Letters-God-Jeffrey-Johnson/product-reviews/B003NKU9AK/ (accessed November 20, 2010).
30. twilightmomforever, "Four star review," Amazon, August 12, 2010, http://www.amazon.com/Letters-God-Jeffrey-Johnson/product-reviews/B003NKU9AK/ (accessed November 20, 2010).
31. Jeffrey Shoell, "5-star review," Amazon, August 11, 2010, http://www.amazon.com/Letters-God-Jeffrey-Johnson/product-reviews/B003NKU9AK (accessed November 20, 2010).
32. http://www.10weststudios.com/#/about (accessed November 20, 2010).
33. John Anderson, "Films in Search of the Faithful," *The New York Times*, August 20, 2010, http://www.nytimes.com/2010/08/22/movies/22christian.html?_r=1&src=me&ref=movies (accessed November 22, 2010).

34. Ibid.
35. Ibid.
36. Ibid.
37. Annie Young Frisbie, "*What If...*," *Christianity Today*, August 20, 2010, http://www.christianitytoday.com/ct/movies/reviews/2010/whatif.html (accessed November 22, 2010).
38. John Beifuss, "Film Review: Faith-based movie *What If...* is tame, shallow," *Memphis Commercial Appeal*, September 1, 2010, http://www.gomemphis.com/news/2010/sep/01/film-review-message-of-faith-based-what-if/ (accessed November 22, 2010).
39. Dallas Jenkins, Weblog comment, September 15, 2010, "*What If...*? What a Guilt Trip," J. Ryan Parker, Pop Theology, September 15, 2010, http://www.poptheology.com/2010/09/what-if/ (accessed January 6, 2011).
40. http://www.memphiscalvary.org/Ministries/WorshipandArts/tabid/48/Default.aspx (accessed August 11, 2010).
41. http://www.memphiscalvary.org/Ministries/WorshipandArts/tabid/48/Default.aspx (accessed August 11, 2010).
42. http://www.graceworkspictures.com/about.php (accessed November 22, 2010).
43. Ibid.
44. Cathy Lynn Grossman, "Churches Making Mainstream Films to Attract Souls," *USA Today*, July 19, 2010, http://www.usatoday.com/news/religion/2010-07-19-churchmovies19_CV_N.htm?csp=34news (accessed January 6, 2011).
45. Unless otherwise noted, all information on the production of *The Grace Card* comes from making-of and behind-the-scenes featurettes available on the DVD version of the film.
46. Kam Williams, "Louis Gossett Jr.: *The Grace Card* Interview," *The Tri-State Defender*, February 24, 2011, http://tri-statedefenderonline.com/articlelive/articles/5835/1/Lou-Gossett-Jr-The-Grace-Card-interview/Page1.html (accessed October 14, 2011).
47. http://www.outreach.com/promo/grace-card.aspx (accessed October 14, 2011).
48. http://www.boxofficemojo.com/movies/?id=gracecard.htm (accessed October 14, 2011).
49. Sean O'Connell, "Sinner Finds Mr. Wright," *The Washington Post*, February 25, 2011, http://www.washingtonpost.com/gog/movies/the-grace-card,1175650/critic-review.html (accessed October 14, 2011).
50. Todd Hertz, Review of *The Grace Card*, *Christianity Today*, February 25, 2011, http://www.christianitytoday.com/ct/movies/reviews/2011/gracecard.html (accessed October 14, 2011).
51. Joe Leydon, Review of *The Grace Card*, *Variety*, February 25, 2011, http://www.variety.com/review/VE1117944720/ (accessed October 14, 2011).
52. Jaimi Thomsen, "Best 'Christian' Film I have seen," IMDb, February 1, 2011, http://www.imdb.com/title/tt1544600/reviews (accessed October 14, 2011).
53. dhenry68, "Worth a Watch!," IMDb, August 17, 2011, http://www.imdb.com/title/tt1544600/reviews (accessed October 14, 2011).
54. Joswircz, "Great Christian Movie!," Amazon, March 21, 2011, http://www.amazon.com/The-Grace-Card/product-reviews/B005CCTIPO/ref=cm_cr_pr_hist_5?ie=UTF8&showViewpoints=0&filterBy=addFiveStar (accessed October 14, 2011).
55. chestnutyouth, "Theological challenges but worth a watch," IMDb.com, March 11, 2011, http://www.imdb.com/title/tt1544600/reviews?start=10 (accessed October 14, 2011).
56. Steve Montgomery, "Highly Disappointing: Only Slightly Christian," Amazon, September 21, 2011, http://www.amazon.com/The-Grace-Card/product-reviews/B005CCTIPO/ref=cm_cr_pr_hist_2?ie=UTF8&showViewpoints=0&filterBy=addTwoStar (accessed October 14, 2011).
57. http://www.ylfc.org/cgi-bin/index.cgi?name=vision (accessed January 6, 2011).
58. http://ylfc.org/cgi-bin/index.cgi?section=worship&name=wcavalues (accessed January 6, 2011).
59. http://ylfc.org/cgi-bin/NewsList.cgi?section=&cat=Events&rec=214 (accessed January 6, 2011).
60. http://web.me.com/criscobueno/Ocean_Avenue_Entertainment/Ocean_Ave.html (accessed January 6, 2011).
61. Ibid.
62. http://web.me.com/criscobueno/Ocean_Avenue_Entertainment/WingCinema.html (accessed November 22, 2010).
63. http://nottodaythemovie.wordpress.com/about-2/ (accessed November 22, 2010).
64. Grossman, "Churches Making Mainstream Films to Attract Souls."

Chapter 9

1. Frank Burch Brown, *Good Taste, Bad Taste, and Christian Taste: Aesthetics in Religious Life* (New York: Oxford University Press, 2000), 146.
2. Ibid., 147.
3. Ibid., 145.
4. Ibid., 12.
5. Barbara Nicolosi, "Facing *Facing the Giants*," Blog Post, October 26, 2006, http://churchofthemasses.blogspot.com/2006/10/facing-facing-giants.html (accessed November 3, 2010).
6. Daniel Radosh, "The Red Hot Christian Blockbuster," The Daily Beast, October 21, 2008, http://www.thedailybeast.com/blogs-and-stories/2008-10-21/the-red-hot-christian-blockbuster/ (accessed January 7, 2011).
7. Nicolosi, "Facing *Facing the Giants*."
8. Leydon, "Facing the Giants."
9. Terry Mattingly, "Birth of Contemporary Christian Cinema?," Get Religion Blog, entry posted October 11, 2006, http://www.getreligion.org/?p=1949 (accessed January 6, 2011).
10. Einstein, 119.
11. Barry Hankins, *American Evangelicals: A Contemporary History of a Mainstream Religious Movement* (Lanham, Maryland: Rowman & Littlefield Publishers, 2008), 8.

12. Ibid., 8, 9.
13. Burch Brown, 147.
14. Nicolosi, "Facing *Facing the Giants*."
15. Radosh, "The Red Hot Christian Blockbuster."
16. Nicolosi, "Facing *Facing the Giants*."
17. Radosh, *Rapture Ready!*, 24–25.
18. Schultze and Woods, "Being Fairly Self-Critical About Evangelical Media," 286.
19. Richard Lindsay, e-mail message to author, October 8, 2011.
20. Quentin J. Schultze and Robert H. Woods, Jr., "Getting the Conversation Going About Media and Culture," in *Understanding Evangelical Media: The Changing Face of Christian Communication*, ed. Schultze and Woods, Jr. (Downers Grove, Illinois: InterVarsity Press, 2008), 21–22.
21. Radosh, *Rapture Ready!*, 93.
22. Joel A. Carpenter, "Contemporary Evangelicalism and Mammon: Some Thoughts," in *More Money, More Ministry: Money and Evangelicals in Recent North American History*, ed. Larry Eskridge and Mark A. Noll (Grand Rapids: Wm. B. Eerdmans Publishing, 2000), 404.
23. Christian Smith, *American Evangelicals: Embattled and Thriving* (Chicago: University of Chicago Press, 1988).
24. Hendershot, 25.
25. Schultze and Woods, "Being Fairly Self-Critical About Evangelical Media," 284.
26. Leslie E. Smith, "Living *in* the World, But Not *of* the World: Understanding Evangelical Support for *The Passion of the Christ*," in *After* The Passion *Is Gone: American Religious Consequences*, ed. J. Shawn Landres and Michael Berenbaum (Walnut Creek, California: AltaMira Press, 2004), 50.
27. Ibid., 54.
28. Mattingly, "Birth of Contemporary Christian Cinema?"
29. Grossman, "Churches Making Mainstream Films to Attract Souls."
30. Burch Brown, 147.
31. Bueno, personal interview.
32. Hendershot, 8.

Conclusion

1. Lindvall, *Sanctuary Cinema*, 216.
2. In my conversation with Chris Bueno, he told me of instances where Hollywood producers and scriptwriters or consultants gutted Christian filmmakers' scripts, downplaying and/or removing their explicit religious messages.
3. See Einstein Chapter 5, "The Course to God."
4. Charles C. Moul and Steven M. Shugan, "Theatrical Release and the Launching of Motion Pictures," in *A Concise Handbook of Movie Industry Economics*, ed. Moul (New York: Cambridge University Press, 2005), 111.
5. Bueno, conversation with the author, October 2010.
6. Radosh, 305.
7. Ibid., 308.
8. Burch Brown, 159.
9. http://www.actoneprogram.com/about-us/who-we-are;keynotes/ (accessed June 8, 2010).
10. Nicolosi, article on-line.
11. Heather Goodman, "In Her Story: Interview with Barbara Nicolosi," *Glimpses* ezine, August 5, 2008, reprint available from http://churchofthemasses.blogspot.com/2008_08_01_archive.html (accessed June 3, 2010).
12. Eleanor Barkhorn, "*Blue Like Jazz*: The Quest to Get Christians to Laugh at Themselves," *The Atlantic*, October 22, 2010, http://www.theatlantic.com/culture/archive/2010/10/blue-like-jazz-the-quest-to-get-christians-to-laugh-at-themselves/64963/ (accessed January 7, 2011).

Bibliography

Abel, Richard. *Americanizing the Movies and "Movie-Mad" Audiences, 1910–1914*. Berkeley: University of California Press, 2006.

Amazing Grace. DVD. Directed by Michael Apted. Bristol Bay Productions, 2007.

Anderson, John. "Films in Search of the Faithful." The *New York Times*. August 20, 2010, http://www.nytimes.com/2010/08/22/movies/22christian.html?_r=1&src=me&ref=movies (accessed August 24, 2010).

Arends, Carolyn. Review of *Letters to God*. *Christianity Today*. April 9, 2010, http://www.christianitytoday.com/ct/movies/reviews/2010/letterstogod.html (accessed November 22, 2010).

Arnold, Robert S. "Definately [sic] a Movie to See!" Amazon. May 31, 2010, http://www.amazon.com/Letters-God-Jeffrey-Johnson/dp/B003NKU9AK/ (accessed November 20, 2010).

"Baptist Faith and Message," http://www.sbc.net/bfm/bfm2000.asp (accessed November 14, 2010).

Barker, Ricki. "*The Love Dare Wedding Edition* is now available." *Albany Herald*. April 4, 2010, http://www.albanyherald.com/home/headlines/89854892.html (accessed November 17, 2010).

Barkhorn, Eleanor. "*Blue Like Jazz*: The Quest to Get Christians to Laugh at Themselves." *The Atlantic*. October 22, 2010, http://www.theatlantic.com/culture/archive/2010/10/blue-like-jazz-the-quest-to-get-christians-to-laugh-at-themselves/64963/ (accessed January 7, 2011).

Basinger, Jeanine. *The Star System*. New York: Vintage Books, 2007.

BBC News. "Profile: Tycoon Philip Anschutz." July 5, 2006, http://news.bbc.co.uk/2/hi/uk_news/5150192.stm (accessed November 10, 2010).

Beal, Timothy K., and Tod Linafelt. Introduction to *Mel Gibson's Bible: Religion, Popular Culture, and* The Passion of the Christ, edited by Beal and Linafelt, 1–7. Chicago: The University of Chicago Press, 2006.

Beifuss, John. "Film Review: Faith-based movie *What If...* is tame, shallow." *Memphis Commercial Appeal*. September 1, 2010, http://www.gomemphis.com/news/2010/sep/01/film-review-message-of-faith-based-what-if/ (accessed September 29, 2010).

Berg, A. Scott. *Goldwyn: A Biography*. New York: Riverhead Books, 1989.

Biskind, Peter. *Easy Riders, Raging Bulls: How the Sex-Drugs-and-Rock 'n Roll Generation Saved Hollywood*. New York: Simon & Schuster, 1998.

Black, Gregory D. *The Catholic Crusade Against the Movies, 1940–1975*. New York: Cambridge University Press, 1998.

Boyd, Danah M., and Nicole B. Ellison. "Social Network Sites: Definition, History, and Scholarship." *Journal of Computer-Mediated Communication*. (13) 1, http://jcmc.indiana.edu/vol13/issue1/boyd.ellison.html (accessed October 21, 2011).

Breimeier, Russ. Review of *One Night with the King*. *Christianity Today*. October 13, 2006, http://www.christianitytoday.com/movies/reviews/2006/onenightwiththeking.html (accessed November 10, 2010).

Brown, Frank Burch. *Good Taste, Bad Taste, and Christian Taste: Aesthetics in Religious Life*. New York: Oxford University Press, 2000.

Brown, Mary. "Wonderful spiritual film very moving." Amazon.com. August 21, 2010, http://www.amazon.com/Letters-God-Jeffrey-Johnson/product-reviews/B003NKU9AK/ (accessed November 20, 2010).

Bruner, Kathy. "Thinking Outside the Tribal TV Box." In *Understanding Evangelical Media*, edited by Quentin J. Schultze and Robert H. Woods, Jr., 46–57. Downers Grove, Illinois: Intervarsity Press, 2008.

Paul Brunick, "Fathers Who Tend to Their Flocks," *The New York Times*, October 2, 2011, http://movies.nytimes.com/2011/10/03/movies/courageous-directed-by-alex-kendrick-review.html?partner=rss&emc=rss (accessed October 24, 2011).

Buckwalter, Ian. "*To Save a Life*: A Sermon Aimed Right at the Choir." NPR.com. January 21, 2010, http://www.npr.com/templates/story/story.php?

storyid=122784345 (accessed on August 10, 2010).

Bueno, Chris. Interview by J. Ryan Parker. October 8, 2010. Skype recording.

Burke, Monte. "Ed Burns, *Nice Guy Johnny*, and a New Way of Distributing Films." *Forbes*. October 20, 2010, http://blogs.forbes.com/monteburke/2010/10/20/ed-burns-nice-guy-johnny-and-a-new-way-of-distributing-films/ (accessed January 6, 2010).

———. "Landing the Big One." *Forbes*. August 9, 2010, http://www.forbes.com/forbes/2010/0809/life-ed-burns-filmmaking-independent-film-landing-big-one.html (accessed January 6, 2010).

Carpenter, Chris. "Facing New Giants: On the Set of *Fireproof*." ChristiansBroadcastingNetwork.com. February 2008, http://www.cbn.com/entertainment/screen/ carpenter-FireproofSet_0208.aspx (accessed November 16, 2010).

Carpenter, Joel A. "Contemporary Evangelicalism and Mammon: Some Thoughts." In *More Money, More Ministry: Money and Evangelicals in Recent North American History*, edited by Larry Eskridge and Mark A. Noll, 399–405. Grand Rapids: Wm. B. Eerdmans Publishing, 2000.

CeilingofsStars. "Good intentions, but falls very flat." IMDb. January 31, 2010, http://www.imdb.com/title/tt1270286/usercomments?start=20 (accessed November 20, 2010).

Chattaway, Peter. Review of *The Chronicles of Narnia: Prince Caspian*. *Christianity Today*. May 16, 2008, http://www.christianitytoday.com/movies/reviews/2008/princecaspian.html (accessed November 10, 2010).

———. Review of *Fireproof*. *Christianity Today*. September 26, 2008, http://www.christianitytoday.com/ct/movies/reviews/2008/fireproof.html (accessed November 16, 2010).

The Chronicles of Narnia: The Lion, the Witch, and the Wardrobe. DVD. Directed by Andrew Adamson. Walt Disney Pictures and Walden Media, 2006.

The Chronicles of Narnia: Prince Caspian. DVD. Directed by Andrew Adamson. Walt Disney Pictures and Walden Media, 2008.

Clark, Jessica. "Grass Roots Effort Brings *Courageous* Movie to St. Augustine." First Coast News. September 26, 2011, http://www.firstcoastnews.com/news/article/220413/3/Grass-Roots-Effort-Brings-Courageous-Movie-to-St-Augustine (accessed October 24, 2011).

Clark, Lynn Schofield. "Identity, Belonging, and Religious Lifestyle Branding (Fashion Bibles, Bhangra Parties, and Muslim Pop)." In *Religion, Media, and the Marketplace*, edited by Schofield Clark, 1–33. Piscataway: Rutgers University Press, 2007.

———. Preface to *Religion, Media, and the Marketplace*, edited by Schofield Clark, ix-xv. Piscataway: Rutgers University Press, 2007.

Clayton, Philip. *Transforming Christian Theology for Church and Society*. Minneapolis:Fortress Press, 2010.

Colson, Charles, and Anne Morse. "The Wilberforce Strategy." *Christianity Today*. February 19, 2007, http://www.christianitytoday.com/ct/2007/february/45.132.html (accessed November 10, 2010).

"Continuing to Pray for Courageous." Courageous Movie Blog. August 25, 2011, http://www.courageousthemovie.com/blog/2011/08/continuing-to-pray-for-courageous%E2%80%94day-4/ (accessed October 24, 2011).

"A Conversation with Evan Williams." Web 2.0 Summit 2009: Evan Williams and John Battelle, O'Reilly Media. October 21, 2009, http://www.youtube.com/watch?v=p5jXcgZnEaO&fmt=18 (accessed May 28, 2010).

Cork, William J. "Passionate Blogging: Interfaith Controversy and the Internet." In *After The Passion Is Gone: American Religious Consequences*, edited by J. Shawn Landres and Michael Berenbaum, 35–46. Walnut Creek, California: AltaMira Press, 2004.

"*Courageous* Could Spark Nationwide Men's Movement." *Baptist Press*. September 30, 2011, http://www.bpnews.net/BPnews.asp?ID=36234 (accessed October 21, 2011).

"*Courageous* Movie to Feature Related Books." Urban Christian News. May 24, 2010, http://www.urbanchristiannews.com/ucn/2010/05/courageous-movie-to-feature-related-books.html (accessed May 28, 2010).

Couvares, Francis G., ed. *Movie Censorship and American Culture*. Amherst: University of Massachusettes Press, 2006.

Coverson, Laura. "Fox Pursues the Flock." ABC News. September 21, 2006, http://abcnews.go.com/Entertainment/story?id=2472082&page=1 (accessed November 14, 2010).

Criswell, David. Review of *The Chronicles of Narnia: Prince Caspian*. Christian Answers. http://christiananswers.net/spotlight/movies/2008/chroniclesofnarnia2008.html?zoom_highlight=prince+caspian (accessed November 10, 2010).

Crowder, Steven. "Why Does Hollywood Hate *To Save a Life*." Fox News. August 17, 2010, http://www.foxnews.com/opinion/2010/08/17/steven-crowder-save-life-jesus-movie-film-hollywood-critics-npr-new-york-times/ (accessed August 23, 2010).

Cyrino, Monica Silveira. *Big Screen Rome*. Malden, Massachusettes: Blackwell Publishing, 2005.

Dans, Peter E. *Christians in the Movies: A Century of Saints and Sinners*. Lanham, Maryland: Rowman & Littlefield Publishers, 2009.

Detweiler, Craig. *Into the Dark: Seeing the Sacred*

in the Top Films of the 21st Century. Grand Rapids: Baker Academic, 2008.

Doherty, Thomas. *Hollywood's Censor: Joseph I. Breen and the Production Code Administration*. New York: Columbia University Press, 2009.

———. *Pre-Code Hollywood: Sex, Immorality, and Insurrection in American Cinema, 1930–1934*. New York: Columbia University Press, 1999.

Easterling, Rebecca. "The Making of *Flywheel, Facing the Giants,* and *Fireproof*." Christian Web News. February 12, 2009, http://www.cwnewz.com/content/ view/589/2/ (accessed July 22, 2010).

Ebert, Roger. Review of *The Chronicles of Narnia: The Lion, the Witch and the Wardrobe*. *Sun Times*. December 8, 2005, http://rogerebert.suntimes.com/apps/pbcs.dll/article?AID=/20051207/REVIEWS/51203001/1023 (accessed November 10, 2010).

Einstein, Mara. *Brands of Faith: Marketing Religion in a Commercial Age*. New York: Routledge, 2008.

Ellis, Carlyle. "The Parson Who Believed in Pictures." *Everybody's Magazine* 36, (February 1917), 140–43. Reprinted in *The Silents of God: Selected Issues and Documents in Silent American Film and Religion, 1908–1925*, edited by Terry Lindvall, 161–66. Lanham, Maryland: Scarecrow Press, 2001.

End of the Spear. DVD. Directed by Jim Hanon. Every Tribe Entertainment, 2006.

The Entertainment Merchants Association, http://www.entmerch.org/annual_reports.html (accessed January 6, 2011).

Eyman, Scott. *Empire of Dreams: The Epic Life of Cecil B. DeMille*. New York: Simon & Schuster, 2010.

———. *Lion of Hollywood: The Life and Legend of Louis B. Mayer*. New York: Simon & Schuster, 2005.

Facing the Giants. DVD. Directed by Alex Kendrick. Sherwood Pictures, 2007.

"*Facing the Giants* Sports Advisory Board Letter," Portable Document Format (PDF), http://www.facingthegiants.com/dvdfaith.php (accessed November 14, 2010).

Fireproof. DVD. Directed by Alex Kendrick. Sherwood Pictures, 2009.

"*Fireproof*: Discussing Filmmaking with Brothers, Writers, Producers, and Director Alex and Stephen Kendrick." Christian Cinema. September 1, 2008, http://www.christiancinema.com/catalog/newsdesk_info.php?newsdesk_id=747 (accessed November 8, 2010).

Flywheel. DVD. Directed by Alex Kendrick. Sherwood Pictures, 2007.

Flywheel Press Release. "The *Flywheel* Time Line." http://www.flywheelthemovie.com (accessed July 22, 2010).

Foust, Michael. "*Amazing Grace* Film About Wilberforce Called Inspirational." *Baptist Press*. February 2, 2007, http://www.bpnews.net/bpnews.asp?ID=24883 (accessed November 10, 2010).

———. "*Courageous* is amazing (& better than *Fireproof*)." *Baptist Press*. June 20, 2011, http://www.bpnews.net/BPFirstPerson.asp?ID=35579 (accessed October 21, 2011).

Frisbie, Annie Young. Review of *What If…*. *Christianity Today*. August 20, 2010, http://www.christianitytoday.com/ct/movies/reviews/2010/whatif.html (accessed September 29, 2010).

Gabler, Neal. *An Empire of Their Own: How the Jews Invented Hollywood*. New York: Anchor Books, 1988.

Gardner, Barry. "Technological Changes and Monetary Advantages." In *More Money, More Ministry: Money and Evangelicals in Recent North American History*, edited by Larry Eskridge and Mark A. Noll, 298–310. Grand Rapids: Wm. B. Eerdmans Publishing, 2000.

Genzlinger, Neil. "Putting Out Fires, Reigniting Passions." *The New York Times*. September 27, 2008, http://movies.nytimes.com/2008/09/27/movies/27proof.html?ref=movies (accessed January 6, 2011).

Goldenberg, Suzanne. "Hollywood Finds Christ as Fox Faith Plans Series of Religious Movies." *The Guardian*. September 20, 2006, http://www.guardian.co.uk/ world/2006/sep/20/religion.media (accessed January 6, 2011).

Goldstein, Gary. "Review: *Courageous*, from Alex Kendrick." *The Los Angeles Times*. October 3, 2011, http://www.latimes.com/entertainment/news/reviews/la-et-courageous-20111003,0,5984643.story?track=rss (accessed October 24, 2011).

Gomery, Douglas. *The Hollywood Studio System: A History*. London: British Film Institute, 2008.

Goodman, Heather. "In Her Story: Interview with Barbara Nicolosi." *Glimpses* e-zine. August 5, reprint available from http://churchofthemasses.blogspot.com/ 2008_08_01_archive.html (accessed June 3 2010).

Grant, Barry K. *American Cinema of the 1960s: Themes and Variations*. Piscataway: Rutgers University Press, 2008.

Greydanus, Steven D. Review of *Courageous*. *Christianity Today*. September 30, 2011, http://www.christianitytoday.com/ct/movies/reviews/2011/courageous.html (accessed October 24, 2011).

Grieveson, Lee. *Policing Cinema: Movies and Censorship in Early-Twentieth-Century America*. Berkeley: University of California Press, 2004.

Grossman, Cathy Lynn. "Churches Making Mainstream Films to Attract Souls." *USA Today*. July 19, 2010, http://www.usatoday.com/news/religion/2010-07-19-churchmovies19_CV_N.htm?csp=34news (accessed August 11, 2010).

Gunning, Tom. "The Cinema of Attractions: Early Film, Its Spectator and the Avant-Garde." In *Early Film: Space, Frame, Narrative*, edited by Thomas Elsaesser and Adam Barker, 56–62. London: British Film Institute, 1989.

Hamilton, Michael S. "More Money, More Ministry: The Financing of American Evangelicalism Since 1945." In *More Money, More Ministry: Money and Evangelicals in Recent North American History*, edited by Larry Eskridge and Mark A. Noll, 104–38. Grand Rapids: Wm. B. Eerdmans Publishing, 2000.

Hananel, Sam. "Lawmakers concerned about Christian film's PG rating." *Fredericksburg Star*. July 15, 2006, http://fredericksburg.com/News/FLS/2006/072006/07152006/203756?rss=local (accessed November 15, 2010).

Hankins, Barry. *American Evangelicals: A Contemporary History of a Mainstream Religious Movement*. Lanham, Maryland: Rowman & Littlefield Publishers, 2008.

Hardy, Michael. Review of *Fireproof*. *Boston Globe*. September 27, 2008, http://www.boston.com/movies/display?display=movie&id=12208 (accessed June 11, 2010).

Hendershot, Heather. *Shaking the World for Jesus: Media and Conservative Evangelical Culture*. Chicago: University of Chicago Press, 2004.

Hertz, Todd. Review of *The Grace Card*. *Christianity Today*. February 25, 2011, http://www.christianitytoday.com/ct/movies/reviews/2011/gracecard.html (accessed October 14, 2011).

_____. Review of *To Save a Life*. *Christianity Today*. January 22, 2010, http://www.christianitytoday.com/ct/movies/reviews/2010/tosavealife.html (accessed August 11, 2010).

Hillier, Jim, ed. *American Independent Cinema: A Sight and Sound Reader*. London: British Film Institute, 2001.

Hoberman, J. *The Dream Life: Movies, Media, and the Mythology of the Sixties*. New York: The New Press, 2007.

Howard, Jay R., and John M. Streck. *Apostles of Rock: The Splintered World of Contemporary Christian Music*. Lexington: The University Press of Kentucky, 1999.

Hurst, Josh. Review of *Facing the Giants*. *Christianity Today*. September 29, 2006, http://www.christianitytoday.com/ct/movies/reviews/2006/facingthegiants.html (accessed June 3, 2010).

Jalsevac, John. "*Facing the Giants* Rated PG for 'Mature Themes' Not Christianity: MPAA." Life Site News. June 20, 2006, http://www.lifesitenews.com/ldn/2006/jun/06062001.html (accessed November 15, 2010).

Jenkins, Dallas. "*What If...?* What a Guilt Trip," J. Ryan Parker. Pop Theology. September 15, 2010, http://www.poptheology.com/2010/09/what-if/ (accessed January 6, 2011).

The Jesus Film Project. "History." http://www.jesusfilm.org/aboutus/history (accessed January 4, 2011).

Jewell, Richard B. *The Golden Age of Cinema: Hollywood 1929–1945*. Malden, Massachusettes: Blackwell Publishing, 2007.

Johnston, Alva. "Pictures Which Have Discarded Satan for Mother Church." *Vanity Fair* 27 (October 1931): 55, 84. Cited in Terry Lindvall, *Sanctuary Cinema: Origins of the Christian Film Industry*. New York: New York University Press, 2007.

Kimball, Josh. "*Love Dare* Racks Up Big Numbers Ahead of *Fireproof* Release." ChristianPost.com. September 15, 2008, http://www.christianpost.com/article/20080915/-love-dare-racks-up-big-numbers-ahead-of-fireproof-release/ (accessed November 17, 2010).

_____. "Southern Calif. Church Enters Movie-Making Business." Christian Post. July 23 2008, http://www.christianpost.com/article/20080723/southern-calif-church-enters-movie-making-business/index.html (accessed August 11, 2010).

Landres, J. Shawn, and Michael Berenbaum. Introduction to *After The Passion Is Gone American Religious Consequences*, edited by Landres and Berenbaum, 1–17. Walnut Creek, California: AltaMira Press, 2004.

Lang, J. Stephen. *The Bible on the Big Screen: A Guide from Silent Films to Today's Movies*. Grand Rapids: Baker Books, 2007.

LaSalle, Mick. "Children Open a Door and Step into an Enchanted World of Good and Evil — the Name of the Place is *Narnia*." *San Francisco Chronicle*. December 9, 2005, http://www.sfgate.com/cgi-bin/article.cgi?f=/c/a/2005/12/09/DDG9QG4FJS1.DTL&type=movies (accessed November 10, 2010).

Laurence, Charles. "After *The Passion*, Hollywood Asks: What About the Sequel?" *The Telegraph*. March 20, 2004, http://www.telegraph.co.uk/news/worldnews/northamerica/usa/1457429/After-The-Passion,-Hollywood-asks-what-about-the-sequel.html (accessed November 10, 2010).

Ledman, Melinda. "Heavy-Handed Messages, But True." Hollywood Jesus. 2006, http://www.hollywoodjesus.com/DVDDetail.cfm/i/2EDA8C02-B003-0230-EB9644DF13B91C59/ia/2EE18AB8-E6AB-A9B4-1(ED520603F1EF70 (accessed January 6, 2010).

Levy, Emmanuel. *Cinema of Outsiders: The Rise of American Independent Film*. New York: New York University Press, 2001.

Leydon, Joe. Review of *Courageous*. *Variety*. October 1, 2011. http://www.variety.com/review/VE1117946281?refcatid=31 (accessed October 24, 2011).

_____. Review of *Facing the Giants*. *Variety*. October 1, 2005, http://www.variety.com/review/VE1117931756.html?categoryid=31&cs=1 (accessed June 2, 2010).

———. Review of *Fireproof*. *Variety*. September 26, 2008, http://www.variety.com/review/VE1117938520.html?categoryid=31&cs=1 (accessed June 11, 2010).

———. Review of *The Grace Card*. *Variety*. February 25, 2011, http://www.variety.com/review/VE1117944720/ (accessed October 14, 2011).

———. Review of *The Ultimate Gift*. *Variety*. March 8, 2007, http://www.variety.com/review/VE1117933023.html?categoryid=31&cs=1 (accessed November 10, 2010).

Lindvall, Terry. "Hollywood Chronicles: Toward an Intersection of Church History and Film History." In *Reframing Theology and Film: New Focus for an Emerging Discipline*, edited by Robert K. Johnston, 126–42. Grand Rapids: Baker Academic, 2007.

———. *Sanctuary Cinema: Origins of the Christian Film Industry*. New York: New York University Press, 2007.

———. *The Silents of God: Selected Issues and Documents in Silent American Film and Religion, 1908–1925*. Lanham, Maryland: The Scarecrow Press, 2001.

——— and Andrew Quicke. *Celluloid Sermons: The Emergence of the Christian Film Industry*. New York: New York University Press, 2011.

——— "Moving from Films to Digital Movies." In *Understanding Evangelical Media*, edited by Quentin J. Schultze and Robert H. Woods, Jr., 58–70. Downers Grove, Illinois: InterVarsity Press, 2008.

———, William J. Brown, and John D. Keeler. "Audience Responses to *The Passion of the Christ*." *Journal of Religion and Media* 6 (2007): 87–107.

Little, William G. "Jesus's Extreme Makeover." In *Mel Gibson's Bible: Religion, Popular Culture, and The Passion of the Christ*, edited by Timothy K. Beal and Tod Linafelt, 169–76. Chicago: The University of Chicago Press, 2006.

Louvish, Simon. *Cecil B. DeMille: A Life in Art*. New York: Thomas Dunne Books, 2007.

Maresco, Peter A. "Mel Gibson's *The Passion of the Christ*: Market Segmentation, Mass Marketing and Promotion, and the Internet." *Journal of Religion and Popular Culture* 8 (Fall 2004), http://www.usask.ca/relst/jrpc/art8-melgibsonmarketing.html (accessed November 10, 2010).

Marquez, Jose. "Lights! Camera! Action!" In *Mel Gibson's Bible: Religion, Popular Culture, and The Passion of the Christ*, edited by Timothy K. Beal and Tod Linafelt, 177–86. Chicago: The University of Chicago Press, 2006.

Mattingly, Terry. "Birth of Contemporary Christian Cinema?" Get Religion Blog. October 11, 2006, http://www.getreligion.org/?p=1949 (accessed January 6, 2011).

May, Larry. *Screening Out the Past: The Birth of Mass Culture and the Motion Picture Industry*. Chicago: The Univeristy of Chicago Press, 1983.

McDannell, Colleen, ed. *Catholics in the Movies*. New York: Oxford University Press, 2007.

Merritt, Greg. *Celluloid Mavericks: A History of American Independent Filmmaking*. New York: Thunder's Mouth Press, 2000.

Minow, Nell. Review of *To Save a Life*. Beliefnet. August 2, 2010, http://blog.beliefnet.com/moviemom/2010/08/to-save-a-life.html (accessed August 11, 2010).

Moore, Roger. Review of *Letters to God*. *Orlando Sentinel*. April 7, 2010, http://blogs.orlandosentinel.com/entertainment_movies_blog/2010/04/movie-review-letters-to-god.html (accessed August 19, 2010).

Morgan, David. *Protestants and Pictures: Religion, Visual Culture, and the Age of American Mass Production*. New York: Oxford University Press, 1999.

Moring, Mark. "Amazing Abolitionist." *Christianity Today*. February 22, 2007, http://www.christianitytoday.com/ct/2007/march/18.34.html (accessed November 10, 2010).

———. "Facing the Critics." *Christianity Today*. September 26, 2006, http://www.christianitytoday.com/ct/movies/interviews/2006/alexkendrick.html (accessed November 15, 2010).

———. "Fox Faith: Is It Working?" *Christianity Today*. October 9, 2007, http://www.christianitytoday.com/movies/news/2007/foxfaithworking.html (accessed November 10, 2010).

———. "Fox Feeds the Flock." *Christianity Today*. October 3, 2006, http://www.christianitytoday.com/movies/interviews/2006/foxfaith.html?start=1 (accessed November 10, 2010).

Morris, Michael. Class Lecture. "Religion and the Cinema." Fall 2006. The Graduate Theological Union, Berkeley, California.

———. E-mail message to author, May 6, 2009.

Motion Picture Association of America. http://mpaa.org/ (accessed January 6, 2011).

Moul, Charles C., and Steven M. Shugan. "Theatrical Release and the Launching of Motion Pictures." In *A Concise Handbook of Movie Industry Economics*, edited by Moul, 80–137. New York: Cambridge University Press, 2005.

The Nativity Story. DVD. Directed by Catherine Hardwicke. New Line Cinema, 2007.

Nicolosi, Barbara. "Facing *Facing the Giants*." Blog Post. October 26, 2006, http://churchofthemasses.blogspot.com/2006/10/facing-facing-giants.html (accessed November 3, 2010).

Niebuhr, H. Richard. *Christ and Culture*. New York: Harper and Row, 1951.

Noah, Mickey. "*Courageous* used to reach first

responders." *Baptist Press.* October 10, 2011, http://www.bpnews.net/BPnews.asp?ID=36307 (accessed October 24, 2011).

O'Connell, Sean. "Sinner Finds Mr. Wright." *The Washington Post.* February 25, 2011, http://www.washingtonpost.com/gog/movies/the-grace-card,1175650/critic-review.html (accessed October 14, 2011).

Olsen, Mark. Review of *The Ultimate Gift. Los Angeles Times.* March 9, 2007, http://www.calendarlive.com/printedition/calendar/cl-et-gift9mar09,0,7711662.story (accessed November 10, 2010).

One Night with the King. DVD. Directed by Michael O. Sajbel. Gener8Xion Pictures, 2007.

One Night with the King Press Release, http://www.8x.com/onenight/epk.html (accessed November 10, 2010).

Paperback Advice Best-seller List. *New York Times.* January 9, 2011, http://www.nytimes.com/best-sellers-books/2011-01-09/paperback-advice/list.html (accessed January 6, 2011).

The Passion of the Christ. DVD. Directed by Mel Gibson. Icon Productions, 2004.

Pinsky, Mark I. "The Reader, the Evangelists, and the Wardrobe." *Harvard Divinity Bulletin* 34 (Winter 2006), http://www.hds.harvard.edu/news/bulletin_mag/articles/34-1_pinsky.html (accessed November 10, 2010).

"Plans for Big Budget *Left Behind* Remake." October 13, 2010, http://www.cloudtenpictures.com/site2/news_article.php?id=42 (accessed November 11, 2010).

Plate, S. Brent, ed. *Re-Viewing the Passion: Mel Gibson's Film and Its Critics.* New York: Palgrave Macmillan, 2004.

Pollock, Melisa. Review of *Facing the Giants.* Christian Answers. http://www.christiananswers.net/spotlight/movies/2006/facingthegiants2006.html?zoom_highlight=facing+the+giants (accessed January 6, 2011).

Radosh, Daniel. *Rapture Ready! Adventures in the Parallel Universe of Christian Pop Culture.* New York: Soft Skull Press, 2010.

_____. "The Red Hot Christian Blockbuster." *The Daily Beast.* October 21, 2008, http://www.thedailybeast.com/blogs-and-stories/2008-10-21/the-red-hot-christian-blockbuster/ (accessed January 7, 2011).

Ravid, S. Abraham. "Film Production in the Digital Age—What Do We Know About the Past and the Future." In *A Concise Handbook of Movie Industry Economics*, edited by Charles C. Moul, 32–58. New York: Cambridge University Press, 2005.

Reduxinflux_1. "Authentic." IMDb. January 23, 2010, http://www.imdb.com/title/tt1270286/usercomments (accessed November 20, 2010).

Reinhartz, Adele. *Jesus of Hollywood.* New York: Oxford University Press, 2007.

Reiss, Jon. *Think Outside the Box Office: The Ultimate Guide to Film Distribution and Marketing for the Digital Era.* New York: Hybrid Cinema Publishing, 2009.

Rogers, Richard. "Special Assignment: *Fireproof.*" WRDW. November 5, 2008, http://www.wrdw.com/entertainment/headlines/33800894.html (accessed November 14, 2010).

Rosenblatt, Josh. Review of *Facing the Giants. Austin Chronicle.* November 16, 2006, http://www.austinchronicle.com/gyrobase/Calendar/Film?Film=oid%3a417777 (accessed June 2, 2010).

Rosin, Hannah. "Can Jesus Save Hollywood?" *The Atlantic.* December 2005. http://www.theatlantic.com/magazine/archive/2005/12/can-jesus-save-hollywood/4398/ (accessed on January 4, 2011).

Rossing, Barbara. *The Rapture Exposed: The Message of Hope in the Book of Revelation.* New York: Basic Books, 2004.

Salzman, Marian. "Why You Need to Twitter." CNBC. Feb 12, 2009, www.cnbc.com/id/29163055/salman_why_you_need_to_twitter (accessed January 7, 2011).

Schatz, Thomas. *The Genius of the System: Hollywood Filmmaking in the Studio Era.* New York: Metropolitan Books, 1996.

Scheck, Frank. Review of *Courageous. The Hollywood Reporter.* September 30, 2011, http://www.hollywoodreporter.com/review/courageous-film-review-242705 (accessed October 24, 2011).

Schultze, Quentin J. Introduction to *Understanding Evangelical Media: The Changing Face of Christian Communication*, edited by Schultze and Woods, Jr., 15–17. Downers Grove, Illinois: InterVarsity Press, 2008.

_____ and Robert H. Woods, Jr. "Being Fairly Self-Critical About Evangelical Media." In *Understanding Evangelical Media: The Changing Face of Christian Communication*, edited by Schultze and Woods, Jr., 282–87. Downers Grove, Illinois: InterVarsity Press, 2008.

_____. "Getting the Conversation Going About Media and Culture." *Understanding Evangelical Media: The Changing Face of Christian Communication*, edited by Schultze and Woods, Jr., 19–32. Downers Grove, Illinois: InterVarsity Press, 2008.

Scott, A. O. "The Virgin Mary as a Teenager with Worries." *The New York Times.* December 1, 2006, http://movies2.nytimes.com/2006/12/01/movies/01nati.html (accessed November 10, 2010).

"Sherwood Pictures Announces Fourth Movie: *Courageous.*" Christians Unite. November 17, 2009, http://news.christiansunite.com/Religion_News/religion08744.shtml (accessed May 28, 2010).

Shone, Tom. *Blockbuster: How Hollywood Learned*

to Stop Worrying and Love the Summer. London: Simon & Schuster, 1997.

Silk, Mark. "Almost a Culture War: The Making of *The Passion* Controversy." In *After* The Passion *Is Gone: American Religious Consequences*, edited by J. Shawn Landres and Michael Berenbaum, 23–34. Walnut Creek, California: AltaMira Press, 2004.

Sklar, Robert. *Movie-Made America: A Cultural History of American Movies*. New York: Vintage Books, 1994.

Smith, Anthony Burke. *The Look of Catholics: Portrayals in Popular Culture from the Great Depression to the Cold War*. Lawrence: University Press of Kansas, 2010.

Smith, Leslie E. "Living *in* the World, But Not *of* the World: Understanding Evangelical Support for *The Passion of the Christ*." In *After* The Passion *Is Gone: American Religious Consequences*, edited by J. Shawn Landres and Michael Berenbaum, 47–58. Walnut Creek, California: AltaMira Press, 2004.

Solomon, Jon. *The Ancient World in the Cinema*. New Haven: Yale University Press, 2001.

Sondag, Monique. "The Love Dare — New Book and #1 iPhone App." Christian News Wire. September 29, 2009, http://www.christiannewswire.com/news/9031711687.html (Accessed November 17, 2010).

The Southern Baptist Convention Cooperative Program. http://www.cpmissions.net/2003/what%20is%20cp.asp (accessed January 5, 2011).

Stern, Richard C. *Savior on the Silver Screen*. Mahwah, New Jersey: Paulist Press, 1999.

Tatum, W. Barnes. *Jesus at the Movies: A Guide to the First Hundred Years*. Polebridge Press, 2004.

"*To Save a Life* Coming to Blu-ray and DVD August 3." *To Save a Life* Website. May 17, 2010, http://www.tosavealifemovie.com/latestnews/ (accessed November 20, 2010.

Tunton, Stuart. "Twitter Earned Dell $9 Million." *PCPro*. March 3, 2010, www.pcpro.co.uk/news/enterprise/356044/twitter-earned-dell-9-million (accessed May 28, 2010).

Turan, Kenneth. Review of *The Chronicles of Narnia: Prince Caspian*. *Los Angeles Times*. May 16, 2008, http://www.latimes.com/entertainment/news/reviews/la-et-narnia16-2008may16,0,1410930.story (accessed November 10, 2010).

"Two Weeks of Filming in the Can!" *Courageous* website. May 7, 2010. Available from www.courageousthemovie.com/blog/. Accessed May 27, 2010.

The Ultimate Gift. DVD. Directed by Michael O. Sajbel. Dean River Productions, 2007.

Unhold, Monica. "Youth pastor draws from life for screenplay." Sign on San Diego. July 18, http://legacy.signonsandiego.com/news/northcounty/20080718-9999-1mc18movie.html (accessed August 11, 2010).

Vasey, Ruth. *The World According to Hollywood, 1918–1939*. Madison: The Unviersity of Wisconsin Press, 1997.

Vu, Michelle A. "*Fireproof* Creators' Next Film About Fatherhood." Christian Post. November 16, 2009, www.christianpost.com/article/20091116/-fireproof-creators-to-make-film-about-fatherhood/index.html (accessed May 28, 2010).

Walsh, Frank. *Sin and Censorship: The Catholic Church and the Motion Picture Industry*. New Haven: Yale University Press, 1996.

Walsh, Richard. *Reading the Gospels in the Dark*. Harrisburg, Pennsylvania: Trinity Press International, 2003.

Wasko, Janet. "Critiquing Hollywood: The Political Economy of Motion Pictures." In *A Concise Handbook of Movie Industry Economics*, edited by Charles C. Moul, 5–31. New York: Cambridge University Press, 2005.

"Watching the Film Develop." *Courageous* Blog Post. May 17, 2010, www.courageousthemovie.com/blog/ (accessed May 27, 2010).

Waxman, Sharon. "Hollywood Rethinking Films of Faith After *Passion*." *The New York Times*. March 15, 2004, http://query.nytimes.com/gst/fullpage.html?res=9906E7DC1F3EF936A25750C0A9629C8B63&sec=&spon=&pagewanted=2 (accessed November 10, 2010).

____. "Hollywood's Newfound Passion for Christ." *International Herald Tribune*. July 20, 2005, http://www.iht.com/articles/2005/07/19/business/christians.php?page=1 (accessed November 10, 2010).

Webster, Andy. "An Athlete in Search of Redemption." *The New York Times*. January 22, 2010. http://movies.nytimes.com/2010/01/22/movies/22tosave.html?partner:RottenTomatoes&ei=5083 (accessed August 10, 2010).

Weisenfeld, Judith. *Hollywood Be Thy Name: African American Religion in American Film, 1929–1949*. Berkeley: University of California Press, 2007.

Williams, Kam. "Louis Gossett Jr.: *The Grace Card* Interview." *The Tri-State Defender*. February 24, 2011, http://tri-statedefenderonline.com/articlelive/articles/5835/1/Lou-Gossett-Jr-The-Grace-Card-interview/Page1.html (accessed October 14, 2011).

Willman, Chris. Review of *Fireproof*. *Entertainment Weekly*. October 10, 2008, http://www.ew.com/wearticle/0..20229911,00.html (accessed June 11, 2010).

Winberg, Charles R. "Profits Out of the Picture: Research Issues and Revenue Sources Beyond the North American Box Office." In *A Concise Handbook of Movie Industry Economics*, edited by Charles C. Moul, 163–97. New York: Cambridge University Press, 2006.

Wright, Greg. "A Film That Doesn't Suck." Hollywood Jesus. 2010, http://www.hollywoodjesus.com/dvddetail.cfm/i/05A963E1-A3C5-1FDF-6FD94DCF973D2FC9/ia/570B0657-CAE9-7E5F-55086E9A3DDCA17E (accessed August 11, 2010).

_____. "Bold Indeed." Hollywood Jesus. 2011, http://www.hollywoodjesus.com/movieDetail.cfm/i/3AAC4D32-98DA-7BC2-098899A8615930B0/ia/BA7E59D7-FF24-D026-B5D3D56F91B6F16D (accessed October 24, 2011).

_____. "Low Budget, Big Heart." Hollywood Jesus. http://www.hollywoodjesus.com/VDDetail.cfm/i/396174A5-B867-6858-42CD4CDF67950CA2/ia/396390CE-EF59-A215-C81DA47F232B19CF (accessed November 8, 2010).

_____. Review of *End of the Spear*. Hollywood Jesus. December 13, 2005, http://www.hollywoodjesus.com/comments/greg/2005/12/end-of-spear.html (accessed January 5, 2011).

Zeitchik, Steven. "Weinsteins Put Faith in Film: Company Forms Christian-based Distribution Label." *Variety*. December 6, 2006, http://www.variety.com/article/VR1117955243.html?categoryid=13&cs=1 (accessed November 10, 2010).

Index

Abraham (1993) 36
Act One Program 12, 181, 185
Adamson, Andrew 42, 44, 55
Addams, Jane 30
Afable, Sean Michael 141
Affirm Films 40, 158, 185
Alcorn, Randy 112
All Pro Dad 110
Allen, Chad 48
Alpha Course 169
Amaya, Robert 116, 124
Amazing Grace (2006) 41, 48–49, 52, 53, 185
An American Carol (2008) 138
Anderson, P.T. 28
Angels with Dirty Faces (1938) 27
Anschutz, Phillip 41, 48
Anschutz Film Group 41, 185
Any Given Sunday (1999) 74
Apocalypse: Caught in the Eye of the Storm (1998) 34
The Apostle (1997) 28
Apted, Michael 49, 53
Arbuckle, Roscoe "Fatty" 33
Arends, Carolyn 148
Arnold, Lisa 61, 66
Association of Marriage and Family Ministries 94, 102, 104

Baehr, Ted 42
Bailey, Robert, Jr. 140
Bancroft, Anne 21
Baptist Faith and Message 58, 104, 105
Baptista, Carlos Octavia 33
Barfield, Warren 88
Barrabas (1961) 40
Bathea, Erin 88, 94, 95, 103, 171
Baugh, Brian 138
Baxter, Anne 24
Beal, Timothy K. 37
Because of Winn-Dixie (2005) 41
Beifuss, John 153
The Bells of St. Mary's (1946) 27
Ben Hur (1907) 25
Ben Hur (1925) 25
Ben Hur (1959) 25
Berenbaum, Mark 38, 55

Bergman, Ingrid 27
Berney, Bob 151
Beta Film Company 36
Better Films Movement 31
Bevel, Ken 94, 113, 116, 124
Beyond the Gates of Splendor (2002) 48
The Bible (1966) 24
Bible Film Company 32
The Birth of Jesus (1909) 20
Black, Gregory D. 30
Black, Jack 26
BlackChristianMovies.com 184
The Blair Witch Project (1999) 11, 131
Blockbuster Video 64
Blue Like Jazz (2012) 12, 182, 183
Bock, Jonathan 42
Bolten, Michael Christopher 147
Boyd, Danah M. 107
Boys Town (1938) 27
Brady, Mary Beattie 54
Breen, Joseph 24, 29, 52
Breen, Joseph I. 24
Breimeier, Russ 46
Breslin, Abigail 50
The Bridge to Terabithia (2007) 41
Bringing Up Bobby (2009) 42
Bristol Bay 41, 48, 185
Britts, Jim 138
Brooks, Richard 27
Brown, Eleanor 117
Brown, Frank Burch 11, 14, 166–167, 168, 170, 174, 176, 180
Brown, William J. 38–39, 55
Bruner, Kathy 41
Brunick, Paul 119
Brynner, Yul 24
Buchter, Andy 172
Buckwalter, Ian 141
Bueno, Chris 75, 82, 164, 174, 177, 180
Burge, Curtis 57
Burnett, Walter 65
Burns, Ed 132
Burton, Richard 25, 27
Bushman, Francis X. 25

Cagney, James 27
Caldwell, Albert 57
Calvary Church of the Nazarene 7, 155, 158, 163, 164, 185
Cameron, James 130
Cameron, Kirk 34, 88, 89, 92, 94, 95, 98, 103, 126
Campus Crusade for Christ 34
Capra, Frank 27, 153
Carmel Entertainment 7, 75, 164, 185
Carmike Cinemas 63, 75
Carpenter, Joel A. 173
Casting Crowns 88
Castle-Hughes, Keisha 45, 52
Catholic Legion of Decency 6, 25, 29, 31; pledge of allegiance 29
Catt, Michael 58, 68, 88, 91, 92, 95, 106, 112, 175
Cave, Bailey 78
Century Films 21
Cera, Michael 26
Chaney, Lon 26
Charlotte's Web (2006) 41
Chattaway, Peter T. 44, 101, 103, 169
Cheatham, Maree 147
Chesterton, G.K. 1
Le Christ marchant sur les flots [*Christ Walking on Water*] (1899) 20
Christian epic films 23–26
The Christian Herald 32, 33
Christian Herald Motion Picture Bureau 9, 32, 156
Christian Network Television 64
ChristianCinema.com 184
The Chronicles of Narnia: The Lion, the Witch, and the Wardrobe (2005) 42–43, 49, 51, 52, 53, 55, 185
The Chronicles of Narnia: Prince Caspian (2008) 42, 43–44, 52, 185
The Chronicles of Narnia: The Voyage of the Dawn Treader (2010) 42
Church Film Company 9

INDEX

Church Film Movement 30–33
CinemaScope 5, 25, 130
Cinerama 21, 130
Citizen Kane (1941) 129
Clark, Lynn Schofield 11, 134, 136
Cloud Ten Pictures 9, 34, 35, 156, 178, 180
Colbert, Claudette 23, 25
Color of the Cross (2006) 22
Color of the Cross 2: The Resurrection (2008) 22
Colson, Charles 53–54
Committee for Better Films 31
Committee on Visual Education 31
Connelly, Marc 24
Contemporary Christian Music (CCM) Industry 55
Coppola, Francis Ford 130
Cork, Matthew 164
Cork, William J. 38
Corman, Roger 11, 130, 172
Courageous (2011) 9, 10, 78, 100, 105, 158, 164, 172, 176, 178, 185; marketing 110–115; plot 116–118; production 108–110; reception 118–122; theology 123–127
Courageous Living: Dare to Take a Stand 112
Courageous novelization 112
Coyle, John T. 20
Criswell, David 44, 52
Crosby, Bing 27
Crouch, Jan 35
Crouch, Matthew 35, 46
Crouch, Paul 35
Crowder, Steven 142–143
Crown Video 64
culture war 10, 180
Curtiz, Michael 23
Cyrino, Monica Silveira 26

Dafoe, Willem 22
Dano, Paul 28
Dans, Peter E. 26, 28
Dapper, Janet Lee 62, 65, 69
Dapper, Steve 62, 74, 87
David (1997) 36
David and Bathsheba (1951) 24
Davies, Ben 116, 124
Dawson, Kim 145
Day-Lewis, Daniel 28
Day of Triumph (1954) 20, 33
Deacon, Brian 34
Dean River Productions 50
De Carlo, Yvonne 24
DeLaurentiis, Dino 24
Deletes (2008) 164
Demetrius and the Gladiators (1954) 25
DeMille, Cecil B. 6, 20, 23, 24, 33, 46, 55, 155; tendency to mix sacred and scandalous 20, 23, 24, 25

DeMille Pictures 6
Dervan, Stephen, 156
Detweiler, Craig 12
Digitalization of Filmmaking 11
A Distant Thunder (1978) 34
Doherty, Thomas 30
Dove Foundation 55, 70
Downes, Kevin 116
DreamWorks 5, 24
Dungy, Tony 110, 113
Dupont, Tiffany 46, 52
Duval, Robert 28

Ebert, Roger 43
ecumenical aesthetics 11
Edison Company 30, 31
Einstein, Mara 11, 83, 84, 94, 136, 169, 178, 179
Eldridge, Rick 50
Ellerbrook, Jason 113
Ellison, Nicole B. 107
Elmer Gantry (1960) 27
End of the Spear (2006) 47, 48, 51, 52, 53, 54, 55, 185
Entertaining Angels: The Dorothy Day Story (1996) 34
Erickson, Rob 158
Esther (1999) 36
Etchells, Lauren 116
evangelical Christian pop culture 10, 11, 128, 133–136, 179, 180
Evans, Dr. David 155, 156, 163
Every Tribe Entertainment 47, 48
Evolutions in Filmmaking 10
Eyman, Scott 26

Facebook 107–108, 109, 110, 123, 138, 140, 158
Facing the Giants (2006) 7, 9, 10, 11, 64, 70, 87, 89, 91, 92, 93, 99, 100, 101, 103, 104, 109, 121, 123, 138, 145, 151, 167, 168, 169, 171, 176, 178, 179, 185; distribution and marketing of 75–78; plot of 78–81; production of 73–75; reception of 81–84; theology of 84–86
Faith TV 64
FamilyLife 94, 104, 111
Familynet 64
Fathers.com 110
Feldstein, Seve 39–40
Fields, Shannen 75, 78
film censorship: Catholic efforts 6, 8, 29–30; Protestant efforts 6, 8, 30
film exhibition sites: changes 10
film ratings 29
filmmaking technology: changes 8, 10–11
Finney, Albert 49
Fireproof (2008) 7, 9, 10, 11, 64, 70, 86, 107, 108, 110, 111, 112, 114, 120, 121, 123, 126, 137, 138,
144, 145, 151, 155, 156, 162, 168, 169, 170, 171, 174, 176, 178, 179, 185; distribution and marketing 89–94; novelization 92; plot 94–99; production 87–89; reception 99–102; theology 102–105
Fireproof Your Marriage study series 92, 94, 178
Fitzgerald, Barry 27
Florence Nightingale (1985) 40
Flywheel (2003) 7, 9, 10, 73, 74, 84, 85, 86, 92, 100, 101, 103, 109, 123, 127, 144, 171, 176, 178, 179, 185; distribution and marketing 63–65; plot 65–67; production 60–63; reception 70–72; theology 67–70
Focus on the Family 94, 100, 104, 111
Foster, Steve 138
Foust, Michael 120
Fox Faith 39, 40, 51, 55, 75, 185
Franco, Nicole 138
Frazier, Jonathan 182
Friday Night Lights (2004) 74
Friedrich, Rev. James K. 21, 33
Frisbie, Annie Young 153
From the Manger to the Cross (1912) 20, 25

Gardner, Ava 24
Gardner, Barry 134
Gener8xion Entertainment 35, 46, 52, 178, 180
Genzlinger, Neil 100
Gibson, Mel 6, 9, 15, 37–39, 42, 53, 55, 56; 151, 180
Girardi, Joe 110
Godspell (1973) 21
Going My Way (1944) 27
Goldenberg, Suzanne 55
Goldstein, Gary 119
Gone with the Wind (1939) 129
Goode, Tracy 61, 62, 65, 78
Gordon, Mac 62
Goss, Luke 46, 52
Gossett, Louis, Jr. 156, 162
The Grace Card (2010) 162, 185; marketing 158; plot 158–159; production 156, 158; reception 159–161; theology 161–163
Grace Hill Media 42, 151, 185
Graceworks Pictures 155, 156, 158, 162, 163, 169, 186
Graham, Billy 9, 33, 36
The Greatest Story Ever Told (1965) 21, 38
Green Pastures (1936) 24, 27
Greydanus, Steven D. 120, 123
Griffith, D.W. 30, 31
Griffud, Ioan 49
Groothuis, Taylor 152
Guber, Peter 38
Gunning, Tom 31

Hachi: A Dog's Tale (2009) 40
Hallelujah! (1929) 27
Hallmark, Clay 122
Hankins, Barry 169, 170
Hanon, Jim 48
Hardwicke, Catherine 45
Hardy, Michael 100
Harmon, William Elmer 32
Harvest Bible Chapel 7, 150
Hatfield, Travis 106
Hawkins, J.T., Jr. 78
Haxan Films 11
Hays, Will H. 29
Hayward, Susan 24
Helfgat, Joseph 54
Hendershot, Heather 11, 14, 34, 35, 55, 134–135, 176
Hertz, Todd 142, 160, 161
Heston, Charlton 21, 24, 25
Heyman, John 34
Hidalgo, Kim 141
The Hiding Place (1975) 34
Higgenbottom, Mike 156, 158, 160, 162
Historical Film Corporation 32
Hollywood: approach to religious subject matter 8, 17–19; assumptions about evangelical Christianity 53–55; failure to replicate success of *The Passion of the Christ* 51–56; reaction to *The Passion of the Christ* 6–7, 9
Holmes, Rev. Lynn 156, 158, 163
Hometown Legend (2002) 150
Honor Begins at Home: The Courageous Bible Study Member Book 112
Hoosiers (1986) 77
Howard, Jay R. 135
Howard, Ron 130
Hull House 30
Hunnewell, Richie 65
Hunter, Jeffrey 21
Hurst, Josh 83
Huston, John 24
Hutcherson, Taylor 126

Icon Pictures 6
Image of the Beast (1981) 34
Impact Entertainment 40
Independent Film Channel 131
Inspiration Network 63
International Bible Students Association 32
International Church Film corporation 9, 32
International Council of Religious Education 31
Isaac, Oscar 45
It Happened One Night (1934) 129
It's a Wonderful Life (1946) 153

Jacob (1994) 36
Jarman, Derek 25

Jaws (1975) 130
The Jazz Singer (1927) 5
Jenkins, Dallas 149, 150, 154
Jenkins, Jerry 149
Jenkins Entertainment 150, 152, 153, 154, 186
Jesus: history of depictions in film 19–23
Jesus (1979) 34
Jesus (1999) 36
Jesus Christ Superstar (1973) 21
Jesus Film Project 34
Jesus of Nazareth (1977) 21
Jewell, Renee 116
Johnson, Alva 5, 6
Johnson, Jeffrey S.S. 145, 147
Joiner, Michael 156, 158, 160
Jones, Shirley 27
Joseph (1995) 36
Judgment (2001) 34

Kazantzakis, Nikos 22
Keeler, John D. 38–39, 55
Keenan, Marc 65
Keitel, Harvey 22
Kelly, Gene 129
Kendrick, Alex 7, 13, 59–60, 61, 62, 63, 64, 65, 67, 69, 70, 73, 74, 75, 78, 80, 84, 85, 86, 87, 88, 89, 91, 92, 99, 101, 103, 104, 105, 106, 109, 113, 116, 117, 118, 119, 123, 124, 127, 137, 150, 151, 162, 168, 170, 171, 173, 175, 176, 177, 179, 180
Kendrick, Stephen 7, 13, 59–60, 61, 63, 64, 69, 70, 73, 74, 75, 84, 85, 86, 87, 88, 89, 91, 92, 101, 103, 104, 105, 106, 109, 116, 118, 119, 123, 125, 127, 150, 151, 162, 168, 170, 171, 173, 175, 176, 177, 179, 180
Kennison, Eddie 110
Kerr, Deborah 25
King, Henry 24, 33
The King of Kings (1917) 6, 20, 23, 38
King of Kings (1961) 21, 43
kitsch 166–167, 176, 180
Klausner, Howard 156, 163
Kreutzberg, Deja 140, 141

Lalonde, Peter and Paul 9, 34, 35
Lamarr, Hedy 24
La Marre, Jean-Claude 22
Lancaster, Burt 27
Land, Richard 53
Landres, J. Shawn 38, 55
Lang, J. Stephen 26
LaSalle, Mick 43
The Last Days of Pompeii (1935) 20
The Last Temptation of Christ (1988) 5, 18, 22
Laughton, Charles 25, 27

The Least Among You (2009) 156
Ledman, Melinda 83
Lee, Spike 174
Left Behind (2000) 34, 93
Left Behind novels 34, 35, 149
Left Behind II: Tribulation Force (2002) 34
Left Behind III: World at War (2005) 34, 156
Letters to God (2010) 146, 147, 171, 185; marketing 148; plot 145, 147; reception 148–149; theology 149
Lewis, C.S. 43
Lewis, Sinclair 27
Leydon, Joe 50, 82, 100, 119, 160, 169
Life of Brian (1979) 18, 21, 26
Lifeway 91, 113
Linafelt, Tod 37
Lindsay, Richard 127, 172
Lindvall, Terry viii, 1, 4, 8, 12, 13, 14, 17, 30, 32, 33, 35, 36, 38–39, 42, 54, 55, 59, 173, 177
Lionsgate 75
Little, William G. 37
Little Miss Sunshine (2006) 50
Litton, Ed 125
Lively, Robyn 147
Lokey, Treavor 65
Lollobrigida, Gina 24
Lord, Daniel 29
The Lord of the Rings film series (2001, 2002, 2003) 43
The Lost and Found Family (2009) 41
Lot in Sodom (1933) 24, 25
Louvish, Simon 26
The Love Dare 87, 89–92, 94, 96, 99, 101, 102, 111, 112, 162, 169, 176, 178
Lucado, Max 40, 77
Lucas, George 130

Madison, Bailee 147
Maguire, Tanner 145, 147
Malcom, Harris 95
Mandalay Entertainment 38
Maresco, Peter A. 38
Mark IV Pictures 9, 14, 34
Marquez, Jose 37
Marriage Commission 94, 104
Martin, Rusty 116
Martz, Brent 164
Mattingly, Terry 169, 173
Mature, Victor 24, 25
McBride, Jim 104, 106, 112, 114, 175
McDannell, Colleen 28
McLeod, Jason 80
Megiddo: The Omega Code 2 (2001) 35
Méliès, Georges 20
Men of Boys Town (1941) 27

Methodist Church "White List" 31
Methodist Committee on Conservation and Advance 31
Methodist Episcopal Centenary (1919) 31
Meyer, Joyce 40
Meyer, Russ 11, 130, 172
MGM 24, 25, 27, 41, 129
Midnight Clear (2006) 150
Miller, Donald 182
ministers: depictions of in film 26–29
Minow, Nell 142
The Miracle Man (1919) 26
The Miracle Woman (1931) 27
Miss Sadie Thompson (1953) 26
Missionary uses of cinema 30
Mitchell, Mark 62
Mitchum, Robert 27, 28
Monty Python 21
Moon, Dr. Irwin 33
Moore, Beth 113
Moore, Joy 158
Moore, Roger 148
Morris, Michael viii, 4, 18, 19, 51
Moses (1995) 36
Motion Picture Producers and Distributors of America (MPPDA) 29
Motive Entertainment 151
Moul, Charles C. 179
Mundroff, Ted 151

Nasraway, John 156
National Board of Review 31
National Fatherhood Initiative 110
The Nativity Story (2006) 44–45, 51, 185
Nelson, Angelita 116
New Era Films 32
New Line Cinema 43, 44, 51, 54
New Song Community Church 7, 40, 143, 185; history 137–138
New Song Pictures 138, 139, 141, 143, 169
Newton, John 48
Nicolosi, Barbara 167, 168, 171, 172, 181, 182
The Night of the Hunter (1955) 27, 28
The Night of the Iguana (1964) 27
Nixon, David 145
Noah, Mickey 122
Noah's Ark (1929) 23
Not Today 164–165, 185
Novarro, Ramon 25

Oberammergau 1
O'Brien, Pat 27
Ocean Avenue Entertainment 164, 186
O'Connell, Sean 160
O'Connor, Donald 129
Olcott, Sidney 20, 25
Old Testament films 23–25, 26
Olsen, Mark 50
The Omega Code (1999) 35
One Night with the King (2006) 46–48, 50, 51, 52, 53, 55, 185
Opie, Rev. Thomas 1
Osteen, Joel 84, 179
O'Toole, Peter 46
Outreach Marketing 65, 77, 91, 94, 158, 164, 178
Overby, Scott 122

Paramount Pictures 6, 27, 41, 129
Paranormal Activity (2007) 131
Pasolini, Pier Paolo 55
La Passion (1897) 20
The Passion of the Christ (2004) 6, 8, 9, 15, 18–19, 48, 51, 53, 54–55, 82, 145, 151; controversy surrounding 37–38; Hollywood's reaction 39–42; marketing 38; religious impact 38–39
Paulist Pictures 34
Peck, Gregory 24
Perry, Tyler 184
Photo-Drama of Creation (1913) 32
Pichel, Irving 20
Pilgrim's Progress 33
Pinsky, Mark I. 53
Pixar 179
Pollock, Melisa 83
Possibility Pictures 145, 146, 147, 148, 179, 186
Powell, Robert 21
Presbyterian Board of Publications 30
The Prince of Egypt (1998) 5, 24
Pritchard, Zack 182
The Prodigal (1955) 24
Production Code 3, 6, 13, 18–19, 23, 29, 52
Production Code Administration 24, 52
Promise Keepers 113
Protestantism and motion pictures: demise of 20th century film programs 9, 33; uses of and expectations for cinema in the early 20th century 6, 8, 30–33
Provident Films 7, 41, 64, 75, 77, 110, 113, 118, 158, 164, 186
Provident Music Group 41, 75
Purpose Driven Life 169

Quicke, Andrew 39, 42, 59
Quo Vadis? (1902) 25
Quo Vadis? (1951) 20, 25

Radosh, Daniel 11, 58–59, 134, 135, 168, 171, 172, 173, 180
Rain (1932) 26
Ramis, Harold 26
rapture: evangelical fears 35; films about 34–35
Ratzenberger, John 152
Ravid, S. Abraham 131–132, 133, 177, 178
Ray (2004) 41
Ray, Nicholas 21, 43
Reeves, Dan 77
Reinhartz, Adele 19, 22
Reisner, Rev. Dr. Christian 31
Reiss, Jon 132–133, 151, 178
Religious Motion Picture Foundation 32
Remember the Titans (2000) 77
The Replacements (2000) 74
Reservoir Dogs (1992) 131
The Resolution for Men 112, 113
The Resolution for Women 112, 113
Revelation (1999) 34
Revell, Perry 96
Reynolds, Debbie 129
Rite of Passage: A Father's Blessing 112
Robbins, Rev. Harry E. 51
The Robe (1953) 5, 25, 130
Robinov, Jeff 55
Romero (1989) 34
Rosenblatt, Josh 82
Rossing, Barbara 35
Ryan, Debby 152

Sacred Films 9, 32
Saddleback Church 179
Sadie Thompson (1928) 26
Sahara (2005) 41
Saint, Eva Marie 27
Saint, Steve 48
Sajbel, Michael O. 46, 50
Salzman, Marian 108
Samson and Delilah (1949) 24
Samson and Delilah (1996) 36
Samuel Goldwyn Films 7, 141, 143
The Sandpiper (1965) 27
Savante, Stelio 152
Scheck, Frank 119
Schultze, Quentin J. 54, 155, 172, 173, 180
Schwartz, Russell 54
Scorsese, Martin 5, 22, 55, 130
Scott, A.O. 45, 51
Scott, Bob 73, 74, 87, 88, 109
Scott, George C. 24
Sebastiane (1976) 25
The Second Chance (2006) 41
Seed, Hal 137
Seed, Lori 137
"Sermons from Science" 33
Sharif, Omar 46
Sherwood Baptist Church 7, 9,

62, 65, 68, 69, 84, 87, 88, 93, 101, 104, 106, 111, 113, 123–124, 125, 133, 137, 138, 150, 175, 179, 185; history of 57–59
Sherwood Christian Academy 57, 75
Sherwood Pictures 8, 13, 15, 35, 40, 42, 64, 66, 67, 70, 72, 77, 78, 86, 89, 94, 95, 98, 100, 102, 104, 105, 106, 107, 110, 111, 112, 114, 117, 118, 119, 120, 121, 123, 124, 125, 126, 127, 128, 133, 136, 137, 138, 140, 145, 150, 151, 156, 158, 163, 164, 167, 169, 170, 171, 174, 175, 177, 178, 179, 180, 186; influence on church-based film production 7, 11, 137; opposition to Hollywood 10, 88, 113, 172–173, 176; reliance on volunteers for film production 7, 10, 59, 74, 87–88, 109; use of prayer and scripture 59–60, 63, 69, 73, 75, 88, 109
Shields, Rev. Dr. James K. 32, 184
Shields, Jim 122
Shmuger, Marc 54
Shugan, Steven M. 179
The Sign of the Cross (1932) 23, 25
Silk, Mark 38
Simmons, Daniel 117
Singin' in the Rain (1952) 129
Sky Angel 63
Smalley, Gary 92
Smith, Anthony Burke 28
Smith, Leslie E. 173
Smith, W.A. 57
social network sites 107
Solomon (1997) 36
Solomon, Jon 26
Solomon and Sheba (1959) 24
Sony Pictures 7, 9, 75, 77, 143
Sorbo, Kevin 151, 152, 153, 154
Southern Baptist Convention 57, 58, 91; Cooperative Program 58; Ethics & Religious Liberty Commission 53
Space Cowboys (2000) 156
Spielberg, Steven 130
Stanwyck, Barbara 27
Star Wars (1977) 130
Stern, Richard C. 22
Stevens, George 21
Stone, Todd 98, 117, 124, 175
The Stream of Life (1932) 32
Streck, John M. 135

Sundance 131
Sunday, Billy 17
Swanson, Kristy 151
Swanson, Tom 145

Tarantino, Quentin 131
Tatum, W. Barnes 22
Taylor, Elizabeth 27
Taylor, Robert 25
Technicolor 21
Teixeira, Mark 110
The Ten Commandments (1923) 23
The Ten Commandments (1956) 6, 23, 24
10 West Studios 150, 186
There Will Be Blood (2007) 28
A Thief in the Night (1972) 14, 34
Third Day 88
Thompson, Donald 9, 34
Thompson, John 91
Though None Go with Me (2005) 150
Thrift, Sandra 145
Titus, Daniel 66
To Save a Life (2010) 139, 141, 171, 176, 185; marketing 138, 140; plot 140–141; production 138; reception 141–143; theology 143–144
Tolkien, J.R.R. 43
Torn, Rip 21
Tracy, Spencer 27
Tribulation (2000) 34
Trinity Broadcasting Network (TBN) 35, 64
True Love Waits 127
Turan, Kenneth 44
Turner, Lana 24
20th Century–Fox 5, 9, 24, 25, 39, 41
20th Century–Fox Home Entertainment 39
Twitter 108, 109, 110, 113, 121, 123, 138, 158, 176, 178
Two a Penny (1967) 33

The Ultimate Gift (2006) 49–51, 138, 185
Universal Pictures 41, 54, 74
Ustinov, Peter 25

Van Dyke, Jon 164
Vidor, King 24, 27, 33
von Sydow, Max 21

Waggoner, Brad 111
Waite, Ralph 147

Walden Media 41, 42, 43, 48, 186
Wales, Ken 48
Walsh, Frank 29
Walsh, Richard 22
Walt Disney Pictures 41, 42, 43, 53, 55, 77, 179
Warner, H.B. 20
Warner Brothers 55, 74, 129
Warren, Rick 53, 84, 179
Washington, Raleigh 113
Wasko, Janet 133
The Waterhorse: Legend of the Deep (2007) 40
Watson, James Sibeley 24, 25
Waxman, Sharon 37–38, 39, 54
Wayne, Randy 140, 141
Webber, Melville 24, 25
Webster, Andy 142
Weigel, Joshua 140
Weinstein, Harvey 40
Weinstein Company 9, 40
What If... (2010) 152, 153, 154, 171, 172, 185; marketing and distribution 151; plot 151–152; reception 152–153; theology 153–155
Wilberforce, William 48, 54
Willard, Mark 62, 88
Williams, Evan 108
Williams, Steve 78
Willman, Chris 100, 101, 103, 169
Willow Creek Church 179
Wilson, Eric 92
Wilson, Robert 21
Winberg, Charles R. 133
WingCinema 164, 186
Winshape 94
The Wizard of Oz (1939) 129
Wood, Ray 79
Woods, Robert H., Jr. 54, 155, 172, 173, 180
Word Australia 64
World Wide Pictures 9, 33, 36
Wright, Greg 48, 52, 70, 120, 123
Wyler, William 25

Yancy, Philip 22
Year One (2006) 26
Yorba Linda Friends Church 7, 164, 165, 185
Yordan, Philip 21

Zapata, Ellie 116
Zapata, Evan 116
Zeffirelli, Franco 21
Zukor, Adolph 31